Fodor's

7th Edition

Thailand

Fodor's Travel Publications • New York, Toronto, London, Sydney, Auckland
www.fodors.com

CONTENTS

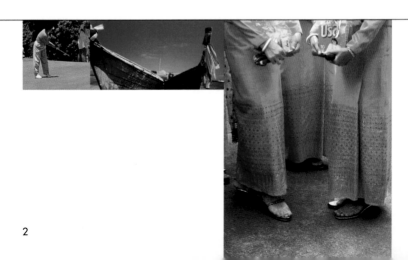

MAPS

Circled letters in text correspond to letters on the photographs. For more information on the sights pictured, turn to the indicated page number **Ⓐ** on each photograph.

DESTINATION THAILAND

Signs of Thailand's hurly-burly rush into the 21st century are overpowering, from the notorious traffic snarls of the capital to the glittering resorts along the sands of Phuket. What endures behind the clamor is a rich culture—untouched by Western influences—that is manifest in the elaborate adornment of architectural marvels, the elegant grace of classic Thai dance, the spiciness of the cuisine, and the gentle seduction of the many as-yet unspoiled beaches. Bridging the gap between the remote countryside, with its sleepy market towns, and the frenetic cities are the eternally amicable Thai people, whose very nature is a testament to co-existence. Whether your aim is hedonism, relaxation, or edification, you'll be captivated by this alluring land and its gracious inhabitants.

22

BANGKOK

Frenzied, frantic, and all the more fascinating for it, Bangkok defies logic as well as easy navigation. Embrace as much of the chaos as possible, and then break from it by taking to the water. A boat trip along the ©**Chao Phraya** and adjoining *klongs* (canals) is a great way to avoid traffic-clogged streets and alleyways, yet still view everything from floating markets and stilt houses to modern shops and high-rises. Bangkok has some of Thailand's most impressive temples, and just inland from the river are Ⓑ**Wat Traimitr,** where you'll find the world's

largest solid-gold Buddha, and ⒜**Wat Phra Keo,** which is the kingdom's most elaborate and most sacred temple. Also near the river is the ⒟**National Museum,** where Thai and Buddhist masterpieces are among the crowning jewels of a world-class Asian art collection. The National Theater next door showcases Thai drama and elegant traditional Thai dancers. Don't worry if you miss one of the theater's all too rare productions; you'll surely stumble onto an impromptu street performance, and there are shows for tourists at the ⒠**Oriental Hotel.** For edge-of-your-seat action, catch one of the daily Thai boxing matches, which are held at the Lumphini and Ratchadamnoen stadiums, and encourage the combatants with shouts of *"O-ay!"* Bangkok does have its seamy side. But as in any other city that never sleeps, its nighttime diversions suit all dispositions—from infamous cabarets to cozy jazz bars, from trendy discos to serene dinner cruises.

AROUND BANGKOK

Ⓐ▷72

Set out from the capital in any direction and you'll soon come upon a natural or man-made marvel that will make your journey worthwhile. Nakhon Pathom is Thailand's oldest city, and its landmark, the Phra Pathom Chedi, is the world's tallest Buddhist monument. At the nearby Ⓒ**Rose Garden,** an ersatz village, the 20,000 blooming specimens are less of an attraction than the traditional Thai dancing. The floating market at Ⓑ**Damnoen Saduak** affords a more authentic glimpse of Thai life—it's your typical traffic jam, albeit one of goods-laden

sampans clogging a canal. Waterfalls cascade through the jungles of Kanchanaburi. Here the landscape is haunted with memories of Allied POWs, who were forced by the Japanese to labor on the so-called Death Railway and who were often buried at the Ⓓ**Kanchanaburi War Cemetery.** The road north from Bangkok leads to Ⓐ**Wat Phanan Choeng** in the kingdom's former capital of Ayutthaya—now better known for its small town charm and hospitality than for its riches or past glories—and to the palace-strewn city of Lopburi, which has also survived many a dynasty. To the east, modern concerns come into play in Ⓔ**Chantaburi,** where gem merchants do a brisk curbside business, and in the beach resort of Pattaya, which has be-

come a playground of tacky diversions. If you truly want a respite from the city, head southwest and hop a ferry to one of the myriad islands—each with its own stretch of tranquil beach—that make up Mu Ko Chang National Park.

Ⓓ 69

Ⓔ 85

9

NORTHERN THAILAND

Ⓐ 107

In the northern regions, you'll find Thailand's most dramatic landscapes, most distinctive temples and palaces, most independent people, and most flavorful food. Make your first stop the walled city of Chiang Mai—where you may see amazing creations at the annual ©**Flower Festival**—to pay a visit to mountaintop Ⓑ**Wat Phrathat Doi Suthep,** one of four royal temple compounds. Among the more remote places, there's the ancient city of Lamphun, where you can sample *lamyai* (a small, sweet fruit), and Doi Inthanon National Park, which rises to the heights of Thailand's tallest mountain and, not to mention

Ⓑ 94

Ⓐ**Mae Hong Son,** which is surrounded by verdant countryside and hill-tribe villages. The biggest attractions in these parts are the Karen Long Necks, who acquire their distinctive appearance by wearing brass neckbands starting at age six. In the far north, more tribal villages surround the market town of Chiang Rai, and forested hills stretch into the Sop Ruak, or Golden Triangle. Once known for opium production and warlords, the region remains exhilarating—even if the most popular pursuit is no more adventurous than enjoying the view of the river valleys and beyond.

© 94

The Thai heartland spans the middle of the country from the border of Myanmar to those of Cambodia and Laos. Here, rice fields and misty uplands are interspersed with ancient ruins. At

THE CENTRAL PLAINS AND I-SAN

Ⓐ**Ban Chiang,** skeletons, jewelry, and pottery are among the artifacts of a civilization that flourished 7,000 years ago. Old Sukhothai is new by comparison; such temples as Ⓑ**Wat Mahathat** evoke the city's 13th-century role in unifying and enlightening the kingdom. The revered Phra That Phanom is one of many sanctuaries on the remote, northeastern plateau of I-san. All around are the scenes of an age-old way of life, from water buffalo working the rice paddies to the tried-and-true production techniques on view at the Ⓒ**Pak Thongchai Silk and Cultural Centre.**

Ⓑ 129

Ⓒ 142

Ⓐ 134

The southern region is paradise—a long peninsula washed by the coral-rich waters of the Gulf of Thailand on one side and the Andaman

Sea on the other. ©Ⓔ**Phuket,** Thailand's largest island, offers worldly pleasures, though at a great price and amidst great excesses of modern development. Here you can succumb to an al fresco *nuat boroan* (traditional massage), watch pearl

SOUTHERN
BEACH RESORTS

Ⓑ>163

workers glean their prizes from local waters, dine poolside at the Ⓐ**Royal Meridien Phuket Yacht Club,** or simply sunbathe on west coast sands. The Phi Phi Islands have also been affected by commercialism, but only Phi Phi Don is inhabited, so the atmosphere is still more laid-back than that on Phuket. The mainland resort of ⒷⒹ**Krabi** also remains very low-key. Surrounded by relatively undiscovered waters, this gateway town provides a playground for snorkelers and a place to catch a long-tail boat for escapes to ever-more-secluded beaches and islands. Phang Nga Bay is a true hideaway, where limestone outcroppings rise 900 feet above the sea and caves accessible only by boat wait to be explored. You can veer still farther off the path by heading to the tranquil

12

Ⓒ>148

fishing island of Ko Pha Ngan, where luxury means a bungalow on the beach. If you're eager for close-up views of extraordinary marine life, sail off to the Similan Islands, where the diving visibility is 60 to 120 feet, or explore the waters around the 40 islets of Angthong Marine National Park, full of astonishing multicolor coral. Both make for perfect day trips. Although few strands and coves in even these remote places are completely untrammeled, many are idyllic nonetheless.

FODOR'S
CHOICE

Even with so many special places in Thailand, Fodor's writers and editors have their favorites. Here are a few that stand out.

BEACHES

Ao Nang Bay, Krabi. Limestone pinnacles grab your attention at this newly discovered stretch of sand. ☞ p.163

Nai Harn, Phuket. On a deep bay, this beach is perfect for swimming, sailing, and sunset-watching. ☞ p.158

Pansea Beach, Phuket. This little beach is a secluded enclave for two of Phuket's most luxurious hotels.☞ p.153

Tong Nai Pan Noi, Ko Pha Ngan. You can shut out the world at this beachcomber's paradise. ☞ p.173

DINING

Le Normandie, Bangkok. Atop the legendary Oriental Hotel, this French restaurant offers river views. $$$$ ☞ p.34

Ⓔ Sala Rim Naam, Bangkok. Sala Rim Naam is a great place to experience royal Thai cuisine while watching a show of classical dancing. $$$ ☞ p.36

Ban Klang Nam, Bangkok. Here superb seafood is served up with a view of ships at anchor on the river. $$–$$$ ☞ p.36

Huen Phen, Chiang Mai. Browse through the many small dining rooms, each full of antiques, then settle in to enjoy good northern Thai fare. $$ ☞ p.97

Spice Market, Bangkok. In this restaurant set up like an old-fashioned spice shop, the superb curries can be prepared at half-strength for sensitive Western palates. $$ ☞ p.38

Prachak, Bangkok. Here, the best roast duck in town is served for less than a dollar. $ ☞ p.34

White Orchid, Phuket. Try this tiny outdoor café at the water's edge for fresh fish and a warm welcome. $ ☞ p.154

LODGING

Chiva-Som, Hua Hin. This spa resort offers rejuvenation with top-notch treatments and peaceful beach accommodations. $$$$ ☞ p.78

Oriental Hotel, Bangkok. The Oriental's prestigious clientele and unbeatable location on the Chao Phraya are just two of the reasons it continues to be an institution. $$$$ ☞ p.42

Rayavadee Premier Resort, Ao Nang. The only way to reach your duplex thatch cottage here is by long-tail boat. $$$$ ☞ p.164

The Regent, Bangkok. For elegance and superb service, the Regent is tops. $$$$ ☞ p.43

Ⓗ Regent Chiang Mai. Luxury is taken for granted here among the Lanna Thai buildings, which encircle rice fields and landscaped gardens. $$$$ ☞ p.99

Santiburi, Ko Samui. Swaying palms shade white sands steps away from your teak-floor bungalow. $$$$ ☞ p.166

Manee's Retreat, Si Saket. This one-of-a-kind luxury guesthouse reveals the real Thailand. $$ ☞ p.138

River View Lodge, Chiang Mai. This small hotel is a charming alternative to the high-rise hotels of the north. $$ ☞ p.100

Tara Mae Hong Son, Mae Hong Son. Whether taking a dip in the pool or enjoying traditional Thai food on the porch, you'll have a full view of a tranquil, terraced valley. $$ ☞ p.109

Ⓓ Panviman Resort, Ko Pha Ngan. This resort's bungalows are staggered up a cliff affording fantastic views of the bay. $–$$ ☞ p.173

Ⓒ The Atlanta, Bangkok. Classical music at teatime and old movies after dinner draw people back to this small, quirky hotel. ¢ ☞ p.52

QUINTESSENTIAL THAILAND

National Museum, Bangkok. Trace Thailand's rich history or view one of the world's best collections of Buddhist and Thai art. ☞ p.27

Night Bazaar in Chiang Mai. One of Thailand's most exciting markets offers much for little, from rural crafts to objets d'art. ☞ p.103

Ⓐ Phang Nga Bay, off Phuket. Limestone rocks rise majestically from the sea at this fascinating spot. ☞ p.162

Suan Pakkard Palace, Bangkok. Five antique teak houses, including the gold-paneled Lacquer Pavilion, magnificently exemplify Thai architecture. ☞ p.29

TEMPLES AND SHRINES

Wat Benjamabophit, Bangkok. The famed Marble Temple has a line of Buddha statues to help harmonize the spirit. ☞ p.29

Wat Chaimongkol, Chiang Mai. The main attraction at this small temple is its unbroken serenity. ☞ p.96

Ⓑ Wat Chedi Luang, Chiang Mai. This massive temple, felled by an earthquake before completion, is a stunning ruin. ☞ p.96

Wat Phanan Choeng. This monument in Ayutthaya commemorates the death of a king's beloved bride. ☞ p.72

Ⓖ Wat Pho, Bangkok. The largest wat in Bangkok houses the largest reclining Buddha in the country as well as a famous massage school. ☞ p.23

Ⓕ Wat Phra Keo, Bangkok. Festooned with murals, glittering gold, and the Emerald Buddha, this is Thailand's most sacred temple. ☞ p.23

Wat Traimitr, Bangkok. The luminous beauty of the world's largest solid-gold Buddha is striking within this otherwise unassuming temple. ☞ p.26

1 BANGKOK

Fascinating, chaotic, congested, polluted, beautiful, seamy, seductive: no single adjective—nor all of them—can properly sum up Bangkok. It's a nightmare, it's a dream, compounded by pungent smells, exotic architecture, and a culture shaped by centuries of Buddhism and independence. You many not like Bangkok, but you'll never forget it.

By Nigel Fisher

Updated by
Mick Elmore
and Nigel
Fisher (Dining
and Lodging)

A FOREIGNER'S REACTION TO THE CAPITAL is often as confused as the city's geography. Bangkok has no downtown, and streets, like the traffic, seem to veer off in every direction. There's even confusion about the city's name: though to Thais it is Krung Thep, the City of Angels, foreigners call it Bangkok. The oldest quarter clusters along the eastern bank of the Chao Phraya River, which snakes between Bangkok and Thonburi, where the capital was first established after the fall of Ayutthaya in 1767. When King Rama I moved his capital across the river in 1782, he chose a site that foreign vessels knew from their navigational charts as the village of Bangkok. This settlement—dominated by the Grand Palace and bordered by the Chao Phraya and semicircular *klongs* (canals)—is called Ratanakosin and is today a jumble of streets that lead to palaces, government buildings, temples, and museums.

In the last 25 years, the city has changed enormously. Before Bangkok became *the* R&R destination for American servicemen during the Vietnam War, it had a population of 1.5 million. Then, as U.S. dollars attracted the rural poor and development began, it grew to more than 10 million, nearly 15% of the population and 40 times the size of any other city in Thailand. Nowadays, space in which to live and breathe is inadequate. Bangkok is infamous for its traffic-jammed streets and *sois* (side streets and alleys), and its air pollution is among the worst in the world (policemen directing traffic wear masks). When the economy collapsed in 1997 the traffic situation improved as people sold their cars instead of driving them, and the population shrunk as many returned to the countryside. But as the economy bounces back so does congestion. The skytrain, which opened in December 1999, makes some difference, and a subway system scheduled to open in 2002 should help. However, some streets, particularly Sukhumvit Road and other major arteries, still look like parking lots during much of the day, and as construction reawakens with the reviving economy, the traffic will only get worse.

Even with its growing pains, though, Bangkok gives you a sense of history and timelessness, perhaps because King Rama I set out to build a city as beautiful as old Ayutthaya before the Burmese sacked it. Bangkok's contrasts require an adjustment on your part, but amid the chaos you soon come to appreciate the gentle nature of the Thais and their genuine respect for other people.

Pleasures and Pastimes

Architecture and the Arts

Bangkok is, without doubt, the chief repository of the nation's religious art and architecture, and the old, refined part of the city is full of unforgettable sights. The *wats* (temple enclosures) contain some of the country's most beautiful buildings and images of Lord Buddha, and the palaces are other splendid examples. The National Museum houses a wonderful cross-section of the arts, and at the National Theater you can watch classic Thai dancing.

Dining

In the Bangkok of today there are endless eating places—from swanky hotel dining rooms (some of Bangkok's best restaurants), to sidewalk stalls for a quick noodle lunch and small, informal restaurants where wonders await the gastronomically curious.

Lodging

Although the troubled economy has slowed the rush to build hotels, 1998–99 still saw two new establishments open in Bangkok—Le Royal

Meridien and the Peninsula. In late 1999 the Concorde in Bangkok opened, and the new Imperial, also in Bangkok, is scheduled to open in 2001.

The half-dozen or so deluxe hotels are superb, offering unparalleled comfort and service, and from those on the Chao Phraya, stunning views. In the past, the Oriental Hotel has been called the world's best, but others such as the Regent now compete for that position. There are also many moderately priced lodgings with excellent facilities and fine service.

Nightlife
The seedy side of Bangkok's nightlife caters to foreigners, and the Patpong area in particular has become synonymous with sex. In fact, much of Bangkok's nightlife is geared towards males, however, more and more bars are opening—sans hostesses—as places where both genders may go to relax, have a drink, and, perhaps, listen to live music.

River Boats and Ferries
Krung Thep used to be the Venice of the East. Sadly, many of the klongs have been paved over, but albeit polluted, all were not lost. The Chao Praya River and several klongs remain, and traveling along these waterways is one of the delights of Bangkok. They have been cleaned up in the last five years, and the water is no longer black and smelly. In the long-tailed boats and ferries, not only do you beat the stalled traffic, but you get to see houses on stilts, women washing, and kids diving in for a splash. One good trip past waterside temples, Thai-style houses, the Royal Barge Museum, and Khoo Wiang Floating Market starts at the Chang Pier near the Grand Palace and travels along Klong Bangkok Noi and Klong Bangkok Yai.

Shopping
In the past, Hong Kong and Singapore were Asia's shopping cities, but now you should hold off until you get to Bangkok, which is much less expensive and offers much more in the way of traditional crafts. And if Bangkok's endless shops are not enough, the markets and sidewalk vendors present bargains wherever you walk.

EXPLORING BANGKOK

Because confusion is part of Bangkok's fascination, learning your way around is a challenge. It may help to think of Bangkok as an isosceles triangle with the base abutting the S curve of the Chao Phraya River and the apex, pointing east, ending on Sukhumvit Road, somewhere around Soi 40.

Sukhumvit, at the apex of this conceptual triangle, was once a residential neighborhood. In the last two decades, it has developed into a district of hotels, shops, nightclubs, and restaurants while retaining some of its residential atmosphere. The new Bangkok Conference Centre attracts more and more hotels and businesses to this area. Ever since Ramkhamhaeng University opened in the 1970s, Bangkok has sprawled even farther east. Now the area known as Bangkapi is a satellite town, attracting industrial and residential complexes.

Westward, toward the Chao Phraya, are spacious foreign embassy compounds, corporate offices, and modern international hotels. To some this is Bangkok's center, symbolized by the Erawan shrine, where everyday Thais worship and traditional dancers perform for a small fee. South of the shrine is Bangkok's largest green area, Lumphini Park, an oasis in an urban jungle. A bit farther still, stores, offices, and more hotels are closely packed. Now you reach the older sections of Bangkok. On the southern flank runs Silom Road, a shopping and financial district; Suriwongse (pronounced *Suriwong*) Road, with more hotels, parallels it. Between them lies the entertainment district of Patpong. Continue farther and you reach the riverbank and four of Bangkok's leading hotels: the Royal Orchid Sheraton, the Oriental, the Shangri-La, and the Peninsula (across the river).

Going west along Rama I Road in the center of the triangle, you pass the Siam Square shopping area and the National Stadium. Continue south toward the Hualamphong Railway Station, and between it and the river lies Chinatown, a maze of streets with restaurants, goldsmiths, small warehouses, and repair shops.

In the northern part of the triangle, moving westward, you pass through various markets before reaching government buildings, the Victory Monument, Chitlada Palace, the Dusit Zoo, the National Assembly, the National Library, and, finally, the river. Slightly south of this route, you can go west from the Democracy Monument to the National Museums and Theatre near the river, and then south to the Grand Palace and Wat Phra Keo.

Knowing your exact destination, its direction, and approximate distance are important in negotiating tuk-tuk (three-wheeled taxi) fares and planning your itinerary. Note, however, that many sights have no precise written address and the spelling of road names changes from map to map and even street sign to street sign, thus Ratchadamri Road can be spelled *Rajdamri,* Ratchadamnoen is also *Rajdamnern,* Charoen Krung can be *Charoennakorn* or even *New Road,* and so on. Crossing and recrossing the city is time-consuming, and many hours can be spent in traffic jams. Above all, remember that Bangkok is enormous, and distances are great; it can take a half hour or more to walk between two seemingly adjacent sites.

Great Itineraries

If you aren't wilted by the heat or jet lag, you can cover Bangkok's attractions in three days, and in another two days make short trips outside the city. But don't rush. It's better to see less and enjoy more. Bangkok is such a maze it would take at least a week to know your way around comfortably, and many months to really get to know it.

IF YOU HAVE 2 DAYS
Numbers in the text correspond to numbers in the margin and on the Exploring Bangkok map.

Start your first day with the most famous of all Bangkok sights, the **Grand Palace** ①, a square mile of royal buildings behind high white walls, mostly used now only for state occasions; then go on, within the same complex, to the gorgeously ornate **Wat Phra Keo** ②, which contains the temple of the Emerald Buddha. Not far south of the Grand Palace is Bangkok's oldest and largest temple, **Wat Pho** ③, famous for its enormous Reclining Buddha and its school of traditional Thai massage. Take a tuk-tuk to Chinatown, to explore its crowded, narrow streets and maybe buy an herbal cure for what ails you, an ancient artifact, or something gold. On the edge of Chinatown, visit **Wat Traimitr** ⑤ and pay respects to this perfectly harmonious and glittering image. At the Chao Phraya, catch a river bus down to the **Oriental Hotel** and have a cup of tea. In the evening, walk bustling **Silom Road** to check out the wares for sale at the stalls and catch a dinner show of Thai dancing. The next day visit **Jim Thompson's House** ⑰, a beautiful reconstruction of several Thai traditional houses, then go to **Wat Benjamabophit** ⑫, where the present king spent early days as a monk and which contains Bangkok's much-photographed Marble Temple. Spend the afternoon in the **National Museum** ⑥ to gain an overview of Thai history and art (free guided tours in English on Wednesday and Thursday).

IF YOU HAVE 3 DAYS

Start your first day with breakfast on the terrace at the **Oriental Hotel,** and then take the river bus up the Chao Phraya to the **Grand Palace** ① and **Wat Phra Keo** ②. Then walk to **Wat Pho** ③ to see the Reclining Buddha and have a massage. Cross the river to **Wat Arun** ④ (Temple of the Dawn) and climb the large *prang* (central tower) for close inspection of its tiles and broken china and for views of the city and river. Then take the river bus upstream to the **Royal Barges** ⑧, which are used on ceremonial occasions. Cross the bridge and visit the **National Museum** ⑥. In the evening, take in Silom Road and a dinner show. On Day Two visit **Jim Thompson's House** ⑰ and **Suan Pakkard Palace** ⑯ to see traditional Thai houses of great classic beauty. Then go on to the **Vimarnmek Mansion** ⑬, the largest teak structure in the world, before visiting **Wat Benjamabophit** ⑫. South of the Marble Temple is the golden *chedi* (the bell-shaped pinnacle where relics are kept) of **Wat Saket** ⑩, elevated on its mound, and the metal temple of **Wat Rachanada** ⑨. Now head for Chinatown to do a little bazaar-style shopping before finding harmony in gazing at **Wat Traimitr**'s ⑤ fabulous 5-ton Golden Buddha. In the evening you might investigate **Patpong.** On the third day go to **Ayutthaya,** the former glorious capital (☞ North from Bangkok, *in* Chapter 2). We recommend going by bus and returning on the same day by boat down the Chao Phraya River. In the evening, if you have the energy, you might explore **Sukhumvit Road** and the bars on Soi Nana and Soi Cowboy.

IF YOU HAVE 5 DAYS

Begin your first day with an early breakfast on the terrace at the **Oriental Hotel** and then take the river bus up the Chao Phraya to the **Grand Palace** ①, **Wat Phra Keo** ②, and **Wat Pho** ③. After lunch cross the river to see **Wat Arun** ④, and then take the river bus to the **Royal Barges** ⑧. Cross the bridge again to end your day at the **National Museum** ⑥. In the evening, do Silom Road and catch a dinner show. On Day Two get an overview of traditional domestic architecture at **Jim Thompson's House** ⑰, **Suan Pakkard Palace** ⑯, and the **Vimarnmek Mansion** ⑬. Check out some sacred architecture at **Wat Benjamabophit** ⑫, **Wat Rachanada** ⑨, and **Wat Sakret** ⑩. Head for Chinatown, and then visit **Wat Traimitr** ⑤ before taking a peek at Bangkok's seamy side at Patpong. On the third day take the trip to **Ayutthaya,** and on the fourth day rise with the dawn and take an early bus tour that goes to **Damnoen Saduak's** floating produce market, a mêlée of exotica, and from there go on to **Nakhon Pathom,** whose main attraction is the ancient Phra Pathom Chedi, the tallest Buddhist monument in the world (☞ West of Bangkok, *in* Chapter 2). By early afternoon a train or bus can get you to **Kanchanaburi,** site of the notorious bridge over the River Kwai (☞ West of Bangkok, *in* Chapter 2). In the evening, stroll along **Sukhumvit Road,** and check out the nightlife in the bars on Soi Nana and Soi Cowboy. Save some time on your last day for shopping and, if it is Saturday or Sunday, go out to the vast **Weekend Market** at Chatuchak, for everything from household goods to instant antiques.

When to Tour Bangkok

November through March is the best time to be in Bangkok. It is at its coolest—85°—and driest. In April the humidity and heat build up to create a sticky melting pot, until the rains begin, in late May.

Old Bangkok Along the Chao Phraya

Bangkok's major sightseeing attractions are within a short distance of the Chao Phraya River in the part of Bangkok that was founded in 1782. Chinatown is also here. On the tour described below you'll experience one of Bangkok's greatest pleasures: after getting good and hot visiting a temple or two, you'll be refreshed by crossing the cool Chao Phraya on a ferryboat before tackling another.

A Good Tour

Start at the **Grand Palace** ①, Bangkok's major landmark, and go on to the adjoining **Wat Phra Keo** ②. Then walk south on Sanamchai Road (or take a taxi) to **Wat Pho** ③. From Wat Pho, walk west to the river and then north (toward the Grand Palace) about 250 yards to the Tha Thien jetty and take the ferry across to **Wat Arun** ④. Return by the same ferry to the eastern shore and take a tuk-tuk to **Chinatown.** Get out at Pahuraht Road, and as you take in the sights, walk east, then zigzag left to Yaowarat Road, and continue east until it leads into Charoen Krung. On the opposite corner stands **Wat Traimitr** ⑤.

Timing

This is a full day's sightseeing. Ideally, you would begin early in the morning, take a break for lunch to escape the heat of midday, and end the excursion in the late afternoon. You might spend as much as 90 minutes each at the Grand Palace and Wat Phra Keo. Wat Pho will only take a half hour, unless you have an hour-long massage. Allow time to climb the prang at Wat Arun (unless you suffer from vertigo). Chinatown is a maze of streets and markets, so two hours of wandering can pass by quickly, though nonshoppers may find 30 minutes sufficient. Wat Traimitr can be a 15-minute stop, or you might like to sit there a while and restore your spirit. Some of Bangkok's sights close in the middle of the day, so plan accordingly. Much of Chinatown closes down during Chinese New Year.

Sights to See

Chinatown. When its buildings were the tallest in the land, Chinatown used to be Bangkok's prosperous downtown, but, as the city grew, new, taller office buildings sprang up farther east, and the neighborhood lost some of its bustle. Red lanterns and Chinese signs still abound, and modest restaurants line the streets. Pahuraht Road is full of textile shops, with nearly as many Indian dealers here as Chinese, and Yaowarat Road, the main thoroughfare, is crowded with gold and jewelry shops. The Thieves Market, at the northwest end of Yaowarat Road, used to sell antiques bargains; it has become more utilitarian in its wares, but it's still fun to browse.

❶ **Grand Palace.** In 1782, when King Rama I moved the capital across the river from Thonburi, he built this palace and walled city, which subsequent Chakri monarchs enlarged. The compound is open to visitors, but all the buildings, which are used only for state occasions and royal ceremonies, are not. The official residence of the king—he actually lives at Chitlada Palace in north Bangkok—is the Chakri Maha Prasart palace, whose state function rooms are sometimes open to visitors on special occasions. The Dusit Maha Prasart, on the right, is a classic example of palace architecture, and Amarin Vinichai Hall, on the left, the original audience hall, is now used for the presentation of ambassadors' credentials. Note the glittering gold throne. ▨ *Admission.* ☉ *Daily 8:30–3:30.*

❹ **Wat Arun.** The Temple of the Dawn is inspiring at sunrise; it is even more marvelous toward dusk, when the setting sun casts amber tones. The temple's architecture is symmetrical, with a square courtyard containing five Khmer-style prangs, the central prang (282 ft) surrounded by its four attendant prangs in the corners. All five are covered in mosaics of broken pieces of Chinese porcelain. Energetic visitors climb the steep steps of the central prang for the view over the Chao Phraya, and the less ambitious linger in the small park by the river, a peaceful spot to take in the sights and smells and watch the sun go down, though the best view is from across the river with the sun setting behind Wat Arun. ✉ *Admission.* ⊙ *Daily 8:30–5:30.*

★ ❸ **Wat Pho, or Wat Phra Jetuphon.** The Temple of the Reclining Buddha, the largest wat in Bangkok, houses the largest—151 ft—Reclining Buddha in the country. Especially noteworthy are his 10-ft feet, with the 108 auspicious signs of the Buddha inlaid in mother-of-pearl.

Walk beyond the chapel containing the Reclining Buddha and enter Bangkok's oldest open university. A hundred years before Bangkok was established as the capital, a monastery was founded to teach classical Thai medicine. The school still gives instruction in natural methods of healing. Around the walls are marble plaques inscribed with formulas for herbal cures, and stone sculptures squat in various postures demonstrating techniques for relieving pain.

The monks still practice ancient cures, and the **massage school of Wat Pho** has become famous. A massage (B200) lasts one hour, growing more and more pleasurable as you adjust to it. Masseurs and masseuses are available daily 8–6. Massage courses of up to 10 days are also available. Don't be perturbed by the tall statues that good-naturedly poke fun at farangs. Referred to as Chinese rock sculptures, these gangling twice-life-size figures depict the most evil demons, which scare away all other evil spirits. With their top hats, they look farcically Western and, in fact, were modeled after the Europeans who plundered China during the Opium Wars.

These statues guard the entrance to the northeastern quarter of the compound and a very pleasant three-tier temple containing 394 seated Buddhas. Usually a monk sits cross-legged at one side of the altar, making himself available to answer questions (in Thai). On the walls, bas-relief plaques salvaged from Ayutthaya depict stories from the *Ramayana*. Around this temple area are four tall chedis, decorated with brightly colored porcelain, each representing one of the first four kings of the Chakri dynasty. ✉ *Admission.* ⊙ *Daily 7–5.*

★ ❷ **Wat Phra Keo.** No building within the Grand Palace compound excites such awe as the adjoining Temple of the Emerald Buddha, the most sacred temple in the kingdom. No other wat in Thailand is so ornate and so embellished with murals, statues, and glittering gold. As your wat experience grows, you may decide that you prefer the simplicity of some other wats, but you'll never quite get over Wat Phra Keo's elaborate richness.

As you enter the compound, take note of the 20-ft-tall helmeted and tile-encrusted statues in traditional Thai battle attire standing guard. They set the scene—mystical, majestic, and awesome. Turn right as you enter, and notice along the inner walls the lively murals depicting the whole *Ramayana* epic (*Ramakien* in Thai).

The main chapel, with its gilded three-tier roof, dazzles your eyes. Royal griffins stand guard outside, and the perfect symmetry of the shining gold stupas in the court gives a feeling of serenity. Inside sits the Emerald Buddha. This most venerated image of Lord Buddha is carved from one piece of jade 31 inches high. No one knows its origin, but history places it in Chiang Rai in 1464. From there it traveled first to Chiang

Exploring Bangkok

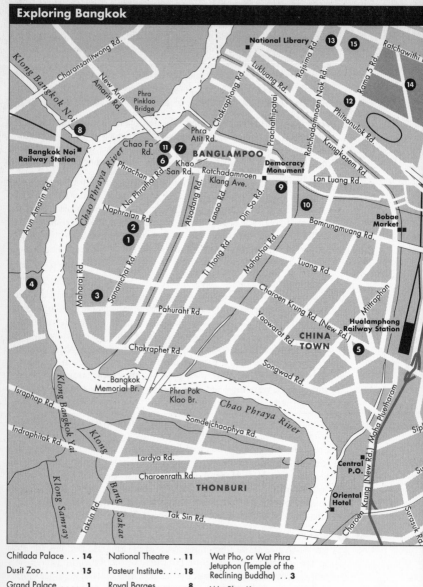

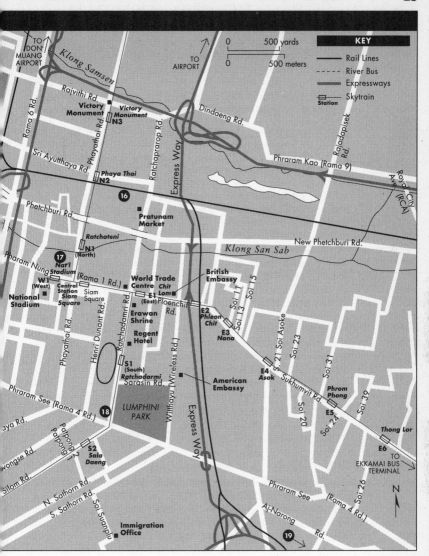

KEY

— Rail Lines
--- River Bus
— Expressways
▢ Skytrain
Station

TO DON MUANG AIRPORT

TO AIRPORT

0   500 yards
0   500 meters

Klong Samsen

Rajvithi Rd.

Rama 6 Rd.

Victory Monument

Victory Monument
N3

Dindaeng Rd.

Phayathai Rd.

Ratchaprarop Rd.

Express Way

Sri Ayutthaya Rd.

Phraram Kao (Rama 9)

Rajdapisek Rd.

Royal City Ave. (RCA)

Phaya Thai
N2

16

Phetchburi Rd.

Pratunam Market

Pharam Nung

Ratchateni
N1 (North)

Klong San Sab

New Phetchburi Rd.

17
Nat'l Stadium

W1 (West)

Central Station Siam Square

(Rama 1 Rd.)

World Trade Centre

British Embassy

National Stadium

Siam Square

Ratchadamri Rd.

Erawan Shrine

E1 (East)

Chit Lom

Ploenchit Rd.

E2
Phleon Chit

E3
Nana

Soi 11

Soi 13

Soi 15

Phayathai Rd.

Henri Dunant Rd.

Regent Hotel

Withayu (Wireless Rd.)

21 Soi Asoke

Soi 23

Soi Asoke

Soi 31

S1 (South)
Ratchadarmi
Sarasin Rd.

American Embassy

E4
Asok

Sukhumvit Rd.

Soi 39

Phrom Phong

Phraram See (Rama 4 Rd.)

18

LUMPHINI PARK

Express Way

Soi 20

E5
Soi 24

Thong Lor

...ya Rd.

Palpong 1
Palpong 2

S2
Sala Daeng

E6

TO EKKAMAI BUS TERMINAL

...wongse Rd.

Silom Rd.

N. Sathorn Rd.

S. Sathorn Rd.

Soi Suanplu

Immigration Office

Phraram See

(Rama 4 Rd.)

Ai-Narong Rd.

Soi 26

N

19

Mai, then to Lamphun, and finally back to Chiang Rai, where the Lao-
tians stole it and took it home with them. Eventually, the Thais sent
an army to get it back, and it reached its final resting place when King
Rama I built the chapel. The statue is high above the altar and visitors
can see it only from afar. Behind the altar and above the window
frames are murals depicting the life and eventual enlightenment of the
Buddha. At the back of the royal chapel you'll find a scale model of
Angkor Wat. ✉ *Admission.* ☺ *Daily 8:30–11:30 and 1–3:30.*

Just east of the Grand Palace compound is the **City Pillar Shrine,** containing the foundation stone (Lak Muang) from which all distances in
Thailand are measured. The stone is believed to be inhabited by a spirit
that guards the well-being of Bangkok.

NEED A BREAK?	When you're ready for refreshment, try the pleasant **snack bar** in the northeastern part of the compound, which serves delicious chilled co- conut milk.

★ ❺   **Wat Traimitr.** The main Temple of the Golden Buddha has little architectural merit, but off to the side, next to the money-changing wagon,
is a small chapel containing the world's largest solid-gold Buddha, cast
about nine centuries ago. Weighing 5½ tons and standing 10 ft high,
the statue gleams with such richness and purity that even the most jaded
are inspired by its strength and power (and value). The statue, sculpted
in Sukhothai style, is believed to have been brought first to Ayutthaya.
When the Burmese were about to sack the city, it was covered in plaster, and two centuries later, still in plaster, it was thought to be just another statue. When it was being moved to a new temple in Bangkok
in the 1950s it slipped from a crane and was left in the mud by work-
men. In the morning, a temple monk, who had dreamed that the statue
was divinely inspired, went to see the Buddha image. Through a crack
in the plaster he saw a glint of yellow, and soon discovered that the
statue was pure gold. ✉ *Admission.* ☺ *Daily 9–5.*

Museums and Wats

Slightly inland from the river and north of the Grand Palace stands a
cluster of government buildings. The neighborhood, in itself not particularly attractive, is made even less appealing by the jammed traffic
on weekdays, but you must not miss the National Museum, with Thailand's most valued historic treasures and a great collection of Southeast Asian art. There are also two unusual temples a little farther east.

A Good Tour

The **National Museum** ⑥ should be seen early in your visit. The **National Art Gallery** ⑦ is opposite. Next, take a ferry across the Chao Phraya
to visit the **Royal Barges** ⑧, coming back the same way. You can walk
or take a tuk-tuk east, past the National Museum and the Democracy
Monument, to **Wat Rachanada** ⑨. Then walk east, across Maha Chai
Road, to **Wat Saket** ⑩, a notable landmark of the old city. Come back
to the **National Theatre** ⑪, next to the National Museum, for a classical Thai dance or drama performance.

Timing

The route is fairly compact. The museums are close together, and
though it's not more than a 15-minute walk, you can take a tuk-tuk
or taxi to Wat Rachanada. Wat Saket is just a block away. Allow a good
two or three hours at the National Museum and just under an hour at
the National Art Gallery. Both are closed on Monday, Tuesday, and
public holidays. Then, after lunch, visit Wat Rachanada and Wat Saket.
It will take at least an hour by taxi from the Sukhumvit area to reach

the National Theatre, and 40 minutes from the Silom Road area via the river bus.

Sights to See

❼ National Art Gallery. Opposite the National Theatre, the National Art Gallery exhibits both modern and traditional Thai art. ⊠ *Chao Fa Rd.,* ☎ *02/281–2224.* ▦ *Admission.* ◷ *Tues.–Thurs. and weekends 9–4.*

★ ❻ National Museum. By far the best place to acquaint yourself with Thai history and art is the National Museum, which has one of the world's best collections of Southeast Asian art in general, and Buddhist and Thai art in particular. Most of the masterpieces of the Sukhothai and Ayutthaya periods and works from the northern provinces are here, leaving up-country museums bare. You'll also have a good opportunity to trace Thailand's long history, beginning with the ceramic utensils and bronzeware of the Ban Chiang civilization (3000–4000 BC). The main building was built in 1783 as a palace for surrogate kings (a position abolished in 1874). You might go first to the artifact gallery, at the left of the ticket counter, for a historical overview. Afterward, explore the galleries that portray the Dvaravati and Khmer periods. These will prepare you for the different styles of Thai art, from the Sukhothai period (1238–mid-14th century) on. ⊠ *Na Phra That Rd.,* ☎ *02/224–1333.* ▦ *Admission.* ◷ *Wed.–Sun. 9–4. Free 90-min orientation tours in English start at the bookshop 9:30 AM Wed.–Thurs.*

⓫ National Theatre. Classical Thai dance and drama can usually be seen here on the last Friday and Saturday of each month, but it is best to call for the schedule or ask your hotel staff (☞ Nightlife and the Arts, *below*). ⊠ *Na Phra That Rd.,* ☎ *02/224–1342.*

❽ Royal Barges. These splendid ceremonial barges are berthed in a shed on the Thonburi side of the Chao Phraya River. The boats, carved in the early part of the 19th century, take the form of mythical creatures in the *Ramayana.* The most impressive is the red-and-gold royal flag barge, *Suphannahongse* (Golden Swan), used by the king on special occasions, including the Royal Barge procession each November. Carved from a single piece of teak, it measures about 150 ft and weighs more than 15 tons. Fifty oarsmen propel it along the Chao Phraya River, accompanied by two coxswains, flag wavers, and a rhythm-keeper. ☎ *02/424–0004* ▦ *Admission.* ◷ *Daily 8:30–4:30.*

❾ Wat Rachanada. Across from Wat Saket, this Temple of the Metal Castle intentionally resembles the mythical castle of the gods. According to legend, a wealthy and pious man built a fabulous castle, Loha Prasat, from the design laid down in Hindu mythology for the disciples of the Buddha. Wat Rachanada, built in metal, is meant to duplicate that castle and is the only one of its kind remaining. There are stalls selling amulets that protect the wearer from misfortune—usually of the physical kind, though love amulets and charms are also sold. They tend to be rather expensive, but that's the price of good fortune. ▦ *Admission.* ◷ *Daily 8–6.*

❿ Wat Saket. East of the Democracy Monument you'll find the Temple of the Golden Mount, a notable landmark of the old city and, for a long time, the highest point in the city. King Rama III started construction of this mound and temple, which were completed by Rama V. To reach the gold-covered chedi, you must climb an exhausting 318 steps winding around the mound. Don't even attempt it on a hot day, but on a cool, clear day, the view from the top is magnificent. Every November, at the time of the Loi Kratong festival, there is a popular temple fair (*ngan wat*), with food stalls and stage shows. ▦ *Admission.* ◷ *Daily 8–5.*

Scattered Bangkok

Bangkok sprawls, seemingly without rhyme or reason, in delightful chaos. Neighborhoods as we know them in the West do not exist. Once you leave the Chao Phraya River, you are in a mix of the old and the new, amidst the glitz of new wealth and the simplicity of poverty. Temples, factories, palaces, office buildings, and private houses may all be found on one block. Unfortunately, getting from one major sight to another takes time, usually spent in stalled traffic.

A Good Tour (or Two or Three)

It makes sense to treat the widely spaced sights in scattered Bangkok as a smorgasbord from which to select a sight or two when you're nearby. You might go first to one of Bangkok's most photographed temples, **Wat Benjamabophit** ⑫, northeast of the Democracy Monument. Then it's a short tuk-tuk ride to **Vimarnmek Mansion** ⑬, the largest teak structure in the world. On your way there, you'll probably pass by **Chitlada Palace** ⑭, on the right. On the other side of the road is the **Dusit Zoo** ⑮. West of the zoo is **Banglampoo,** where backpackers gravitate, a fascinating insight into what Western culture can produce. The **Suan Pakkard Palace** ⑯ is on the south side of Sri Ayutthaya Road, between Phayathai and Ratchaprarop roads; its five traditional Thai houses make a nice contrast to Vimarnmek Mansion. **Jim Thompson's House** ⑰ is west of Siam Square. If cold-blooded reptiles strike your fancy, visit the **Pasteur Institute** ⑱, a snake farm a little west of Lumphini Park. **Muang Boran** ⑲ can give you a one-day tour by miniature of the rest of Thailand if you don't have time to see the real thing.

Sights to See

Banglampoo. Backpackers from around the world gather here, near the Chao Phraya just north of Ratchadamnoen Road. It's not really Bangkok; it's a human zoo, and Thais apparently go there to look at strange Westerners. It's also where the movie *The Beach* begins, as well as a source for the latest in travel tips. Many agencies here can book inexpensive travel and tours. The main thoroughfare, Khao Sahn Road, is full of cafés, secondhand bookstalls, and inexpensive shops. In the evening, the streets are full of food stands catering to young Westerners. Off Khao Sahn Road, hundreds of small guest houses rent tiny rooms for B150 to B300 a night.

⑭ **Chitlada Palace.** When in Bangkok, the king resides at Chitlada Palace, which covers the whole block across from the Dusit Zoo. The public is not permitted, and you are only able to see high walls and the honor guards as you drive by.

☙ ⑮ **Dusit Zoo.** When you are exhausted by Bangkok's traffic and want to rest in a pleasant expanse of greenery, pay a visit to the Dusit Zoo (Khao Din Wana). Children can ride elephants (not the white ones, which are of "royal blood"), and you can sit at one of the shaded cafés. ☎ 02/ 281–0021 ☞ *Admission.* ☉ *Daily 8:30–6.*

⑰ **Jim Thompson's House.** American Jim Thompson, once an architect in New York, joined the OSS in World War II and went to Asia. After the war, he stayed on and took it upon himself to revitalize Thailand's moribund silk industry. His project met with tremendous success, which in itself would have made him a legend. In 1967 Thompson went to the Malaysian Cameron Highlands for a quiet holiday and was never heard from again. Thompson imported parts of up-country buildings, some as old as 150 years, to construct his compound of six Thai houses. Three are exactly the same as their originals, including details of the interior layout. With true appreciation and a connoisseur's eye, Thompson then furnished them with what are now priceless pieces of

Southeast Asian art. The entrance is easy to miss: at the end of an un-prepossessing lane, leading north off Rama I Road, west of Phayathai Road, the house is on your left. It is down the street from the National Stadium skytrain station. ⊠ *Soi Kasemsong 2,* ☎ *02/612–3668.* 🖾 *Admission.* ⊙ *Mon.–Sat. 9–4:30.*

⑲ Muang Boran (Ancient City). About an hour's drive (20 km/12 mi) south-east of the city is a park shaped like Thailand. You enter at the coun-try's southern tip and find throughout the park, placed more or less as in geographical reality, 108 smaller but proportionally correct repli-cas of Thailand's most important architectural sites and monuments. You really need wheels—the area is too vast to cover on foot. Small, discreetly placed restaurants are scattered throughout the grounds, and crafts are sold in a "traditional Thai village." Allow a good four hours to cover most of the sites. By car, take the Samrong–Samut Prakan ex-pressway and turn left at the Samut Prakan intersection onto Old Sukhumvit Road. At km 33, Muang Boran is on your left. Or, take air-conditioned bus No. 11 and get off at Pak Nam to transfer to a small bus, No. 36, which passes in front of the city. You can take a tour arranged by your hotel, or, better yet, four can hire a car and driver for about B1,000. ⊠ *Old Sukhumvit Rd., Samut Prakan,* ☎ *02/323–9252.* 🖾 *Admission.* ⊙ *Daily 8–5.*

👒 ⑱ Pasteur Institute. In 1923, the Thai Red Cross established this snake farm, where venom is milked and stored as an antidote for people kissed by poisonous snakes. At the top end of Suriwongse Road (corner of Rama IV and Henri Dunant), it was the second in the world (the first was in Brazil). There are daily slide shows before the milking sessions at 11 AM, with a second show on weekdays only at 2:30 PM. You can watch the handlers work with deadly cobras, kraits, and pit vipers; you can also get typhoid, cholera, and smallpox vaccinations here. ⊠ *1871 Rama IV Rd.,* ☎ *02/252–0161.* 🖾 *Admission.* ⊙ *Weekdays 8:30–4:30, weekends and holidays 8:30–noon.*

★ ⑯ Suan Pakkard Palace. Five antique teak houses, built high on columns, complement the undulating lawns, shimmering lotus pools, and lush shrub-bery. The serene atmosphere makes Suan Pakkard one of the most re-laxing places in which to absorb traditional Thai culture. The center of attraction, the Lacquer Pavilion, at the back of the garden, contains gold-covered paneling with scenes from the life of the Buddha, and the other houses display porcelains, Khmer stone heads, old paintings, and Bud-dha statues. ☎ *02/245–4934.* 🖾 *Admission.* ⊙ *Daily 9–4.*

⑬ Vimarnmek Mansion. This is the largest teak structure in the world, moved to its present location early last century by King Rama V. The three-story suburban mansion is now in the center of administrative Bangkok, next to the National Assembly building, because the capi-tal has grown so much. The place fits its name, "Castle in the Clouds," its extraordinary lightness enhanced by a reflecting pond. King Rama V's fascination with Western architecture shows in its Victorian style, but the building retains an unmistakably Thai delicacy. Most of the furnishings were either bought in the West or given by European monarchs. Some are exquisite—porcelain, handcrafted furniture, and crystal—and some have novelty value, like the first typewriter brought to Thailand. Exhibitions of Thai dancing take place daily at 10:30 and 2. ☎ *02/628–6300.* 🖾 *Admission.* ⊙ *Daily 9:30–3:15.*

★ ⑫ Wat Benjamabophit. Bangkok's most photographed wat, the Marble Temple, was built in 1899 and is where Thailand's present king came to spend his days as a monk before his coronation. Statues of the Bud-dha line the courtyard, and the magnificent interior has cross beams of lacquer and gold, but Wat Benjamabophit is more than a splendid temple. The monastery is a seat of learning that appeals to Buddhist monks with intellectual yearnings. 🎫 *Admission.* ⊙ *Daily 7–5.*

DINING

Thais are passionate about food—finding the out-of-the-way shop that prepares some specialty better than any place else, then dragging groups of friends to share the discovery, is a national pastime. The tastes and smells of Thai food are all around you, day and night, since Thais always seem to be eating. Until your digestion adjusts to the food, steer clear of stands in markets and at roadsides. Most are safe, but as a general rule, you should stick to cooked food. The clean, well-maintained food shops on major roads and in shopping centers rarely cause problems and will give you a chance to taste authentic versions of popular Thai dishes at very low prices.

Though Bangkok's water is potable, it's best for visitors to drink bottled. Clear ice cubes with holes through them are made with purified water, and most restaurants use them.

Restaurants usually stop serving dinner at 10:30 PM, but you will find many local places stay open until midnight and later. For price categories, *see* Dining *in* Smart Travel Tips A to Z.

Chinese

$$$ ✕ **Dynasty.** Government ministers and the local business establishment come here to feast on outstanding Cantonese cuisine. In addition to the main dining area, 11 quiet rooms provide unsurpassed settings for business lunches or dinners (nine of them accommodate 10 people each, the other two hold up to 50). The red carpeting, heavy traditional Chinese furniture, carved screens, and porcelain objets d'art contribute to the quietly elegant atmosphere. The Peking duck and shark's-fin dishes, prepared by two first-rate Hong Kong chefs, are among the draws. Seasonal specialties include everything from "hairy crab" (October–November) to "Taiwanese eels" (March), with only fresh ingredients used. The service is efficient and friendly without being obtrusive. ✉ *Central Plaza Hotel, 1695 Phaholyothin Rd.,* ☎ *02/541–1234. Reservations essential. AE, DC, MC, V.*

$$$ ✕ **Mayflower.** Captains of industry, royalty, and heads of state are among the regular customers of the five stylishly opulent private rooms and main dining area of the Mayflower. The carved wood screens and porcelain vases set a tone of simple-but-luxurious refinement perfectly in keeping with the outstanding Cantonese food. To provide the best service possible, a computerized record is kept of the guests—of their food preferences, the size of their families, important anniversaries, etc. Two of the best items on the menu are the piquant abalone-and-jellyfish salad, and the Drunken Chinese Chicken—steamed, skinned, and boned chicken doused with Chinese liquor and served with two sauces, one sweet and one spicy. The shark's-fin soup and the dim sum are also worth sampling. An excellent wine list assumes price is no object. Two- to three-day advance notice is required for private rooms. ✉ *Dusit Thani Hotel, Rama IV Rd.,* ☎ *02/236–0450. Reservations essential. AE, DC, V.*

$$$ ✕ **Royal Kitchen.** The Royal Kitchen consists of a number of small, el-
★   egant dining rooms where everything, right down to the silver chopsticks, has been carefully considered. The menu is a reference resource for southern Chinese delicacies, including *mieng nok,* with finely minced, seasoned pigeon served on individual fragrant leaves. At

lunchtime, dim sum is served, and it, too, is probably Bangkok's best, as beautifully presented as it is subtle in taste. ⊠ *N. Sathorn Rd., opposite YWCA and Thai Oil,* ☎ *02/234–3063. Reservations essential. Jacket and tie. AE, DC, MC, V.*

$$$ ✕ **Sui Sian.** The Sui Sian serves great, if a tiny bit inconsistent, Cantonese cuisine. Certainly the decor, the service, and the design of both the main dining area and the private rooms make it a good spot for lunch or dinner meetings. The main dining rooms with bamboo-tile eaves give the feel of a courtyard, an impression reinforced by the jade trees on display. The Peking duck is particularly good. If you're in an extravagant mood, try the pricey Ancient Master Jumps the Wall—a soup incorporating black chicken, deer tendons, abalone, shark's fin, dried scallops, fish maw, turtle, sea cucumber, mushrooms, and a selection of secret Chinese herbs. ⊠ *Landmark Hotel, 138 Sukhumvit Rd.,* ☎ *02/254–0404. AE, DC, MC, V.*

$$–$$$ ✕ **Hok Thean Lauo.** A shuttle boat runs guests across the Chao Phraya from the River City Shopping Centre to one of Bangkok's top Cantonese restaurants. It's nicest to sit at a table by the window, watching the rice barges labor up and down the river. Hok Thean Lauo is known for its dim-sum lunches, especially on Sunday. Waiters continually pass your table offering you small baskets of delicacies. If you're not selective, you'll probably spoil your appetite for the next two days. ⊠ *762 Ladya Rd., Klongsam,* ☎ *02/437–1121. Reservations essential Sun. AE, DC, MC, V.*

$$ ✕ **Jade Garden.** Fine Cantonese cuisine at good value makes this restaurant well worth visiting for dim-sum brunch or dinner. The superb dishes are made without the aid of MSG, a rarity in this part of the world. The decor is similarly assured in its effects, with a remarkable wood-beam ceiling and softly lighted Chinese-print screens. Private dining rooms are available with advance notice; otherwise ask for the corner table in the main dining room—it's partly partitioned off and affords extra privacy. Two good dinner specials are fried Hong Kong noodles and pressed duck with tea leaves. Look for the monthly "special promotion" dish featuring seasonal ingredients. ⊠ *Montien Hotel, 54 Suriwongse Rd.,* ☎ *02/233–7060. AE, DC, MC, V.*

$$ ✕ **Shangrila.** The menu has a wide range of dishes, from Peking duck
★ to thinly sliced pork with garlic, but it is hard to pass up the marvelous dim-sum selection. Waiters will help you choose, but it's difficult to make a mistake. Service is pleasantly attentive even when a high-powered politician comes in and is fawned over. The restaurant's split levels and small size make it a more comfortable Chinese place than many in this neighborhood, and the bright white tablecloths and gleaming glassware make for an upbeat dining experience. ⊠ *154/4–7 Silom Rd.,* ☎ *02/234–9147 or 02/234–9149. AE, DC, MC, V.*

$$ ✕ **Tien Tien.** For years, Tien Tien has catered to a busy business lunch trade. Dinner is good, too, if you happen to be in the neighborhood, but the decor doesn't get much beyond white tablecloths and red walls. The roast pork is superb: have it any way you want, but it's so juicy and tender that simple steamed rice is a sufficient complement. The Peking duck is also a must; its skin is crisp and the pancakes are light and fluffy. ⊠ *105 Patpong, Silom Rd.,* ☎ *02/234–8717. MC, V.*

$ ✕ **Coca Noodles.** On evenings and weekends, this giant, raucous restaurant is full of Chinese families eating a daunting variety of noodle dishes with noisy gusto. Both wheat- and rice-based pastas are available in abundance, in combination with a cornucopia of meats, fish, shellfish, and crunchy Chinese vegetables. Try some of the green, wheat-based noodles called *mee yoke,* topped with a chicken thigh, red pork, or crabmeat. You can also prepare yourself an intriguing Chinese variant of sukiyaki on a gas ring built into the table. ⊠ *In Siam Square Shop-*

Bangkok Dining and Lodging

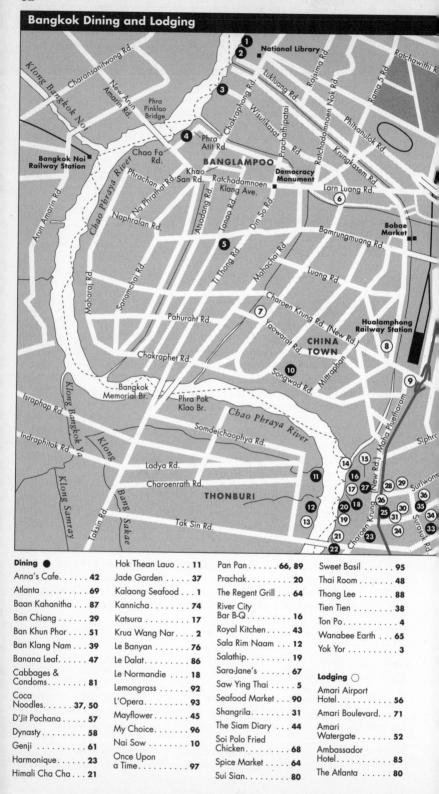

Dining ●

Anna's Cafe	**42**
Atlanta	**69**
Baan Kahanitha	**87**
Ban Chiang	**29**
Ban Khun Phor	**51**
Ban Klang Nam	**39**
Banana Leaf	**47**
Cabbages & Condoms	**81**
Coca Noodles	**37, 50**
D'Jit Pochana	**57**
Dynasty	**58**
Genji	**61**
Harmonique	**23**
Himali Cha Cha	**21**

Hok Thean Lauo	**11**
Jade Garden	**37**
Kalaong Seafood	**1**
Kannicha	**74**
Katsura	**17**
Krua Wang Nar	**2**
Le Banyan	**76**
Le Dalat	**86**
Le Normandie	**18**
Lemongrass	**92**
L'Opera	**93**
Mayflower	**45**
My Choice	**96**
Nai Sow	**10**
Once Upon a Time	**97**

Pan Pan	**66, 89**
Prachak	**20**
The Regent Grill	**64**
River City Bar B-Q	**16**
Royal Kitchen	**43**
Sala Rim Naam	**12**
Salathip	**19**
Sara-Jane's	**67**
Saw Ying Thai	**5**
Seafood Market	**90**
Shangrila	**31**
The Siam Diary	**44**
Soi Polo Fried Chicken	**68**
Spice Market	**64**
Sui Sian	**80**

Sweet Basil	**95**
Thai Room	**48**
Thong Lee	**88**
Tien Tien	**38**
Ton Po	**4**
Wanabee Earth	**65**
Yok Yor	**3**

Lodging ○

Amari Airport Hotel	**56**
Amari Boulevard	**71**
Amari Watergate	**52**
Ambassador Hotel	**85**
The Atlanta	**80**

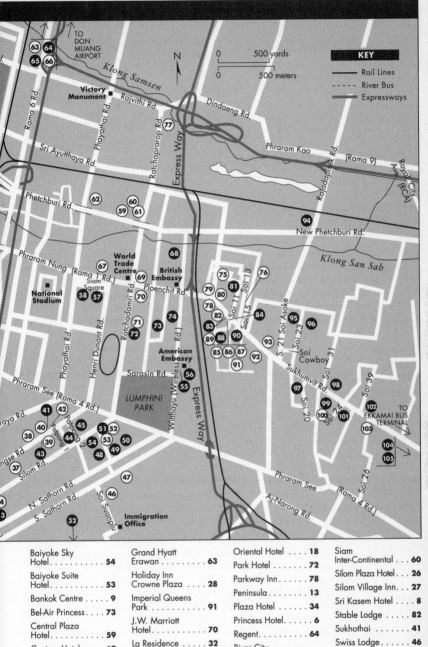

ping Centre facing 461 Henri Dunant Rd., ☎ 02/251–6337 or 02/251–3538. Another branch is at 6 Soi Tantawan, Suriwongse Rd., ☎ 02/236–0107. No credit cards.

$ ✕ **Prachak.** Families from wealthy neighborhoods send their maids here
★ to bring back the superb roast duck (*ped*) and red pork (*moo daeng*)
for dinner. By 6 PM there's often no duck or pork left. Nobody comes
here for the tile floors and bare walls; it may even strike you as a little grungy—but the food is fine. The problem is in *finding* this hole-
in-the-wall restaurant. It is across from Bangrak Market (beside the
Shangri-La hotel), diagonally across the road from a 7-Eleven store.
Two can dine well for $6. The present owner, grandson of the founder,
speaks some English. ✉ *1415 Charoen Krung (New Road), Silom
Bansak, ☎ 02/234–3755. Reservations not accepted. No credit cards.*

Eclectic

$ ✕ **The Siam Diary.** A convenient social spot if you are at the upper end
of Silom or Sathorn roads (it's between the two, one block in from Rama
IV Road), this cozy Thai-style pub and restaurant has a convivial
atmosphere that attracts local expats and Thais. You can sit at the bar
or at tables, and the food is a mixture of Thai and Western, from fried
noodles to hamburgers. On Friday and Saturday, a trio plays jazz until
shortly after midnight. ✉ *14/10 Soi Saladeang, Rama IV, ☎ 02/663–
5348. MC, V.*

$ ✕ **Thai Room.** This time capsule opened during the Vietnam War, in
1966, when it was packed in the evening with GIs on R&R. Not a
molecule of the decor has changed since then, and it is not unusual to
see a veteran of that war quietly reminiscing. Around him, however,
will be local residents and tourists in from the tawdry riot of Patpong.
The Mexican food is a peculiar hybrid of Mexican and Thai cuisines,
and the result is not unpleasing. Some of the Italian items, like the eggplant parmigiana, are very good by any standard, and the Thai food
can be excellent. Local clients feel great affection for this one-of-a-kind
restaurant, which stays open until midnight. ✉ *30/37 Patpong 2 Rd.
(between Silom and Suriwongse Rds.), ☎ 02/233–7920. Reservations
not accepted. AE, DC, MC, V.*

French

$$$$ ✕ **Le Banyan.** Come here—a warm, intimate, and vaguely colonial old
Thai house—for first-rate French cooking. The chef occasionally ex-
periments with Asian influences, adding an accent of lemongrass, ginger, or Thai basil. A large silver-plated duck press normally takes
center stage in the dining room. Pressed duck à la Rouennaise, in a sauce
prepared with the juices of the bird and red wine, is one of the duck
specialties. Pan-fried foie gras and king lobster make delicious alter-
natives. ✉ *59 Sukhumvit Soi 8, ☎ 02/253–5556. Reservations essential. AE, DC, MC, V. Closed Mon. Dinner only.*

$$$$ ✕ **Le Normandie.** This legendary restaurant perched atop the Orien-
★ tal Hotel commands a panoramic view across the Chao Phraya River.
Michelin three-star chef Georges Blanc is the restaurant's permanent
consultant and, periodically, the most highly esteemed chefs in France
take over in the kitchen. These artists usually import ingredients from
home, and at such times the restaurant's patrons feast on phenome-
nal French cuisine. Even when no superstar chef is on the scene, the
food is remarkable, with the menu often including rare dishes taught
to Le Normandie's master chef by the visiting chefs. ✉ *48 Oriental
Ave., ☎ 02/234–8690. Reservations essential. Jacket and tie. AE, DC,
MC, V. No lunch Sun.*

$$$$ ✕ **The Regent Grill.** With a terrace overlooking the imaginatively land-scaped grounds of the Regent of Bangkok Hotel, this is a strikingly designed, high-fashion French restaurant. Though the menu empha-sizes grilled dishes, from time to time it features such memorable en-trées as fresh goose liver in raspberry vinegar (which can be specially ordered a day or so in advance). Excellent endive salads and lobster dishes, one with a subtle goose-liver sauce, are regularly featured. ✉ *155 Ratchadamri Rd.,* ☎ *02/251–6127. Reservations essential. Jacket and tie. AE, DC, MC, V. No dinner weekdays.*

Indian

$$ ✕ **Himali Cha Cha.** Though Cha Cha, the chef who was once Nehru's cook, died in 1996, his recipes live on, now prepared with matching ability by his wife. Northern Indian cuisine is served in a pleasantly informal setting with the usual Mogul decor. The quality of the food, which has kept the place a favorite for a decade, remains top-notch. The tandoori chicken is locally famous, and the daily specials, precisely explained, are usually to be recommended. Always good are the breads and the fruit-flavored *lassis* (yogurt drinks)—especially the mango ones. ✉ *1229/11 New Rd.,* ☎ *02/235–1569. AE, DC, MC, V.*

Italian

$$ ✕ **L'Opera.** Specializing in a variety of homemade pastas, this family bistro draws a loyal clientele of expats. The staff takes pride in work-ing here, and many of them have remained over the years despite cut-throat competition. This is a fine spot to eat when you have a craving for tortelli, large ravioli stuffed with spinach and cheese, or *spadar-rata,* a combination of seafood with garlic-and-white-wine sauce. The bay window table is nice but, given its proximity to the air-conditioner, you might want to wear a sweater. ✉ *53 Sukhumvit Soi 39,* ☎ *02/ 258–5606. AE, DC, MC, V.*

$$ ✕ **Pan Pan.** The two branches of this Italian food and ice-cream chain are enormously popular. They are decorated with Italian kitchen uten-sils and spices, and the relaxed atmosphere in both places invites inti-mate talk. The long list of generous and delicious pasta dishes includes linguine with a sauce of salmon, cream, and vodka that is a taste of high-calorie heaven, and "Chicken Godfather," with a cream-and-mushroom sauce, similarly disappointment-proof. But save room for the ice cream, which is of the thick, dense, Italian type. The branch on Sukhumvit Road offers an antipasto buffet and a large selection of ex-tremely rich desserts. ✉ *6–6/1 Sukhumvit Rd., near Soi 33,* ☎ *02/258–9304 or 02/258–5071;* ✉ *45 Soi Lang Suan, off Ploenchit Rd.,* ☎ *02/ 252–7104. AE, DC, MC, V.*

Japanese

$$$ ✕ **Genji.** Bangkok has many good Japanese restaurants, although a num-ber of them give a chilly reception to outsiders. Genji is a happy ex-ception. The fact that it's in a large international hotel shouldn't deter culinary purists—it has an excellent sushi bar and several small pri-vate rooms. Try especially the succulent grilled eel. Set menus for lunch and dinner are well conceived, and Japanese breakfasts are also served. ✉ *Hilton International, 2 Wireless Rd.,* ☎ *02/253–0123. Reservations essential. AE, DC, MC, V.*

$$$ ✕ **Katsura.** This elegant little place overlooking the Chao Phraya River is favored by Japanese and Westerners alike. Though there are three small private rooms, ask for a table by the river, especially at night. There are teppanyaki and sushi counters in the main dining room, where you'll feel entirely comfortable eating alone. The menu offers a number of the chef's inventions, such as sushi with shrimp eggs, a treat for both the eyes and the palate. The *gyuniku-yudofu* (a hot pot of sliced beef, bean curd, and vegetables) and *dobin mushi* (steamed seafood custard served in earthen teapots) are two other favorites. ⊠ *Royal Orchid Sheraton, 2 Captain Bush La.,* ☎ *02/234–5599. AE, DC, MC, V.*

Thai

$$$ ✕ **Lemongrass.** Elegance and a certain adventurousness have made this restaurant a favorite with Thais and resident Westerners. Embellished with Southeast Asian antiques, the dining rooms and the garden have plenty of atmosphere. Over the years the cuisine has become geared to the milder palate of Westerners, which makes for a good introduction to Thai food. Be sure to try a glass of *nam takrai,* the cold, sweet drink brewed from lemongrass. ⊠ *5/1 Sukhumvit Soi 24,* ☎ *02/258–8637. AE, DC, MC, V.*

$$$ ✕ **Sala Rim Naam.** Definitely an upscale restaurant for visitors, this el-
★ egant *sala* (room), across the river from the Oriental Hotel, realizes many of the images conjured by the word "Siam." The dishes are so beautifully presented that eating them feels like vandalism. Try some of the hot-and-sour salads, particularly the shrimp version called *yam koong.* Make reservations for 7:30 PM and plan to stay on for the beautifully staged Thai dancing. The B1,400 set menu is excellent. Lunch at the Sala Rim's delicious buffet is always less crowded and, during the hot season, special and rarely found light Thai recipes called *Khon Chere* are offered. ⊠ *Use free boat from Oriental Hotel,* ☎ *02/437–6211. Reservations essential weekends and Oct.–late-Feb. AE, DC, MC, V.*

$$$ ✕ **Salathip.** Built as a Thai pavilion, with a veranda facing the Chao Phraya River, this restaurant provides an ambience that guarantees a romantic evening. Be sure to reserve a table outside. Though the food may not have as much hot chili as some like, it hasn't been adulterated to suit Western tastes. On Sunday night, there's possibly the best buffet in Bangkok. ⊠ *Shangri-La Hotel, 89 Soi Wat Suan Phu, New Rd.,* ☎ *02/236–7777. Reservations essential for veranda. AE, DC, MC, V. No lunch.*

$$$ ✕ **Seafood Market.** This vast restaurant still feels like the fish supermarket it used to be. You take a cart and choose from an array of seafood—crabs, prawns, lobster, clams, oysters, flat fish, snapperlike fish, crayfish—and vegetables. The waiter takes it away and cooks it any way you like. Typically your eyes are bigger than your stomach, so select with prudence, not gusto. Though the fluorescent lighting gives it the ambience of a giant canteen, people pack the tables because the prices are reasonable and the fish is fresh. Beware of Johnny-come-latelies who also call themselves Seafood Market and pay taxi and tuk-tuk drivers to divert you to their establishments. ⊠ *388 Sukhumvit Soi 24,* ☎ *02/258–0218. Reservations not accepted. AE, DC, MC, V.*

$$–$$$ ✕ **Ban Klang Nam.** This open-sided restaurant along the river is just
★ upstream from the Hanging Bridge (you'll need a taxi to get here). Choose a table next to the railing overlooking the river; you can also sit out on the patio dock or farther inside. The mee krob, so difficult to make well, is delicious. The fried sea bass in garlic and pepper, snapper in an oyster sauce, and kung paan tod are all superb, as is the smooth tom yam kung. ⊠ *3792/106 Pharam (Rama) 3, Soi 14,* ☎ *02/292–0175 or 02/292-2037. Reservations essential. AE, MC, V.*

$$ ✕ **Baan Kahanitha.** Half the pleasure of eating here is in the ambience and attentive service. Wood paneling, old Thai prints, blooming orchids, antique copper, and tableware from Thai kilns create just the right mood for a relaxing evening. The food is strictly Thai, explained well in the English menu and by the English-speaking waiters, although it has been compromised recently to appeal to Westerners, with a resulting absence of Thai diners. Ask for the complimentary appetizer mieng khum. The fried soft-shell crabs in a hot-and-sour sauce and the gaeng kieuw wan gai are two of the better choices. The tom kha gai is wonderfully rich, with just enough lime and lemongrass. ⊠ *3/1 Sukhumvit 23, Soi Prasan,* ☎ *02/258–4181. MC, V.*

$$ ✕ **Ban Chiang.** The decor here is turn-of-the-century Bangkok, and the painted walls are adorned with prints, photographs, and a pendulum clock. The extensive menu can be quite spicy: examples are the roast-duck curry and the shrimp-and-vegetable herb soup. The fried fish cakes and grilled prawns are milder, as is the gai hor bai toey. The service is not a strong point, and you need to know your way around a Thai menu to order a balanced set of dishes. ⊠ *14 Srivieng Rd.,* ☎ *02/236–7045. MC, V.*

$$ ✕ **Ban Khun Phor.** If you're in the Siam Square area, try this popular bistro diagonally across from the Novotel. The wooden tables mix with European Victoriana and Thai artifacts. The menu is varied, with such standard favorites as tom kha gai, roast duck with red curry, and even spicy stir-fried boar's meat. The best dish is the spicy crab soup. ⊠ *458/7–9 Soi 8, Siam Sq.,* ☎ *02/250–1733. Reservations not accepted. MC, V.*

$$ ✕ **Cabbages & Condoms.** Don't be misled by the restaurant's name or disconcerted by the array of contraceptive devices for sale. C&C fundraises for Thailand's birth-control program, the Population & Community Development Association. You'll find the Thai food here excellently prepared, with such dishes as chicken wrapped in pandanus leaf, crisp fried fish with chili sauce, and shrimp in a mild curry sauce. There's a simply decorated dining room and a pleasant garden with bench tables under shady trees—one of the few places in Bangkok to sit outside without noise and air pollution. ⊠ *10 Sukhumvit Soi 12,* ☎ *02/251–0402. AE, DC, MC, V.*

$$ ✕ **D'Jit Pochana.** This branch of the D'Jit Pochana restaurant chain is convenient for those staying near the airport. The restaurant has numerous rooms—including several large private rooms suitable for business dinners—on different levels. Request a room with a view of the garden and its pond and fountain; other rooms overlook the road. Among the many specialties are gai hor bai toey and tom kha gai. ⊠ *26/368–80 Gp 6 Phaholyothin Rd.,* ☎ *02/531–1644. AE, DC, MC, V.*

$$ ✕ **Harmonique.** You can eat on the terrace or on the ground floor of this small house near the river. The decoration, from flowers tumbling out of vases to chests scattered with bric-a-brac, gives the feeling of casual ease that you could expect in Western Europe, but here it is, down a small soi off Charoen Krung, just left of the General Post Office. The menu is small, but what there is is made with care. Foreign tourists come here from the Oriental and Royal Orchid Sheraton and are ably assisted by Madame in selecting the right courses. Try the crisp fish sautéed in garlic, the mild crab curry, or the Chinese cabbage topped with salted fish—all are excellent. ⊠ *22 Charoen Krung Soi 34,* ☎ *02/ 237–8175. AE.*

$$ ✕ **Kaloang Seafood.** This local favorite is a little off the beaten track, but it's worth the effort if you want the genuine flavor of riverside Bangkok and good seafood as well. Beginning at the National Library, a soi leads down to the open-air restaurant, built on a ramshackle pier. Fans and the breeze off the river keep things comfortably cool most evenings. The more observant customer will notice right away that almost all the waitstaff are transvestites. Service is friendly and competent, if initially somewhat disconcerting. The grilled seafood platter is both generous and cheap, and the grilled giant river prawns are also a bargain. Try the yam pla duk foo. It is rather spicy, but it comple-

ments cold beer as few things in this world do. ✉ *2 Sri Ayutthaya Rd.,* ☎ *02/281–9228. AE, DC, MC, V.*

$$ ✕ **Krua Wang Nar.** This riverside restaurant serves some of the best seafood in town. It is also near the National Museum and Grand Palace. Krua Wang Nar is noisy in the evenings, and the decor is fairly appalling (with pillars and plaster mermaids and several TVs blaring away at once), and the service can sometimes be a little smarmy. However, a prime location on the river, a comfortable, air-conditioned dining section, and high-quality food make this restaurant very popular with Thais and growing numbers of foreigners. Everything listed on the extensive menu is good, particularly the *pla somlee pow* (baked cottonfish with ginger and garlic) and *pae sa pla chon* (steamed serpenthead fish with vegetables). ✉ *17/1 Chao Fa Rd.,* ☎ *02/224–8552. MC, V.*

$$ ✕ **My Choice.** Middle-class Thais with a taste for their grandmothers' traditional recipes flock to this restaurant all day. The *ped aob,* a thick soup made from beef stock, is particularly popular, but foreigners may prefer the *tom kha tala,* a hot-and-sour dish with shrimp, served with rice. The interior is plain, with Formica tables; it's nicer to sit outside. ✉ *Sukhumvit Soi 36,* ☎ *02/258–6174. AE, DC, MC, V.*

$$ ✕ **River City Bar B-Q.** As you're seated on the roof of the River City Shopping Centre, a waiter brings a burner and hot plate, and a mound of different meats and vegetables. You use your chopsticks to grill the food. Order some appetizers to nibble on while dinner is cooking— the northern Thai sausage is excellent. Tables at the edge of the roof have romantic views of the Chao Phraya River. ✉ *5th floor, River City Shopping Centre,* ☎ *02/237–0077 ext. 240. MC, V.*

$$ ✕ **Spice Market.** The decor re-creates the interior of a well-stocked spice ★ shop, with sacks of garlic, dried chilies, and heavy earthenware fishsauce jars lined up as they were when the only way to get to Bangkok was by steamer. The authentic recipes are tempered to suit the tender mouths of Westerners, but you may ask for your dishes to be prepared full-strength; a chili logo on the menu indicates peppery dishes. The curries are superb, and there is a comprehensive selection of old-fashioned Thai sweets. From mid-January to the end of March, try the *nam doc mai* (mango with sticky rice and coconut milk); knowledgeable foreigners arrange trips to Bangkok at this time of year just for this dessert. ✉ *Regent of Bangkok Hotel, 155 Ratchadamri Rd.,* ☎ *02/ 251–6127. Reservations essential. AE, DC, MC, V.*

$$ ✕ **Ton Po.** This is open-air riverside dining without tourist trappings. ★ Ton Po (Thai for the Bo tree, of which there is a large, garlanded specimen at the entrance) has a wide, covered veranda on the Chao Phraya. To get the breeze that blows even on the hottest days, try to wangle a riverside table. Many of the dishes are well known, and none more so than the *tom khlong plaa salid bai makhaam awn,* a delectable, very hot and sour soup made from a local dried fish, chili, lime juice, lemongrass, young tamarind leaves, mushrooms, and a full frontal assault of other herbal seasonings. Less potent but equally good are the gai hor bai toey and *haw moke plaa* (a type of curried fish custard, thickened with coconut cream and steamed in banana leaves). ✉ *Phra Atit Rd.,* ☎ *no phone. Reservations not accepted. AE, DC, MC, V.*

$–$$ ✕ **Anna's Cafe.** When owner Tuay David Wibusin's career in finance abruptly ended with the economic collapse in 1998, he decided to open a restaurant that exuded optimism and cheer. By separating the dining areas with walls and plants, he created an ambience of lighthearted intimacy. Though there is a smattering of European dishes, most of the fare is modern Thai. The gaeng kieuw wan gai is mild and served with a salted boiled egg to counter its sweetness. The *tod mun kung* (fried prawn cakes) served with stir-fried vegetables and fried rice makes for a full and tasty meal. A good appetizer to share is the yam pla duk foo.

✉ *118 Soi Saladaeng (at the top of Silom Rd.),* ☎ *02/632–0619. AE, DC, MC, V.*

$–$$ ✕ **Kannicha.** The contemporary decor of white tablecloths, lighting that highlights the tropical plants, and waiters wearing scarlet braces over their white shirts sets the tone for sophisticated Thai fare. The menu is wide and varied. While reading it, choose an appetizer such as mieng khum or the delicious kung paan tod. Main dishes range from sea bass in "sauce of three tastes" to pork sautéed in garlic and young pepper. ✉ *17 Sukhumvit Soi 11,* ☎ *02/651–1573. AE, MC, V.*

$–$$ ✕ **Once Upon a Time.** This is an inexpensive place to relax and enjoy Thai food on a plant-filled terrace next to a pool. Inside, the dining room has Thai antiques and floor-to-ceiling wood walls decorated with period photos of the Thai royal family, movie stars, and beauty queens. The music is traditional Thai, both taped and live. The menu is good, and authentically Thai. The timid often order the chopped pork with chili sauce or the beef fillet with pickled garlic. *Miang kham,* a traditional snack of dried shrimp, dried coconut, peanuts, pineapple, chili pepper, and sweet tamarind sauce rolled together in a green leaf, makes an excellent appetizer. ✉ *Juladis Tower, 7th floor, Soi 19, Phetchburi Rd.,* ☎ *02/255–4948. AE, DC, MC, V.*

$–$$ ✕ **Sara-Jane's.** Sara, formerly of Massachusetts, married a Thai 20 years ago and started a restaurant in 1986. In 1998 her success led to the opening of a new restaurant just down from the American Embassy. In the ground-floor shopping mall of a large office building, Sara-Jane's open dining room has sparse decor. It is designed to accommodate lots of people for lunch, though many also stop for dinner. The menu celebrates I-san food, with many types of salad served with *larb,* a mince made from pork, chicken, tuna, or other meat and fish. One favorite is the yam pla duk foo. For those who want European fare, Sara-Jane also offers Italian food. ✉ *Ground floor, Sindhorn Tower 1, 130–132 Wireless Rd.,* ☎ *02/650–9992. No credit cards.*

$–$$ ✕ **Wanabee Earth.** White tablecloths and striped wallpaper in gold and white give a bright, fresh feel while the vine-covered trellises separating the tables break up the squareness of the dining room. Thais come here to choose from the range of foods drawn from the four regions of Thailand: for example, spicy salads from the Northeast, southern Thai fried fish, an array of noodle dishes from the Central Plains, and tasty sausages from the North. ✉ *63/12 Soi Langesuan 2, Ploenchit,* ☎ *02/652–2939. MC, V.*

$–$$ ✕ **Yok Yor.** Dine aboard a grounded vessel on the Chao Phraya, reached by a gangplank. The well-cooked Thai food is served with dispatch, and the cool darkness of the river lends a romantic, exotic aura. There's live music from 6 PM on, and Japanese, Chinese, and some European dishes are also served, though few Westerners eat here. The management also runs a dinner-and-music cruise along the Chao Phraya every night (8:30–10:30; B70 plus cost of food) aboard a 400-seat boat. ✉ *Wisutikasat Rd. at Yok Yor Pier (next to Bank of Thailand),* ☎ *02/ 281–1829 or 02/282–7385. No credit cards.*

$ ✕ **Atlanta.** Though simply a coffee shop in a budget hotel, the Atlanta serves Thai cooking that is surprisingly good, thanks to the reclusive innkeeper, Charles Henn, a food fanatic. The menu, which explains the ingredients and their origin, makes interesting, amusing reading. Don't pass up the tom yam kung here—it's especially smooth. Classical jazz is played at dinner, followed by a movie of some repute. New vegetarian dishes are being added every week to the menu. ✉ *78 Sukhumvit Soi 2,* ☎ *02/252–1650 or 02/252–6069. No credit cards.*

$ ✕ **Banana Leaf.** This is not only the best restaurant in this shopping complex, but it's worth making tracks for if you are in the vicinity of upper Silom Road. The people lining up to get in aren't coming for the decor. It's just bare, painted walls, but the harried waiters and waitresses give quick, friendly service, and there's delicious Thai food at low prices. Try the baked crab with glass noodles, hen's fingers salad, spicy papaya salad, grilled black band fish, or grilled pork with a coconut milk dip. ⊠ *Basement level, Silom Complex, Silom Rd.,* ☎ *02/231–3124. No credit cards.*

$ ✕ **Nai Sow.** The best tom yam kung is found here, a Chinese-Thai restaurant next door to Wat Plaplachai in Chinatown. Chefs come and go, but the owner, who never divulges his recipes to his chefs, makes the essential mixture—which includes the fatty juices from the prawns—in secret. Other equally tasty dishes range from curried Thai beef to a mix of sweet-and-sour mushrooms. For an unusual and delicious dessert, finish with the fried taro. Forget decor and ambience: round tables and chairs are about the only furnishings. You come here to eat and talk. ⊠ *3/1 Maitrichit Rd.,* ☎ *02/222–1539. Reservations not accepted. MC, V.*

$ ✕ **Saw Ying Thai.** This place has been open for almost 60 years, and many of its clientele have been regulars for decades. It is rare to find a tourist here, and even long-term expat customers are few. The menus on the wall are in Thai only, and none of the staff speaks English, so try to bring a Thai friend. Be sure to order the *kai toon,* a chicken soup with bamboo sprouts. Also memorable are the *plaa du thawd krawb phad phed* (crisp-fried catfish stir-fried with curry spices and herbs) and the *khai jio neua puu* (an omelette full of crabmeat). This charming restaurant would rate a star if it were more accessible in language or location. ⊠ *Corner of Bamrungmuang and Tanao Rds.,* ☎ *no phone. Reservations not accepted. No credit cards.*

$ ✕ **Soi Polo Fried Chicken.** Although its beat-up plastic tables, traffic
★ noise, and lack of air-conditioning make this small place look like a sure thing for stomach trouble, it is one of the city's most popular lunch spots for nearby office workers. The reason: its world-class fried chicken flavored with black pepper and plenty of golden-brown, crisp-fried garlic. The chicken should be sampled with sticky rice and perhaps a plate of the restaurant's excellent *som tam,* a hydrogen bomb of hot-and-sour raw papaya salad from the Northeast. Try to get here a bit before noon, or landing a table will be a problem. ⊠ *Walk into Soi Polo from Wireless Rd. (the restaurant is the last of the shops on your left as you enter the soi),* ☎ *no phone. Reservations not accepted. No credit cards. No dinner.*

$ ✕ **Thong Lee.** This small but attractive shophouse restaurant has an air-conditioned upstairs dining area. Although prices are very low, Thong Lee has a devoted upper-middle-class clientele. The menu is not adventurous, but every dish has a distinct personality—evidence of the cook's artistry and imagination. Almost everyone orders the *muu phad kapi* (pork fried with shrimp paste); the *yam hed sod* (hot-and-sour mushroom salad) is memorable but very spicy. ⊠ *Sukhumvit Soi 20,* ☎ *no phone. Reservations not accepted. No credit cards.*

Vietnamese

$$–$$$ ✕ **Sweet Basil.** It is worth making the long trek down Sukhumvit to
★ Soi 62 for the splendidly presented Vietnamese fare, in a fresh setting of crisp white tablecloths, glistening silver and glassware, and ferns and flowers. Try the *bo la lat* (brochettes of beef wrapped in a pungent leaf) and the *ban cuon tom* (dumplings stuffed with shrimp and mushrooms), or the more usual but still delicious salads and crunchy *cha gio* (spring rolls with a sweet, tangy sauce). This is a smart restaurant where Thais dress up for a special meal. ⊠ *23 Sukhumvit Soi 62,* ☎ *02/176–5490. Reservations essential. AE, DC, MC, V.*

$$
★
✕ Le Dalat. This very classy Vietnamese restaurant, once a private house, consists of several intimate and cozily decorated dining rooms. Much Vietnamese cuisine is based on flavor juxtapositions striking to the Western palate, and here it's all served up with style. Try *naem neuang,* which requires you to take a garlicky grilled meatball and place it on a round of *mieng* (edible thin rice paper wrapper), then pile on bits of garlic, ginger, hot chili, star apple, and mango, spoon on a viscous sweet-salty sauce, and wrap the whole thing up in a lettuce leaf before eating. The restaurant has become a favorite with Bangkok residents. ⊠ *51 Sukhumvit Soi 23, opposite Indian Embassy,* ☎ *02/260–1849. Reservations essential. AE, DC, MC, V.*

LODGING

The economic and currency crisis of 1997–98 lowered prices in dollars or sterling at hotels whose clientele is mostly Thais and other Asians. Hotels with mostly an American or European clientele (especially the luxury hotels) raised their prices to offset the devaluation of the baht. Now, though, even hotels that quote prices in baht have started to raise their rack rates. Nevertheless, prices fluctuate enormously, and if business is down, huge discounts are offered. The best bargains are probably found in the $$–$$$ categories.

That said, Bangkok hotel prices are still lower than those in Singapore and Hong Kong and are not expensive by European standards. Rates at fabulous deluxe hotels are about the equivalent of $250 for a double. Those in the $80–$100 range also have fine service, excellent restaurants, health clubs, and business facilities. For $40 to $50, you can find respectable lodgings in a hotel with an efficient staff. Rooms in small hotels with limited facilities are available for around $10, and, for those willing to share a bathroom, guest houses are numerous.

The four main hotel districts are next to the Chao Phraya River and along Silom and Suriwongse roads; around Siam Square; in the foreign-embassy neighborhood; and along Sukhumvit Road. Other areas, such as Khao San Road for inexpensive guest houses favored by backpackers, and across the river, where modern high-rise hotels are sprouting up, are not included in the following list. For price categories, *see* Lodging *in* Smart Travel Tips A to Z.

$$$$
▢ Dusit Thani. This low-key 23-story hotel with distinctive, pyramid-style architecture is the flagship property of a Thai group that manages Dusit and Princess hotels. An extensive shopping arcade, a Chinese restaurant, and an elegant Thai restaurant occupy the street level. One floor up, the lobby, reception area, and a sunken lounge overlook a small garden. The pool is in a central courtyard filled with trees, a peaceful oasis amid Bangkok's frenzy. (But be aware that the construction of a subway and the attendant traffic diversion has made the Dusit area a mess.) The Dusit Thani is particularly noted for its spacious though very high-priced Landmark suites, furnished in classical Thai tradition with handcrafted furniture, but the standard rooms are due for refurbishing. The service is not up to past standards. ⊠ *Rama IV Rd., 10500,* ☎ *02/236–0450; 800/223–6800 U.S. reservations; 212/838–3110 in N.Y.,* FAX *02/237–5837. 510 rooms and 30 suites. 7 restaurants, bar, coffee shop, in-room VCRs, pool, health club, shops, nightclub, business services, meeting rooms. AE, DC, MC, V.* ✎

$$$$
▢ Grand Hyatt Erawan. The Grand Hyatt is built on the site of the old Erawan Hotel, next to the Erawan shrine. The typically Hyatt lobby is a stylish four-story atrium with a domed, stained-glass roof and decorated with an extensive art collection. Service is efficient. Guest rooms

are large, with window bays for a desk and a couple of chairs. The wood floors are strewn with area rugs, and each room has original art. Messages are displayed on a TV monitor, and the bathrooms have separate showers, oversize tubs, and dressing areas. The three Regency floors offer concierges and other services. The rooms with the best view look over Lumphini Park and the racetrack, though you can hear the traffic on Ratchadamri Road. With the new skytrain not too far away, the lower-floor rooms can be noisy. Restaurants abound. The Italian fare at Spasso, developed by a Milanese chef, is especially creative and a lunch here is recommended whether you stay in the hotel or not. The pool terrace is covered with ferns and plants, and a physical therapist manages the elaborate health club. ⊠ *494 Ratchadamri Rd., 10330,* ☎ *02/254–1234; 800/233–1234 U.S. reservations,* ℻ *02/253–5856. 389 rooms and suites. 3 restaurants, bar, pool, 2 tennis courts, health club, squash, business services, meeting rooms. AE, DC, MC, V.* 🐾

$$$$ 🏨 **Landmark Hotel.** Though it calls itself high-tech, the Landmark's generous use of teak in its reception areas creates an ambience suggestive of a grand European hotel. Guest rooms, unobtrusively elegant, are geared to the international business traveler, with good desks and TV/video screens that can tune in to information banks linked to the business center. With a staff of 950, service is attentive. The hotel's elegant Hibiscus restaurant has a view of the city and serves European fare, and a jazz trio accompanies drinks and light meals in the Huntsman Pub. ⊠ *138 Sukhumvit Rd., 10110,* ☎ *02/254–0404,* ℻ *02/253–4259. 395 rooms and 55 suites. 4 restaurants, coffee shop, snack bar, pool, sauna, health club, squash, shops, business services, meeting rooms. AE, DC, MC, V.* 🐾

$$$$ 🏨 **Oriental Hotel.** The Oriental has set the standard for which all other
★ Bangkok hotels strive. Part of its fame stems from its past guests, and today's roster features heads of state and film stars. Its location on the Chao Phraya is unrivaled; the original building, now the Garden Wing, has been refurbished, and the rooms here—and the main building's luxury suites—are the hotel's best. Among its well-known restaurants are China House; Sala Rim Naam across the river, renowned for its Thai food; and Le Normandie, the best French restaurant in Bangkok. In addition, the hotel has a riverside barbecue every night. The Oriental radiates elegance and provides superb service, though in recent years some of the crispness and panache have disappeared, perhaps because the staff is continually wooed away by other hotels. You can attend a Thai cooking school here, as well as afternoon seminars on Thai culture. The smart spa across the river (next to the Sala Rim) lets you indulge in all sorts of luxurious treatments. The hotel has a helicopter service ($150) to and from the airport. ⊠ *48 Oriental Ave., 10500,* ☎ *02/236–0400; 71/537–2988 U.K. reservations; 800/223–6800 U.S. reservations,* ℻ *02/236–1937. 398 rooms. 8 restaurants, 2 pools, 2 tennis courts, health club, jogging, squash, nightclub, business services, helipad. AE, DC, MC, V.* 🐾

$$$$ 🏨 **Peninsula.** The Peninsula has all the latest in hotel technology, from fax machines in every room to bedside fingertip controls that operate the lights, TV, and opening and closing of curtains. Bathrooms not only have a separate shower stall but also a TV with a mist-free screen at one end of the bathtub, as well as a hands-free telephone. The spacious rooms look out onto the river and the skyscraper-infested jungle that Bangkok has become. Because the Peninsula is on the Thonburi side of the Chao Phraya, opposite the Oriental, the Shangri-La, and the heart of Bangkok, you'll need to take the free hotel shuttle boat across the river every time you come and go (a possible nuisance, or a retreat from Bangkok's chaos). Dining options at the hotel are adequate, though not exceptional, with the Cantonese (a formal restaurant) and Pacific

Rim (contemporary American cuisine) restaurants, and a dining room–coffee shop. Barbecue buffets are often held in the evening. The hotel has a long, attractive swimming pool stretching inland from the river with *salas* where guests can sit in sun or shade. ⊠ *333 Charoennakorn Rd., Klonsan, 10600*, ☎ *02/861–2888*, FAX *02/861–2355. 370 rooms. 3 restaurants, bar, health club, business center, meeting rooms, helipad. AE, DC, MC, V.* 🐾

$$$$
★ 🏨 **Regent.** Long one of Bangkok's leading hotels, the Regent is in the embassy district, which is now the geographical center of the city. You enter by mounting palatial steps into a formal lobby where local society meets for morning coffee and afternoon tea, and where Thai classical art adds serenity to sophisticated luxury. Service is exemplary. Off a delightful courtyard there are shops and restaurants, including the popular Spice Market. The large rooms are decorated with Thai silk upholstery, and bathrooms have a separate shower. Some of the best rooms overlook the racetrack, but choose one on a high floor, since the new skytrain blocks the view for rooms on the first three floors. There are also four "cabana rooms," whose private patios look onto a small garden with a lotus pond. In the Concierge Club lounge (extra charge), there's an extensive library, concierge services, excellent breakfasts, and complimentary hors d'oeuvres. Be sure to have the Regent's fragrant-oil massage. ⊠ *155 Ratchadamri Rd., 10330*, ☎ *02/251–6127*, FAX *02/253–9195. 363 rooms. 3 restaurants, pool, massage, health club, shops, business services. AE, DC, MC, V.* 🐾

$$$$ 🏨 **Le Royal Meridien.** The new Royal Meridien charges about 20% more than the adjacent 30-year-old Meridien, which has had its day. Because the new hotel is having trouble filling its rooms, special promotional rates often reduce the cost of a hotel room by 50%. The large guest rooms have bathrooms with a separate shower stall. The Executive Floor, which costs 20%–25% more than standard floors, has added amenities including a fax machine with a dedicated line. Executive-floor guests can also use the pleasant lounge with great city views and have complimentary breakfasts and evening cocktails. The hotel, which seems less than oriented to the individual traveler, has a 2,000-person capacity ballroom and meeting rooms with the latest technology. Its leading restaurant, run by a Hong Kong chef, prides itself on tables than can seat 10 to 24 people. The rooftop pool, however, is intimate. ⊠ *973 Ploenchit Rd., Lumphini, Pathumwan, 10330*, ☎ *02/656–0444*, FAX *02/656–0555. 381 rooms. 2 restaurants, pool, spa, health club, business services, meeting rooms. AE, DC, MC, V.* 🐾

$$$$ 🏨 **Royal Orchid Sheraton.** Of the hotels offering riverfront luxury this 28-story palace is more oriented toward tour groups than its neighbors, the Oriental and the Shangri-La. All rooms face the river and are well appointed—the namesake flowers are everywhere. The decor, low-key peaches and creams, is a little boring. Standard rooms tend to be long and narrow, with a slightly cramped feeling, but if you go for a deluxe room, you'll be paying the same price as if you were staying at the Oriental or Shangri-La. The restaurants are almost too numerous to mention, but the Thai Thara Thong is memorable, with subtle classical music accompanying your meal. You could equally well choose Japanese, Indian, or Italian cuisine. A glassed-in bridge leads to the River City Shopping Centre next door. ⊠ *2 Captain Bush La., 10500*, ☎ *02/266–0123 or 02/237–0022*, FAX *02/236–8320. 771 rooms. 3 Restaurants, 2 bars, coffee shop, 2 pools, 2 tennis courts, health club, shops, business services, meeting rooms, helipad. AE, DC, MC, V.* 🐾

$$$$ 🏨 **Shangri-La Hotel.** For decades the Oriental could safely claim to be Bangkok's finest hotel; then came the challenge by a spate of new hotels, of which the Shangri-La was one of the first and best. The initial enthusiasm has passed—it's looking a little tired these days, the smiles

seem permanently fixed, and the fairly large guest rooms, decorated in pastels, are showing signs of age. The staff is nevertheless professional and efficient, and the spacious marble lobby with crystal chandeliers is a relief from the congestion of Bangkok. The lobby lounge, with its floor-to-ceiling windows, offers a marvelous panorama of the Chao Phraya River. The gardens are an oasis whose peace is interrupted only by the riverboat traffic. In the opulent Krungthep Wing, a separate tower across the gardens, all guest rooms have fax outlets and balconies overlooking the river. ⊠ *89 Soi Wat Suan Phu, New Rd., 10500,* ☎ *02/236–7777,* 𝔽𝔸𝕏 *02/236–8579. 801 rooms and 65 suites. 13 restaurants, 4 bars, 2 pools, 2 tennis courts, health club, squash, shops, business services, helipad. AE, DC, MC, V.* ✆

$$$$ ⊞ **Sheraton Grande Sukhumvit.** The Grande Sukhumvit soars 33 floors above the business-shopping-embassy area. The light-flooded guest rooms, on the upper floors, are a far cry from typical boxlike hotel rooms; each has a spacious bathroom angled off the bedroom, and the entrance hall and walk-in wardrobe have interesting diagonals. In these "Deluxe" rooms, a 24-hour butler service will bring you coffee or iron your clothes at the push of a button. You'll never go hungry here: the street-level entrance has Riva's, a restaurant and bar offering live music and contemporary cooking; off the marble lobby on the first floor, the Orchid Café has an international buffet; on the second floor you can choose Italian or Chinese, or have tea in the lounge or cocktails in the rotunda. On the third floor, the health club and the deep-blue, serpentine swimming pool are laid out in an Oriental garden, which is also the setting for the Thai restaurant and, in the winter (dry) months, a barbecue. ⊠ *250 Sukhumvit Rd., 10110,* ☎ *02/653–0333,* 𝔽𝔸𝕏 *02/653–0400. 445 rooms. 4 restaurants, pool, health club, business services. AE, DC, MC, V.* ✆

$$$$ ⊞ **Sukhothai.** On six landscaped acres off Sathorn Road (a high-traffic area with no tourist attractions), this hotel attempts to recapture the glory of Thailand's first kingdom in its architecture and ambience, but it does not quite succeed. It does, however, offer quiet; the clutter and chaos of Bangkok seem a world away from its numerous courtyards. The hotel's Thai restaurant is set in a pavilion in an artificial lake, but for all its elegance, it feels a bit stiff and pretentious. Public areas have stern pillars, sharp right angles, and prim little tables laid for tea. The dining room for Continental and grilled fare is comfortable, but prices are high. Standard rooms are spacious but not exceptionally well furnished. The one-bedroom suites ($400) have splendid, oversize, teak-floor bathrooms with "his and her" washbasins and mirrors. Most of the guest rooms face one of the pond-filled courtyards. ⊠ *13/3 South Sathorn Rd., 10120,* ☎ *02/287–0222,* 𝔽𝔸𝕏 *02/287–4980. 136 rooms and 76 suites. 2 restaurants, pool, massage, sauna, tennis court, health club, squash. AE, DC, MC, V.* ✆

$$$–$$$$ ⊞ **Amari Watergate.** This flagship hotel of the Amari group is at the top range of its price category, with quality to match—ask for the promotional rate. Guest rooms are spacious and comfortable, furnished in rich fabrics. Bathrooms are also quite large, though the separate shower stall is too small for two. The executive floor has a lounge where free breakfast and cocktails are served. The two main restaurants are Italian and Thai; in the latter, the menu has fare from Thailand's four major regions. The coffee shop serves a buffet. The swimming pool is one of the largest in Bangkok hotels. ⊠ *847 Phetchburi Rd., 10400,* ☎ *02/653–9000,* 𝔽𝔸𝕏 *02/653–9045. 575 rooms. 3 restaurants, pool, health club, business services, meeting rooms. AE, DC, MC, V.* ✆

$$$–$$$$ ⊞ **Baiyoke Sky Hotel.** Although the hotel brags that it is the tallest in the world (at 88 stories), completed hotel rooms begin on the 22nd floor and end at the 36th. The empty 40 or so floors don't yet have guest rooms. However, a Japanese restaurant is on the 78th floor and a buffet is on the 79th. Hotel guests must pay B50 to get up there (nonguests pay B100) and that includes a visit to the revolving observation deck on the 84th floor. The rooms are very plainly furnished and not particularly restful to the spirit. However, they are spacious and the bathrooms have a separate shower stall. The one-bedroom suites are disappointing—while they have lots of storage space, the bedrooms may remind you of boarding school. The lobby, on the 18th floor, has a coffee shop open 24 hours. The Baiyoke Sky Hotel is in many ways a symbol of Thailand's billionaires who built for self-glorification until their bubble economy burst. ⊠ *222 Ratchaprarop Rd., Rajthawee, 10400,* ☏ *02/656–3000,* FAX *02/656–3555. 170 rooms and 30 suites. 3 restaurants, pool, business services. AE, DC, MC, V.* ✎

$$$–$$$$ 🏨 **J. W. Marriott Hotel.** The last thing Bangkok needed in late 1997 was a new luxury hotel, but it got this one, and though normally it would be in the $$$$ price category, it has priced itself lower to win some business. Although sparkling with modern technological conveniences, such as two telephone lines per room and a separate shower stall in the bathrooms, the Marriott does not stand out. Rooms are standard, though a firm king-size bed makes for a comfortable stay. It's worth an extra B800 to stay on the Executive Floors (16–24). Though the rooms are the same as others, guests check in and out in the executive lounge and are offered complimentary breakfast, afternoon tea, and evening cocktails. The fitness center is superb, with saunas and the latest equipment for retooling the body. Restaurants include the Cantonese Man Ho, the White Elephant Thai restaurant, and the informal JW's California, with an open kitchen and contemporary cuisine. ⊠ *4 Sukhumvit Soi 2, 10110,* ☏ *02/656–7700,* FAX *02/656–7711. 446 rooms. 3 restaurants, bar, pool, sauna, health club, business services, meeting rooms. AE, DC, MC, V.* ✎

$$$–$$$$ 🏨 **Westin Banyan.** Although the lobby is on the ground floor and the dining room is one floor below, the rest of the hotel starts on the 33rd floor of a skinny building reaching up 60 floors. With no other buildings around and way above the smog level, the light-filled guest rooms—all of which are suites—have sweeping views of the city. The generous use of wood, from large desks to walk-in closets, gives a warm feel to the rooms. With TVs in both the bedroom and the sitting-work area, a two-line telephone system with data port, and an in-room printer-fax-scanner, there is little need for the business center. Large bathrooms have a separate shower stall. For the self-indulgent, there is a fully equipped fitness center and spa, as well as a sun deck on the 53rd floor with a current pool and whirlpool. You can watch the lights on the Chao Phraya River and the city skyline from the excellent Chinese restaurant (on the 60th floor) or the bar lounge (on the 59th). ⊠ *21/100 South Sathorn Rd., 10120,* ☏ *02/679–1200,* FAX *02/ 679–1199. 198 rooms. 2 restaurants, bar, pool, spa, health club, business services, meeting rooms. AE, DC, MC, V.* ✎

$$$ 🏨 **Amari Airport Hotel.** If you need to stay within walking distance of the airport, this is your only option. A covered passageway leads from the International Terminal to the hotel, which is modern and utilitarian, with a helpful staff. Rooms are functional and efficient. The daytime (8 AM–6 PM) rate for travelers waiting for connections is B600 for stays up to three hours, and video screens in public areas display schedules of flight arrivals and departures. ⊠ *333 Chert Wudhakas Rd., Don Muang 10210,* ☏ *02/566–1020,* FAX *02/566–1941. 440 rooms. 2 restaurants, coffee shop, pool, nightclub, meeting rooms. AE, DC, MC, V.* ✎

$$$ 🏨 **Amari Boulevard.** This hotel is just in from Sukhumvit Road, down a one-way soi and close to the tourist action. The original building opened in 1990 and the glass pyramid-shape tower, known as the Krungthep Wing, opened in 1992. The use of dark wood in rooms in the older part give a traditional ambience. Particularly attractive are those overlooking the pool. The new tower is more modern and airy, with pastel furnishings. The bathrooms here are also slightly larger and have a separate shower stall. Rooms in the new wing costs an extra B1,000. The ground floor lobby is vast, with plenty of sitting areas, and the casual Peppermill restaurant serves a range of Thai, Japanese, and international dishes. ⊠ *2 Sukhumvit Soi 5, 10400,* ☏ *02/255–2930,* 🖷 *02/255–2950. 315 rooms. Restaurant, bar, pool, health club, business services, meeting rooms. AE, DC, MC, V.* ♒

$$$ 🏨 **Ambassador Hotel.** This hotel—one of Bangkok's biggest, with three wings of guest rooms, a complex of restaurants, and a shopping center—is virtually a mini-city, which may explain the impersonal service and limited helpfulness of the staff. Milling convention delegates in the colossal lobbies contribute to the businesslike atmosphere. Guest rooms are compact, decorated in standard pastel. The Tower Wing offers the most comfort and should be chosen over the lower-price Sukhumvit Wing, which is exposed to the noise from busy Sukhumvit Road. Be aware that the least expensive rooms are very small. You may also want to select a room above the sixth floor to avoid noise from the hotel's popular clubs: the Dickens Pub garden bar, the Flamingo Disco, and The Club for rock music. ⊠ *171 Sukhumvit Soi 11–13, 10110,* ☏ *02/254–0444,* 🖷 *02/253–4123. 1,026 rooms and 24 suites. 12 restaurants, coffee shop, snack bar, pool, massage, 2 tennis courts, health club, business services, meeting rooms. AE, DC, MC, V.*

$$$ 🏨 **Central Plaza Hotel.** Given its location in the middle of one of the city's fastest-growing business districts, most of the hotel's clientele are business travelers. The west side of the hotel has a view of the former Railway Golf Course; the remaining sides look out on the city's hell-bent horizontal and vertical growth. The refreshingly cool, green lobby is a welcome hideaway, the atmosphere enhanced by the soothing white noise of a cascading waterfall. Rooms are graceful, with understated floral designs; Thai prints, bronze mythological figures, and temple-dog lampstands remind guests that they are in Thailand. The two floors of the Dynasty Club offer even better accommodations, with large, handsomely furnished sitting areas, stereo units, minibars, kitchen facilities, and dining areas plus valet service and lounge access. Among the hotel's numerous restaurants and bars is Dynasty, a popular spot for Chinese cuisine. ⊠ *1695 Phaholyothin Rd., 10210,* ☏ *02/541–1234,* 🖷 *02/541–1087. 421 rooms. 3 restaurants, pool, health club, business services, meeting rooms. AE, DC, MC, V.*

$$$ 🏨 **Holiday Inn Crowne Plaza.** Located next to the Gem Tower, the Holiday Inn has two towers: the smaller of the two, the Plaza Tower, is over 20 years old with cheaper and smaller rooms than the newer Crowne Tower, which opened in 1991. You can usually get a 50% discount on published rates, making a stay here good value. Not so otherwise. Even the newer tower shows signs of wear. The high ceilings and vast spaces of public areas make it seem rather like New York's Grand Central Terminal and the hotel survives by catering to airline staff and tour groups. However, the two executive floors are geared to the business traveler, with check-in and -out at the concierge desk in the executive lounge. Rooms have light color schemes, plenty of lamps, lots of draperies, and a bathroom with separate shower stall. The executive suites are ill-conceived—the bathroom and bedroom are smaller to make up for the extra sitting area. ⊠ *981 Silom Rd., 10500,* ☏ *02/238–4300,* 🖷 *02/238–5289. 385 rooms in the Plaza Tower, 341 rooms in the Crowne Tower. 3 restaurants, pool, 2 tennis courts, health club, business services, meeting rooms. AE, DC, MC, V.* ♒

$$$ ⊞ **Imperial Queens Park.** The largest hotel in Bangkok stands with its two towers just off Sukhumvit and next to a small park (ideal for jogging). With seven restaurants, numerous shops, two swimming pools, a vast lobby, and more space for meetings and conventions than other Bangkok hotels, the Imperial Queens Park is a city in itself. Standard rooms are reasonably spacious and well laid out, with a good-sized desk, but the nicer (more expensive) rooms are the junior corner suites, with a separate work area and plenty of natural light. Many of the rooms have whirlpool tubs (of the dated variety) and a separate shower stall. Rooms have only one telephone line, which doubles as a data port. To fill its 1,400 rooms, management makes special arrangements for long-term (a month or more) guests. ⊠ *199 Sukhumvit Soi 22, 10110,* ☎ *02/261–9000,* ⅎ *02/261–9530. 1,090 double rooms and 310 suites. 7 restaurants, pool, 2 tennis courts, health club, business services, convention center, meeting rooms. AE, DC, MC, V.* ⊛

$$$ ⊞ **Montien.** This hotel across the street from Patpong, convenient to the corporations along Silom Road, has been remarkably well maintained over its two decades. The concierge is particularly helpful. The guest rooms are spacious, though not decoratively inspired. They do, however, have private safes. Prices are slightly higher than you would expect, but the hotel will give discounts. It's also the only hotel with in-house fortune-tellers who will read your palm or your stars for B250. ⊠ *54 Suriwongse Rd., 10500,* ☎ ⅎ *02/234–8060. 500 rooms. 2 restaurants, coffee shop, pool, nightclub, business services, meeting rooms. AE, DC, MC, V.* ⊛

$$$ ⊞ **Narai Hotel.** Conveniently near the business, shopping, and entertainment areas on Silom Road, this friendly, modern hotel offers utilitarian but comfortable rooms. At the low end of this price category, the hotel is a good value, given its cheerful rooms and high level of service. The most distinguishing feature is the revolving restaurant, La Rotonde Grill, on the 15th floor. ⊠ *222 Silom Rd., 10500,* ☎ *02/257–0100,* ⅎ *02/236–7161. 490 rooms and 10 suites. 3 restaurants, coffee shop, pool, health club, nightclub, business services. AE, DC, MC, V.* ⊛

$$$ ⊞ **Siam Inter-Continental.** On 26 landscaped acres in the center of Bangkok, the Siam Inter-Continental has a soaring pagoda roof and beautiful gardens. Its modern Thai architecture, lofty lobby, and sense of space make this hotel stand out. Each of the air-conditioned rooms is stylishly decorated with teak furniture, a trim, upholstered wing chair and love seat, and a cool blue color scheme. Especially attractive are the teak-panel bathrooms with radios, telephones, and hair dryers. ⊠ *967 Rama I Rd., 10330,* ☎ *02/253–0355,* ⅎ *02/253–2275. 411 rooms and suites. 4 restaurants, 2 bars, pool, driving range, putting green, health club, jogging, meeting rooms. AE, DC, MC, V.* ⊛

$$ ⊞ **Bel-Air Princess.** Two hundred yards down Soi 5 from clamorous Sukhumvit is this quiet, well-managed hotel. It gets its fair share of tour groups, but for the most part the lobby and lounge are cool and peaceful, and the downstairs restaurant is a good place to relax over a light meal. Northern Indian cooking, lightly spiced for Western taste, is served in the formal Tiffin Room. Spacious, carpeted guest rooms, with two queen-size beds or one king, are large enough for a round table and chairs as well as the standard TV-cabinet-desk. Personal safes, in-house movies, hair dryers, and tea- and coffeemakers are pluses, and the bowl of fruit on each landing is a nice touch. Rooms at the back of the hotel overlook Soi 7 and beyond; front rooms overlook the pool. ⊠ *16 Sukhumvit Soi 5, 10110,* ☎ *02/253–4300,* ⅎ *02/255–8850. 160 rooms. 2 restaurants, bar, pool, health club. AE, DC, MC, V.* ⊛

$$ ⊞ **Century Hotel.** Its location in the northern part of downtown is convenient to the airport. The rooms, though neat and clean, are small and dark. The coffee shop–bar is open 24 hours, a plus for travelers with early morning flights. ⊠ *9 Ratchaprarop Rd., 10400,* ☎ *02/246–7800. 240 rooms. Bar, coffee shop, pool. AE, DC, MC, V.*

$$ 🏨 **City Lodge.** There are two City Lodges off Sukhumvit, one on Soi 9 and this one, a tad better, on Soi 19. Both are part of the Amari hotel group, but aimed at the frugal traveler. The charmless, compact rooms are functional, designed for efficiency of space. Business services are minimal, but you can use those at the nearby sister hotel, the Amari Boulevard (as well as its pool). The coffee shop–restaurant specializes in Italian food at dinner. ⊠ *Sukhumvit Soi 19, 10110,* ☎ *02/254–4783,* 🖷 *02/255–7340. 35 rooms. Restaurant. AE, DC, MC, V.* 🐾

$$ 🏨 **Grand China Princess.** One good reason for staying in Chinatown is that it's the center of old Bangkok, with lots of exotic turn-of-the-20th-century Asian ambience. Another reason is this hotel. It occupies the top two-thirds of a 25-story tower from which the guest rooms have panoramic views of the city. Room 2202, for example, gives you a morning view of the Temple of the Dawn, the Golden Mount, and Wat Tuk. Since the rooms form a segment of a circle, they are interestingly shaped. The furnishings are unexciting but functional, and all the rooms have safes and satellite TV. The bathrooms are on the small side. Service is friendly, and the reception floor (10th) has a welcoming bar, lounge, and coffee shop. Carpeted in a huge lotus design, the restaurant, Siang Ping Loh (Cantonese and Szechuan fare), is well worth a visit in its own right. ⊠ *215 Corner of Yaowarat and Ratchawongse Rd., Samphantawongse, 10100,* ☎ *02/224–9977,* 🖷 *02/224–7999. 155 rooms. Restaurant, coffee shop, health club, business services. AE, DC, MC, V.* 🐾

$$ 🏨 **La Residence.** You would expect to find this small town-house hotel on the Left Bank of Paris, not in Bangkok. Though it's a little overpriced, La Residence suits the frequent visitor who wants a low-key hotel. The staff, however, can be abrupt at times. The guest rooms are small, but the furnishings—pale-wood cabinets, pastel draperies—give them a fresh, airy feel. The restaurant, with Thai and European food, also serves as a sitting area for guests. ⊠ *173/8–9 Suriwongse Rd., 10150,* ☎ *02/233–3301. 23 rooms. Restaurant, laundry service. AE, DC.*

$$ 🏨 **Swiss Lodge.** This small hotel off Silom Road near the Dusit Thani is the closest equivalent to a boutique hotel in Bangkok. Rooms are furnished in light colors that give a crisp, fresh look. Single rooms are really the size of small doubles; doubles are a bit larger, so as to fit in king-size beds. All rooms have built-in safes, bathrobes, and ample work space, and the telephone line can be transferred to your computer. Bathrooms are compact but fully equipped. Half of the guest-room floors are no-smoking. A very small outdoor pool and sundeck are on the fifth floor, and a helpful business center has computer facilities and a small meeting room for up to six people. The second floor has a bar lounge. On the ground floor, a coffee shop–style dining room serves Thai and Continental food. ⊠ *3 Convent Rd., 10500,* ☎ *02/233–5345,* 🖷 *02/236–9425. 57 rooms. Restaurant, bar, pool, business services. AE, DC, MC, V.* 🐾

$$ 🏨 **Tara Hotel.** This hotel is in the developing restaurant-and-nightlife section of Sukhumvit Road. The lobby is spacious, lined with teak carvings. The check-in lounge serves tea or coffee while formalities are completed. Guest rooms, which are on the small side, are decorated in pastels; many overlook the eighth-floor terrace garden with swimming pool. ⊠ *Sukhumvit Soi 26, 10110,* ☎ *02/259–0053,* 🖷 *02/259–2900. 200 rooms and 20 suites. Restaurant, coffee shop, pool, meeting rooms. AE, DC, MC, V.* 🐾

$$ 🏨 **Tawana Ramada.** Although this hotel has hosted tourists for many years, continual refurbishing keeps the rooms looking smart. You can choose double or king-size beds. Bathrooms are satisfactory rather than grand. Each room has a safe and cable TV, but, unlike many Bangkok

When it Comes to Getting Local Currency at an ATM, Same Thing.

Whether you're in Yosemite or Yemen, using your Visa® card or ATM card with the PLUS symbol is the easiest and most convenient way to get local currency. For example, let's say you're in France. When you make a withdrawal, using your secured PIN, it's dispensed in francs, but is debited from your account in U.S. dollars. This makes it easy to take advantage of favorable exchange rates. And if you need help finding one of Visa's 627,000 ATMs in 127 countries worldwide, visit **visa.com/pd/atm**. We'll make finding an ATM as easy as finding the Eiffel Tower, the Pyramids or even the Grand Canyon.

It's Everywhere You Want To Be.

SEE THE WORLD
IN FULL COLOR

Fodor's Exploring Guides bring all the great sights vividly to life with hundreds of photographs, fascinating historical background, and colorful anecdotes. Detailed maps and practical information keep you headed in the right direction.

Pair a **Fodor's** Exploring Guide with your trusted Gold Guide for a complete planning package.

hotels, no in-room tea/coffeemaker. A few rooms have a balcony (not worth the extra cost) overlooking the very modest pool. Published rates are a hefty B4,000, though the majority of guests—package tour clients—don't pay anywhere near that amount. Ask for a corporate rate. The hotel's location, in the heart of the Silom-Suriwongse business and entertainment district, gives easy access to Bangkok's sights. The coffee shop stays open until 2 AM and the Grill offers an international buffet of some repute for B312. ⊠ *80 Suriwongse Rd., 10500,* ☎ *02/236–0361,* FAX *02/236-3738. 265 room. 2 restaurants, pool, health club, business services, meeting rooms. AE, DC, MC, V.*

$$ ☷ **Wall Street Inn.** Its moderate rates (at the low-end of this price range) and location in the business district make the Wall Street Inn an option. Japanese travelers make up the greatest percentage of guests, due perhaps to the many Japanese offices and nightclubs in the immediate area. Standard rooms are small and windowless, but functional. Furnishings in natural-grain wood are reasonably attractive, though the walls are bare. Bathtubs in the plain bathrooms are cramped. Deluxe rooms have full-size tubs and windows, though the quality of the view may make you wonder if windows are a good thing. There is no pool or health club, but the hotel has a traditional Thai massage parlor, and Lumphini Park is nearby for jogging. ⊠ *37/20–24 Soi Suriwong Plaza, Suriwongse Rd., 10500,* ☎ *02/235–6068,* FAX *02/236–3619. 75 rooms. Coffee shop, massage, business services. AE, DC, MC, V.*

$–$$ ☷ **Baiyoke Suite Hotel.** Many a traveler has passed through this skyscraper hotel and it shows, and its location off Pratunam market and shopping complex may be a tad inconvenient. However, with a promotional price of B1,600, it's good value, especially if you plan to be in Bangkok for some time. The rooms are large and sparsely furnished, with a separate sitting area, pantry-style sink, and cooking area. The hotel's lobby is on the fifth floor, the pool on the 11th. Rooms on the higher floors have panoramic views of the city. At the very top is a revolving restaurant (under separate management). ⊠ *130 Ratchaprarop Rd., Rajthawee, 10400,* ☎ *02/255–0330,* FAX *02/254– 5553. 202 suites. Restaurant, pool, business center. AE, MC, V.*

$–$$ ☷ **Bangkok Centre.** There are few hotels around the Hualamphong Railway Station, in part because it is not a desirable area in which to stay. However, if you do need a place to rest close by, the Bangkok Centre has clean rooms, though the furnishings and decor are in need of a complete overhaul. The main restaurant offers Brazilian fare and is known for its buffet lunch. The day rate (to rest between trains) is B500, less than half the normal rate. ⊠ *328 Pharam 4 (Rama 4), 10500,* ☎ *02/ 238–4848,* FAX *02/236-1862. 80 rooms. Restaurant, coffee shop, pool, meeting rooms. AE, DC, MC, V.*

$–$$ ☷ **Manohra Hotel.** An expansive and spotless marble lobby typifies the pristine efficiency of this hotel between the river and Patpong. Rooms have pastel walls, patterned bedcovers, and dark-green carpets. There is a roof garden for sunbathing and the Buccaneer Night Club for evening action. A word of caution: if the Manohra is fully booked, the staff may suggest its new sister hotel, the Ramada (no relation to the American-managed Ramada) on New Road. Decline unless you are desperate; it is overpriced and has small, poorly designed rooms. The Manohra, on the other hand, is attractive and well run, with a helpful, friendly staff. ⊠ *412 Suriwongse Rd., 10500,* ☎ *02/234–5070,* FAX *02/237–7662. 230 rooms. 2 restaurants, coffee shop, indoor pool, nightclub, meeting rooms. AE, DC, MC, V.*

$–$$ ☷ **Park Hotel.** Although the lobby area, lounge, and bar are far from being designer decorated, this hotel has a fresh crispness to it not often found in its price category. Ample light makes the guest rooms cheerful, and bathrooms are small and clean. The deluxe doubles have space for a desk. There is also a small pool in the garden. ⊠ *Sukhumvit Soi 7, 10110,* ☎ *02/255–4300,* 𝙵𝙰𝚇 *02/255–4309. 139 rooms. Restaurant, bar, coffee shop, pool, travel services. MC, V.*

$–$$ 🏨 **Princess Hotel.** This small, smart hotel in the Grand Palace part of town is close to major tourist attractions. The immediate vicinity, which is dominated by numerous small merchants, is deserted in the evening. You can dine in one of the four hotel restaurants (Chinese, Italian, Japanese, and Thai-Western) or take a short taxi ride to a number of fine riverside restaurants. The small lobby has gardens on two sides, and recessed crystal chandeliers and potted plants complete the tranquil ambience. The rooms have subdued color combinations that set off the dark-wood furnishings. Spacious, well-lighted desks provide adequate work space. The bathrooms and tubs, however, are very small, with rust stains beginning to appear. All the deluxe rooms, costing 8% more, have balconies facing the pool. Executive rooms are on the Princess Floor, which has its own private lobby and breakfast room. Special discounted rates, about half the published rates, are usually available. ⊠ *269 Larn Luang Rd., 10100,* ☎ *02/281–3088,* 𝙵𝙰𝚇 *02/280–1314. 160 rooms. 4 restaurants, pool, business services. AE, DC, MC, V.* 🖂

$–$$ 🏨 **Silom Plaza Hotel.** This hotel in the shopping area on Silom Road has an open lobby area with a lounge. The compact rooms have modern decor in soft colors; the more expensive ones have river views. The hotel caters to business travelers who want to be close to Silom Road. Service is quick. The facilities are limited, but all the entertainment you could wish for is nearby. ⊠ *320 Silom Rd., 10500,* ☎ *02/236–0333,* 𝙵𝙰𝚇 *02/236–7562. 209 rooms. Restaurant, coffee shop, indoor pool, sauna, health club, meeting rooms. AE, DC, MC, V.*

$–$$ 🏨 **Silom Village Inn.** Clean, neat, and friendly, with extremely reasonable ★ prices (about B1,000, with the invariable discount) describes this small hotel. The king-size beds leave just enough space for a desk and a couple of chairs. Bathrooms are new and functional. Choose a room at the back of the hotel to avoid the Silom Road street noise. The reception desk staff is helpful and reliable at taking messages. A small restaurant is good for breakfast and snacks and also serves Italian food, but the Seafood Village Plaza next door is tempting. ⊠ *Silom Village Trade Centre, 286 Silom Rd., 10500,* ☎ *635–6810/7,* 𝙵𝙰𝚇 *02/635–6817. 34 rooms. Restaurant. AE, DC, MC, V.*

$–$$ 🏨 **Tower Inn.** The hotel's name is appropriate; it is a tall skinny building on Silom Road near the Thai International Airways office. The top floor has a health club and swimming pool from which you can glimpse the Chao Phraya River. The reception desk, bar, and small lounge are on the ground floor, and the coffee shop (Thai and Continental food) is on the second floor. The rooms are as spacious as those at the Shangri-La, with plenty of light flooding in from picture windows. The furnishings, however, are utilitarian—two queen-size beds and a cabinet that holds the TV and serves as a desk. The bathroom is smallish—not one to linger in. You can usually negotiate a 30% discount with no trouble at all, which brings the room rate down to about B1,400. ⊠ *533 Silom Rd., 10500,* ☎ *02/237–8300,* 𝙵𝙰𝚇 *02/237–8286. 150 rooms. Restaurant, pool, health club, travel services. AE, DC, MC, V.*

$ 🏨 **Executive House.** Though it offers only limited services, this hotel's reception staff will sometimes help with travel questions, and the coffee shop will deliver food to your room until midnight. The rooms are spacious for the price, the air-conditioning works, and, even if the decor is drab and a bit run-down, the rooms on the upper floors have plenty of light. The penthouse rooms—on the 15th–18th floors—are flooded with it. Rooms with a river view are B200 more than those with a city view. Over the last few years, room prices have steadily increased, with no improvement in facilities, and the lack of tourist services makes this hotel more suited for visitors already familiar with Bangkok. The hotel is next to the Manohra Hotel, down a short driveway. ⊠ *410/3–4 Suriwongse Rd., 10500,* ☎ *02/235–1206,* ℻ *02/236–1482. 120 rooms. Coffee shop. MC, V.*

$ 🏨 **First House.** Tucked behind the Pratunam market on a soi off Phetchburi, the First House offers excellent value for a full-service hotel in this price range. The small lobby serves as a meeting place where guests can read the complimentary newspapers. Off to the left, the Saranyuth coffee shop–restaurant, open 24 hours, serves Thai and Western dishes. The compact rooms are carpeted and amply furnished but so dark as to be depressing during the day. Bathrooms are clean, though patches of rough plaster and drab fixtures don't encourage leisurely grooming. But the reasonable rates, the security, and the helpfulness of the staff all contribute to making this hotel worth noting. ⊠ *14/20–29 Phetchburi Soi 19, Pratunam, 10400,* ☎ *02/254–0303,* ℻ *02/254–3101. 84 rooms. Coffee shop, travel services. AE, DC, MC, V.*

$ 🏨 **Majestic Suites.** On Sukhumvit between Soi 4 and Soi 6, Majestic Suites has no actual suites, only studio, superior, and deluxe rooms. Those barely large enough to fit a queen-size bed run just over B1,000; the much larger deluxe rooms cost B1,800 and have the added touches of coffeemaking facilities and bathrobes. All rooms have safes, minibars, and hair dryers. Furnishings are bright and fresh; rooms at the back are quieter but have no view, whereas the street side, though noisier, has lots of action to watch. ⊠ *110 Sukhumvit Rd., 10110,* ☎ *02/656–8220,* ℻ *02/656–8201. 55 rooms. Bar, coffee shop, business services. AE, DC, MC, V.* ☜

$ 🏨 **New Trocadero.** This hotel, between Patpong and the Chao Phraya River, has been a Westerner's standby for decades—and the furnishings have borne the brunt. The smallish rooms have queen-size-plus beds and clean bathrooms. Service is friendly, and there's a helpful travel-tour desk in the lobby. The New Trocadero is associated with two adjacent, very similar hotels, the Peninsula and the Fuji. ⊠ *343 Suriwongse Rd., 10500,* ☎ *02/234–8920,* ℻ *02/236–5526. 130 rooms. Coffee shop, pool, travel services. AE, DC, MC, V.*

$ 🏨 **Parkway Inn.** Amid the commotion on Sukhumvit stands this small, boutique-style hotel above a tailor's shop and next to the Landmark Hotel. The reception desk, a small bar lounge, and two bedrooms are on the first floor. The other 22 rooms (priced just under B1,000) are on the floors above. Though not very large, the rooms don't seem cramped. Furnishings are comfortable and include cable TV and a refrigerator. The tiled bathrooms are compact but more than adequate. If you can do without looking out on busy Sukhumvit, rooms at the back are the quietest. ⊠ *132 Sukhumvit Rd., 10400,* ☎ *02/255–3711,* ℻ *02/254–2180. 24 rooms. Bar. AE, MC, V.*

$ 🏨 **Plaza Hotel.** This building used to be an apartment complex until fifteen years ago, when it was turned into a hotel—rooms on the seventh floor and above still have a kitchen counter and sink. Though the furnishings are hardly inspiring, the size of the rooms easily accommodates the king-size beds. The staff are low-key and friendly. Though the lobby area and corridors are a little shabby, its convenient location in the heart of the Silom/Suriwongse business and entertainment district makes the Plaza very good value at B1,000 a night. ⊠ *118 Suriwongse Rd., 10500,* ☎ *02/235–1760,* ℻ *02/237–0746. 158 rooms. Coffee shop, pool. AE, DC, MC, V.*

$ 🏨 **Stable Lodge.** Down a small, partly residential street off Sukhumvit Road, this small, quiet hotel seems more like a guest house. Videos are shown in the lounge in the evening. Since the new owners acquired the property (formerly Mermaid's), prices have climbed to around B1,000.

Rooms are clean and neat with queen-size beds. The more expensive rooms have private balconies, and those at the back are the quietest. A pool in the garden is an added attraction. The coffee shop serves Thai and Western food all day, and there is a garden barbecue at night. ⊠ *39 Sukhumvit Soi 8, 10110,* ☎ *02/653–0017,* ℻ *02/253–5125. 40 rooms, most with private baths. Restaurant, pool. AE, MC, V.*

$ 🏨 **Top Inn.** In a busy section of Sukhumvit, this new hotel has small, air-conditioned rooms for B850. Rooms have either twin beds or one queen. A TV, refrigerator, and a couple of chairs make up the furnishings. Bathrooms are compact, but tiled and clean. Notwithstanding the smallness of the rooms, the newness of the hotel and its cleanliness makes it a possible choice if you really want to be close to the nightlife of Sukhumvit and Soi 4. Rooms at the back are the quietest. ⊠ *128 Sukhumvit Rd., 10110,* ☎ *02/656–8290,* ℻ *02/253–6077. 12 rooms. Coffee shop. AE, MC, V.*

¢ 🏨 **The Atlanta.** Charles Henn, a part-time professor, caters to visiting
★ scholars and frugal travelers who often return again and again. The dining room and lobby are straight out of the 1950s, with leatherette banquettes and a circular sofa. Beyond the lobby is the garden, with tables and chairs and even desks for budding authors, as well as an excellent swimming pool. The accommodations are simple and without TV, but they're clean and very spacious for the rock-bottom rates. Some rooms have air-conditioning, some have fans and ventilators, and some have balconies; most have personal safes. In the dining room, classical music is played before 5 PM, jazz thereafter, and a movie from Henn's videotape collection is shown after dinner. The menu, which explains the ingredients of each dish, makes interesting reading (Henn is a food critic), and the Thai food is superb, with a wide vegetarian selection. In the crass glitter of modern Bangkok, the Atlanta is an oasis—and one of the best values in town. ⊠ *78 Sukhumvit Soi 2, 10110,* ☎ *02/252–1650 or 02/252–6069,* ℻ *02/656–8123 or 02/255–2151. 59 rooms. Restaurant, pool, travel services. No credit cards.*

¢ 🏨 **River City Guest House.** It's a shame this small hotel, a block from the water's edge, has no view of the river. But then if it did, the price of a room would probably quadruple. As it is, B500 gives you a modest air-conditioned room with a double bed, and a table and chair. The small bathrooms have showers and exposed plumbing for decoration! Ask for a room with a window. The trick is to find the hotel: walk upriver from the Sheraton, past the River City Shopping Centre, and as the soi bends to the right, the hotel is on the right. This location gives you easy access to the marvelous sois of Chinatown and the river ferries, and puts you within walking distance of Suriwongse and Silom roads. ⊠ *11/4 Soi Rong Nam Khang 1 (Soi 24), Charoen Krung Rd., 10100,* ☎ *02/235–1429,* ℻ *02/237–3127. 17 rooms with bath or shower. Coffee shop. MC, V.*

¢ 🏨 **River View Guest House.** Down a tiny soi on the edge of Chinatown and just one house in from the Chao Phraya River, this family-run hotel is unique for being a budget hotel with river views. The rooms are shabby but clean. The river-view rooms (B450) are fan-cooled and without a full bathroom, and the rooms with only a limited view of the river have air-conditioning and a bath (B700). Tiny rooms with shared bathrooms cost only B150. The coffee shop, on the eighth floor, has a spectacular view, since this is where the Chao Phraya makes a turn. This hotel is not for everyone, and there aren't many Westerners around. It could also use refurbishing. The easiest way to find it is to walk upriver from the Royal Orchid Sheraton, keeping as close to the river as you can. After about 1,000 yards, you'll see the guest house's sign pointing down a soi on the left. ⊠ *768 Soi Panurangsri,*

Songvad Rd., 10100, ☎ 02/234–5429, ℻ 02/236–6199. *37 rooms, half with bath. Restaurant. V.*

¢ 🏠 **Sri Kasem Hotel.** Across the klong from Hualamphong Train Station, this small hotel is ideally located if you come in on a late train or are departing early in the morning. The building is old and so is the hotel—don't expect modern amenities. However, the sparsely furnished rooms are air-conditioned, the bathrooms are clean, the staff is helpful, and the price is right. ⊠ *1860 Krung Kasem Rd., 10500,* ☎ *02/225–0132,* ℻ *02/225–4705. 26 rooms. Coffee shop. No credit cards.*

NIGHTLIFE AND THE ARTS

The English-language newspapers the *Bangkok Post* and *The Nation* have good information on current festivals, exhibitions, and nightlife. TAT's weekly *Where* also lists events. Monthly *Metro* magazine has an extensive listings section and offers reviews of new hot spots.

Nightlife

The law requires that bars and nightclubs close at 2 AM, but Bangkok never sleeps, and many restaurants and street stalls stay open for late-night carousing. The city is awash with bars catering to all tastes, from the Oriental Hotel's classy Bamboo Bar right down to sleazy go-go bars. Soi 55 (also called Soi Thonglor), off Sukhumvit Road, has several good bars and nightclubs. Soi Sarasin, across from Lumphini Park, is packed with friendly pubs and cafés that are popular with yuppie Thais and expats. And it's only in Bangkok that would you ever find a phenomenon like Royal City Avenue (called "RCA"). By about 11 PM this strip, nearly deserted by day, used to be thronged with thousands of young Thais walking up and down between the 160 bars lining the avenue and blaring loud music. With the economic crisis of 1997, RCA lost its wild gaiety and many bars closed, but as the economy regains its strength and newer nightspots go stale, people are returning to RCA and its ever-ready drinking and music joints.

Unfortunately, tourism has fostered the most lurid forms of nightlife geared to the male tourist. Live sex shows, though officially banned, are still found in three areas of Bangkok. Patpong is the biggest, and it includes three streets that link Suriwongse and Silom roads. Patpong 1 and 2 are packed with go-go bars that have hostesses by the dozen. Sex shows are generally found one flight up. Patpong 3 caters mostly to gays but also to lesbians. Note that Patpong is quite safe and well patrolled by police, and it even has a Night Market where Thais take visiting friends to shop. Soi Cowboy, off Sukhumvit Road at Soi 21, is a less raunchy, more easygoing version of Patpong. The bars are considerably tamer; some have go-go dancers, whereas others are good for a quiet beer, with or without a temporary companion. Nana Plaza, at Soi 4 off Sukhumvit Road, is the most popular with expats and expanded in the late '90s. The plaza is now packed with three floors of bars; most of them have hostesses, but there are some quieter places, too. The newest bars have spilled out along Soi 4 itself. All three nightspots are near skytrain stations, but keep in mind that the trains stop just after midnight. Watch out for scams, including aggressive hostesses, touts that promise a lot for a little money, and the copying of credit cards.

Bars and Pubs

You can get a decent pint of (chilled) beer and pub grub at the **Bobbies Arms** (⊠ Car Park Blvd., second level, Patpong 2 Rd., ☎ 02/233–6828). On weekends, a live band plays, and various excuses are made for a party—anything from St. Patrick's Day to St. George's Day. A good place to start carousing is **Brown Sugar** (✉ 231/20 Soi Sarasin, ☎ 02/250–0103). The popular **Bull's Head Pub** (✉ Sukhumvit Soi 33, near the Phrom Phong skytrain station, ☎ 02/259–4444) offers a Quiz Night on the second Tuesday of each month. Amid the swinging nightlife of Nana (Soi 4), **Bus Stop** (✉ 14 Sukhumvit Soi 4, ☎ 02/251–9222) is a pleasantly relaxed pub with outdoor seating and grilled fare. Two large TVs play sports channels, and hostesses are not pushy.

For years now, **Delaney's Irish Pub** (✉ 1/5–6 Convent Rd., near the Sala Daeng skytrain station, ☎ 02/266-7160) has been standing room only during evening music hours. Beers include Guinness on tap, and good Western food is served. The **Hard Rock Cafe** (✉ Siam Sq., ☎ 02/254–0830) remains popular for Western food and music. **The Hemingway Bar & Grill** (✉ Sukhumvit Soi 55, ☎ 02/392–3599), modeled on a log cabin, is popular with Thais and expats. **The Londoner Brew Pub** (✉ 591 UBCH Building, in the basement, Sukhumvit Rd. at the corner of Soi 33, ☎ no phone) makes its own "real ale." British fare is served at tables, booths, and the bar.

The Old Dragon (✉ 29/78–81 Royal City Ave., ☎ 02/203–0972), or Old Leng, is filled with oddities, from wooden cinema seats to etchings of Chinese characters on old mirrors. The owner claims that only the music machines, cash register, and most of the guests are younger than 50 years. The food served is a mix of Chinese and Thai (snacks are also available). **Route 66** (✉ 29/37 Royal City Ave., ☎ 02/203–0407 or 02/203–0407) celebrates the famous American highway and is often packed. **Saxophone Pub & Restaurant** (✉ 3/8 Victory Monument, Phayathai Rd., near the Victory Monument skytrain station, ☎ 02/246–5472) offers great music and good food and proves popular with locals and expats. The **Old West Saloon** (✉ 231/17 Soi Sarasin, ☎ 02/252–9510) re-creates the atmosphere of America's Old West aided by a four-piece band and a happy hour.

Cabaret

The largest troupe of performing transvestites is reputed to be the **Calypso Cabaret** (✉ In the Asia Hotel, 296 Phayathai Road, ☎ 02/653–3960 or 02/653–3962 before 6 PM; 02/216–8937 or 02/216–8938 after 6), with nightly shows at 8:15 and 9:45. For live bands and internationally known nightclub artists, try the **Tiara** (✉ Rama IV Rd., ☎ 02/236-0450, ext 2449), the Dusit Thani's penthouse restaurant.

Cultural Shows

Silom Village (✉ 286 Silom Rd., ☎ 02/234–4448), open 10 AM–10 PM, may be rather touristy, but it appeals also to Thais. The block-size complex has shops, restaurants, and performances of classical Thai dance. At a couple of the restaurants, chefs cook tasty morsels in the open—you select what suits your fancy or order from a menu. Silom Village also has a cultural show at **Ruan Thep** (☎ 02/635–6313). Dinner starts at 7 and showtime is at 8:30. Dinner and a show costs B450; the show only is B350.

Dance Clubs

Although most hotels have discos that were popular in the mid '90s, there are better places to dance, including several good dance bars on RCA (☞ *above*). **Concept CM2** (✉ Siam Square 392/44 Rama 1, Soi 6, ☎ 02/255–6888) is a posh nightclub in the Novotel Siam. If you want to really cut loose try **Deeper** (✉ 82 Silom Rd. Soi 4, ☎ 02/233–2830). The in-crowd goes to **Taurus** (✉ Sukhumvit Soi 26, ☎ 02/261–3991).

Dinner Cruises

Boats built to look like traditional Thai houses or refurbished rice barges serve a Western or Thai dinner while cruising the Chao Phraya River.

Hotel staff make reservations, as these two-hour evening cruises are usually strictly for tourists. **The Horizon** (⊠ Shangri-La Hotel, 89 Soi Wat Suan Phu, New Rd., ☏ 02/236–7777) has cruise departures at 8 PM. **The Manohra Moon** (⊠ Marriott Royal Garden Riverside Hotel, 257/1–3 Charoen Krung Rd., Thonburi ☏ 02/476–0021 or 02/476–00222, ext. 1416) has lunch (B800) and dinner (B1,200) cruises. **Yok Yor** (☞ Dining, *above*) is one of the few cruises likely to be all Thai.

Jazz Bars

For a quiet drink accompanied by easy-listening live jazz try the Oriental Hotel's **Bamboo Bar** (⊠ Oriental Lane, ☏ 02/236–4000). **Fabb Fashion Cafe** (⊠ In the Mercury Tower, 540 Ploenchit Rd., near the Chidlom skytrain station, ☏ 02/658–2003) plays jazz in the early evening and offers good Thai and Western food. **Witch's Tavern** (⊠ Sukhumvit Soi 55, down from the Thong Lor skytrain station, ☏ 02/391–9791) has classical jazz in a cozy Victorian atmosphere. It also serves hearty English fare.

The Arts

Classical Thai Dance

Thai classical dance is the epitome of grace. Themes for the dance drama are taken from the *Ramayana*. A series of controlled gestures uses eye contact, ankle and neck movements, and hands and fingers to convey the stories' drama. It is accompanied by a woodwind called the *piphat*, which sounds like an oboe, and percussion instruments.

Various restaurants offer a classical dance show with dinner. **Baan Thai** (⊠ Sukhumvit Soi 22, ☏ 02/258–5403) is popular for those staying at hotels in the eastern part of Bangkok. At the **National Theatre** (⊠ Na Phra That Rd., ☏ 02/221–5861 or 02/224–1342), performances are given most days at 10 AM and 3 PM, and special performances are also held on the last Friday of each month at 5:30 PM. The **Sala Rim Naam** (☞ Dining, *above*) in the Oriental Hotel puts on a beautiful show with an excellent dinner.

OUTDOOR ACTIVITIES AND SPORTS

Participant Sports

Golf

There are good golf courses in and around Bangkok, and although weekend play requires advance booking, tee times are usually available during the week. Greens fees are approximately B700 weekdays and B1,500 weekends, with caddy fees about B100. **Krungthep Sports Golf Course** (⊠ B.P. 522, 10 Huamark, ☏ 02/374–6063) is attractively laid out with fairways flanked by bougainvillea and pine trees, and elevated greens surrounded by sand traps. The **Navatanee Golf Course** (⊠ 22 Mul Sukhaphiban 2 Rd., Bangkapi, ☏ 02/374–7077), designed by Robert Trent Jones, is thought to be the area's most challenging. The **Rose Garden Golf Course** (⊠ 4/8 Sukhumvit Soi 3, ☏ 02/253–0295) is a pleasant, undemanding course.

Health Clubs

The **Clark Hatch Athletic Club** has branches at Thaniya Plaza (⊠ Silom Rd., ☏ 02/231–2250); Charn Issara Tower II (☏ 02/308–2779); Amari Watergate Hotel (☏ 02/653–9000); Amari Atrium Hotel (☏ 02/718–2000); Century Park Hotel (☏ 02/246–7800); and Chaengwatana Sports Club (☏ 02/962–6100). The **Grand Hyatt Erawan** (⊠ 494 Ratchadamri Rd., ☏ 02/254–1234, ext 4437) has the best health-and-fitness facility of any Bangkok hotel. The **Peninsula** (⊠ 333 Charoennakorn Rd., Klonsan, ☎ 02/861–1111, ext. 6011) also has a good fitness center.

Jogging

For a quick jog, the small running track at many hotels may be the best bet. Stay off the grass in all city parks; you can run alone safely in the parks during the day but not at night. **Chatuchak Park's** loop is 4 km (2½ mi), but it is north of the city. **Lumphini Park,** whose pathways are paved, is about 2 km (1¼ mi) around and is popular with serious joggers. **Sanam Luang,** in front of the Grand Palace, is a popular park for runners. The **Siam Inter-Continental Hotel's** jogging track in its parkland gardens is one of the most attractive.

Massage

Traditional Thai massage is very common in Bangkok and will generally be Wat Pho style. Go for two hours for the full effect. Hotel staff can usually recommend where to go.

The massage (B200) given at the famous **Wat Pho school** is the best bargain and an experience not to be missed. A very gentle massage in very genteel surroundings may be had at the new **Oriental Spa** (⊠ In the Oriental Hotel, 48 Oriental Ave., ☎ 02/236–0400). Here in wood-paneled sophistication you can get facials, hydrotherapy, mud and seaweed wraps, and herbal treatments, from the "Jet Lag Solution" at B2,000 to a full day's pampering for $200. A most relaxing massage, with oils, is available at the **Regent Hotel** (⊠ 155 Ratchadamri Rd., ☎ 02/251–6127).

Spectator Sports

Horse Racing

Horse racing is a popular pastime in Bangkok, where each meeting has up to 12 races, and public betting is permitted. The **Royal Bangkok Sports Club** (⊠ Henri Dunant Rd. between Rama I and Rama IV roads, ☎ 02/251–0181) and the **Royal Turf Club** (⊠ On the north side of Phitsanulok Rd. just east of Rama V Rd., ☎ 02/280–0020) hold races on alternating Sundays.

Thai Boxing

The national sport of Thailand draws an enthusiastic crowd in Bangkok, where bouts are the real thing, unlike some Thai boxing shows you may see in tourist resort areas. Understanding the rules is difficult; it's fast and furious, and the playing of traditional music heightens the drama. Daily matches alternate between the two main stadiums. **Lumphini stadium** (⊠ Rama IV Rd., ☎ 02/251–4303) has matches on Tuesday, Friday, and Saturday at 6 PM and Sunday at 1 PM. **Ratchadamnoen stadium** (⊠ Ratchadamnoen Nok Rd., ☎ 02/281–4205) has bouts on Monday, Wednesday, and Thursday at 6 PM. Tickets (B100–500) may be bought at the gates.

SHOPPING

Even if you don't feel like buying, browsing through the markets is fascinating. Everything is for sale—from fake Rolex watches for the equivalent of a few bucks to Paris originals costing thousands. And aside from the wonderfully cheap mass-produced knockoffs of international brands, you'll find good-quality merchandise made in Thailand: jewelry, silks, silverware, leather, and Oriental antiques are just some examples.

Tourists can now reclaim the 7.5% VAT (Value Added Tax) at the airport on store-bought items if they have a receipt for the merchandise. Ask about the VAT refund when you buy goods. If you still want the convenience of a big duty-free shop try **King Power International Group** (✉ 4 Ratchadamri Rd., 7th floor, Patumwan, ☎ 02/252–3633 up to 8), which has a large array of goods on the top floor of the World Trade Centre and is open daily 9:30 AM to 10:30 PM. The merchandise is rather expensive, and you miss the fun of bartering at street stalls. Most clerks speak a bit of English. You pay for the items at the shop, then pick them up at the airport when you leave. To buy, you need your passport and airline ticket, and you need to pay for goods at least eight hours before leaving the country.

Districts

The main shopping areas are along Silom Road and at the Rama IV end of Suriwongse for jewelry, crafts, and silk; along Sukhumvit Road for leather goods; along Yaowarat Road in Chinatown for gold; and along Silom Road, Oriental Lane, and Charoen Krung Road for antiques. The Oriental Plaza and the River City Shopping Centre have shops with collector-quality goods; the shops around Siam Square and at the World Trade Centre attract middle-income Thais and foreigners. Peninsula Plaza, across from the Regent Hotel, has very upscale shops, and the newest and glitziest complex is Thaniya Plaza, between Silom and Suriwongse roads, near Patpong. If you're knowledgeable about fabric and cut, you can find bargains at the textile merchants and tailors who compete along Pahuraht Road in Chinatown and Pratunam off Phetchburi Road. Although prices are inflated for tourists, Patpong 1 is a lively market for cheap goods. You'll see locals buying here, too, from 6 PM until well into the night. Stalls are also set up in the afternoon and evening along Silom Road, selling tourists knock-off designer ware.

Markets

You can buy virtually anything at the **Chatuchak Weekend Market** (✉ Chatuchak Park, Phaholyothin Rd.), across the street from the northern terminus of the skytrain and near the Northern Bus Terminal. Sometimes you'll find great fashion buys, including items made from *mudmee* silk (ikat weave, where thread is tie-dyed before weaving) that would sell in America for five times the price. Even if you don't buy, a visit will open your eyes to exotic foods, flowers, and Thai life. Though open on Friday from 5 to 9 PM and weekends from 9 AM to 9 PM, Bangkok's largest market is best visited on Saturday and Sunday in the late morning.

Pahuraht Cloth Market (✉ Off Yaowarat Rd.), operated mostly by Indians, is known for its bargain textiles, batiks, and buttons. An auctioneer with a microphone announces when everything at a particular stall will be sold at half price, and the shoppers surge over to bid. Hundreds of stalls and shops jam the sidewalk daily at **Pratunam Market** (✉ Corner of Phetchburi and Ratchaprarop Rds., near the Indra Regent and Amari Watergate hotels). The stacks of merchandise consist mainly of inexpensive clothing—jeans for $5 and shirts for $4. It's a good place to meet Thais, who come in the evening to shop and eat tasty, inexpensive Thai and Chinese street food.

Soi Sampeng (✉ Parallel to Yaowarat Rd.) has toys, household goods, clothes, and lots of fabrics—it is Bangkok's best-known and oldest textile center. Antiques (both old and new) are found on **Ta Chang Road,** where there's also jewelry made by Thailand's northern hill tribes. **Ta Phra Chan** (✉ Near Wat Phra Keo), where the Weekend Market used to be, still has booths selling antiques and assorted goods. Between Yaowarat and Charoen Krung in Chinatown lies the so-called **Thieves**

Market (Nakorn Kasem), an area of small streets with old wood houses, where you can buy anything from hardware to porcelains. Bargains are hard to find nowadays, but these small, cluttered streets are fascinating. Bargain hard!

Specialty Stores

Art, Crafts, and Antiques

Note that Thai antiques and old images of the Buddha need a special export license. Suriwongse Road, Charoen Krung Road, and the Oriental Plaza (across from the Oriental Hotel) have many art and antiques shops, as does the River City Shopping Centre. Original and often illegal artifacts from Angkor Wat are sometimes sold there too.

Don't miss **123 Baan Dee** (⌧ 123 Fuengnakorn Rd., ☎ 02/221–2520) in the old town, in a restored small teak house. Antique silks, ceramics, beads, pictures, and other fascinating artifacts abound on two floors, and there's a small ice-cream parlor at the back. **Peng Seng** (⌧ 942 Rama IV, at the Suriwongse Rd. intersection, ☎ 02/234–1285) is one of the most respected dealers of antiquities in Bangkok. Prices may be high, but articles are likely to be genuine. **Rasi Sayam** (⌧ 32 Sukhumvit Soi 23, ☎ 02/258–4195), in an old teak house in a garden, has a wonderful collection of fine Thai crafts.

Clothing and Fabrics

Thai silk gained its world reputation only after World War II, when technical innovations were introduced. Two other fabrics are worth noting: mudmee silk, produced in the Northeast, and Thai cotton, which is soft, durable, and easier on the wallet than silk.

Design Thai (⌧ 304 Silom Rd., ☎ 02/235–1553) has a large selection of silk articles in all price ranges—a good place for that gift you ought to take home (you can usually manage a 20% discount here). For factory-made clothing, visit the **Indra Garment Export Centre** (⌧ Ratchaprarop Rd., behind the Indra Regent Hotel), where hundreds of shops sell discounted items.

The **Jim Thompson Thai Silk Company** (⌧ 9 Suriwongse Rd., ☎ 02/234–4900) is a prime place for silk by the yard and ready-made clothes. There is no bargaining and the prices are high, but the staff is knowledgeable and helpful. A branch store has opened in the Oriental Hotel's shopping arcade.

Napajaree Suanduenchai studied fashion design in Germany; 20 years ago she started the **Prayer Textile Gallery** (⌧ Phayathai Rd., near Siam Square, ☎ 02/251–7549) where her mother's dress shop had been for 14 years before that. She makes stunning traditional clothes in naturally dyed silks and cottons and in old fabrics from the north, Laos, and Cambodia.

The custom-made suit in 24–48 hours is a Bangkok specialty, but the suit often hangs on the shoulders just as one would expect from a rush job. If you want an excellent cut, give the tailor more time. The best in Bangkok is **Marco Tailor** (⌧ 430/33 Siam Square, Soi 7, ☎ 02/252–0689), where, for approximately B17,000, your suit will equal those made on Savile Row.

For women's apparel, **Stephanie Thai Silk** (⌧ 55 Soi Shangri-La Hotel, New Rd., Bangrak, ☎ 02/234–0590 or 02/233–0325) is a respected shop which can deliver in 24 hours, though allowing more time is recommended. It has its own wide selection of silks but you can bring your own material. A skirt with blouse and jacket made of Thai silk starts at B5,000.

Jewelry

Thailand is a world center for gems, exporting more colored stones than anywhere in the world, and the jewelry trade has taken off in the past decade. Be wary of deals that are too good to be true; they probably are. Scams are common and it's best to stick with established businesses. If you have any complaints, see the tourist police. There are countless gem and jewelry stores on Silom and Suriwongse roads, with a large concentration of gem dealers in the Jewelry Trade Centre on Silom Road.

A long-established jewelry firm is **Johny's Gems** (⊠ 199 Fuengnakorn Rd., ☎ 02/224–4065). If you telephone, he'll send a car to pick you up (a frequent practice among the better Bangkok stores), or you can walk to the shop if you are in the vicinity of Wat Phra Keo. **Oriental Lapidary** (⊠ 116/1 Silom Rd., just across and a little down the street from the Jewelry Trade Centre, ☎ 02/238–2718) has a long record of good service. **Pranda Jewelry** (⊠ 333 Soi Rungsang, Bangna-Trad Rd., ☎ 02/361–3311) is a well-established store with separate branches for gems and jewelry. **Than Shine** (⊠ 84/87 Sukhumvit Soi 55, ☎ 02/381–7337), run by sisters Cho Cho and Mon Mon, offers classy and New Wave designs.

Leather

Leather is a good buy in Bangkok, with some of the lowest prices in the world, especially for custom work. Crocodile leather is popular, but be sure to obtain a certificate that the skins came from a domestically raised reptile; otherwise U.S. Customs may confiscate the goods. The River City Shopping Centre has a number of leather shops. For shoes and jackets, try the 20-year-old **Siam Leather Goods** (⊠ In the River City Shopping Centre, ☎ 02/233–4521).

Precious Metals

Chinatown is the place to go for gold. Most shops are authentic (they wouldn't survive there as anything but); still, insist on a receipt. There is no bargaining for gold. For bronze try **Siam Bronze Factory** (⊠ 1250 Charoen Krung Rd., ☎ 02/234–9436).

BANGKOK A TO Z

Arriving and Departing

By Airplane

At **Don Muang Airport international terminal,** next to the Domestic Terminal, you'll find an array of desks where you can arrange for taxis into Bangkok and transport to other destinations; a reservation desk for Bangkok hotels (no fee); and a **Tourist Authority of Thailand (TAT)** desk with free brochures and maps. Both terminals have luggage-checking facilities (☎ 02/535–1250, but only Thai is spoken).

There's a tax of B500 for international departures and B30 for domestic departures.

Thai Airways International (⊠ 485 Silom Rd., ☎ 02/280–0060) is the national airline, and most of its flights go through Don Muang. It has direct flights from the West Coast of the United States and from London, and it also flies daily to Hong Kong, Singapore, Taiwan, and Japan.

The U.S. carrier with the most frequent flights is **Northwest Airlines** (⊠ 153 Ratchadamri Rd., Peninsula Shopping Plaza, 4th floor, ☎ 02/254–0789). It has service through Tokyo (with a minimal stopover) from New York, Detroit, Seattle, Dallas, San Francisco, and Los Angeles. Northwest also has a round-Asia fare, in conjunction with local airlines, which lets you hop from one capital to another. **Singapore Air-**

lines (⊠ Silom Centre Building, 2 Silom Rd., ☎ 02/236–0440) flies to Bangkok through Singapore. **British Airways** (⊠ 990 Rama IV Rd., ☎ 02/636–1747) flies nonstop to Bangkok from London. The three airlines are among the 70 or so now serving Bangkok, with more seeking landing rights. A new international airport, southeast of the city, is scheduled to open in 2004.

The airport has more than its share of hustlers out to make a quick baht, who often wear uniforms and tags that make them seem official. They will try to get you to change your hotel to one that pays them a large commission, perhaps claiming your intended hotel is overbooked. They will hustle you into overpriced taxis or limousines. Do not get taken in.

Between the Airport and Town

BY BUS

An airport bus service (B70) runs approximately every 30 minutes between Don Muang and four sectors of downtown Bangkok. A1 travels to Ratchadamri and Silom roads. A2 covers the central area that includes the Victory Monument and Chinatown. A3 goes down Sukhumvit. A4 weaves its way to Hualamphong, the main train station. A detailed listing of each route is available from the airport TAT office and at the bus stop outside the arrivals hall. You can also catch local air-conditioned buses (B15) on the main road that passes the airport.

BY HELICOPTER

For about $150, with a three person minimum, you can fly between the airport and the Peninsula, Oriental, Royal Orchid Sheraton, and Shangri-La hotels, but new expressways have greatly diminished the need for this service.

BY TAXI

Don Muang is 25 km (15 mi) from the city center. The highways are often congested, and the trip can take from 30 minutes to more than an hour. State your destination at the counter on the curb (at either terminal) and obtain a voucher; a driver will lead you to the taxi. The fare on the meter (be sure that the meter is turned on) for downtown Bangkok depends on the exact destination and, to some extent, the time of day. Count on B200–B250 plus a B50 expressway toll charge and a B50 airport surcharge. Taxis to the airport from downtown Bangkok do not have the airport surcharge, and will cost approximately B200.

BY TRAIN

Bangkok Airport Express trains make the 35-minute run every 90 minutes from 8 AM to 7 PM. Check the schedule at the tourist booth in the arrival hall. The fare is B100. You can also take the regular trains from 5:30 AM to 9 PM. The fare is B5 for a local train and B13 for an express. The train is rarely convenient as there are few hotels near the train station.

By Bus

Bangkok has three main bus terminals. **Northern Bus Terminal** (⊠ Phaholyothin Rd., behind Chatuchak Park, ☎ 02/279–4484), called Morchit, serves I-san, Chiang Mai, and the north. **Southern Bus Terminal** (⊠ Pinklao-Nakomchaisri Rd., Talingchan, ☎ 02/391–9829), in Thonburi, is for Hua Hin, Ko Samui, Phuket, and points south. **Eastern Bus Terminal** (⊠ Sukhumvit Soi 40, ☎ 02/391–2504), called Ekkamai, is for Pattaya, Rayong, and Trat province.

By Train

Hualamphong Railway Station (⊠ Rama IV Rd., ☎ 02/223–0341), the city's main station, serves mostly long-distance trains. **Bangkok Noi**

(✉ Arun Amarin Rd., ☏ 02/411–3102), on the Thonburi side of the Chao Phraya River, is used by local trains to Hua Hin and Kanchanaburi.

Getting Around

Both the skytrain, which opened along two central city routes in December 1999, and the river, when available, are good options to beat the traffic. New expressways have eased the congestion somewhat, particularly from the airport to hotels on the river. If you do join the traffic, timing is a consideration, with roads at their worst during rush hours, 7–10 AM and 4–7 PM. A subway system is scheduled to open in 2002.

By Boat

Water taxis and ferries ("river buses") ply the Chao Phraya River. The taxis are long-tail boats (so called for the extra-long propeller shaft that extends behind the stern) that you can hire for about B400 an hour. The river-bus fare is based on zones, but B5 will cover most trips that you are likely to take. At certain ferry piers (*tha*) you will also pay a B1 jetty fee. The jetty adjacent to the Oriental Hotel is a useful stop. You can get to the Grand Palace in about 10 minutes and half a dozen stops, or to the other side of Krungthon Bridge in about 15 minutes. It is often the quickest way to travel north–south. It is also a few degrees cooler on the water.

By Bus

Though buses can be very crowded, they are convenient and inexpensive. For a fare of only B3.50 (any distance) on the ordinary non-air-conditioned buses and B6 to B16 on the air-conditioned ones, you can go virtually anywhere in the city. Micro Buses are smaller, air-conditioned, do not permit standing passengers, and charge B20 for any distance. Buses operate from 5 AM to around 11 PM. The routes are confusing, but usually someone at the bus stop will know the number of the bus you need to catch. You can pick up a route map at most bookstalls for B35. Be alert for purse snatchers and pickpockets on buses.

By Mototaxi

At the head of many sois you will often find a gang of motorbikers. These "soi boys" began by taking passengers down the sois, but their operations have expanded to take you anywhere in Bangkok, although they can still pick up passengers only at their soi. The physical risk and discomfort limit their desirability, but, if you are late for a date, they are the fastest means of transport in congested traffic. Ask for a helmet. Fares, to be negotiated, are about the same as, or perhaps a little less than, taxi fare.

By Samlor

These unmetered three-wheeled polluters, called tuk-tuks, are slightly cheaper than taxis and are best used for short trips in congested traffic. But the drivers are tough negotiators, and unless you are good at bargaining you may well end up paying more than for a metered taxi. Tuk-tuk drivers often offer "tours" at a bargain rate and take the unsuspecting to gem shops and tailors who, of course, give the drivers a commission.

By Skytrain

The skytrain opened on December 5, 1999, the King's birthday. With two intersecting lines, it covers 23 km and has 25 stations. It has shrunk the city for those who can pay the fare (B10 to B40), determined by the distance you travel. The routes above Sukhumvit, Silom, and Phaholyothin roads make traveling in those areas a breeze. The skytrain does not go through the old part of town, however, because it is considered too unsightly (you certainly can't miss the huge concrete pillars). The skytrain runs from 5 AM to midnight.

By Taxi

Nowadays most taxis are metered, and you should take only these. The tariff for the first 2 km (1.2 mi) is set at B35 and then increases a baht for about every 50 meters. If the speed drops to under 6 kph, there is a surcharge of one baht per minute. A typical journey of about 5 km (3 mi) runs B60.

Contacts and Resources

Emergencies

Ambulance: ☎ 02/252–2171 up to 5. **Fire:** ☎ 199. **General emergencies:** ☎ 1155. **Police:** ☎ 191.

In an emergency, you are advised to contact the **Tourist Police** (✉ Tourist Service Centre, 4 Ratchadamnoen Rd., ☎ 02/1155) rather than the local police. There are Tourist Police mobile units in major tourist areas.

Dentists: Bangkok has a number of dental clinics, among them **Ambassador Dental Clinic** (✉ 171 Sukhumvit Soi 11, Ambassador Plaza, ☎ 02/255–2279) and **Thaniya Dental Centre** (✉ 4th floor, Thaniya Plaza, 52 Silom Rd., ☎ 02/231–2100). If you want a private dentist, see **Khun Phira Sithiamnuai** (✉ President Park Dental Clinic, Mahogany Tower, President Park, Sukhumvit 24, ☎ 02/661–1156), who did his training and internship in Massachusetts.

Hospitals: Bangkok Adventist Hospital (✉ 430 Phitsanulok Rd., ☎ 02/281–1422). **Bangkok Christian Hospital** (✉ 124 Silom Rd., ☎ 02/233–6981 or 02/233–6989). **The Bangkok Nursing Home** (✉ 9 Convent Rd., ☎ 02/233–2610 or 02/233–2609). **Chulalongkorn Hospital** (✉ Rama IV Rd., ☎ 02/252–8181). **Nonthavej Hospital,** (✉ 30/8 Ngam-wong-wan Rd., Bangkhen Nonthaburi, ☎ 02/951–8575), out toward Don Muang Airport, has qualified doctors and an excellent staff accustomed to overseas patients.

Pharmacies: There is no shortage of pharmacies in Bangkok. Compared with the United States, fewer drugs require prescriptions, but if you need one, the prescription must be written in Thai. Be aware that over-the-counter drugs are not necessarily of the same chemical composition as those in the United States. **Foodland Supermarket Pharmacy** (✉ No. 9 Patpong 2 Rd., ☎ 02/233–2101; ✉ 1413 Sukhumvit Soi 5, ☎ 02/254–2247) stays open all night. The ubiquitous **7-Eleven, AM/PM,** and other 24-hour stores carry nonprescription medications.

English-Language Bookstores

The English-language dailies the *Bangkok Post* and *The Nation* and the monthly *Metro* are available at newsstands.

Asia Books has a wide selection of books and magazines at branches throughout the city. Two convenient locations are 221 Sukhumvit Soi 15) ☎ 02/651–0428) and the Peninsula Plaza, adjacent to the Regent Hotel (☎ 02/253–9786). **Bookazine** is a chain with a good selection and several locations, including one in the CP Tower (✉ 313 Silom Rd., ☎ 02/231–0016). **Kinokuniya Books** (✉ Emporium Shopping Complex, Sukhumvit Rd., at the corner of Soi 24 and connected to the Phrom Phong skytrain station, ☎ 02/664–8554) has one of the largest selections of books.

Guided Tours

Virtually every major hotel has a travel desk that books tours in and around Bangkok, though you can easily visit many of the sights independently. With slight variation, the following tours of the city are usually offered: the half-day City and Temples tour (Wat Pho, Wat Benjamabophit, Wat Traimitr, but not the Grand Palace); the Grand Palace and Emerald Buddha tour; and a Thai Dinner and Classical Dance tour.

Telephones

The level of English remains limited even in Bangkok, so patience will serve you well. Telephone information from an English-speaking operator is available by dialing 13, but getting through is often difficult.

Travel Agencies

For significant purchases, you may want to use a large, established agency. Major hotels can arrange itineraries or recommend a good travel agent. **Diethelm** (⊠ Kian Gwan Building 11, 140/1 Wireless Rd., across from the U.S. Embassy, ☎ 02/255–9150). **East West Siam** (⊠ Building One, 11th floor, 99 Wireless Rd., ☎ 02/256–6153 or 02/256–6155). **World Travel Service** (⊠ 1053 Charoen Krung Rd., ☎ 02/233–5900).

Visitor Information

The **Tourist Authority of Thailand (TAT)** (⊠ Le Concord Building, 202 Ratchadaphisek Rd., Huay Kwang, 10320, ☎ 02/694–1222, FAX 02/694–1220), open 8:30 to 4:30, tends to have more in the way of colorful brochures than hard information, but it can supply useful material on national parks and various routes to out-of-the-way destinations. A tourist hot line (dial 1155—open 24 hours a day) provides information on destinations, accommodations, festivals, arts, and culture. You may also use the hot line to register complaints or request assistance from the tourist police. There is also a TAT branch at the international terminal at **Don Muang Airport** (☎ 02/523–8973), open 8 AM to half-past midnight.

2   SIDE TRIPS OUT OF BANGKOK

Spend a day among ancient ruins in the cities north of Bangkok, explore national parks strewn with waterfalls in the west, or head to the coast to find an unspoiled beach.

T HOUGH THE FASCINATION OF BANGKOK never really dulls, there comes a time when you want to escape the clouds of pollution and find fresher fields. Sophisticated seaside resorts at Cha' Am and Hua Hin are a few hours away, pristine beaches on Ko Samet and Ko Chang, a day's journey. But exotic markets in Damnoen Saduak, religious centers at Nakhon Pathom, Kanchanaburi's forested jungles laced with waterfalls, and ancient temples and palaces in Ayutthaya and Lopburi can all be seen on day trips from the City of Angels.

Updated by
Mick Elmore

Pleasures and Pastimes

Architecture
Classic Thai architecture achieved its zenith in the 16th century when Ayutthaya was the capital. Though it was destroyed by the Burmese in 1767, extensive restoration lets us see and appreciate the magnificence of that era. And, if that is not enough, we can find traces of the Khmer influence in Lopburi, two hours farther north.

Beaches
Along the Gulf of Thailand, beaches come in all shapes and sizes. You can relax by the shore in genteel surroundings at Cha' Am and Hua Hin; you can find raunchy discos, bars, and fairgrounds at Pattaya. If you seek idyllic beaches, go south of Hua Hin or far down the Eastern Seaboard. For the Robinson Crusoe in us all, deserted islands await discovery, from Ko Samet to Ko Chang.

Dining
Wherever you go, there is always good Thai food, and along the Gulf, seafood is king. An array of the day's catch is spread out on ice in front of many restaurants. Pick and choose, but be sure to establish the price before you make the final selection. In the full-blown resorts of Hua Hin and Pattaya, many restaurants serve elaborate Western fare, but elsewhere the options for "steak and chips" are limited. For price categories, *see* Dining *in* Smart Travel Tips A to Z.

Lodging
In Pattaya, Cha' Am, and Hua Hin, there are lodging choices aplenty, from luxury resorts to basic guest houses. In Kanchanaburi, accommodations are often chalets that cater mostly to Thai families. In Ayutthaya, since most tourists come only on day trips out of Bangkok, the hotels are more for the business traveler or stranded tourist. Beyond Pattaya, with its 500 or so hotels, the Eastern Seaboard lodgings are more modest—often simple bungalows, a few with air-conditioning.

Nightlife
Pattaya offers the lot, from discos to Thai classic dancing. Elsewhere nightlife is limited, except for the large resorts in Cha' Am and Hua Hin.

Outdoor Activities and Sports
Resorts on the Gulf have come of age and have something for everyone. Both Hua Hin and Pattaya have excellent golf courses. Water sports from windsurfing to snorkeling and scuba diving are available on both Gulf coasts. In Kanchanaburi, you can go river rafting and hiking.

Exploring Around Bangkok

From all points of the compass, out of Bangkok, the rest of Thailand beckons. To the west lie the exotic floating market at Damnoen Saduak; the tallest Buddhist monument, at Nakhon Pathom; and the bridge over the River Kwai, in Kanchanaburi's lush countryside. Continue south on the west coast of the Gulf of Thailand to Cha' Am and Hua Hin, two courtly resorts, or try the other coast, the Eastern Seaboard, for gaudy Pattaya, Ko Samet, and hideaway beaches on Ko Chang. North lies Ayutthaya, the former capital (said to have been more beautiful than any city in Europe) and the ancient Khmer city of Lopburi.

Great Itineraries

If you love beaches and the lazy life, allow a week or so to chill out far from the big city, at a resort with lots of activity or on a deserted strand. Otherwise, you could cover the ruins north of the city, the floating market, Nakhon Pathom's architecture, and the tawdriness of Pattaya all in three days.

IF YOU HAVE 2 DAYS
Numbers in the text correspond to numbers in the margin and on the Around Bangkok map.

Leave Bangkok early to visit the floating market at **Damnoen Saduak** ①, and you'll be finished by 10:30 AM. Rather than returning, go on to see the huge *chedi* (graceful tower containing relics) at ancient **Nakhon Pathom** ②, and continue to **Kanchanaburi** ③ and the bridge over the River Kwai, returning late to Bangkok. The next day, make a trip up the Chao Phraya River to the old capital of **Ayutthaya** ⑤ and the **Bang Pa-In** ⑥ summer palace, by boat and coach.

IF YOU HAVE 5 DAYS
Go first to either **Cha' Am** or **Hua Hin** ⑧, resort towns on the west gulf coast, and spend two or three days soaking up the rays. Devotees of modern history should next go up to ⊡ **Kanchanaburi** ③; nature lovers to the **Erawan Waterfall** ④; and en route back to Bangkok stop at the **Rose Garden,** a reconstructed Thai village with cultural shows. Architecture buffs should instead choose the excursion north from Bangkok, going on from ⊡ **Ayutthaya** ⑤ to ⊡ **Lopburi** ⑦ and spending the night in either one. From there they can continue north to Phitsanulok or Chiang Mai.

IF YOU HAVE 8 DAYS
Spend the first two or three days north amid ancient ruins or west with modern history, as above. Then venture southeast down the eastern seaboard; spend a day and night in ⊡ **Pattaya** ⑨, then find R&R on a sparkling beach at ⊡ **Ko Samet** ⑩ or the remote islands of ⊡ **Ko Chang** ⑫ before returning to Bangkok.

When to Tour
Remember, the rainy season is from the end of May through October.

WEST OF BANGKOK

Don't bother visiting the floating market in Bangkok; head out through rice paddies and water buffalo to Damnoen Saduak in the province of Ratchaburi, where the colorful scene is a photographer's fantasy. The area around Nakhon Pathom has been settled for millennia—the city was founded before the time of Christ. Kanchanaburi Province, farther west, is so beautiful that you may want to go hiking and thoroughly explore its gorges and waterfalls, or even take an overnight rafting trip.

Damnoen Saduak

❶ *109 km (65 mi) southwest of Bangkok.*

At Damnoen Saduak, hire a *ruilla pai* (sampan) for about B300. Then, for an hour or more, lazily travel the canal and witness true gridlock: a mess of boats trying to shove their way along the klong as sampan vendors sell fresh vegetables, meats, and clothes. Farmers' wives dressed

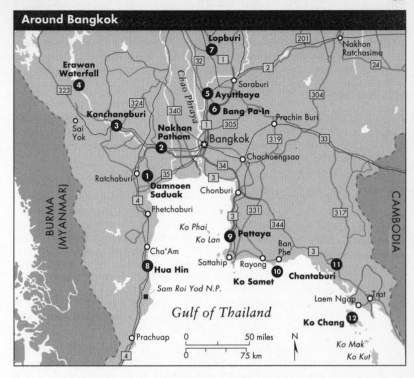

in baggy pants, long-tail shirts, and straw hats sell produce from their boats, paddling back and forth, or rather pushing and barging their way through the congestion. Other women, cooking tasty treats on little stoves, sit ready to ferry sustenance to the hungry.

If you want to rest, a wharf alongside the klong has tables and chairs. Buy your drinks from the stall and your food from any one of the ruilla pai. Go early, because by 11 AM you will have seen the best of Damnoen Saduak; any longer and the novelty of exotica wears thin and irritation at the vendors' aggressive commercialism sets in.

Nakhon Pathom

2 *56 km (34 mi) west of Bangkok.*

Nakhon Pathom is reputed to be Thailand's oldest city, dating from 150 BC. Its main attraction is **Phra Pathom Chedi,** the tallest Buddhist monument in the world—at 417 ft, it stands a few feet higher than the Shwe Dagon Chedi in Burma. The first chedi on this site was erected in the 6th century, but the large chedi you see today, built in 1860, encases the ruins of the original. It also marks the first center of Buddhist learning on the Thai peninsula, established here about 1,000 years ago.

The man responsible for reconstructing the chedi was King Monghut (Rama IV), who, when he was a monk, understood the historical role Phra Pathom Chedi had played in the the establishment of Buddhism in Thailand. Believing that the chedi, then in a state of disrepair, contained the Buddha's holy ashes, he ordered that it be incorporated into the new one. In the outer courtyard are four viharn facing in different directions and containing images of Lord Buddha in various postures. The terraces around the temple complex are full of fascinating statuary, including a Dvaravati-style Buddha seated in a chair, and the museum contains some interesting Dvaravati (6th–11th century) sculpture. Occasionally, classical Thai dances are performed in front of the temple, and during the Loi Krathong festival, bazaars and a fair are set up in the adjacent park. ☉ *Museum Wed.–Sun. 9–noon and 1–4.*

Sanan Chan Palace, just west of Phra Pathom Chedi, was built during King Rama IV's reign. The palace is closed to the public, but the surrounding park is a lovely place to relax in the shade before heading back to Bangkok.

Rose Garden

🍃 *25 km (15 mi) east of Nakhon Pathom, 32 km (19 mi) west of Bangkok.*

On the Bangkok Road out of Nakhon Pathom is the Rose Garden, a complex that replicates a Thai village. Amid flowering gardens of 20,000 rosebushes, there are traditional Thai houses and a stage where a "cultural show" of dance, Thai boxing, sword fighting, and a wedding ceremony is performed at 2:45. The park also has a hotel, restaurants, swimming pools, and playground activities. The B250 admission is fairly steep, but you can while away a few pleasant hours, especially with children, in this somewhat sterile re-creation of Thailand. There is a daily afternoon tour from Bangkok. ⊠ *195/15 Soi Chokchai Chongchamron, Rama III Rd. (Bangkok booking office),* ☎ *02/295–3261.* 🎫 *Admission.* ☉ *Daily 8–6.*

Next door to the Rose Garden and equally as commercial are the ele-
🍃 phant roundups and crocodile shows at the **Samphran Elephant Ground & Zoo.** Though there is lots else to see, the elephants steal the day. A score of these great pachyderms haul logs, play football, and dance on their hind legs. The finale reenacts the Yutha Harti, the 16th-century elephant-back battle between King Naresuan and a Burmese prince-invader. During the 40-minute show a soundtrack explains the role of elephants in Thai history, including their centuries-long role as domestic beasts of burden. ⊠ *Km 30, Petchkasem Rd.,* ☎ *02/295–2938 or 02/295–2939 for reservations.* 🎫 *Admission.* ☉ *Daily 10–4.*

Kanchanaburi

❸ *140 km (87 mi) west of Bangkok.*

Kanchanaburi Province's jungles, rivers, and waterfalls make it one of Thailand's most beautiful regions. But it is also known for the Death Railway built during World War II and immortalized in the movie *The Bridge Over the River Kwai,* adapted from Pierre Boulle's novel. About 16,000 Allied prisoners-of-war and between 50,000 and 100,000 slave laborers were forced by the Japanese to construct a rail link through the jungles of Thailand and Burma. One person died for every railway tie on the track. There are two Allied cemeteries where the remains of 8,732 POWs are buried.

Don't expect to see the bridge from the 1954 movie, which was filmed in a river gorge in Sri Lanka. A reconstructed bridge, still in use, is in Kanchanaburi town where the Kwai Noi and Kwai Yai rivers meet to form the Mae Khlong River. It has arched steel spans which the Japanese brought from Java late in the war. They rebuilt the two square center sections after the war to replace those destroyed by Allied bombs. The original bamboo bridge that inspired the book and movie was a few hundred meters downstream. You can walk across the new bridge, which is next to a plaza, with restaurants, souvenir shops, and jewelry stores.

The **Kanchanaburi War Cemetery,** next to noisy Saengchuto Road just south of the train station, has row upon row of neatly laid-out graves of 6,982 Australian, British, and Dutch prisoners of war. The remains of the American POWs were returned to the United States during the Eisenhower administration. They are all remembered at a commemorative service here every April 25, Australia's Anzac Day.

The **Japanese War Memorial Shrine** is near the bridge, 1 km (½ mi) northwest of the Kanchanaburi War Cemetery. Be sure to read the plaque on the Japanese War Memorial—it has an English translation.

About 2 km (1 mi) downriver from the bridge and in town is the **JEATH War Museum** (JEATH is an acronym for Japan, England, America, Australia, Thailand, and Holland). Founded by a monk from the adjoining temple, the museum consists of a reconstructed bamboo hut—the type used to house the POWs—and a collection of utensils, railway spikes, clothing, aerial photographs, newspaper clippings, and illustrations designed to show the conditions under which the POWs lived during the construction of the Death Railway. ▣ *Admission.* ☉ *Daily 8–5.*

The **Chong-Kai War Cemetery,** on the grounds of a former POW hospital and graveyard, is a sadly serene site with simple, neatly organized grave markers of Commonwealth soldiers. Though rarely visited because it's a little out of the way, it is worth the trek. Hire a tuk-tuk, or take the ferry across the river from the pier below the park off Patana Road and walk just over 500 meters down the road. The cemetery will be on your left.

Walk inland from Chong-Kai about 1 km (½ mi) to find **Wat Thum Khao Pun,** one of the best cave temples in the area. A small temple stands outside and a guide entices you into the cave, where calm images of the Buddha sit between the stalagmites and stalactites.

Dining and Lodging

Most of the restaurants for tourists are near the River Kwai Bridge or farther downstream where the Kwai Noi and Kwai Yai join to form the Mae Khlong. Because most foreigners visit Kanchanaburi on day trips, hotels, which line the riverbanks, are designed primarily for Thai families. A few of the resorts offer thatched bungalows on the river that have river views by day but tend to be hot and muggy at night.

$ ✕ **Pae Karn Floating Restaurant.** For authentic Thai food, try this little restaurant on a floating dock at the river's edge just at the confluence of the Kwai Noi and Kwai Yai rivers. The food is better than in tourist restaurants around the bridge, but the decor amounts to no more than plain walls and a few tables. ▣ *Song Kwai Rd.,* ☎ *no phone. No credit cards.*

$ ✕ **River Kwai Floating Restaurant.** The most attractive—and crowded—open-air restaurant is to the right of the bridge. Fish dishes, either cooked with Thai spices or lightly grilled, dominate the menu. The specialty is *yeesok,* a fish found in the Kwai Yai and Kwai Noi rivers. Try to arrive before the tour groups, and request a table alongside the river. ▣ *River Kwai Bridge,* ☎ *034/512595. No credit cards.*

$$ ✕▣ **River Kwai Village.** Nestled in the heart of the jungle in the River Kwai Valley, this resort village consists of five one-story log cabins and a few guest rooms on rafts. All non-raft rooms have air-conditioning and are simply furnished in teak, with colored stones embedded in the walls. The cafeteria-style restaurant offers a combination of Thai and Western dishes, but it's more fun to eat at the casual restaurant on one of the anchored floating rafts. The resort will supply transportation from Bangkok and arrange tours of the area. ▣ *72 Moo 4, Tambon Thasao, Amphoe Sai Yok, Kanchanaburi 71150,* ☎ *034/634454 up* *to 6; 02/251–7552 Bangkok reservations, FAX 034/591054. 60 rooms and 7 raft houses. 2 restaurants, pool, meeting rooms, travel services. AE, DC, V.*

$$$ 🏨 **Felix River Kwai Resort.** This luxury hotel was first managed by Sofitel and then by a Thai group. It is still going through growing pains, but it does have a tranquil setting along the bank of the river in sight of the bridge. Polished wood floors and wicker headboards give a cool airiness to the rooms. Each has two queen beds or one king, as well as a private safe and cable TV. A large free-form pool amid tropical plants sets the relaxing scene. The hotel is within walking distance of most of Kanchanaburi's attractions. ⊠ *9/1 Moo 3, Tambon Thamakham, Kanchanaburi 71000,* ☎ *034/515061 or 034/515002; 02/675–6990 Bangkok reservations,* FAX *034/515095. 150 rooms. Restaurant, pool, massage, health club. AE, DC, MC, V.*

$$–$$$ 🏨 **The Pavilion Rim Kwai Thani Resort.** Between downtown Kanchanaburi and the Erawan Waterfall, this new resort caters to upscale Bangkok residents wanting to retreat into the country and still have their creature comforts. Tropical flora surrounds the hotel, and the infamous River Kwai flows serenely past. Guest rooms are sparsely furnished, which, along with the shining wood floors, gives a fresh, sparkling ambiance. The large dining room serves Thai and Western dishes. ⊠ *79/2 Moo 4, Km 9 Ladya-Erawan Rd., Tambon Wangdong, Kanchanaburi 71190,* ☎ *034/515772,* FAX *034/515774. 200 rooms. Restaurant, pool, 2 tennis courts, exercise room. AE, MC, V.*

$$ 🏨 **Kasem Island Resort.** Within view of the town is this resort, perched on an island in the middle of the river. You can choose to stay in a room, bungalow, or raft-house. ⊠ *44 Thaichumpon St., Kanchanaburi 71000,* ☎ *034/513359; 02/255–3604 Bangkok reservations. 29 rooms, 10 bungalows, and 19 rafts. Restaurant. MC, V.*

$$ 🏨 **River Kwai Hotel.** On the main road through town is Kanchanaburi's first big hotel. It is a comfortable place, but far from the river and popular with tour groups. ⊠ *284/4–6 Saengchuto Rd., Kanchanaburi 71000,* ☎ *034/513348,* FAX *034/511269. 150 rooms. Restaurant, travel services. AE, MC, V.*

Outdoor Activities and Sports

RAFTING

Rafting trips on either the Kwai Yai or Mae Khlong river, which take at least a full day, let you experience the tropical jungle in a leisurely way. The rafts, which resemble houseboats, are often divided into sections for eating, sunbathing, and diving. Be careful when swimming— the currents can have a whirlpool effect and suck a swimmer down. The cost of a one-day trip starts at about B300. Longer trips are also available. Make advance reservations through the TAT office or a travel agent. Booking through a responsible travel agent may cost more, but you'll be more likely to get a raft in good condition and a skipper familiar with the currents.

Shopping

Blue sapphires from the Bo Phloi mines, 45 km (28 mi) north of Kanchanaburi, are generally a good buy, but prices are marked up at the shops in the plaza before the bridge. You're better off buying the sapphires at the small shops in the center of town or in Bangkok.

Erawan Waterfall

4   *65 km (40 mi) northwest of Kanchanaburi (Rte 3199).*

If you want to visit some of the spectacular countryside of Kanchanaburi Province, make the trip out to the Erawan Waterfall, perhaps the most photographed in Thailand. It is in the beautifully forested

Khao Salop National Park and is at its best in early autumn. You can take a tour bus from Kanchanaburi or the public bus (No. 8170), which leaves every hour for the 90-minute journey. It's a 1½-km (1-mi) walk or taxi ride to the foot of the falls. Allow two hours to climb up all seven levels of the falls, and wear tennis shoes or similarly appropriate footwear. The rock at the top is shaped like an elephant; hence the name Erawan, which refers to the god Indra's three-headed elephant.

Five kilometers (3 miles) up the road from the Erawan Waterfall is the 300-ft **Sri Nakharin Dam,** with its power station and vast reservoir. A tour boat makes a two-hour excursion on the reservoir to the **Huay Khamin Falls.**

OFF THE **SAI YOK NOI –** The trip out of Kanchanaburi to this waterfall (also called
BEATEN PATH Kao Phang) is a memorable one, since you travel the 77 km (46 mi) on the Death Railway. The train leaves each day at 10:33 AM, passing through jungle landscape and by rushing waterfalls as it clings to the mountainside on a two-hour run that is not for the faint-hearted. From Nam-Tok, the last stop, it's a 1½-km (1-mi) walk to Sai Yok Noi. Although a lot smaller than the Erawan falls, it offers pools for swimming during the rainy season (May–Aug.), the best time to visit. On weekends the area is packed with Thai families. The bus back to Kanchanaburi takes half the time of the train.

NORTH FROM BANGKOK

Thailand's most glorious period began when Ayutthaya became the kingdom's seat of power in 1350. Toward the end of the 16th century, Europeans described the city, with its 1,700 temples and 4,000 golden images of the Buddha, as more striking than any capital in Europe. In 1767, the Burmese conquered Ayutthaya and destroyed its temples with such vengeance that little remained standing. The city never recovered, and today it is a small provincial town with partially restored ruins. The site is particularly striking at sunset, when the silhouetted ruins glow orange-brown and are imbued with a melancholy charm.

People usually visit these sites on excursions from Bangkok or on the way to Thailand's northern provinces. Try to get an early start for Ayutthaya to see as much as possible before 1 PM, when the heat becomes unbearable. Then take a long lunch and, if you have time, continue into the late afternoon and catch the sunset before you leave. Most people, though, find that a morning is sufficient. For a three-hour tour of the sights, tuk-tuks can be hired for about B500; a four-wheel samlor (small bicycle cab) costs a bit more than B700. English-speaking guides can be hired around the station. A popular excursion to Ayutthaya from Bangkok, run by the Oriental, Marriott Royal Garden Riverside, and Shangri-La hotels, takes you by cruise one way and bus the other; going by bus and coming back by boat is the better choice. A tour of a couple of Ayutthaya's sights and of the Bang Pa-In Palace is included, along with lunch on the cruise boat. It makes for a hassle-free day, and the boat trip is wonderful, but it gives you very little time actually visiting what you spend most of the day traveling to see.

Ayutthaya

⑤ *72 km (45 mi) north of Bangkok.*

Ayutthaya lies within a large loop of the Chao Phraya River as it meets the Pa Sak and Lopburi rivers. To completely encircle their capital by water, the Thais dug a canal along the northern perimeter, linking the

Chao Phraya to the Lopburi. Although the new provincial town of Ayutthaya, which has a railway station, is on the east bank of the Pa Sak, most of Ayutthaya's ancient temples and ruins are on the island. An exception is Wat Yai Chai Mongkol, a B20 tuk-tuk ride southeast of the railway station.

Wat Yai Chai Mongkol was built in 1357 by King U-Thong for meditation. After King Naresuan defeated the Burmese by beheading their crown prince in single-handed combat on elephants in 1593, he enlarged the temple. The complex was totally restored in 1982, and with the neatly groomed grounds, smart new monks' quarters, and contemporary images of the Buddha lining the courtyard it looks a little touristy, an impression not helped by several souvenir shops, a beverage stand, and a host of tour buses from Bangkok. Notice how the chedi is leaning; it was restored without replacing the foundations and is, under the increased weight, sinking. Linger a while to pay your respects to the Reclining Buddha, and be sure to enter the new sala to look at a painting (1988) of the battle with the Burmese (Thai soldiers are dressed in red uniforms). ▨ *Admission.* ⊙ *Daily 8–5.*

★   The road continues to **Wat Phanan Choeng,** a small temple on the bank of the Lopburi, which predates Ayutthaya's flowering. In 1324, one of the U-Thong kings, who had arranged to marry a daughter of the Chinese emperor, came to this spot on the river; instead of entering the city with his fiancée, he arranged an escort for her. But she, thinking that she had been deserted, threw herself into the river in despair and drowned. The king tried to atone for his thoughtlessness by building the temple. The story has great appeal to Thai Chinese, many of whom make romantic pilgrimages here. ▨ *Admission.* ⊙ *Daily 8–6.*

From the main road, go left and cross over the bridge to the island. Continue on Rojana Road for about 1½ km (1 mi) to the **Chao Phraya National Museum.** Though Ayutthaya's best pieces are in Bangkok's National Museum, a guided visit here can highlight the evolution of Ayutthaya art over four centuries. ▨ *Admission.* ⊙ *Wed.–Sun. 9–noon and 1–4.*

Just beyond the Chao Phraya National Museum, turn right onto Si Samphet Road. Pass the city hall on the left and continue for 1 km (½ mi) to **Wat Phra Si Samphet,** easily recognizable by the huge parking lot. The shining white-marble building south of Wat Phra Si Samphet not only looks modern, it is. Built in 1956, **Viharn Phra Mongkol Bopitr** houses a large bronze image of the Buddha, one of the few that escaped the destruction wrought by the Burmese.

Wat Phra Si Samphet was the largest wat in Ayutthaya and the temple of the royal family. Built in the 14th century, in 1767 it lost its 50-ft Buddha, Phra Sri Samphet, to the Burmese, who melted it down for its gold—374 pounds' worth. The chedis, restored in 1956, survived and are the best examples of Ayutthaya architecture. Enshrining the ashes of Ayutthaya kings, they stand as eternal memories of a golden age. The architectural design of Wat Phra Si Samphet was used in the construction of Wat Phra Keo at Bangkok's Grand Palace. Beyond the monuments is a grassy field where the royal palace once stood. The field is a cool, shady place in which to walk and picnic. The foundation is all that remains of the palace that was home to 33 kings. ⊙ *Daily 8–5.*

Before you leave, visit some of the stalls in the **market** behind the souvenir stands; you'll find a marvelous array of vegetables, fruits, and other foods. After wandering around, stop at the café at the viharn end of the market for refreshments—try the chilled coconut in its shell.

From the large coach park, Naresuan Road crosses Si Samphet Road and continues past a small lake to nearby **Wat Phra Mahathat,** at the intersection with Chee Kun Road. Built in 1384 by King Ramesuan, the monastery was destroyed by the Burmese, but in 1956, during a restoration project, a buried chest was found containing a relic of Lord Buddha, golden Buddha images, and other objects in gold, rubies, and crystal that are now housed in Bangkok's National Museum. If you climb up what is left of the monastery's 140-ft prang, you'll be able to envision just how grand the structure must have been. You can also admire neighboring **Wat Raj Burana,** built by the seventh Ayutthaya king in memory of his brother.

Continue east on Naresuan Road, now called Chao Phnom Road, to the Pa Sak River. Either go left up U-Thong Road to **Chandra Kasem Palace,** or go right to the bridge. The reconstructed 17th-century palace is Ayutthaya's second national museum.

For an educational overview of the Ayutthaya period, stop in at the new **Ayutthaya Historical Study Centre,** near the Teacher's College and the U-Thong Inn. Financed by the Japanese government, the center functions as a museum and a place of national research. Models of the city as a royal capital, as a port city, as an administrative and international diplomatic center, and as a rural village are displayed. ⊠ *Rotchana Rd.,* ☎ *035/245123.* ⊡ *Admission.* ☉ *Tues.–Sun. 9–4:30.*

About 5 km (3 mi) north of Ayutthaya is the **Elephant Kraal,** Thailand's only intact royal kraal, last used during King Chulalongkorn's reign in 1903 to hold wild elephants to be trained for martial service.

Dining and Lodging

Romantics may want to stay in Ayutthaya to see the ruins at night. Since most tourists arrive from Bangkok around 10 AM and depart at 4 PM, those who stay are treated to genuine Thai hospitality. Don't expect luxury, however; Ayutthaya has only modest hotels and simple Thai restaurants.

$$ ✕ **Pae Krung Kao.** If you want to dine outdoors on Thai food and watch the waters of the Pa Sak, this is the better of the two floating restaurants near the bridge. You can also come here for a leisurely beer. ⊠ *4 U-Thong Rd.,* ☎ *035/241555. AE, MC, V.*

$ ✕ **Tevaraj.** For good, spicy Thai food, head for this unpretentious restaurant behind Ayutthaya's railway station. The fish dishes and the tom kha gai are excellent. ⊠ *74 Wat Pa Kho Rd.,* ☎ *no phone. No credit cards.*

$$$$ ✕🖾 **The Manohra Song.** The 60-ft wreck of an old teak rice barge has, with the help of lots of taste and even more money, been brought back to life as a luxury cruiser on the Chao Phraya. For a day and a half, eight passengers are pampered by a chef and their own guide, amid mahogany, silks, and antique furnishings, as they watch the world drift by between Bangkok and Ayutthaya. ⊠ *Manohra Cruises, Marriott Royal Garden Riverside Hotel, 257/1–3 Charoen Nakorn Rd., Thonburi, Bangkok 10600,* ☎ *02/476–0021 or 02/276–0022 Bangkok reservations,* FAX *02/4761120 or 02/460–1805. 4 suites. AE, MC, V. AP.*

$$ 🖾 **Krungsri River Hotel.** The Krungsri is a welcome addition to Ayutthaya's hotels, and it is conveniently close to the train station. The spacious marble-floor lobby is refreshingly cool, and the rooms, albeit not special in any way, are clean, fresh, and furnished with modern amenities. For atmosphere, choose a room overlooking the river. Because Ayutthaya has few overnight visitors, try to negotiate a discounted rate. ⊠ *27/2 Rojana Rd., Ayutthaya 13000,* ☎ *035/242996,* FAX *035/243777. 200 rooms. Restaurant. MC, V.*

Bang Pa-In

⑥ *20 km (12 mi) south of Ayutthaya.*

A popular attraction outside Ayutthaya is the Bang Pa-In Summer Palace, within well-tended gardens in an architectural complex of striking variety. The original palace, built by King Prusat (1630–55) on the bank of the Pa Sak, was used by the Ayutthaya kings until the Burmese invasion. After being neglected for 80 years, it was rebuilt during the reign of Rama IV (1851–68) and became the favored summer palace of King Chulalongkorn (Rama V, 1868–1910) until tragedy struck. Once, when the king was delayed in Bangkok, he sent his wife ahead on a boat, which capsized, and she drowned. She could easily have been saved, but because a royal person was sacrosanct she could not be touched by a commoner on pain of death. The king could never forgive himself. He built a pavilion in her memory; be sure to read the touching inscription engraved on the memorial.

King Chulalongkorn was interested in Europe and its architecture, and many Western influences are evident here. The most beautiful building, however, is the **Aisawan Thippaya,** a Thai pavilion that seems to float on a small lake, its series of staggered roofs leading to a central spire. It is sometimes dismantled and taken to represent the country at worldwide expositions.

Phra Thinang Warophat Phiman, nicknamed the Peking Palace, stands to the north of the Royal Ladies Landing Place in front of a stately pond. The replica of a palace of the Chinese imperial court, it was built from materials custom-made in China—a gift from Chinese Thais eager to win the king's favor. It contains a collection of exquisite jade and Ming-period porcelain.

Take the cable car across the river to the **Wat Nivet Thamaprawat,** built by King Chulalongkorn in Gothic style. Complete with a belfry and stained-glass windows, it looks as much like a Christian church masquerading as a Buddhist temple. ✉ *Admission to Bang Pa-In Palace Complex.* ☉ *Tues.–Thurs. and weekends 8–3.*

The **Bang Sai Folk Arts and Craft Centre** was set up by the queen in 1976 to train and employ families in handicraft skills. Workers at the center demonstrate their technique and make and sell products available throughout Thailand at the Chitrlada handicraft shops. The crafts on sale include fern-vine basketry, wood carvings, dyed silks, and handmade dolls. It also has a small restaurant and a park, a pleasant place for a picnic, although it is crowded on weekends with Thai families. ✉ *24 km (14½ mi) south of Bang Pa-In on the Chao Phraya River,* ☏ *035/366092.* ✉ *Admission.* ☉ *8:30–4, closed Mon.*

Lopburi

⑦ *75 km (47 mi) north of Ayutthaya, 150 km (94 mi) north of Bangkok.*

Lopburi is one of Thailand's oldest cities: the first evidence of its habitation dates from the 4th century. After the 6th century, its influence grew under the Dvaravati rulers, who dominated northern Thailand until the Khmers swept in from the east. From the beginning of the 10th century until the middle of the 13th, when the new Thai kingdom drove them out, the Khmers used Lopburi as their provincial capital. During the Sukhothai and early Ayutthaya periods, the city's importance declined until, in 1664, King Narai made it his second capital to escape the heat and humidity of Ayutthaya. He employed French architects to build his palace; consequently, Lopburi is a strange mixture of Khmer, Thai, and Western architecture.

Lopburi is relatively off the beaten track for tourists. Few foreigners stay overnight, but there is one reasonable hotel, the Lopburi Inn. The rarity of foreigners may explain why locals are so friendly and eager to show you their town—and to practice their English! Bicycle samlors are available, but most of Lopburi's attractions are within easy walking distance.

Wat Phra Si Mahathat, built by the Khmers, is behind the railway station. It underwent so many restorations during the Sukhothai and Ayutthaya periods that it's difficult to discern the three original Khmer prangs—only the central one is intact. Several Sukhothai- and Ayutthaya-style chedis are also within the compound. ☒ *Admission.* ◷ *Daily 8:30–4:30.*

Walk diagonally through Wat Phra Si Mahathat to **Narai Ratchaniwet Palace.** The preserved buildings, which took from 1665 to 1677 to complete, have been converted into museums. Surrounding the buildings are castellated walls and triumphal archways grand enough to admit an entourage mounted on elephants. The most elaborate structure is the **Dusit Mahaprasat Hall,** built by King Narai to receive foreign ambassadors. The roof is gone, but you'll be able to spot the mixture of architectural styles: the square doors are Thai and the domed arches are Western.

The next group of buildings in the palace compound—the **Chan Phaisan Pavilion** (1666), the **Phiman Monghut Pavilion** (mid-19th century), and the row of houses once used by ladies of the court—are now all museums. The ladies' residences now house the **Farmer's Museum,** which exhibits regional tools and artifacts seldom displayed in Thailand. ☒ *Admission.* ◷ *Wed.–Sun. 9–noon and 1–4.*

North across the road from the palace (away from the station), you'll pass through the restored **Wat Sao Thong Thong.** Notice the windows of the viharn, which King Narai changed to imitate Western architecture. Beyond the wat and across another small street is **Vichayen House,** built for Louis XIV's personal representative, De Chaumont. The house was later occupied by King Narai's infamous Greek minister, Constantine Phaulkon, whose political schemes eventually caused the ouster of all Westerners from Thailand. When King Narai was dying in 1668, his army commander, Phra Phetracha, seized power and beheaded Phaulkon. In the attack, the Vichayen House and its ancillary buildings, including a Roman Catholic church, were nearly destroyed. ☒ *Admission.* ◷ *Wed.–Sun. 9–noon and 1–4.*

Walk east on the road between Wat Sao Thong Thong and Vichayen House to **Phra Prang Sam Yot,** a Khmer Hindu shrine and Lopburi's primary landmark. The three prangs symbolize the sacred triad of Brahma, Vishnu, and Shiva. King Narai converted the shrine into a Buddhist temple, and a stucco image of the Buddha sits serenely before the central prang once dedicated to Brahma.

About 250 meters down the street facing Phra Prang Sam Yot and across the railway tracks is the **San Phra Kan shrine.** The respected residents of the temple, Samae monkeys, often perform spontaneously for visitors. These interesting animals engage in the human custom of burying their dead.

Dining and Lodging

Accommodations in Lopburi are used mostly by Thai traveling salesmen. Except for the hotel dining rooms, Lopburi restaurants are sidewalk cafés serving Thai and Chinese food. Menus are written in Thai, but you can point to what you want in glass cases at the front of the restaurant.

$$ ⊡ **Lopburi Inn.** This is the only hotel in Lopburi with air-conditioning and modern facilities. Even so, don't expect your room to have much more than a clean bed and a private bath. The dining room serves Thai and Chinese food, and the hotel has achieved a certain fame by having an annual dinner party for the town's resident monkeys. ✉ *28/9 Narai Maharat Rd.,* ☎ *036/412300,* ℻ *036/411917. 142 rooms. Restaurant, coffee shop. AE, DC, V.*

THE WESTERN GULF COAST

In the 1920s the royal family built a palace at Hua Hin on the western shore of the Gulf of Thailand. The royal entourage would travel from Bangkok on special trains, and high society followed. Those were Hua Hin's glory days. After World War II, Pattaya's star ascended, and Hua Hin became a quiet town once more, but Pattaya's seedy reputation has made Thais and foreign visitors reconsider Hua Hin and its neighbor Cha' Am as desirable beach resorts close to the capital. After a building boom in the 1990s, the coastline is now dotted with high-rise hotels and weekend condominiums.

During the day, Hua Hin is a busy market town, but most tourists are at the beach. They come into town in the early evening to wander through the bazaars before dinner. There is no beachfront road to attract boisterous crowds, so stretches of beach remain deserted. The drop-off slopes down gently, and the waters are usually calm. The only drawback is the occasional invasion of jellyfish—check for them before you plunge in. The nightlife here is restricted mostly to hotels, though a few bars have opened in recent years. Most foreign visitors stay at hotels in Hua Hin rather than at self-contained resorts, where you need a car or taxi to take you into town.

Hua Hin

❽ *189 km (118 mi) south of Bangkok.*

The king and queen spend the month of April and celebrate their wedding anniversary at the royal summer palace, on the northern boundary of Hua Hin. The palace was completed in 1928 by King Rama VII, who named it Klai Kangwol ("far from worries"). Four years later, while he was staying at Klai Kangwol, the army seized control in Bangkok and demanded that he relinquish absolute power in favor of a constitutional monarchy. He agreed, and the generals later apologized for their lack of courtesy.

The highway to the southern provinces passes through the center of Hua Hin. In fact, it's the town's main street, with shops and cafés lining the sidewalk; a congested street of market stalls and buses runs parallel to it. The **Chatchai street market** is fun to walk through. In the morning vendors sell meats and vegetables; then, from early evening, all sorts of wares, from food to trinkets, are offered. Toward the southern end of town, across the tracks from the quaint wooden railway station, lies the respected **Royal Hua Hin Golf Course** (✉ Damnernkasem Rd., Prachchuabkirikhan, ☎ 032/512475). Nonmembers can play the par-72 course for B800–B1,200; you can rent clubs, and there's a coffee lounge for refreshments.

Tourist shops and moderately priced hotels line both sides of Damnernkasem Road, leading to the **public beach.** On your way to the beach, keep your eyes open for Naresdamri Road, just before the Sofitel, where Damnernkasem Road becomes closed to traffic. Turn left down Naresdamri Road, which is parallel to and a block from the beach, and walk past several inexpensive hotels and the 17-story Melia Hua Hin, and a few hundreds meters farther you'll find **Fisherman's Wharf.** It's abuzz in the morning, when the catch comes in. Naresdamri Road is active at night with restaurants and a few bars.

Near the intersection of Damnernkasem and Naresdamri roads is the **Sofitel Central Hua Hin Resort,** formerly the Royal Hua Hin Railway Hotel, which put up royalty and Thailand's elite during the town's heyday. The magnificent Victorian-style colonial building was portrayed as the hotel in Phnom Penh in the film *The Killing Fields.* Be sure to wander through its well-tended gardens and along its verandas.

If you look south along the coast, you'll see a small headland, **Khao Takiab,** and a small island, **Ko Singto.** You can reach the headland by *songthaew* (a pickup truck with two benches), but the best way to get there is to hire a pony and trot along the beach. The 7-km (4-mi) stretch passes hotels and villas and then becomes virtually deserted until you eventually reach Khao Takiab's beach, where three tall condominiums have been built. At the end of the beach, where restaurant stalls abound, dismount for the steep climb past a large statue of the Buddha to the small Buddhist monastery—the views are worth the climb. Then, try to rent a fishing boat at the base of Khao Takiab to cross over to Ko Singto, where you are guaranteed a catch within an hour.

OFF THE
BEATEN PATH

KHAO SAM ROI YOD NATIONAL PARK – The rice fields, sugar palms, pineapple plantations, and crab farms that make up this park are about 40 km (25 mi) south of Hua Hin. The plains of the park were depicted in the movie *The Killing Fields* as the site of Pol Pot's murderous reeducation schemes. The charming fishing village of **Wang Daeng** is typical of coastal Thailand 20 years ago, and south of Wang Daeng, the countryside is even more magnificent, with jungle-clad hills and a curving shoreline. Try to get as far south as the picturesque fishing village of **Ao Noi.** Beyond that is the pleasant, sleepy town of **Prachuap** (about 90 km/56 mi south of Hua Hin), which has little appeal for the tourist except for staggering panoramic views from the hills behind its bay.

Dining and Lodging

The restaurants along Naresdamri Road in Hua Hin offer a warm ambience and good value, especially for fresh seafood. For Western food, it's best to eat at one of the major hotels. On Thai holiday weekends, reservations are a must. During peak season—October through mid-March—the prices at hotels are nearly double those in the off-season.

$$$ ✕ **Fisherman's Seafood Restaurant.** The nautical decor sets the tone of the Royal Garden Resort's restaurant, which serves excellently prepared clams, lobsters, mussels, sea tiger prawns, and crabs. Depending on your taste, these can be cooked with Thai spices (such as lobster with garlic and peppers) or simply grilled. ✉ *107/1 Phetkasem Rd.,* ☎ *032/511881. AE, DC, MC, V.*

$$ ✕ **Sang Thai.** For interesting seafood dishes—from grilled prawns with bean noodles to fried grouper with chili and tamarind juice—this open-air restaurant down by Fisherman's Wharf is popular with Thais. The extensive menu is appealing, but you need to ignore the ramshackle surroundings and floating debris in the water. Don't miss the *kang* (mantis prawns). ✉ *Naresdamri Rd.,* ☎ *032/512144. DC, MC, V.*

$–$$ ✕ **Chao Lay.** Of the many outdoor pier restaurants, this one is consistently good. The fish is fresh, the cooking exact, and the service friendly (many of the staff speak English). The pier stretches out into the sea a little farther than at the other restaurants, which seems to allow for more cooling breezes. There is an ample selection of dishes, from spicy to tame, from prawns to snapper, and from hot pork curry to mild chicken in coconut milk. ✉ *15 Naresdamri Rd.,* ☎ *032/513436. No credit cards.*

$$$$ 🏨 **Chiva-Som.** Chiva-Som has become a world-class spa. The resort cen-
★ ters on health treatments and a wholesome diet, but the setting on the beach in tasteful and comfortable lodging will do you a world of good, too. ✉ *73/4 Petchkasem Rd., Hua Hin 77110,* ☎ *032/536536; 02/381–4459 or 02/381–4460 Bangkok reservations,* FAX *032/381154. 57 rooms and suites. Restaurant, pool, massage, spa. AE, DC, MC, V.* 🕸

$$$$ 🏨 **Royal Garden Resort.** Adjacent to the Sofitel, this hotel has ac-commodations and service equal to those of its neighbor, but because it doesn't have the colonial ambience, the rates are a few hundred baht less. The hotel tends to draw a younger set, attracted by the nightclub and the proximity to the beach. Guest rooms are decorated with mod-ern, unimaginative furniture. The Market Seafood Restaurant is less elegant than Sofitel's Salathai, but it serves better food. ✉ *107/1 Phetkasem Rd., Hua Hin 77110,* ☎ *032/511881; 02/476–0021 Bangkok reservations,* FAX *032/512422. 215 rooms. 2 restaurants, bar, coffee shop, pool, 4 tennis courts, snorkeling, boating, nightclub, play-ground. AE, DC, MC, V.* 🕸

$$$$ 🏨 **Sofitel Hua Hin Resort.** Even if you don't stay here, the Old World
★ charm of this tasteful hotel is worth a visit. Wide verandas fan out in an arc, following the lines of the wooden building, and open onto gar-dens leading down to the beach. The gardens are splendidly maintained by 30 gardeners, with scores of different plants and topiary figures that look like shadows at night. The lounges around the reception area are open to sea breezes. The best guest rooms are those on the second floor with sea views, though the newest are in the 60-room modern wing. The units in an annex across the street, run by the Central Village Hotel, offer 41 less attractive but also less expensive one- and two-bedroom bungalows. ✉ *1 Damnernkasem Rd., Hua Hin 77110,* ☎ *032/512021; 02/233–0974 Bangkok reservations,* FAX *032/511014. 214 rooms. 2 restaurants, bar, coffee shop, pool, 4 tennis courts, snorkeling, boat-ing, nightclub, meeting rooms. AE, DC, MC, V.* 🕸

$$$–$$$$ 🏨 **Dusit Resort & Polo Club.** Although this resort opened in early 1991,
★ the polo grounds and riding stables have yet to be added. Perhaps not so many guests will actually play polo, but the game establishes the tone—smart, exclusive, and luxurious. The spacious lobby serves as a lounge for afternoon tea and evening cocktails, drunk to the soft tunes of house musicians. Beyond an ornamental lily pond is the swimming pool with bubbling fountains, and beyond that is the beach. The main dining room serves Thai, Chinese, and European fare. Off to the left is the San Marco, an alfresco Italian restaurant; to the right is the Ben-jarong, in a traditional Thai-style pavilion. All guest rooms have pri-vate balconies and a pool or sea view. There's shuttle service to Hua Hin and car service to Bangkok. ✉ *1349 Petchkasem Rd., Cha' Am, Petchburi 76120,* ☎ *032/520009; 02/636–3333 Bangkok reserva-tions,* FAX *032/520296. 298 rooms and 10 suites. 5 restaurants, 2 bars, in-room safes, pool, wading pool, 5 tennis courts, steam room, exer-cise room, squash, boating, parasailing, waterskiing, meeting rooms. AE, DC, MC, V.* 🕸

$$$–$$$$ 🏨 **Melia Hua Hin.** Towering over Hua Hin, this 17-story hotel has great rates during the off-season, as low as B1,000. In-season rates are a lit-tle lower than the Sofitel's. The Melia is a mass-market hotel, popu-lar with many European tour groups. Its rooms are spacious (a minimum of 42 square meters [450 square ft]), modern, and functional. The lagoon-like pool dominates the garden, and the small sandy beach shares its limited space with vendors and tourists from other hotels. ✉ *33 Naresdamri Rd., Hua Hin 77110,* ☎ *032/511612,* 🖷 *032/511135. 297 rooms. 3 restaurants, pool, 2 tennis courts, health club, squash, nightclub, meeting rooms. AE, DC, MC, V.* ✧

$$$–$$$$ 🏨 **Regent Cha' Am.** This beach resort has everything from water sports to gourmet dining to shopping arcades. Some guest rooms are in bungalows, a number of which face the beach, while others are in one of two 12-story buildings set back from the beach. Gardens separate the bungalows, the main building, two large outdoor pools, and two smaller outdoor pools. The Lom Fang restaurant, overlooking the lake at the back, serves excellent fish with a spiced curry-and-lime sauce. The more formal restaurant, the Tapien Thong Grill Room, offers seafood and steak. In the evening, a small group sings Western songs in Thai. The hotel has its own car service from Bangkok. ✉ *849/21 Cha' Am Beach, Petchburi,* ☎ *032/451240; 02/251–0305 Bangkok reservations,* 🖷 *032/471492; 02/253–5143 Bangkok reservations. 630 rooms and 30 suites. 3 restaurants, coffee shop, 4 pools, snorkeling, boating, nightclub. AE, DC, MC, V.* ✧

$$$ 🏨 **Pran Buri Seaview Beach Resort.** A collection of small bungalow units facing the beach south of Hua Hin comprises this isolated holiday complex. The first row, facing the beach, is the best. Though simply furnished, guest rooms have their own terraces, minibars, telephones, and TV with VCR. The main lodge contains the bar-lounge and dining room, where Thai, Chinese, and Western dishes are served. The atmosphere is laid-back and fun. ✉ *9 Parknampran Beach, Prachuapkhirikhan 77220,* ☎ *032/631765; 02/233–3871 Bangkok reservations,* 🖷 *02/235–0049. 60 rooms. Restaurant, bar, pool, 2 tennis courts, health club, snorkeling, boating, meeting rooms. AE, DC, MC, V.*

$ 🏨 **Jed Pee Nong.** This hotel, on the main tourist street, has bungalow cottages in its courtyard. Rooms have huge beds and not much else, but the price is right. The terrace restaurant facing the street stays open late and is a popular spot from which to watch the parade of vacationers walking past. ✉ *17 Damnernkasem Rd., Hua Hin 77110,* ☎ *032/512381,* 🖷 *032/53063. 44 rooms. Restaurant, coffee shop. MC, V.*

$ 🏨 **Sirin.** At B1,500 during high season, B890 in low season, this ordinary hotel with a helpful staff is a bargain. It's on the main tourist avenue, a block from the beach. The air-conditioned rooms are plain but clean and light, and the bathrooms are reasonably large. Although there is a dining room (which doubles as a lounge), you'll probably want to go out for dinner. ✉ *18 Damnernkasem Rd., Hua Hin 77110,* ☎ *032/511150 or 032/512045,* 🖷 *032/513571. 35 rooms. Restaurant. AE, DC, MC, V.*

¢ 🏨 **All Nations.** Of the backpacker hangouts in Hua Hin, this is about the best. You'll find local expats coming by for a drink or breakfast. Rooms are clean, and while none have private bathrooms, there is a large bathroom on each floor, and only two or three rooms per floor. The expat owner has set up a computer corner where guests and nonguests can, for a fee, access e-mail. ✉ *10–10/1 Dechanuchit Rd., Hua Hin 77110,* ☎ *032/512747,* 🖷 *032/53474. 11 rooms. Restaurant, bar. No credit cards.*

THE EASTERN SEABOARD

As the Bangkok metropolitan area becomes more and more congested, the Eastern Seaboard is growing rapidly, with most of the economic development around Chonburi and Rayong. The coast—chiefly the resort of Pattaya—has long been the attraction, with water sports, fairgrounds, and nightlife, but Pattaya has so exemplified the seedier aspects of tourism and so rapidly outpaced its infrastructure that many travelers continue into Chantaburi and Trat provinces. Not all the coast-line is particularly attractive, and cultural sites are few and far between, but there are fishing villages along the way, a few decent beaches, de-lightful islands offshore, and inland provincial capitals for supplies. Ex-cept for buying gemstones in Chantaburi and Trat, tourists come for beach pleasures. The following destinations are arranged in order of their proximity to Bangkok.

Pattaya

9 *147 km (88 mi) southeast of Bangkok.*

Five decades ago, Pattaya was a fishing village on an unspoiled natu-ral harbor. Discovered by affluent Bangkok residents, it became a weekend playground, replacing the southwest coast as a vacation des-tination. Then came the Vietnam War, when thousands of American soldiers sought recreation. With air and naval bases nearby, U.S. ser-vicemen hit the beaches at Pattaya in droves, and the resort became a boomtown of uncontrolled development.

Pattaya's unbridled sex trade, its crowds, and its water pollution began to erode its appeal, and business dropped off. Now, after a few years in the doldrums, Pattaya is getting busier, with conventioneers and many tourists from Eastern Europe. Pattaya has something tacky for every-one, the most obvious being its many bars and nightclubs catering to foreign males (conveniently located on the side streets are dozens of clinics to treat venereal diseases). The highway from Bangkok was re-cently expanded but still remains congested; on weekends the two-hour trip often takes four. Raw sewage still seeps into the once crystal-clear bay, though the government and private enterprises have started a cleanup process with water- and sewage-treatment plants. Most of the hotels are now connected to a sewage system and the water quality is slowly improving. But another problem now faces Pattaya: foreign underworld gangs, generally referred to by Thais as the "Mafia," are a law unto themselves, with the Russian mafia coming out on top.

If Pattaya were anywhere else but Thailand, it would be positively dis-tasteful. But it *is* in Thailand, and somehow what is gross is made ac-ceptable by the smiling Thais. Pattaya can be divided into three sections: the northernmost, Naklua Beach, still attracts locals but has recently expanded, with bars and restaurants that cater to foreigners—partic-ularly Germans and some backpackers. On a small promontory south of the Dusit Resort Hotel is the curving bay of Pattaya, along which runs Beach Road, lined with palm trees on the beach side and modern resort hotels on the other. At the southern end of the bay is the fun part of town—bars, nightclubs, restaurants, and open-front cafés dom-inate both Sunset Avenue (the extension of Beach Road) and side streets.

Parallel to Beach Road runs Pattaya 2 Road, the main commercial street, which becomes more crowded with traffic and shops the farther south you go. Continuing through town, Pattaya 2 Road climbs a hill lead-ing past Buddha Park on the left and then descends to quieter Jontien Beach, which has attracted condominium developers and hotels along its stretch of white sand.

Tourist attractions abound in Pattaya. The number of open-air bars will astound you. Massage parlors line Pattaya 2 Road. And there are a dozen or so attractions designed for families. One such diversion is the **Elephant Kraal,** where 14 pachyderms display their skill at mov-ing logs in a two-hour show. There are also demonstrations by war elephants, an enactment of ceremonial rites, and the capture of a wild elephant. Everything is staged, but it's always fun to see elephants at work and at play, and though it's unsettling to see them in the city, they and their mahouts have little other choice in making a living. ⊠ *On main hwy., 5 km (3 mi) from Pattaya,* ☎ *038/249818. Tickets and transport: Tropicana Hotel Elephant Desk, Pattaya 2 Rd.,* ☎ *038/ 428158.* 🖭 *Admission.* ⊘ *Show daily at 2:30.*

Ⓒ **Nong Nuch Village** has a folklore show, an exhibition of monkeys picking coconuts, elephants bathing, and a small zoo and aviary. Two restaurants, one Thai and one Western, serve refreshments on rolling grounds covered with coconut trees. Despite its touristy nature, the village provides a pleasant break from sunbathing on the beach, particularly if you're traveling with children. Hotels will arrange transportation for morning and afternoon visits, since it is 15 km (9 mi) south of Pattaya, at the 163-km marker on Highway 1. Or you can contact the **office in Pattaya** (☎ 038/429321) opposite the Amari Nipa Resort on Pattaya Klang Road. ⊠ *163 Sukhumvit Hwy., Bang Saray,* ☎ *038/709358.* 🖭 *Admission.* ⊘ *Daily 9–5:30; folklore show daily 10 AM and 3 PM.*

Ⓒ **Ripley's Believe It or Not Museum** (⊠ Royal Garden Plaza, 218 Beach Rd., South Pattaya, ☎ 038/710294) offers an adventure through 10
Ⓒ theme galleries that lasts about an hour. The **Million Years Stone Park and Crocodile Farm** (⊠ 22/1 Mu, Nongplalai, Banglamung, ☎ 038/ 422957) has gigantic, grotesque-shape rocks decorating a large garden, and a man-catching-crocodile show performed every hour from
Ⓒ 11 AM to 5 PM. The **Pattaya Monkey Training Centre** (⊠ 151 Km., Soi Chaiyapruk, Sukhumvit Rd., ☎ 038/756367) has shows at 9, 11, noon, 1, 2, and 5. The pig-tailed monkeys, who live about 40 years, are trained for harvesting coconuts, a 12-month course, but are also taught a few other entertaining tricks and are popular with tour groups.

Ⓒ The **Bottle Museum** is actually quite special. Pieter Beg de Leif, a Dutchman, has devoted 14 hours a day for the last 15 years to creating more than 300 miniatures—tiny replicas of famous buildings and ships—in bottles. ⊠ *79/15 Moo 9, Sukhumvit Rd.,* ☎ *038/422957.* 🖭 *Admission.* ⊘ *Daily 10–9.*

Dining and Lodging

$$$ ✕ **Bruno's.** This restaurant and wine bar, which replaced Dolf Riks, a Pattaya institution, is well on its way to being an institution itself. Bruno promises to keep the same warm, friendly atmosphere; you can still chat at the bar and dine on top-quality food. The difference is in the cooking. Riks was Indonesian-influenced; Bruno's uses Swiss recipes. ⊠ *463/28 Sri Nakorn Centre, N. Pattaya (turn down cul-de-sac beside Pattaya Bowl),* ☎ *038/361073. AE, DC, MC, V.*

$$$ ✕ **Peppermill Restaurant.** Tucked away next to P. K. Villa, this distinctly French restaurant takes a classical approach to dining, with an emphasis on flambéed dishes. More creative dishes such as fresh crab in a white-wine sauce and poached fillet of sole with a lobster tail are also served. Dinner is a special occasion here, particularly if complemented by a good bottle of wine from the respectable cellar. ⊠ *16 Beach Rd.,* ☎ *038/428248. AE, DC, MC, V. No lunch.*

$$ ✕ **Angelo's.** For Italian food, this is a good choice. The Milanese owner presides over the dining room, and his Thai wife is the chef. Her fortes are lasagna and a wonderful fish casserole. ⊠ *N. Pattaya Rd.,* ☎ *038/429093. MC, V.*

$$ ✕ **Nang Nual.** Next to the transvestite nightspot Simon Cabaret is one of Pattaya's better places for seafood, cooked Thai-style or simply grilled. A huge array of fish is laid out as you enter the restaurant. Point out what you want and say how you want it cooked. There's a dining room

upstairs, but you may want to eat on the patio overlooking the sea. For carnivores, the huge steaks are an expensive treat. Menu photographs of the finished products will overcome any language barrier. Similar dishes are found at Nang Nual's Jontien Beach branch, near the Sigma Resort. ⊠ *214–10 S. Pattaya Beach Rd.,* ☎ *038/428478. AE, MC, V.*

$$ ✕ **PIC.** Dine in classic teak pavilions on a wide range of Thai dishes like delicious deep-fried crab claws and spicy eggplant salad. The food can be hot or mild, and if you are averse to chilies, try the succulent white snapper on vegetables, scented with ginger and salted prunes. ⊠ *Soi 5, Beach Rd.,* ☎ *038/428387. AE, DC, MC, V.*

$$ ✕ **Tak Nak Nam.** This floating restaurant in a Thai pavilion at the edge of a small lake has an extensive menu of Chinese and Thai dishes. Live classical Thai and folk music plays while you dine on such specialties as steamed crab in coconut milk or blackened chicken with Chinese herbs. ⊠ *252 Pattaya Central Rd., next to Pattaya Resort Hotel,* ☎ *038/429059. MC, V.*

$ ✕ **Sportsman Inn.** If you want some down-home English cooking, this is the best spot in Pattaya. The steak-and-kidney pie, bangers-and-chips, and fish-and-chips are well prepared, as testified to by the many expats who get their daily sustenance here. ⊠ *Soi Yod Sak (Soi 8),* ☎ *038/361548. No credit cards.*

$$$$ 🏨 **Royal Cliff Beach Hotel.** Pattaya's most lavish hotel, 1½ km (1 mi) south of town on a bluff jutting into the Gulf, is a self-contained resort with three wings. The 84 one-bedroom suites in the Royal Wing (double the price of standard rooms in the main building) have butler service, in-room breakfast at no charge, and reserved deck chairs. The Royal Cliff Terrace wing has two-bedroom and honeymoon suites with four-poster beds. The swimming pool sits on top of a cliff overlooking the sea. ⊠ *Jontien Beach, Pattaya, Chonburi,* ☎ *038/250421; 02/282–0999 Bangkok reservations,* 🆁🅰🆇 *038/250141. 700 rooms and 100 suites. 4 restaurants, 3 pools, sauna, miniature golf, 2 tennis courts, jogging, squash, 2 beaches, windsurfing, boating, shops. AE, DC, MC, V.* 🏖

$$$ 🏨 **Dusit Resort.** On a promontory at the northern end of Pattaya
★ Beach, this large hotel has superb sea views. The beautifully laid-out grounds with two pools that run around the promontory add to the pleasure. Though the rooms are in need of some cheerful refurbishing, they have large bathrooms, balconies, oversize beds, and sitting areas. The Landmark Rooms are larger and have extensive wood trim. The Empress restaurant serves sophisticated Cantonese fare against the panoramic backdrop of Pattaya Bay. This retreat is only a B5 song-thaew ride from all of Pattaya's tourist action. ⊠ *240/2 Pattaya Beach Rd., Pattaya, Chonburi 20260,* ☎ *038/425611; 02/236–0450 Bangkok reservations,* 🆁🅰🆇 *038/428239. 500 rooms and 28 suites. 4 restaurants, 2 pools, massage, sauna, 3 tennis courts, health club, Ping-Pong, squash, windsurfing, boating, shops, billiards. AE, DC, MC, V.* 🏖

$$$ 🏨 **Montien.** Though not plush, this hotel is centrally located and designed to take advantage of the sea breezes. With the hotel's generous off-season discounts, a room with a sea view can be one of the best values in town. The air-conditioned section of the Garden Restaurant has a dance floor and stage for entertainment. ⊠ *Pattaya Beach Rd., Pattaya, Chonburi 20260,* ☎ *038/361340 up to 54; 02/233–7060 Bangkok reservations,* 🆁🅰🆇 *038/423155. 320 rooms. 2 restaurants, bar, coffee shop, snack bar, pool, 2 tennis courts, meeting rooms. AE, DC, MC, V.*

$$$ 🏨 **Royal Garden Resort.** This modern resort in downtown Pattaya, a block from the beach, gives the feeling of great space by having both a large, open lobby and lounge and a garden full of trees with a pool in its center. The carpeted bedrooms are standard, furnished in light colors with enough room for a coffee table and two chairs; a balcony looks over the pool and garden to the sea. Next door is the Royal Garden Plaza, a shopping and entertainment complex. ⊠ *218 Beach Rd., Pattaya, Chonburi 20260,* ☎ *038/412120; 02/476–0021 Bangkok reservations,* FAX *038/429926. 300 rooms. 2 restaurants, bar, pool, beauty salon, 4 tennis courts, health club, business services, meeting rooms, travel services. AE, DC, MC, V.* ✉

$–$$ 🛏 **Palm Lodge.** This started as a no-frills hotel, but its central yet quiet location has prompted the owners to expand and improve the facilities. Now the hotel offers modern rooms with TVs and minibars. Bathrooms are tiled and clean. The outdoor pool is smallish but pleasantly laid out in a shady garden; besides, the sea is just across the road. ⊠ *Mu 9, Beach Rd., Pattaya, Chonburi 20260,* ☎ *038/428780,* FAX *038/421779. 80 rooms. Coffee shop, pool, laundry service. MC, V.*

$ 🛏 **Chris Guest House.** Owned by an Englishman, this small hotel offers clean, inexpensive (B500), air-conditioned rooms with private baths—ask for one of the new rooms. The friendly atmosphere makes this the top choice in the budget category. On the ground floor there's an open-front lounge-restaurant-bar where old roués gather at a round table chaired by Chris. Though it's only half a block from the sea, it is nevertheless quietly secluded, with its own garden down a small soi. ⊠ *185 Soi 13, Pattaya Beach Rd., Pattaya, Chonburi 20260,* ☎ *038/ 429586,* FAX *038/423653. 15 rooms. Restaurant, bar. No credit cards.*

$ 🛏 **Diamond Beach Hotel.** In the heart of Pattaya's nightlife, amid discos and cafés, this hotel is a bastion of sanity. Rooms are clean, and security guards help female guests feel safe. The staff, however, is not particularly friendly or helpful—perhaps that's why you can often find a room here when other hotels are full. ⊠ *373/8 Pattaya Beach Rd., Pattaya, Chonburi 20260,* ☎ *038/428071,* FAX *038/424888. 126 rooms. Restaurant, massage, travel services. No credit cards.*

Nightlife and the Arts

Entertainment in Pattaya revolves around its hundreds of bars, cafés, discos, and nightclubs, most of which are at the southern end of the beach and a couple of blocks inland. Bars and clubs stay open past midnight, and some are open much later. Pattaya has confronted its AIDS problem, but the disease is still a serious concern. The city is also the center of criminal gangs. Caution is therefore advised for night revelers! For something other than the go-go bars try **Tony's Entertainment Complex** (⊠ Walking Street Rd., South Pattaya, ☎ 038/425795), next to the Royal Garden Plaza, which has live bands, a beer garden, and a disco. **Dalaney's Pattaya** (⊠ In the Royal Garden Resort, 218 Beach Rd., ☎ 038/710641) has food, beer, and a large-screen TV for sports fans.

Outdoor Activities and Sports

BUNGEE JUMPING

If you like the thrill, try **Kiwi Thai Bungee Jump** (⊠ Off the main road to Jontien Beach, ☎ 038/250319). You are hoisted in a metal cage to a height of 150 ft; then you jump. Just remember to attach your rubber harness first.

GOLF

Laem Chabang International Country Club (⊠ 106/8 Moo 4 Beung, Srirach, Chonburi, ☎ 038/372273) has a professionally maintained course near Pattaya. Thailand's longest course (6,800 yards), the **Royal Thai Navy Course** (⊠ Phiu Ta Luang Golf Course, Sattahip, Chonburi, ☎ 02/466–1180 or 02/466–2217, ext. Sattahip), is 30 km (18 mi) from Pattaya. With rolling hills and dense vegetation, it's considered one of the country's most difficult. The **Siam Country Club** (⊠ 50 Moo 9 T. Poeng A., Banglamong, Chonburi, ☎ 038/418002), close to Pattaya, offers a challenging course with wide fairways but awkward water traps and wooded hills.

WATER SPORTS

All kinds of water sports are available, including windsurfing (B200 per hr), waterskiing (B1,000 per hr), and sailing on a 16-ft Hobie catamaran (B500 per hr). Private entrepreneurs offer these activities all along the beach, but the best area is around the Sailing Club on Beach Road. Jet skiing and parasailing are dangerous and shouldn't be tried for the first time here. Operators of parasailing boats tend to be inexperienced, making sharp turns or sudden stops that bring the parachutist down too fast. Be on the lookout for unscrupulous operators who rent a defective machine and hold the customer responsible for its repair or loss. The water near the shore is too polluted for diving and snorkeling.

En Route   Take highway H3 south for about 20 km (12 mi) and turn right at the 165-km marker for **Bang Saray.** The village consists of jetties, a fishing fleet, a small temple, and two narrow streets running parallel to the bay. Fully equipped game-fishing crafts are tied to the jetty, and photos to prove fishermen's stories are posted in the area's two hotel bars, Fisherman's Lodge and Fisherman's Inn. It costs about B2,500 to charter one of the faster fishing boats for the day. If you just want to soak up the scene, stop next to the main jetty at the Ruam Talay Restaurant. Windsurfers can be rented at the beach, just north of the bay at the Sea Sand Club. H3 goes through Sattahip, a Thai naval base. Avoid it by taking bypass H332, which passes through countryside full of coconut groves and tapioca plantations, to **Rayong** (50 km/31 mi east of Sattahip), a booming market town famous for seafood and nam plaa, the fermented fish sauce Thais use to salt their food. Since the early 1990s, this area has become a center of economic growth, with industrial estates offering tax and customs breaks to investors. About 20 km (12 mi) east of Rayong is the small village of **Ban Phe,** whose beaches and self-contained resorts attract Thai families. Ban Phe is the jumping-off point for Ko Samet.

Ko Samet

⓾ *30 mins by ferry from Ban Phe, which is 223 km (139 mi) southeast of Bangkok.*

Two ferries (B30) from Ban Phe make the crossing to Ko Samet. One goes to Na Duan on the north shore, the other to An Vong Duan halfway down the eastern shore. All the island's beaches are an easy walk from these villages. Indeed, from the southern tip to the north is a comfortable three-hour walk. Ko Samet is known for its beaches; its other name is Ko Kaeo Phitsadan ("island with sand like crushed crystal"), and its fine sand is in great demand by glassmakers. The island has many bungalows and cottages, with and without electricity. Make sure that yours has mosquito netting: come dusk, Ko Samet's mosquitoes take a fancy to tourists. Restaurants set up along the beach in the late afternoon offer an opportunity to laze a little more. Seafood is the best choice but menus cater to all tastes. While you dine, the tide will inch its way up to your table in the sand, and your feet could be wet before you leave.

Lodging

¢   🏨 **Vong Duan Resort.** Vong Duan (also spelled Wong Deuan) beach is a cove with lots of bungalow accommodation. The Vong Duan Resort is the biggest and has the largest staff. Its bungalows, which are on stilts and have air-conditioning and fans, are a degree better than its neighbors'. The beach has a smaller, more relaxed crowd than some other parts of the island. Although the hotel has a restaurant, all the seafood restaurants lining the beach are pretty good. ⊠ *Vong Duan Beach,* ☎ *038/651777. 30 bungalows. Restaurant. No credit cards.*

Chantaburi

⑪ *100 km (62 mi) east of Rayong; 180 km (108 mi) east of Pattaya.*

Buses from Rayong and Ban Phe make the 90-minute journey to the pleasant provincial town of Chantaburi. Its gem mines are mostly closed now, but it has become renowned as a trading center for gems. Rubies and sapphires still rule, but stones from all corners of the world are now traded here. Gem Street, in the center of town, is fascinating: in small storefronts, you'll see traders sorting through gems and making deals worth hundreds of thousands of baht. The street becomes a gem market on Fridays and Saturdays with buyers and sellers from all over the world. The province of Chantaburi has few beach resorts of note, and those cater mostly to Thais. Laem Sadet, 18 km (11 mi) from Chantaburi, is the most popular, and its accommodations range from small bungalows to low-rise hotels. Chantaburi is once again becoming a gateway to the western part of Cambodia as Thailand's neighbor opens up.

Lodging

$$ 🏨 **KP Grand Hotel.** Though this 18-story business hotel has no charm, it does have modern facilities, large guest rooms with two single beds or a king, and attentive service. It's on the eastern side of town, but within walking distance of Gem Street. ✉ *35/200–201 Theerat Rd., 22000,* ☎ *039/323201,* FAX *039/323214. 200 rooms. 2 restaurants, bar, pool, health club, meeting rooms. AE, DC, MC, V.*

En Route Beyond Chantaburi lies Trat, Thailand's easternmost province. Hemmed in by the Khao Banthat mountain range, the region is waiting to be discovered by tourists. The provincial capital, **Trat,** two hours plus from Chantaburi, is a small town whose interest is as a market and transport center. For travelers, it is where buses arrive from and depart for Bangkok, and where songthaews leave for the 20-minute trip to Laem Ngop, the port for ferries to Ko Chang.

Ko Chang

★ ⑫ *1 hr by ferry from Laem Ngop, which is 15 km (9 mi) southwest of Trat; Trat is 400 km (250 mi) southeast of Bangkok.*

Ko Chang (Elephant Island) is Thailand's second largest island (Phuket is the biggest). It is also the largest and most developed of the 52 islands that make up Mu Ko Chang National Park, many of which are not much more than hummocks protruding from the sea. These islands are still being discovered by Westerners and local tourists and have not yet been spoiled by the honky-tonk commercialism found in Pattaya, Phuket, and Ko Samui. The infrastructure is basic and accommodations are rustic. You can book lodgings on these islands in Laem Ngop, where you buy your ferry ticket. Most of the tourists who make the trip here (a good eight hours from Bangkok) are backpackers and young Thais looking for inexpensive vacations.

Ko Chang's best beaches are on the western shore. Haad Sai Khao (White Sand Beach) attracts mostly backpackers who pay B100 a night for a cot in huts crammed together along the narrow beach. Haad Khlong Phrao is next, with a long, curving beach of pale golden sand. Accommodations here are spaced farther apart and tend to be larger and more expensive. Farther down and at the end of the only road on the island is Haad Kai Bae. Here, the beach, with both sand and pebbles, has a very gentle drop-off—safe for nonswimmers. A couple of small, uninhabited islands offshore make the views attractive, and accommodations range from a few air-conditioned bungalows to small huts.

One of the most beautiful islands is tiny **Ko Wai** (three hours by ferry from Laem Ngob), resplendent with idyllic beaches, tropical flora, and fantastic coral reefs. **Ko Ngam,** also small, is shaped like a butterfly and has waters of different hues. **Ko Kradat** has little development except for one bungalow resort. **Ko Mak,** a little larger than the other islands, has a small village and a couple of basic resorts with bungalows. **Ko Kut,** the second largest of the Ko Chang group, is mountainous.

Lodging

Booking agents at travel agencies in Laem Ngob port can make reservations for you on the Ko Chang islands.

$$$ ⊞ **Ko Chang Resort.** One of the first comfortable resorts to be built on Ko Chang is a self-contained complex on the edge of the bay, with clean, rustic bungalows around a reception lounge and dining room. The rate for the air-conditioned units is fairly steep, and the small ones are very cramped. The advantage of the resort is that you can make the booking in Bangkok; it also has its own boat service to the island. ⊠ *Ko Chang, Trat 23120,* ☎ *01/211–3834; 02/276–1233 Bangkok reservations,* FAX *02/276–6929 in Bangkok. 45 rooms. Restaurant. MC, V.*

$–$$$ ⊞ **Sea View Resort.** Choose either a small, fan-cooled thatched bungalow just back from the sands of Kai Bae Beach or a larger air-conditioned unit with a private bath 100 yards inland on a slight rise. The resort is at the far end of the beach and is therefore quieter than the others. It has an attractive terrace restaurant and a very gentle, sloping, sandy beach—too gentle for many. ⊠ *Ko Chang, Trat 23120,* ☎ *038/538055; 02/256–7168 Bangkok reservations,* FAX *02/276–6929 in Bangkok. 32 rooms. Restaurant. MC, V.*

¢–$$ ⊞ **Kae Bae Hut Bungalows.** Accommodations run the gamut from tiny ★ B50 bungalows back from the beach to much larger ones with air-conditioning and private baths facing the beach. Because the bungalows are near the center of Kae Bae Beach, guests can wander over to nearby restaurants for meals and entertainment, although the restaurant's food is the best on the beach and the staff the friendliest. ⊠ *Ko Chang, Trat 23120,* ☎ *No phone. 25 rooms. Restaurant, dive shop. No credit cards.*

SIDE TRIPS OUT OF BANGKOK A TO Z

Arriving and Departing

By Airplane

HUA HIN AND CHA' AM

The Hua Hin airport will open again in 2001 after an expansion and renovation. Charter flights and private aircraft will be welcome, and Bangkok Airways or another of Thailand's airlines may return with regular flights. The airport is near town.

PATTAYA

Bangkok Airways (⊠ 60 Queen Sirikit National Convention Centre, New Ratchadaphisek Rd., Bangkok, ☎ 02/229–3434) has a daily flight from Ko Samui, which lands at U-Tapao Airport, 50 km (30 mi) east of Pattaya. **Silk Air** (☎ 02/236–0440 in Bangkok; 053/276–459 in Chiang Mai; 076/213891 in Phuket) has flights between Singapore and Pattaya every Tuesday, Wednesday, Friday, and Saturday. There are also chartered flights from Europe.

By Boat

AYUTTHAYA

Though you can go by rail or road, the nicest way to get there (at least one-way) is by tourist boat along the Chao Phraya River (☞ Tour Operators, *below*).

By Bus and Minibus

AYUTTHAYA

Buses leave Bangkok's Northern Terminal every 30 minutes between 6 AM and 7 PM for Ayutthaya and Lopburi. Minibuses frequently leave Ayutthaya's Chao Prom Market for Bang Pa-In starting at 6:30 AM. The 50-minute trip costs B10.

DAMNOEN SADUAK, NAKHON PATHOM, AND KANCHANABURI

Public buses, some air-conditioned, leave from Bangkok's Southern Bus Terminal every 20 minutes starting at 6 AM for Damnoen Saduak's bus station. The fare is B30, B90 air-conditioned. From there, walk along the canal for 1½ km (1 mi) to the floating market or take a taxi boat at the pier for B10. Buses leave Bangkok from the same terminal every 20 minutes for the 2½-hour trip to Kanchanaburi. Buses also run to Nakhon Pathom from Damnoen Saduak.

HUA HIN AND CHA' AM

Buses, air-conditioned and non-air-conditioned, leave Bangkok's Southern Bus Terminal every half hour during the day for the three-hour trip to **Hua Hin's terminal** (⊠ Srasong Rd., ☎ 032/511654).

KO CHANG

For the various islands of the Ko Chang group, take a bus from Bangkok's Eastern Bus Terminal for the five- to six-hour trip to Trat, where you pick up a songthaew for the 20-minute run to the ferries at Laem Ngob. Schedules vary, but if you can get to Laem Ngob by 1 PM (take the first bus from Bangkok, at 6 AM), you should find a ferry that afternoon going to Ko Chang and the other islands. The last bus out of Bangkok is at 11 PM, which gets you to Trat at 4 or 5 AM, in time for coffee at the market before a songthaew, usually loaded with housewives and vegetables, leaves for Laem Ngob to connect with the 7 AM ferry.

PATTAYA AND KO SAMET

Buses depart every half hour from Bangkok's Eastern Bus Terminal, arriving at **Pattaya's bus station** (⊠ North Pattaya Rd., ☎ 038/429877). The fare is B77. From the bus station, songthaews will take you into downtown Pattaya for B30—tell the driver where you want to go. A bus runs between Don Muang Airport and Pattaya (B120) every two hours from 7 AM to 5 PM, and direct buses run between Nakhon Ratchasima (Korat) and Pattaya's northern bus station on Central Pattaya Road.

Most hotels in Bangkok and Pattaya have a travel desk that works directly with a minibus company. Minibuses leave approximately five times a day and cost B200 per person. An Avis minibus that departs from Bangkok's **Dusit Thani Hotel** (⊠ Rama IV Rd., ☎ 02/236–0450) for its Pattaya property is open to nonguests.

Direct buses make the three-hour trip between Pattaya's hotels and Bangkok's Don Muang Airport every two or three hours from 6 AM to 9 PM. **Thai Limousine Service** (⊠ ticket desk at airport, or in Pattaya, ☎ 038/421421) has the cleanest, most reliable air-conditioned buses. The cost is B200.

For Ko Samet, buses leave frequently from Bangkok's Eastern Bus Terminal for Ban Phe to connect with the ferry. From Pattaya, try the **Malibu Travel Centre** (⊠ Post Office La., ☎ 038/423180), which has daily 8 AM departures for B150. You can also take the local bus or a car to Ban Phe.

By Car and Taxi

DAMNOEN SADUAK, NAKHON PATHOM, AND KANCHANABURI

You can arrange to be picked up by a private car or taxi in Bangkok and reach the Damnoen Saduak market by 9 AM, before the tours arrive. Speak to your concierge, who will usually have a good resource. The cost for two people will be no more than a tour-bus fare and can be as low as B1,500 round-trip. If you keep the car to visit both Nakhon Pathom and Kanchanaburi, the cost will be about B2,000.

HUA HIN AND CHA' AM

A few hotels, such as the Regent and Dusit Thani, run minibuses (which nonguests may use) between their Bangkok and Cha' Am or Hua Hin properties for a flat fee of B450. Otherwise, you can hire a car and driver for approximately B2,500 to or from the Bangkok airport.

PATTAYA

Taxis to Pattaya from either Don Muang Airport or downtown Bangkok will ask B2,500, which can be quickly renegotiated to B1,800 or less. Coming back costs about B1,000.

By Train

AYUTTHAYA

Between 4:30 AM and late evening, trains depart frequently from Bangkok's Hualamphong station, arriving in Ayutthaya 80 minutes later. Since Don Muang Airport lies between the two cities, many travelers coming back from Chiang Mai visit Ayutthaya and then get off at the airport to fly to their next destination. Trains from Bangkok regularly make the 70-km (42-mi) run to Bang Pa-In railway station, from which a minibus runs to the palace. Three morning and two afternoon trains depart from Hualamphong station for the three-hour journey to Lopburi. The journey from Ayutthaya takes just over an hour. Trains back to Bangkok run in the early and late afternoon.

DAMNOEN SADUAK, NAKHON PATHOM, AND KANCHANABURI

Trains from Bangkok's Hualamphong and Noi stations stop in Nakhon Pathom. Trains for Kanchanaburi leave Noi Station at 8 AM and 1:55 PM. The State Railway of Thailand also runs a special excursion train (B75) on weekends and holidays; it leaves Hualamphong Station at 6:15 AM and returns at 7:30 PM, stopping at Nakhon Pathom, the River Kwai Bridge, and Nam-Tok, from which point minibuses take you to Khao Phang Waterfall. There is no train to Damnoen Saduak.

HUA HIN AND CHA' AM

The train from Bangkok's Noi Station takes four long hours to reach Hua Hin's delightful wooden **train station** (✉ Damnernkasem Rd., ☎ 032/511073). Trains leave Bangkok at 12:45 PM and 2:45 PM and depart Hua Hin for the return trip at 2:20 PM and 4 PM.

Getting Around

Ayutthaya

For a three-hour tour of the sites, tuk-tuks can be hired within the city for about B400.

Hua Hin and Cha' Am

Local buses make it easy to travel between Cha' Am and Hua Hin, as well as to points south of Hua Hin. Taxis are available, but samlors are more convenient for short distances. You can walk to most of the sights in town, but if you are staying at a resort hotel in Cha' Am, use the hotel shuttle bus or take a taxi. Tours to nearby attractions can be arranged through your hotel.

Kanchanaburi

Attractions around Kanchanaburi are accessible both on foot and by samlor. Buses leave from the town's **terminal** (✉ Saeng Chuto Rd., ☎ 034/511387) every half hour for most of the popular destinations.

Pattaya

Songthaews cruise the two main streets, parallel to the beach. The fare is B5 in town, and B10 between Naklua and Pattaya; for the Royal Cliff Resort, the fare is about B50, and to Jontien Beach it's at least B100. Sedans and jeeps can be rented for B700–B900 a day, with unlimited mileage. **Avis** (✉ Dusit Resort Hotel, Pattaya, ☎ 038/429901) and **Budget** (✉ Sai 2 Rd., Pattaya, ☎ 038/720613) offer insurance, though not all rental companies do. Motorbike rentals cost about B250 a day but getting around by bike is risky.

Contacts and Resources

Emergencies

AYUTTHAYA

Tourist Police (☎ 035/242352). **Ratcha Thani Hospital** (✉ 111 Moo 3, Rotchana Rd., ☎ 035/335555 or 035/335560).

HUA HIN AND CHA' AM

Tourist Police (☎ 032/515995). **Hua Hin Hospital** (✉ Phetkasem Rd., ☎ 032/511743).

PATTAYA

Tourist Police (✉ Pattaya 2 Rd., ☎ 038/429371; 1699 for emergencies). **Hospital and ambulance** (☎ 191).

Tour Operators

Tours of Ayutthaya and Bang Pa-In take a full day. You can travel the 75 km (46 mi) both ways by coach or in one direction by cruise boat and the other by coach. The best combination is to take the morning coach to Ayutthaya for sightseeing before the day warms up, and return down the river. The most popular trip is aboard the overnight **Manohra Song** (✉ Managed by the Marriott Royal Garden Resort, 257/1–3 Charoen Nakorn Rd., Thonburi, Bangkok, ☎ 02/476–0021/2). Day trips with the **Oriental Queen** (✉ Managed by the Oriental Hotel, 48 Oriental Ave., Bangkok, ☎ 02/236–0400) cost B1,900. You can book either of these cruises with any travel agent.

The **Chao Phraya Express Boat Co.** (✉ 2/58 Aroon-Amarin Rd., Maharat Pier, Bangkok, ☎ 02/222–5330) runs a Sunday excursion to Bang Pa-In Summer Palace, which leaves the pier at 8:30 AM and arrives in time for lunch. On the downriver trip, it stops at the Bang Sai Folk Arts and Craft Centre and arrives in Bangkok by 5:30 PM.

All major hotels have arrangements with tour operators who organize morning trips to Damnoen Saduak, sometimes combined with the Rose Garden, or Kanchanaburi and the bridge over the River Kwai. These tours pick you up at about 8 AM and cost B700. A full day is usually necessary to visit the Allied war cemeteries and the infamous bridge, and to tour the gorgeous countryside.

Visitor Information

Ayutthaya Tourist Authority of Thailand (TAT) (✉ Si Sanphet Road, ☎ 035/246076 or 035/246077), open daily 9–5. **Cha' Am TAT** (✉ 500 Petchakasem Rd., ☎ 032/471005 or 032/471006), open daily 8:30–4:30. **Kanchanaburi TAT** (✉ Saeng Chuto Rd., ☎ 034/511200). **Pattaya TAT** (✉ 382/1 Mu 10 Chaihat Rd., ☎ 038/427667 or 038/428750), open daily 9–5.

3 NORTHERN THAILAND

Here in the misty mountains, hill tribes still grow the poppy, but the notorious Golden Triangle, once the battleground of opium warlords, has been tamed. Resorts now look out to the Mae Khong River and where the frontiers of Thailand, Myanmar, and Laos meet. In the ancient Lanna Thai capital of Chiang Mai, condominiums and luxury hotels vie for space with 12th-century Buddhist temples. Pedicabs meet the jets at Mae Hong Son's airport and mahouts work their elephants alongside bulldozers carving out new highways.

NORTHERN THAILAND IS THE SCENE of an ancient sophisticated culture and intellectual center existing side by side with agrarian peoples stepping slowly into the industrial age. Chiang Mai is the gateway to the region: many travelers stay a month or longer, making excursions and returning there to rest. Guest houses and smart hotels accommodate them, and well-worn tracks lead into the surrounding tribal villages. The opium trade still flourishes, flowing illegally into southern Thailand en route to the rest of the world. For the tourist, however, the attractions are trekking in forested hills laced with rivers, the cultures of the hill tribes, and the cool weather. (Those who also seek the poppy often find themselves languishing in a Chiang Mai prison.)

Updated by
Nigel Fisher

The hill tribes around Chiang Mai have been visited so frequently that they have lost some of their unique character. You need to go farther afield, to areas around Tak, near the Burmese border, and Nan to the east, to find villages untainted by tourism. Two paved highways from Chiang Mai and daily flights have opened up the region, and even Mae Hong Son, west of Chiang Mai, known for its sleepy pace and the regular gathering of hill tribes, is developing its tourist trade.

The Golden Triangle (*Sop Ruak* in Thai), the area where Thailand, Laos, and Burma meet, has long captivated the Western imagination. The opium poppy still grows here, albeit on a much diminished scale, and the hill tribes that cultivate it are semiautonomous, ruled more by warlords than by any national government. Today, the tribes of Laos and Burma retain their autonomy, but Thailand's corner of the Golden Triangle has become a tourist attraction, with the tribes caught up in the tide of commercialism. Chiang Rai is the closest city. In 1990 it had only one luxury hotel; now there are at least three resort complexes, and two more have been built where the rivers converge, overlooking Laos and Burma.

Pleasures and Pastimes

Dining
Northern Thai food differs from mainstream Thai, and most restaurants serve both. For a start, the glutinous "sticky rice" is preferred over plain *khao suay* (white rice). Red curry of beef is a popular traditional dish, as are crispy pork and spicy sausages. Everywhere you'll find yellow egg noodles in a broth mixed with coconut milk, curry, red onions, and lemon. Western food is served at virtually all hotels, and in Chiang Mai and Chiang Rai countless stalls at large food courts sell excellent, inexpensive Thai and Chinese fare. For price categories, *see* Dining *in* Smart Travel Tips A to Z.

Lodging
More and more, the countryside around Chiang Mai is becoming known as a resort area. As if to prove it, the Regent Chiang Mai, an architectural wonder, recently opened about 18 km (12 mi) north of the city. Other luxury resort hotels are in Chiang Rai and in Chiang Saen (Bop Sop Ruak), and a four-star hotel in Mae Sai caters to tourists and businesspeople. Elsewhere, accommodations are in guest houses, usually separate thatched bungalows consisting of a small room (most without bath) and an eating area. For price categories, *see* Lodging *in* Smart Travel Tips A to Z.

Shopping
Northern Thailand is seventh heaven for shoppers. Not only does the region produce a wide range of goods—from silver to handwoven silk

and from bronzeware to leather—but the hill tribes also produce many handicrafts. Chiang Mai is the center for all these wares; shops, showrooms, demonstration factories, and bazaars abound. Pa Sang has cotton goods; Chiang Rai has a night bazaar selling mostly artifacts made by nearby hill tribes; Mae Sai has Burmese goods slipped across the border; and in Chiang Khong you can find handmade lace imported from Laos.

Trekking

Since the 1960s, more and more visitors to Thailand have gone trekking to the villages of the hill tribes. In ever greater numbers they put up with rudimentary accommodations, basic food, and often arduous hiking to pursue their fascination with the culture of the hill people. The trick nowadays is to find a knowledgeable guide who can take you to a village that has not already been overrun by tourists. The best way to do this is to speak to tourists who have just completed a trek—the more people you ask, the better equipped you will be to choose an honest and knowledgeable guide.

Exploring Northern Thailand

Chiang Mai, Thailand's second most popular city, is the region's cultural center, its transportation hub, and the major base for travelers. Venture south and southeast to visit Lamphun and Lampang, with dazzling wats and ancient architecture, and southwest to Doi Inthanon National Park. About 90 km (56 mi) northwest of Chiang Mai in the mountains along the Burmese border is the little market town of Mae Hong Son—the base from which you visit the Karen Long Neck villages. Another base for tours into the countryside and treks to villages is Chiang Rai, at Thailand's northern tip near the Golden Triangle; nowadays, you can take a hydrofoil up the Mae Khong into Laos.

Great Itineraries

To see all the sights and get a feeling for northern Thailand, it would be ideal to spend two weeks. This would allow time to make a trek to one or two hill villages.

IF YOU HAVE 2–3 DAYS
Numbers in the text correspond to numbers in the margin and on the Northern Thailand and Chiang Mai maps.

Stay in and around ⊞ **Chiang Mai** ①–⑫. On the first day, explore the wats of the inner city, and in the afternoon check out the crafts stores along Sankamphaeng Road (extension of Charoenmuang Road). In the evening have a Thai massage and follow it by a *khantoke* (northern Thai) dinner and cultural show. On the second day rise early and go to **Wat Phrathat Doi Suthep** ②, the temple on a mountain overlooking Chiang Mai. On the way back, visit the **Elephant Training Centre** at **Mae Sa.** In the afternoon see **Wat Chedi Yot** ⑥ and the **National Museum** ⑦. For the evening's entertainment go to the Night Bazaar. If life has granted you one more day, spend it on an excursion south to see the wats at **Lamphun** ⑬ and buy cottons at **Pa Sang** ⑭, then go on to see the Burmese architecture and stay overnight in ⊞ **Lampang** ⑮.

IF YOU HAVE 5 DAYS
On your first two days cover the major sights of ⊞ **Chiang Mai** ①–⑫, not forgetting to shop and have a massage. On the third day, fly to ⊞ **Mae Hong Son** ⑯ and take a tour to the nearby Karen Village. On the fourth day fly to ⊞ **Chiang Rai** ⑰, take a ride on the Mae Kok river in a long-tail boat, and visit the night market. On the fifth day make a circular tour: first to **Chiang Saen** ⑱ to see its wats and museum, next

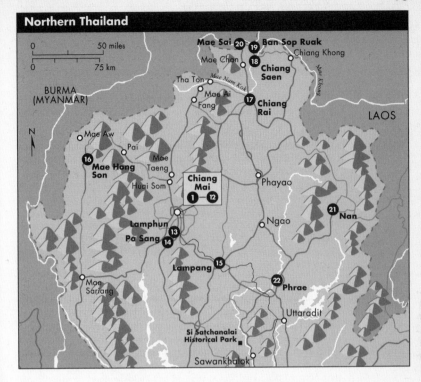

Northern Thailand

0 — 50 miles
0 — 75 km

BURMA
(MYANMAR)

LAOS

Mae Sai ⑳ ⑲ Ban Sop Ruak
Mae Chan ⑱ Chiang Khong
Tha Ton ⑱ Chiang Saen
Mae Nam Kok
Mae Ai
Fang ⑰ Chiang Rai

Mae Aw
Pai
Mae Taeng
⑯ Mae Hong Son
Huai Som
Chiang Mai ① ⑫
Phayao

⑬ Lamphun
Pa Sang ⑭
Ngao
⑮ Lampang
㉑ Nan

Mae Sariang
㉒ Phrae

Uttaradit

Si Satchanalai
Historical Park

Sawankhalok

to **Ban Sop Ruak** ⑲ at the Golden Triangle, then along the Mae Khong to **Mae Sai** ⑳ for Burmese wares and perhaps a peek into Myanmar.

IF YOU HAVE 8 DAYS

Spend the first two nights in ☒ **Chiang Mai** ①–⑫; on day three travel by raft to ☒ **Chiang Rai** ⑰ for two nights, and make the circular trip around the Golden Triangle, as above. On the fifth day fly to ☒ **Mae Hong Son** ⑯, and make a three-day/two-night trek among the hill tribes. Fly back to Chiang Mai in the early morning and go by road to **Lamphun** ⑬ and **Pa Sang** ⑭, then head for **Lampang** ⑮ to visit the wats and perhaps an elephant training camp.

When to Tour Northern Thailand

The northern part of Thailand has three seasons. It's hottest and driest from March to May, and the rainy season—June to October—makes unpaved roads difficult, especially in September. The best season to visit is winter. From November to May the weather is cool in the hills at night; take a sweater and a windbreaker if you are trekking.

CHIANG MAI AND WEST TO THE BORDER

Most visitors fly from Bangkok to the walled, moated city of Chiang Mai (though many are discovering the pleasant overnight train) and make short excursions to the smaller towns south and southeast; we cover those spots in that order. People also come to see Chiang Mai's ancient buildings and stay to shop. Then, if there's time, they drive or fly west to Mae Hong Son to visit the nearby hill-tribe villages.

Chiang Mai

❶ *696 km (430 mi) north of Bangkok.*

Chiang Mai's rich culture stretches back 700 years to the time when several small tribes, under King Mengrai, banded together to form a new "nation" called Anachak Lanna Thai. They first made Chiang Rai (north of Chiang Mai) their capital but moved it in 1296 to the fertile plains between Doi Suthep mountain and the Mae Ping River and called it Napphaburi Sri Nakornphing Chiang Mai.

Lanna Thai eventually lost its independence to Ayutthaya and, later, Burma. Not until 1774—when the Burmese were driven out—did the region revert to the Thai kingdom. After that, it developed independently of southern Thailand. Even the language is different, marked by a relaxed tempo. In the last 50 years communications have grown between Bangkok and Chiang Mai; the small, provincial town has exploded beyond its moat and gates, and some of its innocence has gone. Chiang Mai can be explored easily on foot or by bicycle, with the occasional use of buses, tuk-tuks, or taxis. Most wats are free and are usually open sunup to sundown.

❷ **Wat Phrathat Doi Suthep** is perched high up—3,542 ft—on Doi Suthep, a mountain 16 km (10 mi) northwest of Chiang Mai that overlooks the city. It is a 30-minute drive—you can take a songthaew from Chuang Puak Gate at the corner of Manee Napparat and Chotana roads on the north side of the city—and then a cable-car ride (if the cable car is completed) or steep climb up 304 steps to the chedi. The stone balustrade, added in 1577, is in the form of *nagas* (mythical snakes that control the irrigation waters in rice fields), inlaid with scales of brown and green tiles.

A special relic here makes Wat Phrathat one of the four royal wats: in the 14th century, when a relic of Lord Buddha was being installed at Wat Suan Dok, it split into two, and a white elephant was sent to find a new location for the second piece. The animal stomped his way up Doi Suthep, circled three times in a counterclockwise direction and knelt down, marking the chosen spot. A chedi was built, then later enlarged and followed by other shrines to make a large and glorious complex that dazzles the eyes with gold, red, and green mosaics and a glittering gold-plated chedi. Murals depict scenes from Buddha's life.

❸ **Phuping Palace,** the summer residence of the Thai royal family, is across a valley from Wat Phrathat. Though the palace cannot be visited, the gardens are open on Friday, Sunday, and public holidays, unless any of the royal family is in residence. The blooms are at their best in January.

❹ **Wat Umong,** south off Suthep Road, is the most fun temple in Chiang Mai. According to local lore, a monk named Jam liked to go wandering in the forests. This irritated King Ku Na, who often wanted to consult with Jam. To seek advice at any time, the king built this forest wat for the monk in 1380. Along with the temple structures, tunnels were constructed and decorated with paintings, fragments of which may still be seen. Beyond the chedi is a pond filled with hungry carp. Throughout the grounds are snippets of "wisdom" on posted signs.

❺ **Wat Suan Dok,** on Suthep Road, is one of the largest of Chiang Mai's temples, said to have been built on the site where bones of Lord Buddha were found. Some of these relics are reportedly housed in the chedi; the others went to Wat Phrathat. At the back of the viharn is the bot housing Phra Chao Kao, a superb bronze Buddha cast in 1504. Chiang Mai aristocrats are buried in stupas in the graveyard.

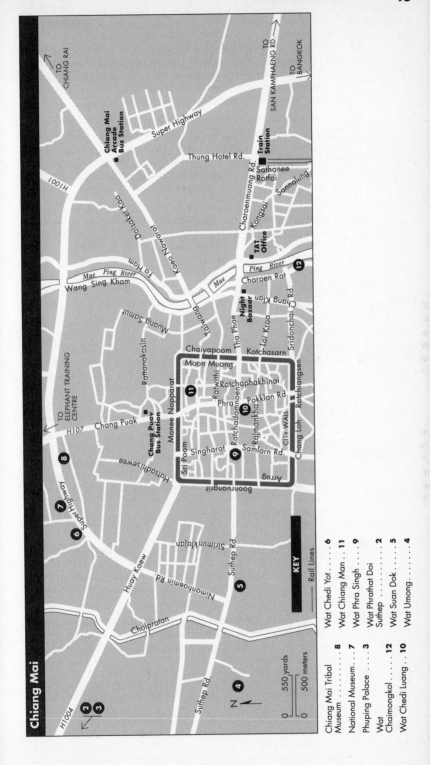

Chiang Mai

KEY

Rail Lines

0   550 yards
0   500 meters

N

Chiang Mai Tribal
Museum **8**

National Museum . . . **7**

Phuping Palace **3**

Wat
Chaimongkol **12**

Wat Chedi Luang . . **10**

Wat Chedi Yot **6**

Wat Chiang Man . . . **11**

Wat Phra Singh **9**

Wat Phrathat Doi
Suthep **2**

Wat Suan Dok **5**

Wat Umong **4**

6 On the superhighway between its intersection with Huay Kaew Road and Highway 107 stands Wat Photharam Maha Viharn, more commonly known as **Wat Chedi Yot.** Meaning Seven-Spired Pagoda and built in 1455, it is a copy of the Mahabodhi temple in Bodh Gaya, India, where the Buddha achieved enlightenment; the seven spires represent the seven weeks that he subsequently spent there. The sides of the chedi have marvelous bas-relief sculptures of celestial figures.

7 From Wat Chedi Yot you can walk to the recently renovated **National Museum,** a northern Thai–style building containing many statues of Lord Buddha and a huge Buddha footprint of wood with mother-of-pearl inlay. The upper floor's archaeological collection includes a bed with mosquito netting used by an early prince of Chiang Mai. ⌦ *Admission.* ⊙ *Weekdays 8:30–noon and 1–4:30.*

8 Up Chang Puak Road (take a tuk-tuk) are Rachanangkla Park and the **Chiang Mai Tribal Museum.** Until 1998, more than 1,000 pieces of traditional crafts from the hill tribes, collected over the past 30 years, had been hidden away in a small museum at Chiang Mai University. This fine collection—farming implements, colorful embroidery, weapons, hunting traps, and musical instruments—is now displayed in its own building by the lake in the park. ⊠ *Rachanangkla Park, Chang Puak Rd.,* ☎ *053/221933.* ⌦ *Admission.* ⊙ *Mon.–Sat. 8:30–4.*

★ 9 Chiang Mai's city walls contain several important temples—all within walking distance of one another. At the junction of Ratchadamnoen and Singharat roads, in the middle of town, stands Chiang Mai's principal monastery, **Wat Phra Singh,** containing the Phra Singh Buddha image. Its serene and benevolent expression has a radiance enhanced by the light filtering into the chapel. Be sure to note the temple's facades of splendidly carved wood, the elegant teak beams and posts, and the masonry. In a large teaching compound, student monks often have the time and desire to talk.

★ 10 On Phra Pokklao Road, between Rajmankha and Ratchadamnoen roads, stands **Wat Chedi Luang.** In 1411, a vision commanded King Saen Muang Ma to build a chedi "as high as a dove could fly." He died before it was finished, as did the next king, and, during the following king's reign, an earthquake knocked down 100 ft of the 282-ft chedi. It is now a superb ruin. Don't miss the naga balustrades at the steps to the viharn, considered the finest of their kind.

11 **Wat Chiang Man,** Chiang Mai's oldest (1296) monastery and typical of northern Thai architecture, has massive teak pillars inside the bot. Two important images of the Buddha sit in the small building to the right of the main viharn. Officially, they are on view only on Sunday, but sometimes the door is unlocked.

★ 12 The rarely visited **Wat Chaimongkol,** along the Mae Ping River and near the Chiang Mai Plaza Hotel, is small, with only 18 monks in residence. Its little chedi contains holy relics, but its real beauty lies in the serenity of the grounds.

☾ If you have not seen an "elephant camp" elsewhere, visit the **Elephant Training Centre** about 20 km (12 mi) northwest of Chiang Mai at Mae Sa. As commercial and touristy as it is, elephants are so magnificent that the show (B80) cannot fail to please. Action begins at 9:40 AM, when mahouts bring their animals to the river for a frolic in the water and a thorough wash down. The elephants then stage a dull demonstration of dragging in 20-ft teak logs and nudging them into a pile. At the end of the show, the audience feeds them bananas. You can also ride an elephant around the camp or take a one-hour trek through the forest. Lunch at the **Mae Sa Valley Resort** (⊠ In the valley, ☎ 053/ 291051, 🖷 053/290017), which has thatched cottages in beautiful gardens where vegetables are grown. The owner's honey-cooked chicken with chili is particularly good.

Dining

All the top hotel dining rooms serve good Continental and Thai food, but for the best Thai cuisine go to the restaurants in town. Several good bistro-style restaurants serving northern Thai cuisine are across from the Rincome Hotel on Nimanhaemin Road, about 1½ km (1 mi) northwest of downtown. Also try the food at the Anusan Market.

$$–$$$ ✕ **Baen Suan.** Off the San Kamphaeng Road (the shopping-factory street), and a B40 tuk-tuk ride from downtown, sits a northern-style teak house in a peaceful garden. The excellently prepared food is from the region. Try the hot Chiang Mai sausage, broccoli in oyster sauce, and shrimp-and-vegetable soup. ⊠ *51/3 San Kamphaeng Rd.,* ☎ *053/ 242116. Reservations essential. No credit cards.*

$$–$$$ ✕ **The Gallery.** North along the Mae Ping from the Riverside and the Good View is the third in a line of pleasant, shaded, waterside restaurants. This one is also an art and antiques gallery. The terraces down toward the river have a secluded feeling, and the food is Thai, with some northern Thai dishes to spice up the menu. ⊠ *25–29 Charoen Rat Rd.,* ☎ *053/248601. AE, DC, MC, V.*

$$ ✕ **Arun Rai.** This is the best-known restaurant in Chiang Mai for northern Thai cuisine. Its success has inspired the owner to roof half of his space, but you still should not expect great ambience; the focus is on the food. Try the papaya salad, *tabong* (boiled bamboo shoots fried in batter), *sai oua* (pork sausage with herbs), or the famous frogs' legs fried with ginger. The menu is available in English. The Arun Rai often has the delicacy *rod fai* (fried banana worms), which you may want to try. ⊠ *45 Kotchasarn Rd.,* ☎ *053/276947. Reservations not accepted. No credit cards.*

$$ ✕ **The Good View.** Of the three terraced restaurants in a row along the Mae Ping River, this one in the middle is the prettiest and the quietest and has the best view. You can sit on the shaded deck just outside the restaurant or down toward the water on varying levels. A broad menu with both Thai and Western dishes should satisfy all comers. ⊠ *13 Charoen Rat Rd.,* ☎ *053/302764. MC, V.*

$$ ✕ **Hong Tauw Inn.** Linger in the relaxing, intimate atmosphere as you try dishes from northern Thailand and the Central Plains. There is an English menu, and the owner speaks English fluently. Excellent Thai soups, crispy *pla mee krob* (fried fish with chili), and *nam phrik ong* (minced pork with chili paste and tomatoes) are among the popular dishes. ⊠ *Across from Rincome Hotel, 95/17–18 Nantawan Arcade, Nimanhaemin Rd.,* ☎ *053/218333. MC, V.*

$$ ✕ **Huen Phen.** The small rooms in this restaurant, once a private
★ home, are full of old handicrafts which, if not antiques, are wonderfully decorative artifacts. Be sure to browse through each dining room before settling in, either inside or in the garden, to study the extensive menu. The *kaeng hang lae* (northern pork curry) with *kao neeu* (sticky rice) is a specialty; *larb nua* (spicy ground beef fried with herbs) and deep-fried pork ribs are two more good dishes to try. ⊠ *112 Rachamongka Rd., Phrasing,* ☎ *053/277103. MC, V.*

$$ ✕ **Kaiwan.** Not many Westerners come here, but the food is held in
★ high esteem by Thais. The best place to sit is upstairs at one of the picnic tables under the stars. Try the not-so-spicy beef curry (*kaeng mat sa man*) or the zesty fried fish (*pla tot na phrik*). ⊠ *181 Nimanhaemin Rd. Soi 9, near the Rincome Hotel,* ☎ *053/221147. MC, V.*

$$ ✕ **Len Pae.** If you've made the shopping trip along San Kamphaeng Road and want a relaxing lunch, try this floating restaurant on an artificial lake. Gentle breezes off the water keep the temperature down. The best tables are those on the piers extending into the lake. The fare is northern Thai with a variety of spicy sausages and fried freshwater fish, as well as less spicy Chinese food. ✉ *114 Moo 2 Sanklang, Chiang Mai–San Kamphaeng Rd.,* ☎ *053/338641. No credit cards.*

$$ ✕ **Nang Nuan.** Though this large restaurant has tables indoors, it's pleasant to sit on the terrace facing the Mae Nam Ping. Because it's 3 km (2 mi) south of Chiang Mai, you'll need to take a tuk-tuk or taxi, but the tom kha gai and the *yam nua* (beef salad) are worth the trip. Grilled charcoal steaks and fresh seafood (displayed in tanks) are also on the menu. ✉ *27/2 Ko Klang Rd., Nonghoy,* ☎ *053/281955. AE, DC, MC, V.*

$$ ✕ **Riverside.** In a 100-year-old teak house on the bank of the Mae Nam Ping, this restaurant serves primarily Western food given zest by the Thai chef. The casual, conversation-laden atmosphere attracts young Thais and Westerners, and with lots of beer flowing the food gets only partial attention. Choice tables are on the deck, with views of Wat Phrathat on Doi Suthep in the distance. There's live light jazz and pop music after 7 PM. ✉ *9–11 Charoen Rat Rd.,* ☎ *053/243239. Reservations not accepted. No credit cards.*

$$ ✕ **Whole Earth.** On the second floor of an attractive old Thai house in a garden, this long-established restaurant serves delicious vegetarian and health foods and a few nonveg dishes for the carnivorous, such as *kai tahkhrai* (fried chicken with lemon and garlic). Many are Indian dishes—try the eggplant masala. The inside dining room is air-conditioned, and the balconies take full advantage of any breezes (but you should ask for a mosquito coil under your table). The service is sometimes slow. ✉ *88 Sridonchai Rd.,* ☎ *053/282463. Reservations not accepted. No credit cards.*

$ ✕ **Supotana Kaun.** For superb northern Thai food you must travel 7
★ km (4½ mi) north on the Chiang Dao road (Hwy. 107) and also put up with traffic noise, zero decor, and crates of empty bottles lying around, but the food is worth it. The *phad thai* (stir-fried noodles) is so crisp and delicate it melts in your mouth, and the fish with a hot-and-sour sauce is delicious. Try the "1,000-year-old eggs" (actually eggs buried in mud for three months and called *kai yean ma,* which means "eggs washed in horse's urine"). ✉ *Chiang Dao Rd., at traffic light where road from Chiang Mai Sports Complex joins from left,* ☎ *053/210980. No credit cards.*

Lodging

With Chiang Mai on every tourist's itinerary, a variety of hotels flourishes, and construction is ongoing. Some hotels add a surcharge in January and February, which brings prices here close to those in Bangkok. Lodgings cluster in four districts. The commercial area, between the railway station and the Old City walls, holds little interest for most tourists. The area between the river and the Old City has the largest concentration of hotels and is close to most of the evening street activity. Within the city walls small hotels and guest houses offer simple, inexpensive accommodations. The west side of town, near Doi Suthep, has attracted the posh hotels; it's quieter but also far from many points of interest. Taxi and tuk-tuk drivers will try to get you to change your hotel for one they recommend (which gives them a commission), and hotels that don't pay them off (the River View Lodge and Gap's House are two) often have their clients misrouted.

$$$$ **Ⓗ Regent Chiang Mai.** In the lush Mae Rim Valley, 20 minutes north
★   of Chiang Mai, the most attractive hotel in northern Thailand nestles
in 20 acres of landscaped gardens amid lakes, lily ponds, and terraced
rice paddies. An arc of 16 two-story buildings in traditional Lanna style
contains the suites, each with an outdoor *sala* (Thai gazebo) just perfect for breakfast and cocktails. Rooms are furnished with rich Thai
cottons and Thai art; floors are polished teak. Huge bathrooms overlook a garden. The main restaurant, Sala Mae Rim, serves beautifully
presented Thai dishes and offers sweeping views of the valley. Another
restaurant beside the pool is popular for light meals. Once you're here,
even catching the shuttle bus to Chiang Mai center seems too much
effort, and therein lies its disadvantage: isolation from the rest of the
world. ⊠ *Mae Rim-Samoeng Old Rd., 50180,* ☎ *053/298181,* 🖷 *053/
298189. 67 suites. 2 restaurants, bar, pool, 2 tennis courts, health club.
AE, DC, MC, V.* ☙

$$$ **Ⓗ Chiang Mai Orchid Hotel.** This is a grand hotel in the old style, with
teak pillars in the lobby. Rooms are tastefully furnished and trimmed
with wood. The Honeymoon Suite is often used by the Crown Prince.
You can choose to eat at either the formal Continental restaurant, Le
Pavillon; the Japanese restaurant; or the informal Thai coffee shop. You'll
find entertainment in the lobby bar or the cozy Opium Den. The hotel
is a 10-minute taxi ride from Chiang Mai center. ⊠ *100–102 Huay
Kaeo Rd., 50000,* ☎ *053/222099; 02/245–3973 Bangkok reservations,*
🖷 *053/221625. 260 rooms and 7 suites. 2 restaurants, coffee shop, 2
bars, pool, beauty salon, sauna, health club, business services, meet-
ing room. AE, DC, MC, V.*

$$$ **Ⓗ Imperial Mae Ping Hotel.** Festoons of lights sweep down from the
building's towering heights to the vast courtyard and gardens below.
Here, in the outdoors, buffet dinner is served and, in the beer garden
Philippine bands drown out any street noise. Classical and hill-tribe
dancing are performed at the far end of the garden. Inside the hotel
are three more restaurants—European, Chinese, and Japanese. With
371 rooms to fill in the center of town, the Imperial caters to package
tours, particularly Japanese, but the modern, functional bedrooms are
well kept and the staff is surprisingly even-tempered. ⊠ *153 Sridonchai Rd., 50100,* ☎ *053/270160; 02/261–9460 Bangkok reservations,*
🖷 *053/270181. 371 rooms. 4 restaurants, bar, beer garden, coffee shop,
pool, meeting rooms. AE, DC, MC, V.* ☙

$$$ **Ⓗ Royal Princess.** Formerly the Dusit Inn and still part of the chain,
this hotel is ideal if you'd like to step out of the front door and into
the tumult of Chiang Mai's tourist center. The famous Night Bazaar
is a block away, and street vendors are even closer. The rooms lack nat-
ural light, making them a little dreary, but the staff is well trained and
helpful, the lobby is pleasant, the cocktail lounge has a pianist in the
evenings, and the Jasmine restaurant serves the best Cantonese fare in
Chiang Mai. ⊠ *112 Chang Rd., 50000,* ☎ *053/281033; 02/233–
1130 Bangkok reservations,* 🖷 *053/281044. 200 rooms. 2 restaurants,
pool, meeting rooms, airport shuttle. AE, DC, MC, V.* ☙

$$ **Ⓗ Chiang Inn.** Behind the Night Bazaar and set back from the street,
the Chiang Inn has quiet rooms (the higher up the better). They are
reasonably spacious and decorated in local handwoven cottons. La Gril-
lade serves Thai-influenced French cuisine in a formal atmosphere, and
the more casual Ron Thong Coffee House serves Thai and Western
dishes. The hotel is usually swamped with tour groups, to which its
facilities are geared. ⊠ *100 Chang Khlan Rd., 50000,* ☎ *053/270070;
02/251–6883 Bangkok reservations,* 🖷 *053/274299. 170 rooms and
4 suites. 2 restaurants, pool, nightclub, meeting rooms, travel services.
AE, DC, MC, V.*

$$ ✕ **River View Lodge.** Facing the Mae Nam Ping across a grassy lawn,
★ this lodge is an easy 10-minute walk from the Night Bazaar. Some sea-
soned travelers say it's the best place to stay in the city. The rooms are
tastefully done with wood furniture crafted in the region and terra-cotta
floor tiles; the more expensive ones have private balconies overlook-
ing the river. Though neither elegant nor luxurious, there's a restful
simplicity here that's a far cry from the standard uniformity in most
of the city's high-rise hotels. The small restaurant is better for break-
fast than for dinner, and the veranda patio overlooking the pool and
river is good for relaxing with a beer or afternoon tea. The owner speaks
nearly fluent English and will assist in planning excursions. ✉ *25
Charoen Prathet Rd. Soi 2, 50000,* ☎ *053/271109,* FAX *053/279019.
36 rooms. Restaurant, pool. AE, DC, MC, V.*

$$ ✕ **Zenith/Suriwongse.** Around the corner from the Royal Princess, near
the Night Bazaar, this hotel recently underwent a refurbishment that
brought it up to first-class standards. Its association with the French
hotel chain attracts European tour groups, and the staff makes a game
attempt to speak French. The rooms, done in pastels, are bright and
cheery, and the hotel compares favorably with the Royal Princess. ✉
110 Chang Khlan Rd., 50000, ☎ *053/270051; 02/251–9883 Bangkok
reservations; 800/221–4542 U.S. reservations,* FAX *053/270063. 166
rooms and 4 suites. Restaurant, coffee shop, travel services, airport shuttle. AE, DC, MC, V.*

$–$$ ✕ **Galare Guest House.** This guest house on the Mae Ping riverfront
★ has many advantages: its good location (within five minutes' walk of
the Night Bazaar); small but clean rooms with air-conditioning and fans;
a shady garden; and a restaurant facing the river. It offers more charm
and personal service than many of the other city hotels, and it's the
best value in town. ✉ *7 Charoenprathet Rd. Soi 2, 50100,* ☎ *053/
818887,* FAX *053/279088. 35 rooms. Restaurant. MC, V.*

$–$$ ✕ **Grand Apartments.** With reasonable rates by the day or the month
(B4,000 per month), this new building in the old city is good for an
extended stay. Its air-conditioned rooms are efficient and clean, and
guests have access to telex and fax machines and a laundry room. ✉
24/1 Prapklao Rd., Chang Puak Gate, 50000, ☎ *053/217291,* FAX *053/
213945. 36 rooms. Café, coin laundry. MC, V.*

$–$$ ✕ **Montri Hotel.** Near the Tha Pae Gate, the Montri has clean, utili-
tarian rooms with adequate bathrooms. Rooms at the back are quietest. The coffee shop–restaurant opens at 6 AM for those wanting
breakfast. ✉ *2-6 Ratchadamnoen Rd., 50200,* ☎ *053/211069,* FAX *053/
217416. 46 rooms. Restaurant. MC, V.*

$–$$ ✕ **River Ping Palace.** The complex of Thai buildings at this welcom-
ing little guest house shows you what Chiang Mai was like 50 years
ago. It's owned by a Frenchman and his Thai wife. Food is served at
anytime in the pleasant open-air restaurant. The wooden structures have
smallish rooms decorated with old Thai furnishings and artifacts—very
personal, if a bit fussy. The best room, No. 3, costs B1,600; in the smaller
ones (B1,200), there's very little space around the double bed. The guest
house is a B30 tuk-tuk ride south of the Night Bazaar. ✉ *385/2
Charoen Phrathat Rd., Chang Klan 50100,* ☎ *053/274932,* FAX *053/
204281. 5 rooms, most with bath. Restaurant. MC, V.*

$ ✕ **Gap's House.** This collection of traditional wood houses is like a
tiny shady village within the walls of old Chiang Mai. Room No. 5
overlooks a junglelike plant nursery and tiny vegetable garden; one room
has a fishpond, another an old Thai bed on its veranda. A lively rooster
and a bilingual mynah bird add to the rural atmosphere, and antique
bric-a-brac is scattered around the open breakfast-sitting area. Mr. Gap,
the owner, either likes you or not—immediately. The rooms are furnished with an odd assortment of antiques, giving a homey, well-worn

feel. Bathrooms are basic, with cement floors and rudimentary showers, and breakfast comes with the room. Treks or excursions can be arranged, and the garden bar is often full of happy travelers swapping stories. English is spoken here, but don't speak it too loudly or get too rowdy—Gap might throw you out! ⊠ *4 Ratchadamnoen Rd. Soi 3, 50200,* ☎ *053/278140. 18 rooms. Bar. MC, V.*

$ 🏠 **Mountain View Guest House.** Within the Old City and just inside the Chang Puak Gate is this oasis of a guest house with simple but clean rooms. It has its own garden and a little restaurant where the friendly staff will prepare basic food for you. ⊠ *105 Sriphum Rd., 50200,* ☎ *053/212–8666,* ℻ *053/222635. 15 rooms. No credit cards.*

$ 🏠 **Roong Ruang Hotel.** You step into the courtyard of this little garden hotel right off Tha Pae Road, the scene of a lot of Chiang Mai's action. Two-story wings with overhanging eaves and galleries for sitting flank the courtyard, where motorbikes and a few cars can be parked. All rooms have hot water and satellite TV; some have fans (B350) and some are air-conditioned (B450). The owner, who speaks English, owns the neighboring cybercafé and will order breakfast if you want it. ⊠ *398 Tha Pae Rd., 50000,* ☎ *053/234746 or 053/232017,* ℻ *053/ 252409. 25 rooms. No credit cards.*

¢ 🏠 **Lai Thai.** On the edge of the Old City walls, a 10-minute walk from the Night Bazaar, this friendly guest house has air-conditioned or fan-cooled rooms around a garden courtyard. Bare, polished floors and simple furniture give them a fresh, clean look, and those at the back are quietest. The casual open-air restaurant serves Thai, Western, and Chinese food. ⊠ *111/4–5 Kotchasarn Rd., 50000,* ☎ *053/271725,* ℻ *053/272724. 120 rooms. Restaurant, motorbikes, coin laundry, travel services. MC.*

Nightlife and the Arts

BARS AND PUBS

Aside from go-go bars of which Chiang Mai has its share, there are several pubs and bars, some with live music and food. To listen to live jazz, drop in at the casual European-style **Bantone** (⊠ 99/4 Moo 2, Huay Kaew Rd., ☎ 053/224444). **Bubbles** (⊠ Charoen Prathet Rd., ☎ 052/270099), in the Pornping Tower Hotel, is a lively disco for the young at heart. The Chiang Mai Orchid Hotel's dance club, **Club 66** (⊠ 100–102 Huay Kaeo Rd., ☎ 053/222099), aspires to attract a stylish, sophisticated crowd. At the **Cozy Corner** (⊠ 27 Moon Muang Rd., ☎ 053/277964), the pub atmosphere, chatty hostesses, and beer garden with a waterfall are all popular with the patrons, who come for hamburgers and beer.

You may leave messages for fellow travelers at **The Domino Bar** (⊠ 47 Moon Muang Rd., ☎ 053/278503), an English-style pub serving snacks. For those who want to visit each branch of the famous chain, there is a **Hard Rock Cafe** (⊠ 66/3 Loi Kroh Rd., near Thape Gate, ☎ 053/206103) in Chiang Mai. Described by *Newsweek* as "one of the world's best bars," **The Pub** (⊠ 189 Huay Kaew Rd., ☎ 053/211550) can get a little crowded. Still, for draft beer, good grilled steak, and a congenial atmosphere, this place is hard to beat. With its location next to the Mae Ping River and small bands that perform throughout the evening, the **Riverside** (☞ Dining, *above*) is popular.

At **The Hill** (⊠ 92–93 Bumrungburi Rd., ☎ 053/277968), in a large, mostly covered courtyard, Thais while away the evening listening to a live band (usually with Thai vocalists). The cement floors are scattered with bench tables, a wooden bridge crosses a stream that divides the cavernous area, and a balcony attracts the more demonstrative couples. Entertainers perform on an artificial hill with rocks and ferns. You buy tickets at a kiosk, then collect your food, beer, and soft drinks from stands (bring your own bottle and pay a corkage fee if you want the hard stuff).

KHANTOKE DINNER AND DANCING

No first visit to Chiang Mai should omit a khantoke dinner. The menu is usually sticky rice, which you mold into balls with your fingers; delicious *kap moo* (spiced pork skin); a super-spicy dip called *nam phrik naw,* with onions, cucumber, and chili; and *kang ka,* a chicken-and-vegetable curry—all accompanied by Singha beer. The dinner usually includes performances of Thai or hill-tribe dancing (or both). An evening's diversion usually starts at 7, costs B650 for two, and requires reservations.

Tour buses deposit middle-aged Westerners at the **Blue Moon** (✉ 5/3 Moon Muang Rd., ☎ 053/278818) for a very routine performance of a dance show that includes a troupe of transvestites. One much-publicized "dinner theater" puts on a repertory of dancing and a khantoke dinner at the back of the **Diamond Hotel** (✉ 33/10 Charoen Prathet Rd., ☎ 053/272080). Tour groups come here because there are good explanations of the symbolism in the dancing. The best place in the center of Chiang Mai to eat a khantoke dinner and see hill-tribe and classical Thai dances is the **Khum Kaew Palace** (✉ 252 Pra Pok Klao Rd., ☎ 053/214315). The symbolism of each dance is explained in Thai and English. The building is a distinctive traditional northern Thai house, where you sit cross-legged on the floor or at long tables. The **Old Chiang Mai Cultural Centre** (✉ 185/3 Wualai Rd., ☎ 053/275097), designed like a hill-tribe village, has nightly classical Thai and authentic hill-tribe dancing, after a khantoke dinner.

MASSAGE

Chiang Mai is a good place to try a **traditional Thai massage,** practiced since the time of the Buddha and believed to ameliorate problems ranging from epilepsy to backaches and tension. A simple hour massage costs B200, a two-hour rubdown is B400. **Petngarm Hat Wast** (✉ 33/10 Charoen Prathet Rd., ☎ 053/270080), in the Diamond Hotel, offers a range of traditional and herbal massages. Good massages with or without herbs are given at **Suan Samoon Prai** (✉ 105 Wansingkham Rd., ☎ 053/252716).

Shopping

Chiang Mai, Thailand's foremost shopping center, is known for many crafts. Lacquerware was traditionally used to make betel-nut sets; the bamboo frame would be covered with layer upon layer of red lacquer and decorated with black. Nowadays trays and jewelry boxes are popular items. Jade comes from Burma: the softer jade is carved into chopsticks, figurines, and Buddha images, the harder and more translucent jade is used for jewelry. Silver is hammered into plates and cups as well as chunky jewelry, priced according to weight (silver runs about B10 per gram). Paper made from silk, cotton, or mulberry leaves is used to make writing paper and umbrellas. Celadon, often known as greenware, is a variety of stoneware developed in China over 2,000 years ago. Much of Chiang Mai's wood carving is pretty junky, but fine workmanship can be found in **Baan Tawai,** a village of small workshops devoted to wood carving (go 13 km/8 mi south down Highway 108 to Hang Dong and then east for a couple of km). Silk prices are higher here than in I-san, and for mudmee, wait until you get to the Northeast. Two-ply silk for shirts and skirts runs about B375 a meter and four-ply silk for suits runs about B500 a meter. Rough cotton, usually from Pa Sang, is B60 a meter. Even if merchandise is priced, there is always room for negotiation. Most shops honor major credit cards, and a discount for cash is often possible.

The **Golden Mile** is a 16-km (10-mi) stretch of the road that runs east to San Kamphaeng. Large emporiums on both sides sell silver, ceramics, cottons and silks, wood carvings, hill-tribe crafts and artifacts, lacquerware, bronzeware, and hand-painted umbrellas. You can watch the goods being made at factory workshops, which is alone worth the trip. Taxi drivers know the stores and any of them will happily spend a couple of hours taking you around for B50 to B100. The driver receives a commission each time he brings tourists to a store, whether they buy or not.

★ The **Night Bazaar** is a congestion of stalls and one of Thailand's most exciting markets. There are crafts made in rural villages throughout Burma, Laos, and northern Thailand—but inspect the goods thoroughly for minor flaws. The clothing can be very inexpensive, and, at times, good quality. Some objets d'art are instant antiques, but there are real ones, too. **Lanna Antiques** (⌧ Booth No. 2 on the second floor) has a good selection. Behind the stalls is a sort of courtyard, with restaurants and some good hill-tribe products.

Some of your best buys can come from patient browsing among the downtown shops north of Tha Pae Road, but there are also larger shopping venues. The **Chiang Inn Plaza** (⌧ Chiang Khlan Rd.), across from the Chiang Inn in the center of town, is a modern shopping center where you can buy well-crafted goods. At the **Rimping Superstore Chotana** (⌧ 171 Chang Puak Rd., ☎ 053/210377), established retailers sell quality goods at fixed prices.

En Route A few miles south of Chiang Mai, before you reach Lamphun, a small road marked by a Shell station on the corner leads west to **Wat Chedi Liem,** a five-tier wat built by King Mengrai in the 13th century, and probably copied from Wat Chama Devi in Lamphun. Approximately 3 km (2 mi) past Wat Chedi Liem, on a small island in the Mae Nam Ping, is the **McKean Leprosarium,** which has treated leprosy sufferers since 1908 and is internationally recognized as a model self-contained community clinic. Don't worry about catching the disease—visitors are perfectly safe. The community itself is inspiring: some 200 patients have their own cottages on 160 secluded acres, with medical facilities, occupational therapy workshops, stores, and a church. The Leprosarium is open weekdays 8 to noon and 1 to 4, and Saturday 8 to noon; donations are requested.

Lamphun

⓭ *26 km (16 mi) south of Chiang Mai.*

Minibus songthaews (B10) go from Chiang Mai to Lamphun. It's also a pleasant day's trip to drive south on Highway 106, a shady road lined by 100-ft rubber trees, past Lamphun to Wat Phra Baat Takpa.

Lamphun claims to be the oldest existing city in Thailand (but so does Nakhon Pathom). Originally called Nakhon Hariphunchai, it was founded in AD 680 by the Chamdhevi dynasty, which ruled until 1932. Unlike Chiang Mai, Lamphun has remained a sleepy town, consisting of a main street with stores, several food stalls, and not much else. The town is known for its *lamyai* (longan), a sweet cherry-size fruit with a thin shell. The fruit is celebrated in early August with the Ngam Lamyai festival, with floats, a beauty pageant, and a drum-beating competition. In the nearby village of **Tongkam,** the "B10,000 lamyai tree" nets its owner that sum in fruit every year. Buy yourself a jar of lamyai honey; you'll be in for a treat.

Lamphun's architectural prizes are two temple monasteries. Two kilometers (1¼ miles) west of the town's center is **Wat Cham Devi**—often called Wat Kukut (topless chedi) because the gold at its top has been removed. You'll probably want to take a samlor down the narrow residential street to the wat. Since it is not an area where samlors generally cruise, ask the driver to wait for you.

Despite a modern viharn at the side of the complex, the monastery has a lovely weathered look. Suwan Chang Kot, to the right of the entrance, is the most famous of the two chedis, built by King Mahantayot to hold the remains of his mother, the legendary Queen Cham Devi, first ruler of Lamphun. The five-tier sandstone chedi is square; on each of its four sides, and on each tier, are three Buddha images. The higher the level, the smaller the images. All are in the 9th century Dvaravati style, though many have obviously been restored. The other chedi was probably built in the 10th century, though most of what you see today is the work of 12th-century King Phaya Sapphasit.

Wat Phra That Hariphunchai is dazzling. Enter the monastery from the river, through a parking lot lined with stalls selling food, clothing, and mementos. Through the gates, guarded by ornamental lions, is a three-tier, sloping-roof viharn, a replica (built in 1925) of the original, which burned in 1915. Inside, note the large Chiang Saen–style bronze image of the Buddha and the carved *thammas* (Buddhism's universal principals) to the left of the altar.

Leave the viharn by walking to the right, past what is reputedly the largest bronze gong in the world, cast in 1860. The 165-ft Suwana chedi, covered in copper plates and topped by a golden spire, dates from 847. A century later, King Athitayarat, the 32nd ruler of Hariphunchai, raised it and added more copper plating to honor the relics of Lord Buddha inside. On top of the chedi, he added a nine-tier umbrella, gilded with 14 pounds of pure gold. The monk who brought the relics from India is honored with a gold statue in a nearby chamber. He's also remembered for his potbelly—legend has it that he made himself obese so that his youthful passion for women wouldn't interfere with his concentration on the Buddha's teachings.

At the back of the compound—which leads to a shortcut to the center of town—there's another viharn with a standing Buddha, a sala housing four Buddha footprints, and the old museum. The new museum, just outside the compound, has a fine selection of Dvaravati stucco work and Lanna antiques. ▦ *Admission.* ☉ *Museum: Wed.–Sun. 8:30–4.*

NEED A
BREAK?
For lunch or a cold drink, go back through Wat Hariphunchai to the main road along the Kwang River and choose any one of the string of cafés.

Pa Sang

 12 km (7½ mi) south of Lamphun, 38 km (19 mi) south of Chiang Mai.

Many visitors go to Pa Sang, down Highway 106 from Lamphun, to shop for locally produced cottons with traditional designs and to watch the weaving. Songthaews (B10) ply the route all day. Although in recent years the better stores have moved to Chiang Mai and the selection has diminished, you can find both cloth by the yard and ready-made clothing. A shirt with a batik pattern goes for B100, while dresses run about B175. More contemporary clothing and household items can be found at **Nandakwang Laicum,** a market on the right-hand side as you enter town.

Five kilometers (3 miles) south of Pa Sang on Highway 106 is **Wat Phra Bhat Takpa,** commonly known as the Temple of Buddha's Footprint. The energetic can climb the 600 steps to the hilltop chedi, but the main attraction is the two huge imprints of Lord Buddha's foot, indented in the floor, inside the temple at the right of the car park. As you enter, buy a piece of gold leaf (B20), which you can paste in the imprint and make a wish.

Lampang

⑮ *65 km (40 mi) southeast of Lamphun, 91 km (59 mi) southeast of Chiang Mai.*

During Rama VI's reign, carriage horses were imported from England. The quaint image of horse-drawn carriages in the town's streets is still promoted by tourism officials, but the 21st century has come to Lampang, and a superhighway connects this busy metropolis to Chiang Mai and Bangkok. Concrete houses and stores have replaced the wooden buildings, cars and buses have taken over the streets, and only a few horses remain. Still, its wats, shops, and the few old-style wooden houses are sufficiently pleasant that you may wish to spend the night. Hotels in Lampang are the best you'll find between Chiang Mai and Phitsanulok.

Despite its modernization, Lampang has some notable Burmese architecture remaining. Opposite the Thai International Airways office is **Wat Phra Fang,** easily recognizable by its green corrugated-iron roof on the viharn and its tall white chedi, decorated with gold leaf. Surrounding the chedi are seven small chapels, one for each day of the week. Inside each chapel is a niche with images of the Buddha.

A well-preserved example of Lampang's Burmese architecture is **Wat Sri Chum.** Pay particular attention to the viharn: the eaves have beautiful carvings, and its doors and windows have elaborate decorations. Inside, gold-and-black lacquered pillars support a carved-wood ceiling, and to the right is a bronze Buddha cast in the Burmese style. Red-and-gold panels on the walls depict country temple scenes.

North of town, on the right bank of the River Wang, is **Wat Phra Kaeo Don Tao,** dominated by its tall chedi, built on a rectangular base and topped with a rounded spire. Of more interest, however, are the Burmese-style shrine and adjacent Thai-style sala. The 18th-century shrine has a multi-tier roof. Inside, the walls are carved and inlaid with colored stones; the ornately engraved ceiling is inlaid with enamel. The Thai sala, with the traditional three-tier roof and carved-wood pediments, houses a Sukhothai-style reclining Buddha.

Legend suggests that the sala was also home to the Emerald Buddha (Phra Keo). In 1436, when King Sam Fang Kaem was transporting the statue from Chiang Rai to Chiang Mai, his elephant reached Lampang and refused to go farther. The statue remained here for the next 32 years, until the succeeding king managed to get it to Chiang Mai.

If you are driving to Chiang Mai and want a tranquil rural rest stop, stop on the north side of town at **Wat Chedi Sao,** a charming, peaceful monastery named after its 20 small white chedis.

Ⓒ Farther up the road toward Chiang Mai, at the 32 km post, is the **Elephant Conservation Centre** at Baan Tung Kiewn. Not only was this the first center to train elephants and to have a hospital specializing in pachyderm care, but it is one of the best places to see an elephant show. The elephants are first bathed; then, under instructions from mahouts, they drag and stack logs. (By the time elephants are 15 years old they understand some 40 different commands.) There are daily shows at

9:30 and 11 and an extra show on weekends at 2. Money from admission (B75) and elephant rides goes toward supporting the hospital. ☎ 054/227051. ☒ *Admission.* ⊙ *Daily 8–4. Closed Mar.–May.*

Wat Phra That Lampang Luang, south of Lampang, is one of the most venerated temples in the north. You'll spot the chedi towering above the trees, but the viharn to the left is more memorable. The carved wood facade and two-tier roof complement its harmonious proportions; note the painstaking workmanship of the intricate decorations around the porticoes. The temple compound was once part of a fortified city founded in the 8th century by the legendary Princess Chama Devi of Lopburi and destroyed about 200 years ago by the Burmese. The temple museum has excellent wood carvings, but its treasure is a small emerald Buddha, which some claim was carved from the same stone as its counterpart in Bangkok. ☒ *Admission.* ⊙ *Tues.–Sun. 9–4. Closed Mon.*

Dining and Lodging

$$$ ✕ **Krua Thai.** Take a samlor to this stylish and popular restaurant in a northern Thai–style house. Locals gather in the many small, heavily timbered dining rooms to eat spicy northern Thai food. There are some Chinese dishes to offset the heat of chilies. ☒ *Phahonyothin Rd.,* ☎ *054/226766. MC, V.*

$$ ✕ **Baan Rim Nam.** The name means "home by the river," and that is exactly what this traditional wood house was before it became an atmospheric restaurant. The menu offers good, not-too-spicy Thai food and international dishes. ☒ *328 Thip Rd.,* ☎ *054/322501. MC, V.*

$ ✕ **Riverside.** A clutter of wooden rooms with verandahs over the riverbank gives a charm to this pub-style restaurant, which serves tasty Thai and European fare at moderate prices. Or just come in for a relaxing beer. ☒ *328 Tipchang Road,* ☎ *no phone. No credit cards.*

$ ✕ **U-Ping.** The fun local place to eat is this open-sided restaurant on the main street, across from the access road to the Thip Chang hotel. Sports fans gather here to dine on the varied and well-prepared Thai food and drink the evening away while watching local and international matches on the half dozen TVs suspended from the ceiling. ☒ *Thakraw Noi Rd.,* ☎ *054/226824. No credit cards.*

$$–$$$ ☷ **Lampang River Lodge.** Set on the banks of the Wang River and a small lake, this resort is 6 km (3½ mi) south of town. A tremendous effort has been made to develop the gardens and build the hotel to blend in with nature. Wood furnishings give the ambience of a rustic retreat, and there are serene bungalows overlooking the lake. The other rooms are set in rows among the gardens and are usually assigned to tour groups, which flock into the hotel just before dinner. The restaurant is a vast, open-sided room; the set dinner is pricey and not very good. It's better to eat in town, but first, have a cocktail at the bar overlooking the river. ☒ *330 Mu 11, Tambol Champoo, 52000,* ☎ *054/226922,* FAX *054/226922. 47 rooms. Restaurant, bar. AE, MC, V.*

$$ ☷ **Thip Chang.** Stay here only if the Wienthong Hotel is full, since the Thip Chang has aged badly and is in need of a complete overhaul. Most rooms have two double beds, a coffee table, and a couple of chairs. A few of the staff members speak some English, but often not with a smile. The coffee shop stays open until 1 AM, and the restaurant serves respectable Western, Thai, and Chinese food. It is sometimes fully booked by tour groups. ☒ *54/22 Thakraw Noi Rd., 52000,* ☎ *054/226501,* FAX *054/ 225362. 120 rooms. Restaurant, bar, coffee shop, pool. AE, MC.*

$$ ☷ **Wienthong Hotel.** Currently the best city hotel, the Wienthong has comfortable rooms and public areas. Rooms are kept clean and fresh, despite the continual flow of tour groups. The restaurant is the best in town for Western food. ☒ *138/109 Phahonyothin Rd.,* ☎ *054/225801,* FAX *054/225803. 178 rooms. Restaurant. AE, MC, V.*

¢ ▣ **No. 4 Guest House.** The friendly owner of this old, Thai-style teak house with a garden teaches English at the local school. ⊠ *54 Pamai Rd., Vieng Nuea,* ☏ *no phone. 25 rooms with shared bath. Breakfast room. No credit cards.*

Shopping

Lampang is known for its blue-and-white pottery, which is sold in Bangkok and Chiang Mai at a hefty markup. Buy it here at shops in the city center, or visit any of the 60 factories in town. Generally, a samlor driver will take you to these factories for a few baht, since he receives a commission if you buy something. **Ku Ceramic** (⊠ 167 Mu 6, Phahonyothin Rd., ☏ 054/218313) has a good selection.

Doi Inthanon National Park

57 km (36 mi) southwest of Chiang Mai.

Doi Inthanon is Thailand's highest mountain (8,464 ft) and the habitat of many species of plants, animals, and birds. You can drive the steep, 48-km (30-mi) toll road to the top from the park entrance on the main road, or take a minibus from Chom Thong, beyond the park's turnoff. It's best to rent a minibus if you wish to see the Mae Ya waterfall, because the road there—12 km (7½ mi) of unpaved tracks—can be impassable. An easier waterfall to reach is Mae Klang, which has three tiers of falls. The turnoff is 6 km (3½ mi) from the entrance.

Mae Hong Son

⑯ *270 km (169 mi) northwest of Chiang Mai via Pai, 368 km (230 mi) via Mae Sariang, 924 km (574 mi) north of Bangkok.*

This sleepy market town close to the Burmese border where villagers trade vegetables and wares is like the Chiang Mai of 30 years ago, but it is developing quickly. Already it has two comfortable hotels, several small resorts, and at least a dozen guest houses. Tourists usually spend only a night or two here, though a few foreign travelers have embraced the gentle pace and stayed a month or more. Mae Hong Son means "province of the three mists," and it is a good base from which to trek through the jungles to less commercialized hill-tribe villages. A word of warning: around late March and April, farmers set brush fires in the surrounding hills to clear the land. The smoke can make breathing unpleasant and often prevents the scheduled Thai International Airways planes from landing at Mae Hong Son airport.

If you take a 15-minute walk up the winding stepped path to the top of Doi Kong Mu, Mae Hong Son's highest hill, you will be rewarded first by restful views as you sit in the small shaded pavilion, then by the marvelously varied structures of **Wat Phra That Doi Kong Mu,** a gleaming white temple inhabited by white plaster demons with gaping scarlet mouths. A kiosk sells bottled water and film. In town, after you stroll around the lake and look at the two temples, there is little to do but have coffee or eat at one of the restaurants on the main street and observe daily life. A few stores sell hill-tribe jewelry, textiles, and a few garments, but the merchandise is more of the souvenir variety than art. (Art objects are bought by dealers directly from the villages and shipped to Chiang Mai or Bangkok.) In the morning the local market has a colorful array of fruits, vegetables, and people.

Aside from the lush countryside, waterfalls, and caves around Mae Hong Son, the tourist lure is **visiting hill-tribe villages,** especially those of the Karen Long Necks (also called Padong), whose women wear brass bands around their necks, making them exceptionally long. Most of the

Karen Long Necks are in Burma—an estimated 3,000 families. In Thailand there are three villages, all near Mae Hong Son, with a total of 36 Long Neck families, all of whom are accustomed to posing for photographs. Some visitors find there's an ethical dilemma in going to these villages, since tourism may perpetuate what some find to be a rather barbaric custom. At the same time, tourist dollars also help to feed these Karen refugees from Burma. There is a B300 fee for entering a village; half of it goes to the village, the other half to the local warlord, who uses the money to fund his army. With as many as 150 tourists a day in peak season, a village can make good money by exhibiting their long-neck women.

Long Neck Karens have a legend that their ancestors were descended from the god of wind and a female dragon, and it is thought that the women extend their necks to imitate the dragon. The brass bands may also be a sign of wealth. Girls start to wear bands at six, adding another every three years until they are 21. They are never removed, even after death, except for cleaning, or in the case of adultery, when the woman's relatives, out of shame, will forcibly remove them.

The easiest village to reach is one with six families, upriver from Mae Hong Son beyond the village of Nam Pieng Din. By arrangements made through your hotel or a local guide, you travel by boat, with a guide, for the 90-minute trip. The cost is approximately B1,300.

The second village is near the Shan village of Nai Soi. Getting there is a two-hour, four-wheel-drive journey, followed by a 30-minute hike (an experienced rider traveling with a guide can go by motorbike, over a rough trail and a swinging bridge). The cost is B1,500.

Families living in the third village, at Huey Sautea, arrived in 1995, fleeing factional fighting in Burma. The village is relatively easy to reach by a 50-minute drive in the dry season, but if it rains the track becomes extremely muddy and waters must be forded. The cost is B1,000.

Within a three-hour drive of Mae Hong Son, the Shans, Lanna Thais, Karens, and Hmongs (Meo) also have villages, which are usually visited on guided treks of three or more days. You can leave the choice of village up to the guide—each has his favorites—but you should ask him whether he speaks the village language and discuss fully with him what is planned and how strenuous the trek will be. Since guides come and go, and villages tend to change in their attitude toward foreigners, what is written today is out of date tomorrow (☞ Outdoor Activities and Sports, *below*).

Dining and Lodging

$–$$ ✕ **Bai Fern.** For food and live music together this is the most popular restaurant in town, both with Thais and foreigners. The dining room is large, with paneled walls and teak columns. Subdued lights and whirling fans add to the festive mood. The staff is surprisingly helpful, anxious for you to enjoy the food. Most of the menu is Thai, and spicy dishes can be adapted to Western tastes on request. ⊠ *87 Khun Lum Praphas Rd.,* ☎ *053/611374. MC, V.*

$ ✕ **Kai-Mook.** Just off the main street, this is the best restaurant for alfresco dining and excellent northern Thai cooking. Of the 10 or so restaurants along this street, Kai-Mook has the freshest and tastiest food. ⊠ ★ *71 Khun Lum Praphas Rd.,* ☎ *053/612092. No credit cards.*

$$–$$$ ▥ **Rooks Holiday Hotel and Resort.** This former Holiday Inn, about 1½ km (1 mi) out of town off the main road to Khun Yuam, teems with tour groups; activity focuses around the pool in the daytime and in the disco at night. Rooms are standard, boring, slightly depressingly furnished in blue, and well worn but clean. The best of them have private balconies that overlook the gardens and the pool. Service is a little sloppy, but many of the staff speak English. ⌧ *114/5–7 Khun Lum Praphas Rd., 58000,* ☎ *053/611390,* 𝖥𝖠𝖷 *053/611524. 144 rooms. Restaurant, pool, nightclub, travel services. AE, DC, MC, V.*

$$
★ 🏨 **Tara Mae Hong Son.** Though slightly less expensive than the Rooks Holiday Hotel, this hotel is considerably more attractive. Its classic northern Thai architecture, with a huge lobby and broad open porches, makes it very airy. The restaurant, which serves good Thai food—both northern and Bangkok—has a glassed-in section for chilly mornings and evenings. It faces the terraced valley, as does the beautifully landscaped pool. The decor emphasizes wood, with polished floors and bamboo chairs and tables. The service is enthusiastic and helpful. The hotel is 3 km (2 mi) out of town, slightly beyond Rooks. ⌧ *149 Moo 8 Tambon Peng Moo, 58000,* ☎ *053/611473; 02/254–0023 Bangkok reservations,* 𝖥𝖠𝖷 *053/611252. 104 rooms. Restaurant, pool, travel services. AE, DC, MC, V.*

$–$$
🏨 **Rim Nam Klang Doi.** On the Pai River, 5 km (3 mi) out of town, is one of the better rural resorts that offers good value. Many of the rooms overlook the river; others have views of the tropical landscaped grounds. There are fan-cooled rooms with a private hot-water shower—you really don't need the more expensive air-conditioned rooms. A minivan shuttles you to town or back for B100. ⌧ *Ban Huay Dua, 58000,* ☎ *053/ 612142,* 𝖥𝖠𝖷 *053/612086. 34 rooms. Restaurant. MC, V.*

$
🏨 **Piya Guest House.** The most comfortable guest house in the area, with the best location, faces serene Jong Kham lake in the center of Mae Hong Son. The owner, Piya Grongpherpoon, has let the fan-cooled rooms around the courtyard deteriorate slightly (they cost only B250) and paid more attention to the air-conditioned rooms, each with a clean private bath, that face the garden and cost B550. Outside tables at the restaurant face the lake; those inside share space with a pool table. ⌧ *1 Soi 6, Khun Lum Praphat Rd., 58000,* ☎ *053/611260,* 𝖥𝖠𝖷 *053/612308. 11 rooms, most with bath. Restaurant. No credit cards.*

¢
🏨 **Jean's Guest House.** This is truly a basic bungalow guest house for backpackers on the cheap, where a tiny room with a fan goes for B100. The advantage of staying here is that Jean speaks fluent English and can often serve as a good resource for finding local guides. ⌧ *6 Prachautith Rd., 58000,* ☎ *053/611662. 9 rooms. No credit cards.*

Outdoor Activities and Sports

TREKKING

In the 1960s a few intrepid travelers in northern Thailand started wandering the hills and staying at the villages; by 1980, tour companies were organizing guided groups and sending them off for three- to seven-day treks. Days are spent walking forest trails between villages, where nights are spent as paying guests. Accommodation is in huts, and at best a wooden platform with no mattress is provided. Food is likely to be a bowl of sticky rice and stewed vegetables. Travel light, but be sure to take sturdy hiking shoes, warm clothes (it can become very cold at night), mosquito repellent, and perhaps some disinfectant soap, in case the huts are grubby.

The level of difficulty varies: you might traverse tough, hilly terrain for several hours, or travel by jeep, and then take an easy 30-minute walk to a village. An elephant ride or a half day on a raft may be thrown in to give a sense of adventure.

Typically, the easier the trek the more commercial the village, though the number of villages unsaturated by Westerners is ever-dwindling. Because areas quickly become overtrekked and guides come and go, the only way to select a tour is to talk to other travelers and try to get the latest information. What was good six months ago may not be good today.

Unless you speak some Thai, know the local geography, and understand something of the native customs, don't go alone: you risk being robbed, or worse, by bandits. Use a certified guide, and since he determines the quality of the tour, it's important to pick one who's familiar with local dialects and who knows which villages are the least tourist-ridden. He should also speak English well. It is also imperative that you discuss the villages and route; that way you'll at least seem to know the ropes. You can usually tell whether the guide is knowledgeable and respects the villagers, but question him thoroughly about his experience before you sign up.

CHIANG RAI AND THE GOLDEN TRIANGLE

Chiang Rai's raison d'être is as a base for visiting tribal villages and exploring the Golden Triangle. This area, remarkable for its natural beauty and friendly villagers, is relatively easy to explore on your own. The following itinerary goes from Chiang Rai to Chiang Saen and up to the apex of the triangle, Sop Ruak. It then continues west along the Burmese border to Mae Sai and back to Chiang Rai. You can hire a taxi or take a public bus, though many people rent jeeps or motorbikes.

Chiang Rai

⑰ *180 km (112 mi) northeast of Chiang Mai, 780 km (485 mi) north of Bangkok.*

King Mengrai, who founded the Lanna kingdom, built Chiang Rai in 1256. According to legend, a runaway royal elephant stopped to rest on the bank of the Mae Nam Kok River. Considering this an auspicious sign, King Mengrai placed his capital where the elephant stopped. In the 15th century the area was overrun by the Burmese, who stayed until 1786. Architecturally, little can be said for this city of two-story concrete buildings. Most of the famous old structures are gone. Wat Phra Keo once housed the Emerald Buddha that is now in Bangkok's Grand Palace, and a precious Buddha image in the 15th-century Wat Phra Singh has long since disappeared. Today, Chiang Rai is a market town that works during the day and is fast asleep by 10 PM, though a recently established night bazaar, just off Phaholyothin Road, has crafts stalls and open-air dining.

The Akha, Yao, Meo, Lisu, Lahu, and Karen tribes all live within Chiang Rai province. Each has a different dialect, different customs, handicrafts, costumes, and a different way of venerating animist spirits. Only in the past two decades have the tribes been confronted with global capitalism. Now, the villagers are learning to produce their handicrafts commercially for eager buyers in exchange for blue jeans and other commodities. You can visit some villages on day trips or make two- to five-day guided treks to the more remote ones (☞ Outdoor Activities and Sports, *above*).

Dining and Lodging

$ ✕ **Honarira.** If you decide not to eat at the night bazaar, then this restaurant is by far Chiang Rai's best for a casual outdoor meal under an umbrella of small trees. The extensive menu (also in English) is a mix of northern and mainstream Thai, so you might start with some spicy sausages and follow with *pla tod chon* (deep-fried serpent-head fish) and red curry beef. ✉ *402/1–2 Banphaprakan Rd.,* ☎ *053/715722. No credit cards.*

$$$–$$$$ ❒ **Dusit Island Resort.** Sitting on 10 acres on an island in the Kok river, ★ the Dusit Island has all the amenities of a resort, including the largest outdoor pool in the north, plus quick access to town. The building's three wings give all the guest rooms a stunning view of the river. Furnished in a modern rendition of traditional Thai, the spacious rooms have private safes and large marble baths. The formal dining room offers Western cuisine and a panoramic view; a Chinese restaurant serves Cantonese food; and the Island Cafe, where a buffet breakfast is served, has rather disappointing Thai and Continental food all day. If you arrive in Chiang Rai by river, the boatman can drop you off at the hotel's pier, except in periods of low water. ✉ *1129 Kraisorasit Rd., Chiang Rai 57000,* ☎ *053/715777; 02/238–4790 Bangkok reservations,* 🖷 *053/715801 or 02/238–4797. 271 rooms. 3 restaurants, 4 bars, pool, beauty salon, massage, 2 tennis courts, health club, shops, nightclub, meeting rooms, airport shuttle, car rental. AE, DC, MC, V.*

$$$ ❒ **Little Duck Hotel.** The first luxury resort in Chiang Rai screams its modernity. Guests are often conventioneers who mill around the huge lobby, far removed from the world outside. The rooms are bright and cheery, with light-wood fixtures and large beds. Service is brisk and smart, and the travel desk organizes excursions into the neighboring hills. ✉ *450 Super Highway Rd., Amphoe, Muang, Chiang Rai 57000,* ☎ *053/715620; 02/255–5960 Bangkok reservations,* 🖷 *053/712639. 350 rooms. 2 restaurants, coffee shop, pool, tennis court, meeting rooms, travel services. AE, DC, MC, V.*

$$–$$$ ❒ **Rimkok Resort.** Because it's across the Mae Nam Kok river and a 10-minute drive from town, the hotel, on extensive grounds, has more appeal for tour groups than for independent travelers. The main building is designed in modern Thai style with palatial dimensions—a long, wide lobby lined with boutiques leads to a spacious lounge and dining area. Guest rooms are in wings on both sides, and most have views of the river from their picture windows. ✉ *6 Moo 4 Chiang Rai Tathorn Rd., Rimkok Muang, Chiang Rai 57000,* ☎ *053/716445; 02/ 279–0102 Bangkok reservations,* 🖷 *053/715859. 248 rooms. 4 restaurants, bar, pool, shops, meeting rooms, car rental. AE, DC, MC, V.*

$$–$$$ ❒ **Wiang Inn.** In the heart of town, this comfortable, well-established hotel has a small outdoor pool, a pleasant sitting area, and a restaurant serving Chinese, Thai, and Western food. Spacious bedrooms, now slightly worn, made this the top hotel in Chiang Rai until the two resort hotels opened; it is still the best hotel within the town itself. ✉ *893 Phaholyothin Rd., Chiang Rai 57000,* ☎ *053/711543,* 🖷 *053/ 711877. 260 rooms. Restaurant, pool, health club, nightclub, travel services. AE, DC, V.*

$ ❒ **Golden Triangle Inn.** Don't confuse this guest house with the backpackers hangout at Ban Sop Ruak. This is a comfortable little place that is all too popular—advance reservations are necessary—since it is ideally situated in the center of town. Rooms have private bathrooms and are either air-conditioned or fan-cooled, and since the guest house is set back from the road, there is no traffic noise. The restaurant-lounge offers Thai and Western fare. Next door is a travel agency of the same name that arranges treks and visas into Laos. ✉ *590 Phaholyothin Rd., Chiang Rai 57000,* ☎ *053/711339,* 🖷 *053/713933. 20 rooms. No credit cards.*

Chiang Saen

⑱ *59 km (37 mi) north of Chiang Rai, 239 km (148 mi) northeast of Chiang Mai, 935 km (581 mi) north of Bangkok.*

An hour outside Chiang Rai, on the banks of the Mae Khong River, is Chiang Saen, a one-street town that in the 12th century was home to the future King Mengrai. Only fragments of the ancient ramparts survived destruction by the Burmese in 1588, and the remainder was ravaged by fire in 1786, when the last of the Burmese were ousted.

Only two ancient chedis remain standing. Just outside the city walls is the oldest chedi, **Wat Pa Sak,** whose name (*sak* means "teak") reflects the 300 teak trees that were planted around it. The stepped pyramid, which narrows to a spire, is said to enshrine holy relics brought here when the city was founded. Inside the walls stands the imposing octagonal 290-ft high 14th-century **Wat Phra That Luang.**

Next door to Wat Luang is the **National Museum,** which houses artifacts from the Lanna period (Chiang Saen style), as well as some Neolithic finds. The museum also has a good collection of carvings and traditional handicrafts from the hill tribes. ⊠ *Admission.* ⊗ *Wed.–Sun. 9–4.*

Lodging

¢ 🏠 **Chiang Saen Guest House.** One of several guest houses in this area, the Chiang Saen was among the first on the scene and is still a gathering point for travelers, especially at its riverside restaurant. However, the rooms have become very shabby. The helpful owner is well informed on trips in the area. ⊠ *45 Tambon Wiang, Amphoe Chiang Saen, Chiang Rai 57150,* ☎ *053/650146. 10 rooms and 3 bungalows. No credit cards.*

¢ 🏠 **Gin's Guest House.** The best guest house in Chiang Saen is a couple of kilometers north of town and is run by a local schoolteacher. The main house has attractively furnished, spacious rooms. Less-expensive smaller rooms are available in A-frame buildings in the garden. A simple breakfast is offered and, if you give advance notice, dinner is available. ⊠ *Sop Ruak Rd., Chiang Saen, Chiang Rai 57150,* ☎ *053/650847. 12 rooms. No credit cards.*

....

OFF THE
BEATEN PATH

CHIANG KHONG AND BAN HOUIE SAN – The recently paved road east out of Chiang Saen parallels the Mae Khong en route to **Chiang Khong,** with magnificent views of the river and Laos on the other side. Bus songthaews plough the 53-km route; make the trip in the morning to avoid crowded midday songthaews. You can also hire a speedboat to go down the river, a thrilling three hours of slipping between the rocks and rapids. Not too many tourists make the journey, especially to villages inhabited by the local Hmong and Yao tribes. Across the river from Chiang Khong is the Laotian town of **Ban Houie Sai,** from which beautiful antique Lao textiles and silver jewelry are smuggled to Thailand. Locals are permitted to cross the river; foreigners require Laotian visas. Fifteen-day visas can be acquired in Chiang Khong from **Ann Tour** (⊠ 6/1 Moo 8, Saiklang Road, ☎ 053/655198) within one business day. Numerous guest houses in Chiang Khong accommodate overnight visitors. **The Bamboo** (⊠ 71/1 M.1 Huaviang, ☎ 053/791621), on the riverside, has thatched bungalows with hot and cold water (B250) and a pleasant restaurant-lounge. If you don't go to Laos, you could drive directly back to Chiang Rai, but retracing your steps north from Chiang Khong will give you a different view of the wild, rugged, and beautiful scenery along the Mae Khong that is actually more dramatic than that around the Golden Triangle.

....

Bureau de change

Cambio

外国為替

In this city, you can find money on almost any street.

NO-FEE FOREIGN EXCHANGE

The Chase Manhattan Bank has over 80 convenient
locations near New York City destinations such as:

- Times Square
- Rockefeller Center
- Empire State Building
- 2 World Trade Center
- United Nations Plaza

Exchange any of 75 foreign currencies

CHASE

THE RIGHT RELATIONSHIP IS EVERYTHING.®

Ban Sop Ruak (The Golden Triangle)

⑲ *8 km (5 mi) north of Chiang Saen.*

Turning left (north) at the T junction in Chiang Saen will take you to Ban Sop Ruak, a village in the heart of the Golden Triangle where the opium warlord Khun Sa once ruled. A decade ago, Thai troops forced him back to Burmese territory, but visitors still flock here to see this notorious region, and the village street is lined with souvenir stalls to lure them from their buses. The only evidence of opium that you are likely to see will be at the new **Opium Museum** in the center of town that's open daily from 7 to 6. A commentary in English details the growing, harvesting, and smoking of opium, and many of the exhibits, such as carved teak opium boxes and jade and silver pipes, are fascinating. Even if you don't stay overnight, pay a visit to the new **Golden Triangle Resort Hotel,** which has some of the best views over the confluence of the Mae Sai, Mae Ruak, and Mae Khong rivers, and into the hills of Burma and Laos. Another good viewing point is the pavilion along the path leading from behind the police station.

Lodging

$$$ 🏨 **Le Meridien Baan Boran Hotel.** This distinctive resort hotel, on a
★ hill off the Mae Sai road 12 km (7 mi) out of Chiang Saen, looks out over the confluence of the Ruak and Mae Khong rivers to the mysteries of Burma and Laos. All the hilltop guest rooms share the hotel's panoramic views. They have corner table-desks, couches, coffee tables, and picture windows opening onto balconies. Bedside panels hold controls for the TV and lights. The central building houses the Yuan Lue Lao restaurant, serving Thai and Western fare, and in high season the more formal Suan Fin offers elaborate Thai and European dishes. People meet in the evening in the cocktail bar and the Opium Den bar. ⊠ *Chiang Saen, Chiang Rai 57150,* ☎ *053/784084; 02/653–2201 Bangkok reservations,* 📠 *053/784090 or 02/653–2208. 106 rooms and 4 suites. 2 restaurants, 2 bars, in-room safes, pool, 2 tennis courts, health club, squash, meeting rooms, travel services, airport shuttle, car rental. AE, DC, MC, V.*

$$–$$$ 🏨 **Imperial Golden Triangle Resort Hotel.** The views of the forested hills across the rivers are splendid from this resort. The architecture is northern Thai, with plenty of wood throughout. The superior ("executive") rooms have private balconies overlooking the Golden Triangle; third-floor rooms have the best view. The hotel has an elegant dining room called the Border View, but it's more fun sitting out on the deck, sipping Mae Khong whiskey and imagining the intrigues in villages across the border. Classical Thai dance is performed in the evening. ⊠ *222 Ban Sop Ruak, Chiang Saen, Chiang Rai,* ☎ *053/784001; 02/261–9000 Bangkok reservations,* 📠 *053/784006 or 02/261–9518. 74 rooms. 2 restaurants, pool, travel services. AE, DC, MC, V.*

Mae Sai

⑳ *25 km (15 mi) west of Ban Sop Ruak, 60 km (36 mi) north of Chiang Rai.*

By minibus—or your car or motorbike—from Ban Sop Ruak you can travel west on a semipaved, dusty, but easy road to Mae Sai, along the Mae Sai River. Mae Sai is a border market town where merchants trade goods with Burmese from Tha Kee Lek village. For the best view across the river into Burma, climb up to **Wat Phra That Doi**—the 207-step staircase starts from behind the Top North Hotel.

Non-Thais may cross the river to visit **Tha Kee Lek** on a one-day visa, obtainable at the bridge for $10. It's a smaller version of Mae Sai, selling the same goods. For $30 plus a mandatory purchase of $100 worth of Burma's Foreigner Exchange Certificates, you can get a three-night visa that lets you travel north to **Kengtung,** a quaint town with British colonial structures alongside old Buddhist temples. The trip on the unpaved road (163 km/101 mi) takes four to five hours in the dry season and up to eight from June through November.

Dining and Lodging

$$ ✕ **Rabiang Kaew.** Set back from the main road by a wooden bridge, this restaurant built in the northern style has a certain Old World charm. Artifacts adorning the dining room add to its rustic style, and the Thai fare is well prepared. ⌧ *356/1 Phaholyothin Rd. (across from the Krung Thai Bank),* ☎ *053/731172. MC, V.*

$ ✕ **Rim Nam (Riverside) Restaurant.** Its open terrace above the Mae Sai, overlooking Burma, makes this restaurant a good choice for relaxing with a beer. The Thai food, however, is only passable. ⌧ *Phaholyothin Rd.,* ☎ *053/731207. No credit cards.*

$$ ▨ **Wang Thong.** This hotel on the riverbank opened in 1993, hoping to cash in on the relaxing of trade restrictions with Burma. Choose a guest room high up on the river side, and you can spend the day idly watching the flowing waters and the flowing pedestrian traffic across the bridge. The hotel is designed for upscale business travelers. Its rectangular rooms are modern and functional, and though the restaurant offers only average fare, it has Western dishes as well as Thai and Chinese. ⌧ *299 Phaholyothin Rd., Mae Sai, Chiang Rai 57130,* ☎ *053/ 733388,* ⒻⒶⓍ *053/733399. 148 rooms. Restaurant, coffee shop, pool. MC, V.*

$ ▨ **Mae Sai Guest House.** Backpackers rank this riverside guest house, 1 km (½ mi) west of the bridge, as the best in Mae Sai. It has clean bungalows and some river views. A small garden area surrounds the bungalows, and the main building housing the office also has a casual dining room. ⌧ *688 Wiengpangkam, Mae Sai, Chiang Rai 57130,* ☎ *053/732021. 20 cottages with communal showers. No credit cards.*

$ ▨ **Northern Guest House.** When the Mae Sai Guest House is full, this is a good second choice, with a helpful owner. It's on the way back to town from the Mae Sai, and it has small (there's just enough room for a bed) but clean bungalows. A few have their own shower and toilet. The veranda-style dining room is pleasant in the evenings, and the river flows at the edge of the garden. ⌧ *402 Tumphajom Rd., Mae Sai, Chiang Rai 57130,* ☎ *053/731537. 26 cottages, a few with bath. Dining room. No credit cards.*

$ ▨ **Tip Sukon House.** Just down the road to the left (west) of the bridge is this concrete structure, on the left and perched on the hill. Most rooms face Burma, but the ones on the top floor have the best view from their balconies. The rooms are bare but clean, and there is hot and cold water in the bathroom. There is no restaurant, but breakfast coffee is served in the reception area. ⌧ *774 Moo 1, Shailamjay Rd., Mae Sai, Chiang Rai 57130,* ☎ *053/642816. 23 rooms. No credit cards.*

Shopping

Thais take household goods and consumer products across the river, and the Burmese bring sandalwood, crafts, raw jade, and rubies. Though you may want to set a foot in Burma, the prices and quality of the goods will not be better than in Mae Sai, which has better prices than Chiang Mai. **Mengrai Antique** (⌧ Phaholyothin Rd., close to the bridge, ☎ 053/731423) is a good store. On the east side of Phaholyothin Road, opposite the Tourist Police, is the **Thong Tavee Jade factory.** Mae Sai is also justifiably proud of its sweet strawberries, which ripen in December or January.

Cheng Dao Cave

5 km (3 mi) from Mae Sai.

From Mae Sai, it's a 1½-hour local bus ride back to Chiang Rai, or you can take an air-conditioned express bus to Chiang Mai (via Chiang Rai) that takes about five hours. If you are traveling back to Chiang Rai by car or motorbike, drive to the **Cheng Dao Cave Temple,** known for its Buddha carvings and monstrous stalactites. Farther up the dirt road you come to the **Monkey Temple,** where playful monkeys will snatch anything that sparkles.

OFF THE
BEATEN PATH

DOI TUN – Just south of Mae Chan, between Mae Sai and Chiang Rai, look for the right-hand turnoff to Highway 149, a steep, rough road that runs 17 km (11 mi) up to **Phra That** on Doi Tun, one of the highest peaks in northern Thailand. En route, stop at the Akha Guest House to inquire about road conditions to the top. The drive is awe-inspiring; at the summit, mist cloaks monks chanting at the temple, which was built in 911. This has become one of the area's most revered shrines. If you don't feel like driving, you can arrange in Mae Chan for a car to take you.

Nan

㉑ *270 km (167 mi) southeast of Chiang Rai, 318 km (197 mi) east of Chiang Mai.*

Near the Laos border lies the city of Nan, a provincial capital founded in 1272 by the court of Laos—though according to local legend, the Lord Buddha, passing through Nan valley, spotted an auspicious site for a temple to be built. By the late 13th century Nan was brought into Sukhothai's fold, but it maintained a fairly independent status into the 20th century. Only in the last two decades has a modern road been cut from Phrae to bring this region into closer communication with authorities in Bangkok. Nan province is rich in teak plantations and fertile valleys that produce rice and superb oranges. The town of Nan itself is small; everything is within walking distance, and daily life centers on the morning and evening markets. The Nan River, which flows past the eastern edge of town, is ignored by the tourist industry, except for a couple of riverbank restaurants with overpriced food. The most popular time to visit the Nan is in October during the traditional boat races.

To get a sense of the region's art visit the **National Museum,** housed in the former palace of the Nan royal family. The collection has a good array of wood and bronze Buddha statues, textiles, musical instruments, ceramics, and other works of Lanna art, all of which are explained in English. ✉ *Phalong Rd.* 🎫 *Admission.* ⊙ *Wed.–Sun. 9–12 and 1–5.*

★ The most astounding temple in Nan is the beautiful **Wat Pumin** on Phalong Road. The cruciform bot, built in 1596, is small and quite intimate. You climb a flight of steps flanked by two superb nagas, their heads guarding the north entrance and their tails the south. The temple was extensively renovated in 1865 and 1873, and at the end of the 19th century murals picturing everyday life and the commoner's view of the world were painted on the inner walls. The images range from the traumas of Buddhist hell and men with oversize testicles to a starving farang clasping a tool for premasticating food; from hunting scenes to views of courtly life. These are simple murals totally unlike the sophisticated art found in Bangkok's Grand Palace. The unknown artist is presumed to be from southern Yunan. The bot's central images are also quite unusual—four Sukhothai Buddhas in the vanquishing Mara position, facing the cardinal compass points.

Nan is dotted with other wats. **Wat Hua Wiang Tai** on Sumonthewarat Road is the gaudiest, with a naga running along the top of the security wall and lively murals painted on the viharn's exterior. **Wat Suan Tan** in Tambon Nai Wiang district has a 15th-century bronze Buddha image and is the scene for fireworks during Songkran. **Wat Ming Muang** on Suriyaphong Road contains the city pillar (lak muang). **Wat Chang Kham** on Suriyaphong has a large chedi supported by elephant buttresses.

Lodging

$–$$ ☷ **Dhevaraj.** The first international hotel in Nan has been modernized to become the hotel of choice. While the City Park Hotel is newer and has a pool, it is a good mile out of town and has a deserted, empty feel unless a tour group has descended on it. Dhevaraj, on the other hand, is in the center of town across from the market and is a meeting point for locals as much as tourists. A coffee shop is open from 6 AM to midnight and the courtyard dining room serves dinner in a romantic setting. The rooms are quite respectable, with small but modern bathrooms. ⊠ *T44 Sumonthevaraj Rd., 50000,* ☎ *054/710094,* ⨳ *054/710212. 154 rooms with bath. 2 restaurants. MC, V.*

$ ☷ **Nanfah Hotel.** This old wooden Chinese hotel, a relic of the past, is worth a visit, even if you are disinclined to stay in its rather dark, bare rooms with their dated bathrooms. A live band plays in the lounge-restaurant at night. That, of course, does not help those trying to sleep in the rooms above, but rooms at the back of the hotel are quiet. The wide-plank floors are of a bygone age and a balcony overlooks the street. Marvelous antiques are scattered around the hotel, and the owner, who also has a souvenir and artifact shop in the lobby, is a delightful host. ⊠ *438 Sumonthevaraj Rd., 55000,* ☎ *054/772640. 14 rooms with shower. No credit cards.*

Phrae

㉒ *235 km (145 mi) south of Chiang Rai, 201 km (125 mi) southeast of Chiang Mai, 118 km (73 mi) southwest of Nan.*

Phrae (pronounced "prayer") is off the main tourist beat, a market town in a narrow rice valley on the road to Nan. The town's recorded history starts in the 12th century, when it was called Wiang Kosai, the Silk Cloth City. It remained an independent kingdom until the Ayutthaya period. Remains of these former times are seen in the crumbling city walls and moat, which separate the old city from the new commercial sprawl. On the northeastern edge of town stands **Wat Chom Sawan,** a beautiful monastery built during the reign of King Rama V (1868–1910) and designed by a Burmese architect. The bot and viharn are combined to make one giant sweeping structure. Phrae's oldest building is **Wat Luang,** near the city wall and moat. Though it was founded in the 12th century, renovations and expansions completely obscure the original design, and the only original section is a Lanna chedi with primitive elephant statues. A small museum on the grounds contains sacred Buddha images, swords, and texts; a monk will take you around, but he is likely to speak only Thai.

On a hilltop in Tambon Pa Daeng, 10 km (6 mi) southeast of town, stands another ancient wat, **Wat Phra That Cho Hae.** It was built in the late 12th century, and its 108-ft chedi is coated in gold sheet. The chedi is linked to the viharn, a later construction, which has a series of murals depicting scenes from the Buddha's life. The revered Buddha image is said to increase a woman's fertility. Cho Hae is the name given to the cloth woven by the local people, and in the fourth lunar month (June) the chedi is wrapped in this cloth and an annual fair is held. Two kilometers (1 mile) from Wat Cho Hae is another smaller wat, **Wat Phra That Chom Chang,** whose chedi is said to contain a strand of Lord Buddha's hair.

About 9 km (6 mi) west of Phrae's center, in the hamlet of Tambon Pa Maet on highway 1023, is **Ban Prathap Chai,** billed as one of the largest teak structures in the world. Although that may be an exaggeration, this composite of nine old houses was constructed from 130 huge teak posts, and the rooms inside are a beautiful example of traditional Thai housing. Much of the compound is given over to shops, some of which have weaving and crafts of good quality.

There is a **Night Market** at Pratuchai Gate with numerous stalls offering cheap, tasty food.

Lodging

$–$$ 🏨 **Nakorn Phrae Tower Hotel.** Although Phrae is not a tourist town, you'll find all the creature comforts one might expect in the leading hotel of a provincial capital. Bedrooms have either two queen-size beds or a king and are furnished with chairs, desks, minibars, and TVs. Bathrooms are small, tiled, and functional. The restaurant serves Thai, Chinese, and Western fare, and you can have drinks in the lounge or at a small bar. ⊠ *3 Muanghit Rd., 54000,* ☎ *054/521321,* ℻ *054/523503. 139 rooms. Restaurant, bar, meeting rooms. AE, DC, MC, V.*

NORTHERN THAILAND A TO Z

Arriving and Departing

The State Railway links Chiang Mai to Bangkok and points south but goes no farther north. As the trip from Bangkok takes about 13 hours and there's little to see but paddy fields, overnight sleepers are the best trains to take, and they are very comfortable. On most routes buses are faster and cheaper than trains, but if time is short, take a plane. Don't leave your valuables unattended on either bus or train. Petty thievery is common.

By Airplane

CHIANG MAI AND NEARBY; MAE HONG SON

In peak season, flights to Chiang Mai are heavily booked. The airport is about 10 minutes from downtown, a B80 taxi ride. **Thai Airways International** (⊠ 240 Prapokklao Rd., ☎ 053/211044; 02/234–3100 in Bangkok) has 10 or more flights daily from Bangkok (about one hour; B1,700), and direct daily flights from Phuket. It also has a twice weekly service to Kumming, China. **Bangkok Airways** (☎ 053/281519; 02/229–3434 in Bangkok) flies daily from Bangkok, with a stopover in Sukhothai. **Lao Aviation** (☎ 053/418258) offers two flights a week to Vientiane.

Silk Air (☎ 053/276459) has direct flights from Singapore. **Air Mandalay** (☎ 053/818049) flies three times a week from Mandalay, Burma (book through a travel agent).

Thai Airways International has a daily flight between Bangkok and Lampang. It also has several flights between Bangkok and Mae Hong Son, and two flights daily between Chiang Mai and Mae Hong Son. In March and April, smoke from slash-and-burn fires often prevents planes from landing at the airport.

CHIANG RAI

Thai Airways International (☎ 054/711179) has two nonstop flights daily from Bangkok (B1,820) and two from Chiang Mai (B230). Taxis meet incoming flights, but most tourist hotels have their own shuttle vans waiting for guests.

By Boat
CHIANG RAI

The most exciting way to reach Chiang Rai is on a combination bus and boat trip. You leave Chiang Mai at 6:30 AM for a four-hour trip on a local bus to Tha Thon, north of Fang (or you can hire a car and driver for about B1,200 and leave your Chiang Mai hotel at 8 AM). In Tha Thon, after lunch at the restaurant opposite the landing stage, you leave on a long-tail boat at 12:30 PM (buy your ticket at the kiosk). These public boats hold about 12 passengers, sitting in the bottom, and the fare is B160 per person. You may hire your own boat for B1,600, which you will have to do if you arrive after 12:30 PM. The trip down the Mae Nam Kok River to Chiang Rai takes five hours, going through rapids and passing a few hill-tribe villages. Bring bottled water, an inflatable cushion, and a sun hat. The more adventurous can travel by unmotorized raft (best during October and November, when the water flows quickly), staying overnight in villages on the three-day journey.

By Bus
CHIANG MAI AND NEARBY; MAE HONG SON

The trip between Bangkok and Chiang Mai takes about 11 hours and costs approximately B300. More comfortable, privately run air-conditioned buses cost B470. State-run buses leave from Bangkok's **Northern Bus Terminal** (✉ Phaholyothin Rd., ☎ 02/279–4484). Some of the private buses use Bangkok's Banglampoo section of town as the drop-off and pick-up point. An express bus to Mae Hong Son leaves in the morning for the five- to six-hour trip (B175) from Chiang Mai's **Arcade bus terminal** (☎ 053/274638 or 053/242664), which also serves Bangkok, Chiang Rai, and Chiang Rai province. **Chiang Phuak terminal** (☎ 053/211586) serves Lamphun, Fang, Tha Ton, and destinations within Chiang Mai province.

The easiest way to reach Lamphun from Chiang Mai is to take the minibus songthaew (B10), which leaves every 20 minutes from across the TAT office on Lamphun Road. Both air-conditioned and non-air-conditioned buses connect Lampang to Thailand's north and northwest and to Bangkok. The bus station is 3 km (2 mi) away—take a samlor into town—but the ticket offices are in Lampang.

CHIANG RAI

Buses run throughout the day from Chiang Mai. The express takes 2½ hours and costs about B80; the local takes 3½ hours and is even cheaper.

By Car
MAE HONG SON

The road to Mae Hong Son from Chiang Mai has 1,273 arm-wrenching bends but is also very scenic; the northern route through Pai (4 hours) is shortest and most attractive; the southern route—Highway 108 through Mae Sariang—is easier driving but takes about two hours longer.

By Train
CHIANG MAI AND NEARBY

Trains for the north depart from Bangkok's Hualamphong Railway Station and arrive in **Chiang Mai station** (✉ Charoenmuang Rd., ☎ 053/245563). Overnight sleepers leave Hualamphong at 3 PM, 6 PM, 8 PM, and 10 PM, arriving at 5:35 AM, 7:20 AM, 9:05 AM, and 1:05 PM. Return trains leave at 2:50 PM, 4:25 PM, 5:25 PM, and 11:30 PM and arrive in Bangkok at 5:55 AM, 6:25 AM, 6:50 AM, and 2:55 PM. (Departure times are subject to minor changes.) The overnight trains are invariably well maintained, with clean sheets on the rows of two-tier bunks. The second-class carriages, either fan-cooled or air-conditioned, are comfortable (the fare is B625). First class (two bunks per compartment) is twice the price. The Nakhonphing Special Express (no first class) leaves Bangkok at 7:40 PM and arrives in Chiang Mai at 8:25 AM (return trip departs at 9:05 PM and arrives in Bangkok at 9:40 AM). The tuk-tuk fare to the center of town is about B25.

Most Bangkok–Chiang Mai trains stop at Phitsanulok and at Lamphun, where a bicycle samlor can take you the 3 km (2 mi) into town for B30. The train to Lampang from Chiang Mai takes approximately 2½ hours; from Bangkok, it takes 11 hours, and from Phitsanulok, 5 hours.

Getting Around

Chiang Mai and Nearby

Compact Chiang Mai can be explored easily on foot or by bicycle, with the occasional use of public or other transport for temples, shops, and attractions out of the city center. A car, with a driver and guide, is the most convenient way to visit the five key temples outside Chiang Mai, the elephant camp, the hill-tribe villages, and the Golden Mile craft factory–shopping area. If you hire a taxi for a day (B1,000–B1,400, depending on mileage), negotiate the price in advance or, better yet, arrange it the evening before and have the driver collect you from your hotel in the morning. Do not pay until you have completed the trip. More and more tourists are renting four-wheel-drive vehicles. Driving is easier than it may first appear, though pedestrians and unlighted vehicles make it hazardous at night. Two major car-rental agencies in Chiang Mai are **Avis** (⊠ Chiang Mai Airport, ☎ 053/201574) and **Hertz** (⊠ 90 Sridornchai Rd., ☎ 053/279474).

Motorcycles are also popular. Rental agencies are numerous, and most small hotels have their own agency. Shop around to get the best price and a bike in good condition. Remember that any damage to the bike that can be attributed to you will be, including its theft. Most trips in a tuk-tuk within Chiang Mai should cost less than B30. Songthaews follow a kind of fixed route, but will go elsewhere at a passenger's request. Name your destination before you get in. The cost is B5.

In the small town of Lamphun all the sights are within a B20 bicycle samlor ride.

Chiang Rai

Taxis and bicycle samlors are always available in Chiang Rai and in the surrounding small towns. Buses depart frequently for nearby towns (every 15 minutes to Chiang Saen or to Mae Sai, for example), or you can commission a taxi for the day.

Lampang

Horse-drawn carriages are available for tourists at a rank outside the government house, although some are usually waiting at the train station. The price for a 15-minute tour of central Lampang is B30. The hourly rate is approximately B100. The easiest and least expensive way to get around, however, is by samlor.

Mae Hong Son

Mae Hong Son is very small; everything is within walking distance, although you may need a tuk-tuk or taxi to take you into town from your hotel. Tourists usually take trips to the outlying villages and sights with a guide and chauffeured car. Should you hire a jeep, be sure that its four-wheel drive is in working order. Less expensive, if you want to explore on your own, are motorbikes, which can be rented from one of the shops along the town's main street. Be careful: the main roads have gravel patches, the side roads are rutted and, in the rainy season, you must also contend with mud.

Contacts and Resources

Emergencies

CHIANG MAI AND NEARBY

Police and ambulance (☎ 191). **Tourist Police** (✉ 105/1 Chiang Mai–Lamphun Rd., ☎ 053/248974 or 1699). There are also tourist police boxes in front of the Night Bazaar and in the airport. **Lanna Hospital** (✉ 103 Superhighway, ☎ 053/211037).

CHIANG RAI

Police (☎ 053/711444). **Chiang Rai Hospital** (☎ 053/711300). **Over Brook Hospital** (☎ 053/711366).

MAE HONG SON

Thai Tourist Police (✉ Rajadrama Phithak Rd., ☎ 053/611812).

Tour Operators

Every other store in Chiang Mai seems to be a tour agency, so you'd be wise to pick up a list of TAT-recognized agencies before choosing one. Each hotel also has its own travel desk and association with a tour operator. Since it is the guide who makes the tour great, arrange to meet yours before you actually sign up. This is particularly important if you are planning a trek to the hill-tribe villages. Prices vary quite a bit, so shop around, and carefully examine the offerings. Unreliable tour operators often set up shop on a Chiang Mai sidewalk and disappear after they have your money, so *use* your TAT-approved list. **Summit Tour and Trekking** (✉ Thai Charoen Hotel, Tapas Rd., ☎ 053/233351) and **Top North** (✉ 15 Soi 2, Moon Muang Rd., ☎ 053/278532) offer good tours at about B350 a day (more for elephant rides and river rafting). **World Travel Service** (✉ Rincome Hotel, Huay Kaeo Rd., ☎ 053/221–1044) is reliable.

The four major hotels in Chiang Rai and the Golden Triangle Resort in Chiang Saen organize minibus tours of the area. Their travel desks will also arrange treks to the hill-tribe villages with a guide. Should you prefer to deal directly with a tour agency, try **Golden Triangle Tours** (✉ 590 Phaholyothin Rd., Chiang Rai 57000, ☎ 053/711339).

Travel Agencies

In Chiang Mai, **ST&T Travel Centre** (✉ 193/12 Sridonchai Rd., ☎ 053/251922), on the same street as the Chiang Plaza Hotel, is good for plane, train, or bus tickets.

Visitor Information

In Chiang Mai you'll find an office of the **Tourist Authority of Thailand** (TAT) (✉ 105/1 Chiang Mai-Lamphun Rd., ☎ 053/248604) on the far side of the river. For information in Chiang Rai try the **Tourist Information Centre** (✉ Singhakhlai Rd., ☎ 053/711433).

4 THE CENTRAL PLAINS AND I-SAN

Thailand's fertile rice bowl is studded with the ruins of its ancient capitals, and in the northeast plateau you'll find Khmer sanctuaries and a rural way of life.

Updated by
Nigel Fisher

NASMUCH AS BANGKOK IS THE ECONOMIC HEART of Thailand, and the south its playground, the soul of the country lives in the vast central area, symbolized by rice fields worked by farmers and their water buffalo, that stretches from the Burmese border to Cambodia. In the western part of this region, at Sukhothai, Thailand's first kingdom was established when the Khmer empire was defeated. The eastern part, known as the I-san, close to Cambodia and the Khmer capital of Angkor Wat, was slower in being absorbed into the new Thai nation. Its many Khmer ruins present a different aspect of Thailand. Other parts of the I-san have been influenced by the culture of what is now Laos.

The shift of power, first to Ayutthaya and then to Bangkok, left both the western and eastern regions of this central area to become rural backwaters. Modern international hotels are few and far between, yet some of Thailand's most fascinating historic sites are here. Sukhothai takes first place, since it was the nation's first capital, but there are other architectural treasures that span half a millennium of Thai history.

Pleasures and Pastimes

Architecture

In the Central Plains, the Thai nation was born at Sukhothai, and the art reflects the optimism of the age. Strongly influenced by Sri Lankan Buddhism, Sukhothai's architecture became the foundation of what is now known as classic Thai. Its art, mostly exemplified in statues of the Buddha, is light, smiling, serene, and innovative—e.g., the walking Buddha. The Northeast, in contrast, was under the influence of the Khmer Empire, which in the 12th and 13th centuries ruled most of the Korat plateau. Scattered through the southern part of the I-san are *phrasat*, the Thai word for Khmer complexes, loosely translated as "castles," though Khmer kings did not live in them. They were used as Hindu sanctuaries or for retreats or as rest stops for travelers en route from Angkor. A few of these have been restored, but many are in a romantic, ruinous state that evokes a strong feeling for the past.

Dining

The Central Plains is not known for a particular cuisine, and the restaurants aren't notable. Most travelers dine in their hotels and rely on local markets and food stalls, which are full of delicious things to eat.

Food in the I-san is influenced by Laos and the harsh climate—hot and dry until the rains flood the land from May through October. The I-san is poor and the people have learned to make a little go a long way. Glutinous rice (*khao niaw*) rather than plain steamed rice (*khao suay*), for example, is the staple; it sticks to the stomach. The food is often hot and spicy, including the delicious sausages. Pork is popular and is eaten as *moo pan,* beaten flat and roasted over charcoal, and as *moo yor,* ground and wrapped in a banana leaf. Beef slices are lightly grilled and garnished with shallots, rice flour, dried chilies, lemon juice, and fresh mint leaves (*nua namtok*). Each province claims to have the best *kai yang* (roast chicken) and sticky rice, but Si Saket and Udon Thani brag the loudest. Especially popular in Korat is *sai krog I-san,* a sausage filled with minced pork, garlic, and rice, which is cooked and eaten with sliced ginger, dry peanuts, and grilled chilies. It is very spicy, not to say hot. You will probably want to stay away from *balah,* a vile-smelling fermented fish sauce that's widely offered. For price categories, *see* Dining *in* Smart Travel Tips A to Z.

Lodging

Although there are no luxurious hotels in the Central Plains, and charming ones are scarce, you can find decent, clean lodging. With the exception of two hotels in Nakhon Ratchasima, accommodations in the Northeast are mostly city hotels catering to Thai business travelers. But as more tourists discover the region, hotels are gradually adapting to the needs of the vacationer. Expect polite and friendly service, but do not count on an English-speaking staff or for the hotel to arrange tours. Expect the guest rooms to be mopped clean but furnished modestly, with faded paint on the walls. In rural areas, expect only basic bathroom facilities; in budget accommodations, there is no hot water. For price categories, *see* Lodging *in* Smart Travel Tips A to Z.

National Parks

Two of the most popular national parks are in the I-san: cool, misty Phu Kra Dueng, in mountainous Loei province, and Khao Yai, southwest of Korat, which covers 2,168 square km (833 square mi) in four provinces. Another favorite is Ban Phue, northwest of Udon Thani, a 1,200-acre park covered with rocks of all sizes, some shaped into Buddhist and Hindu mythical figures.

Shopping

Villagers in the Northeast have a tradition of spending time on handicrafts, which continues today, and some of them have become well-known for their skills. So, although the Northeast has no major tourist shopping center like Chiang Mai or Bangkok, there are wonderful things to buy: the village of **Renu Nakhon** produces cheerful quilted blankets and highly patterned ceramics; pottery made with rust-colored clay is found in the village of **Ban Kwian;** straw baskets are woven at **Ban Butom;** and **Ban Choke** produces fine silver bracelets and necklaces. Along the Mae Khong you'll find markets, like the one in **Mukdahan,** selling crafts brought over from Laos; look for fine handmade embroidery and lace. The village of **Chonnabot** weaves high-quality mudmee silk, as does the area around **Si Chiang.** More silk comes from **Chiang Khan** and from villages south of Korat.

Exploring the Central Plains and I-san

In the best of all possible worlds you'd spend at least two weeks in this region, browsing through the mysterious temples and sanctuaries, the ruined cities and streets. You'd shop till you dropped in the markets and crafts villages. But on any trip, you'll find wonderful classic Thai architecture at Sukhothai, the first capital, and Khmer sanctuaries of another world in the southern I-san. Shoppers can pursue exotic bargains along the Mae Khong River and in villages throughout the northeast.

Great Itineraries

IF YOU HAVE 2 DAYS

Numbers in the text correspond to numbers in the margin and on the Central Plains and I-san and Old Sukhothai maps.

From Bangkok, take the train or plane to **Phitsanulok** ① to see the Phra Buddha Chinnarat and the Pim Buranaket Folklore Museum. Three hours should be enough time before boarding a bus for the hour-long trip to 🏨 **New Sukhothai.** You'll need the best part of a day to see Thailand's first capital, **Old Sukhothai** ②–⑪. Spend the night nearby or in the new town, and the next morning take the hour's trip to **Si Satchanalai Historical Park** ⑫, an ancient satellite city, then take a plane from the new, nearby airport back to Bangkok or on to Chiang Mai.

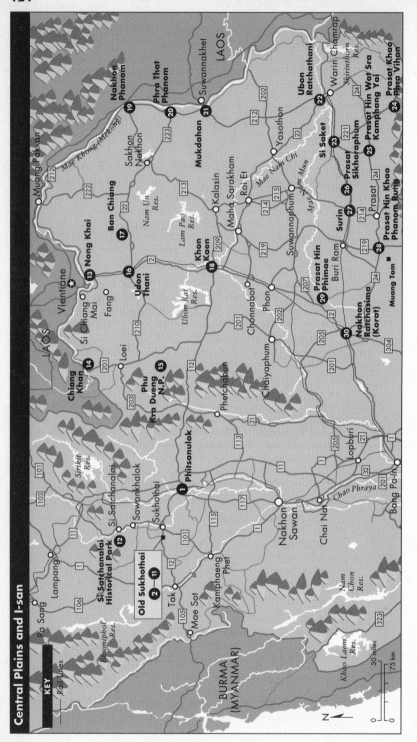

KEY

Rail Lines

LAOS

Muang Pakxan

Nakhon Phanom **19**

Phra That Phanom **20**

Suwannakhet

Mukdahan **21**

Ubon Ratchathani **22**

Warin Chamrap

Si Saket **23**

Prasat Hin Wat Sra Kamphang Yai **24**

Prasat Khao Phra Vihan **24**

Prasat Sikhoraphum **25**

Prasat **26**

Surin **27**

Prasat Hin Khao Phanom Rung **28**

Muang Tam

Prasat Hin Phimae **29**

Nakhon Ratchasima (Korat) **30**

Buri Ram

Roi Et

Yasothon

Kalasin

Maha Sarakham

Khon Kaen **18**

Sakon Nakhon

Nakhon Phanom

Ban Chiang **17**

Nam Un Res.

Lam Pao Res.

Mae Nam Chi

Nam Mun

Mae Nam Mun

Suwannaphum

Phon

Chonnabot

Nong Khai **13**

Si Chiang Mai **13**

Udon Thani **16**

Vientiane

Chiang Mai

Fang

Ubon Rat Res.

Mae Khong (Mekong)

Loei

Chiang Khan **14**

Phu Kra Dueng N.P. **15**

Phetchabun

Chaiyaphum

Lopburi

Bang Pa-In

Chao Phraya

Chai Nat

Nakhon Sawan

Phitsanulok **1**

Sirikit Res.

Lampang

Pa Sang

Si Satchanalai **12**

Si Satchanalai Historical Park

Sawankhalok

Sukhothai

Old Sukhothai **2–11**

Tak

Kamphaeng Phet

Mae Sot

Bhumiphol Res.

BURMA (MYANMAR)

Khao Laem Res.

Nam Chon Res.

50 miles

75 km

N

From Bangkok take the night train or an early morning flight to ⛫ **Nakhon Ratchasima** ㉚, or Korat, where you'll spend two nights, and go by car or bus to **Prasat Hin Phimae** ㉙ to visit the late 11th-century Khmer sanctuary. In the evening, be sure to go to Korat's Night Bazaar. On the next day take a car or bus to **Prasat Hin Khao Phanom Rung** ㉘, a supreme example of 12th-century Khmer architecture. On the third day take either a direct bus or fly via Bangkok to ⛫ **Phitsanulok** ① and spend the night there. On the fourth and fifth days visit ⛫ **Old Sukhothai** ②–⑪ and **Si Satchanalai** ⑫, as above, before flying out.

Take the overnight sleeper train to explore and shop in ⛫ **Nong Khai** ⑬, a gateway to Vientiane and Laos. On the next day travel south to **Udon Thani** ⑯ and its Udon Cultural Center, then go east to **Ban Chiang** ⑰, where archaeological finds suggest a civilization more than 7,000 years old. Continue on to ⛫ **Nakhon Phanom** ⑲, on the banks of the Mae Khong, leaving early on day three for **Phra That Phanom** ⑳, northeast Thailand's most revered shrine. Continue south to ⛫ **Mukdahan** ㉑, on the Mae Khong, for great shopping. Spend the night here or three hours south in ⛫ **Ubon Ratchathani** ㉒, southern I-san's largest city, where you can visit two wats. On the fourth day, travel west from Ubon to **Si Saket** ㉓, turn south to visit **Prasat Hin Wat Sra Kamphang Yai** ㉕, go on to **Prasat Sikhoraphum** ㉖, a five-prang Khmer pagoda built in the 12th century, and end the day at ⛫ **Surin** ㉗, famous for its annual Elephant Roundup in the third week of November. On day five, push on to the restored hilltop sanctuary of **Prasat Hin Khao Phanom Rung** ㉘, a supreme example of 12th century Khmer art. ⛫ **Nakhon Ratchasima** ㉚ (Korat) should be the resting place for your last two nights in the I-san. Take a car or a bus up to **Prasat Hin Phimae** ㉙, a marvelous late 11th-century Khmer sanctuary, and in the evening, go to the Night Bazaar. On day seven take a direct bus from Korat or a plane via Bangkok to ⛫ **Phitsanulok** ①, and spend the night, before putting in a day at ⛫ **Old Sukhothai** ②–⑪ and the day after that at **Si Satchanalai** ⑫, as above, before flying out.

When to Tour the Central Plains and I-san

The dry months between November and March are also the coolest and therefore the best time to visit. After March, this central area of Thailand becomes almost unbearably hot and is only slightly cooled by the rains that fall between June and early October.

CENTRAL PLAINS

The early history of Thailand lies in the plains due north of Bangkok, where the Thai nation was founded at Sukhothai in 1238. After 112 years the seat of government was transferred briefly to Phitsanulok, then south to Ayutthaya. In recent times, Phitsanulok has grown into a major provincial capital, whereas Sukhothai has become a small farming community. Fortunately, the wats and sanctuaries of Old Sukhothai still remain, and their careful restoration displays the classical art of early Thailand.

Phitsanulok

❶ *377 km (234 mi) north of Bangkok.*

For a brief span, Phitsanulok was the kingdom's capital, after the decline of Sukhothai and before the consolidation of the royal court at Ayutthaya in the 14th century. Farther back in history, Phitsanulok was a Khmer outpost called Song Kwae—only an ancient monastery remains.

The new Phitsanulok, which had to relocate 5 km (3 mi) from the old site, is a modern provincial administrative seat with few architectural blessings. Two outstanding attractions, however, merit a visit: Phra Buddha Chinnarat and the Pim Buranaket Folklore Museum. Phitsanulok is also the closest city to Sukhothai with modern amenities and communications, which makes it a good base for exploring the region.

A major street runs from the railway station to the Kwae Noi River. The newer commercial area is along this street and a little farther south, around the TAT office. North of this main street are the market and **Wat Phra Si Ratana** (commonly known as Wat Yai). Take a samlor to Wat Yai from the railway station or your hotel, but pay no more than B20. The temple is close to the river, on the city side of Naresuan Bridge.

Built in 1357, Wat Yai has developed into a large monastery with typical Buddhist statuary and ornamentation. Particularly noteworthy are the viharn's wooden doors, inlaid with mother-of-pearl at the behest of King Boromkot in 1756. Behind the viharn is a 100-ft prang that you can climb, but you cannot see the Buddha relics, which are in a vault.

All this is secondary, however, to what many claim is the world's most beautiful image of the Buddha, **Phra Buddha Chinnarat,** cast during the late Sukhothai period. The statue, in the Mara position, was covered in gold plate by King Eka Thossarot in 1631. According to folklore, the king applied the gold with his own hands. The statue's grace and humility are overpoweringly serene. The black backdrop, decorated with gilded angels and flowers, only increases this impression. It's no wonder that so many copies of the image have been made, the best known of which resides in Bangkok's Marble Temple. The many religious souvenir stands surrounding the bot make it hard to gain a good view of the building itself, but the bot has a fine example of the traditional three-tier roof with low sweeping eaves, designed to diminish the size of the walls, accentuate the nave, and emphasize the image of the Buddha. ▣ *Free.* ⊙ *Daily 8–6.*

From Wat Yai, walk south along the river, where numerous tempting food stalls line the bank, particularly in the evening. On the far side of the bank you'll see many houseboats, which are popular among Thais. Disregarding the Naresuan Bridge, some Thais still paddle across in sampan ferries. Two blocks after the post office and communications building—from which you can make overseas calls—is a small park. Turn left and the railway station is straight ahead.

Phitsanulok also has an unheralded museum that alone justifies a visit to the city. The **Pim Buranaket Folkcraft Museum** (Sergeant-Major Thawee Folk Museum) is a 15-minute walk south of the railway station, on the east side of the tracks. In the early 1980s, Sergeant-Major Khun Thawee traveled to small Thai villages, collecting traditional tools, cooking utensils, animal traps, and crafts that are rapidly disappearing, and crammed them into a traditional Thai house and barn. For a decade nothing was properly documented; visitors stumbled through tiger traps and cooking pots. Then Khun Thawee's daughter graduated from college and came to the rescue: The marvelous artifacts are now systematically laid out, and displays show how the items were used—from the simple wood pipes hunters played to lure their prey to elaborately complex rat guillotines. The daughter or her assistant will explain the ingenuity of the contraptions and the cultural norms embedded in the household implements. ▣ *Donations requested.* ⊙ *Daily 9–5.*

Dining and Lodging

Phitsanulok lacks fine dining establishments, and most travelers eat at their hotels, though the Night Market, along the river by Naresuan Bridge, has food stalls and carts.

$$ 🏨 **Amarin Nakhon.** Only two blocks from the train station, this hotel fulfills all the basic needs. The staff is helpful and the rooms are clean. Each has two queen-size beds, leaving little space for other furniture. The coffee shop stays busy 24 hours a day, serving late-night customers from the hotel's basement disco. U.S. Army personnel use this hotel during visits to the Thai military base on the outskirts of town. ✉ 3/1 Chao Phraya Rd., ☎ 055/258588, 📠 055/258945. 130 rooms. Restaurant, coffee shop, nightclub. AE, DC, MC, V.

$$ 🏨 **Pailyn Hotel.** Phitsanulok sprouted several hotels in the late 1990s and this is the best, if only because it's downtown and within walking distance of most of the city's attractions. Rooms are quite large, with picture windows—choose a higher floor for a view of the Nan River. Furnishings are in pastels and the larger rooms have two queen beds. The large lobby and coffee shop can be a scene of great activity in the morning as tour groups depart, and in the evening the disco attracts locals and tourists. ✉ 36 Baromatrailokart Rd., 65000, ☎ 055/253411; 02/215–7110 Bangkok reservations, 📠 055/258185. 125 rooms. 2 restaurants, nightclub, meeting rooms. AE, DC, MC, V.

$–$$ 🏨 **Rajapruk Hotel.** Of the modest hotels in town, this one is quieter and more refined, with newer furnishings. The owner's wife is American, and many staff members speak a little English. Guest rooms are decorated with wood and warm colors that accentuate the hotel's intimacy. The small restaurant off the lobby is good for light meals; a formal restaurant serves Thai and Chinese food. The hotel's main drawback is its location, away from the town center on the east side of the railroad tracks. ✉ 99/9 Pha-Ong Dum Rd., ☎ 055/258477; 02/251–4612 Bangkok reservations, 📠 055/251395. 110 rooms. Restaurant, coffee shop, pool, beauty salon, nightclub, car rental. AE, DC, MC, V.

Old Sukhothai

❷ 56 km (35 mi) northwest of Phitsanulok, 427 km (265 mi) north of Bangkok.

An hour from Phitsanulok by road, Sukhothai has a unique place in Thailand's history. Until the 13th century, most of Thailand consisted of many small vassal states under the suzerainty of the Khmer Empire based in Angkor Wat. But the Khmers had overextended their resources, allowing the princes of two Thai states to combine forces. In 1238 one of the two princes, Phor Khun Bang Klang Thao, marched on Sukhothai, defeated the Khmer garrison commander in an elephant duel, and captured the city. Installed as the new king of the region, he took the name Sri Indraditya and founded a dynasty that ruled Sukhothai for nearly 150 years. His youngest son became the third king of Sukhothai, Ramkhamhaeng, who ruled from 1279 to 1299 (or possibly until 1316), and through military and diplomatic victories expanded the kingdom to include most of present-day Thailand and the Malay peninsula.

The Sukhothai (Sukhothai means "the dawn of happiness") period was relatively brief—a series of eight kings—but it witnessed lasting accomplishments. The Thais gained their independence, which was maintained despite the empire building of Western powers. King Ramkhamhaeng formulated the Thai alphabet by adapting the Khmer

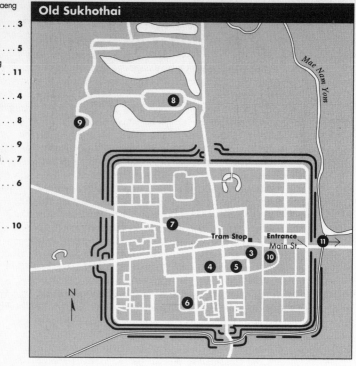

Old Sukhothai

script to suit the Thai tonal language; Theravada Buddhism was established and became the dominant national religion; and, toward the
end of the Sukhothai dynasty, such a distinctive Thai art flourished that
the period is known as Thailand's Golden Age of Art.

By the mid-14th century, Sukhothai's power and influence had waned,
and Ayutthaya, once its vassal state, became the capital of the Thai kingdom. Sukhothai was gradually abandoned to the jungle, and a new town
of Sukhothai developed 10 km (6 mi) away. In 1978, a 10-year restoration project costing more than $10 million created the Sukhothai His-
torical Park. New Sukhothai, where all intercity buses arrive, is a
small, quiet market town where most inhabitants are in bed by 11 PM.
The vast historical park (70 square km/27 square mi) has 193 historic
monuments, of which about 20 can be classified as noteworthy and
six have particular importance.

Frequent songthaew buses from New Sukhothai will drop you on the
main street just outside the park entrance, about 500 yards from the
museum. The best way to tour the park is by bicycle; you can rent one
from a store along the main street.

The restaurant across the street from the museum is your last chance
for refreshment until you reach the food stalls at the center of the Historical Park. It's a good idea to take a bottle of water with you into
the park—cycling in the sun is hot work. The park's main entrance is
at the east end of the main street, and the terminus for the tourist tram
is at this entrance. The admission ticket does not permit reentry. Begin
your tour with the museum.

❸ Most of the significant pieces of Sukhothai art are in Bangkok's National Museum, but the **Ramkhamhaeng National Museum** has enough to demonstrate the gentle beauty of this period. The display of historic artifacts helps visitors form an image of Thailand's first capital city, and a relief map gives an idea of its geographical layout. ▨ *Admission.* ☉ *Wed.–Sun. 9–noon and 1–4.*

For the modern Thai, Sukhothai represents a utopian state in which man is free, land is plentiful, and life is just. The spiritual center of this ❹ utopia is magical **Wat Mahathat.** Sitting amid a tranquil lotus pond, it is the largest and most beautiful monastery in Sukhothai. Enclosed in the compound are some 200 tightly packed chedis, each containing the funeral ashes of a nobleman, and towering above them, a large central chedi, notable for its bulbous, lotus-bud prang. Around the chedi are friezes of 111 Buddhist disciples, hands raised in adoration. Probably built by Sukhothai's first king, Wat Mahathat owes its present form to a 1345 remodeling by King Lö Thai, who erected the lotus-bud chedi to house two important relics—the Hair Relic and the Neck Bone Relic— brought back from Sri Lanka by the monk Sisatta. This Sri Lankan– style chedi became the symbol of Sukhothai and classical Sukhothai style. Copies of it were made in the principal cities of its vassal states, signifying a magic circle emanating from Sukhothai, the spiritual and temporal center of the empire.

Thais imagine Sukhothai's government as a monarchy that served the people, stressing social needs and justice. Slavery was abolished, and people were free to believe in their local religions, Hinduism and Buddhism (often simultaneously), and to pursue their trade without hindrance. In the 19th century, a famous stone inscription of King ❺ Ramkhamhaeng was found among the ruins of the **Royal Palace** across from Wat Mahathat. Sometimes referred to as Thailand's Declaration of Independence, the inscription's best-known quote reads: "This Muang Sukhothai is good. In the water there are fish, in the field there is rice. The ruler does not levy tax on the people who travel along the road together, leading their oxen on the way to trade and riding their horses on the way to sell. Whoever wants to trade in elephants, so trades. Whoever wants to trade in horses, so trades."

❻ Sukhothai's oldest structure may be **Wat Sri Sawai.** The architectural style is Khmer, with three prangs—similar to those found in Lopburi— surrounded by a laterite wall. (Laterite, made from red porous soil that hardens when exposed to air, is the building material used most in Sukhothai.) The many stucco Hindu and Buddhist images and scenes suggest that Sri Sawai was probably first a Hindu temple, later converted to a Buddhist monastery, and that Brahmanism probably played an important role throughout the Sukhothai period.

Another one of Sukhothai's noteworthy attractions is the striking and ❼ peaceful **Wat Sra Sri,** which sits on two connected islands encircled by a lotus-filled lake; the rolling, verdant mountains beyond add to the monastery's serenity. The lake, called Traphong Trakuan Pond, supplied the monks with water and served as a boundary for the sacred area. A Sri Lankan-style chedi dominates six smaller chedis, and a large, stucco, seated Buddha looks down a row of columns, past the chedis, and over the lake to the horizon.

Even more wondrous is the **walking Buddha** by the Sri Lankan-style chedi. The walking Buddha is a Sukhothai innovation and the most ephemeral of Thailand's artistic styles. The depiction of the Buddha is often a reflection of political authority and is modeled after the ruler. Under the Khmers, authority was hierarchical, but the kings of Sukhothai represented the ideals of serenity, happiness, and justice. The walking Buddha is the epitome of Sukhothai's art: Lord Buddha appears to be floating on air, neither rooted on this earth nor placed on a pedestal above the reach of the common people. Later, after Ayutthaya had become the capital, statues of Buddha took on a sternness that characterized the new dynasty.

⑧ Just beyond the northern city walls is **Wat Phra Phai Luang,** second in importance to Wat Mahathat. This former Khmer Hindu shrine was converted into a Buddhist temple. Surrounded by a moat, the sanctuary is encircled by three laterite prangs, similar to those at Wat Sri Sawai—the only one that's intact is decorated with stucco figures. In front of the prangs are the remains of the viharn and a crumbling chedi with a seated Buddha on its pedestal. Facing these structures is the *mondop* (square structure with a stepped pyramid roof, built to house religious relics), once decorated with Buddha images in four different poses. Most of these are now too damaged to be recognizable; only the reclining Buddha still has a definite form.

⑨ The **Wat Si Chum,** southwest of Wat Phra Phai Luang, is worth visiting for its sheer size. Like other sanctuaries, it was originally surrounded by a moat. The main sanctuary is dominated by the Buddha in his Mara position. The huge stucco image is one of the largest in Thailand, measuring 37 ft from knee to knee. Enter the mondop through the passage inside the left inner wall. Keep your eyes on the ceiling: more than 50 engraved slabs illustrate scenes from the *Jataka* (stories about the previous lives of Lord Buddha).

⑩ On the east side of the park, the most notable temple is **Wat Traphang Thong Lang.** The square mondop is the main sanctuary, the outer walls of which boast beautiful stucco figures in niches—some of Sukhothai's finest art. The north side depicts the Buddha returning to preach to his wife; on the west side, he preaches to his father and relatives. Note the figures on the south wall, where the story of the Buddha is accompanied by an angel descending from Tavatisma Heaven.

⑪ Also on the east side of the park beyond the moat is **Wat Chang Lom.** The bell-shape chedi is raised on a square base atop now-damaged elephant buttresses (a few of the elephants have been reconstructed). In front of the chedi are a viharn and solitary pillars; the remains of nine other chedis have been found within this complex.

Dining and Lodging

Old Sukhothai has no smart restaurants, but there are many inexpensive cafés and food stalls. Old Sukhothai also has one hotel, but most visitors stay in New Sukhothai, where there's some evening entertainment and where, across from the long-distance bus stop, there are a number of good Thai food eateries in and around the covered marketplace. For the best coffee in the province, visit the rustic **Dream Coffee Shop** (✉ Singhawat Road), across from the Sawat Phong Hotel.

$$ ✕⌂ **Northern Palace.** The best of New Sukhothai's indifferent lodgings is this small, modern hotel on the Phitsanulok road, close to the town center. Rooms have twin beds and are furnished in light colors and kept clean. The staff speaks a little English, and the bar and dining room serve as an evening gathering spot—often with live music—for locals and foreigners. The dining room offers mostly Chinese and Thai food. ✉ *43 Singhawat Rd., 64000,* ☏ *055/612081,* ℻ *055/612038. 81 rooms. Restaurant, pool, nightclub. MC, V.*

$$ ⌂ **Pailyn Sukhothai Hotel.** This modern building tries to incorporate Thai architecture, but the result is characterless. Nevertheless, it has the most creature comforts of any hotel in the area and most of the better tour groups stay here. It has a shuttle to the historic area. The big negative is that it's off by itself between Old and New Sukhothai, with no place of interest in the vicinity. ✉ *Jarodvithithong, Sukhothai 64210,* ☎ *055/613310; 02/215–5640 Bangkok reservations,* 🖷 *055/613317. 238 rooms. 3 restaurants, pool, massage, sauna, health club. MC, V.*

$–$$ 🏨 **Thai Village House.** This compound of thatched bungalows is usually stuffed with tour groups. Consequently, the staff is impersonal and unhelpful. The hotel's advantage is its location—a five-minute bicycle ride from the Historical Park. Guest rooms (most are air-conditioned) have two queen-size beds and little else except for private bathrooms. The open-air dining room is pleasantly relaxing when tour groups aren't around. ✉ *214 Jarodvithithong Rd., Muang Kao 64000,* ☎ *055/ 611049 or 055/612075,* 🖷 *055/612583. 123 rooms. Restaurant, shops. MC, V.*

$ 🏨 **Anasukho.** Down a narrow soi on the south side of the river in New Sukhothai, this small guest house is run by a friendly Thai couple. The wood floors and beams and the small garden add to the feeling that this could be your home away from home. No food is served, but tea and coffee are always available. ✉ *234/6 Jarodvithithong Rd. and Soi Panison, Sukhothai 64000,* ☎ *055/611315. 3 rooms with shared bath. No credit cards.*

$ 🏨 **River View Hotel.** Steps away from the private bus terminal in the center of the new town, this very basic and rather institutional hotel is currently the best and most convenient budget choice. (Neighboring Chinawat has deteriorated in the last couple of years.) The air-conditioned rooms are clean, and each has a private shower. There is a restaurant, but it's better to eat in the market across the street. ✉ *92 Nikorn Kasem Rd., 64000,* ☎ *055/61156,* 🖷 *055/613373. 32 rooms. Dining room. No credit cards.*

Si Satchanalai Historical Park

⑫ *57 km (35 mi) north of Sukhothai.*

With its expanse of mown lawns, Sukhothai Historical Park is sometimes criticized for being too well groomed—even the ruins are neatly arranged. Si Satchanalai is less so; spread out on 228 acres on the right bank of the Mae Yom River, it remains a quiet place with a more ancient, undisturbed atmosphere. Si Satchanalai may be reached either as part of a tour from Sukhothai—Chinawat Hotel offers a day minibus tour—or by local bus. If you go by bus, get off in Sawankhalok and take a taxi to the historical park, using it to visit the various sites inside. For the more energetic, bicycles may be rented from the shop close to the signpost for Muang Kao Si Satchanalai. Accommodations near the park are only expensive bungalow-type guest houses.

Si Satchanalai, a sister city to Sukhothai, was usually governed by a son of Sukhothai's reigning monarch. Among its many monuments are a few to search out. At the right of the entrance, **Wat Chang Lom,** with its 39 elephant buttresses, shows strong Sri Lankan influences. The main chedi was completed by 1291; as you climb the stairs, you'll find seated images of the Buddha. The second important monument, **Wat Chedi Jet Thaew,** across the road and to the south of Wat Chang Lom, has seven rows of lotus-bud chedis, in a ruinous state, that contain the ashes of members of Si Satchanalai's ruling family. **Wat Nang Phya,** to the southeast of Wat Chedi Jet Thaew, has well-preserved floral reliefs on its balustrade and stucco reliefs on the viharn wall. On your way back out, stop at **Wat Suam Utayan** to see a Si Satchanalai image of Lord Buddha, one of the few still remaining.

I-SAN

The sprawling northeast plateau, known as I-san, is rarely visited by tourists. Comprising one third of Thailand's land area, 17 provinces, and four of the kingdom's most populous cities, the Northeast is also Thailand's poorest region. Life, for the most part, depends on the fickleness of the monsoon rains; work is hard and scarce. For many, migration to Bangkok has been the only option. Most tuk-tuk drivers in Bangkok are from I-san, and the bars of Patpong are filled with its daughters, sending their earnings back home.

The people of the Northeast, burned by the scorching sun and weathered by the hard life, are straightforward and direct, passionate and obstinate. Their food is hot and spicy, their festivals are robust, and their regional language reflects their closeness to Laos. I-san's attractions are: the Khmer ruins, which have been only partially restored; national parks; the Mae Khong river; and the traditional way of life. While there are hotels in every major town, they are mostly characterless, designed for the business traveler. In Si Saket, however, in the heart of the I-san's Khmer ruins, a boutique guest house called Manee's Retreat recently opened, paving the way for a new way to see rural, traditional Thailand.

Travelers in Bangkok who are short on time may want to limit their visit to Nakhon Ratchasima (Korat), only four hours away by train, which can serve as a base for trips to the nearby Khmer ruins at Phimae. Surin and Si Saket, a little farther away, are also good bases from which to visit more Khmer ruins. Our itinerary begins in the far north at Nong Khai on the Mae Khong, then loops west via Loei and the national park, to Udon Thani and Khon Kaen, then back to the Mae Khong at Nakhon Phanom. Next it roughly follows the Mae Khong south along the Laotian border to Ubon Ratchathani before turning west to Si Saket and Surin along the Mun River and the Cambodian border, through an area full of Khmer ruins, and back to Korat.

The new bridge into Laos at Nong Khai has stimulated local trade, and shoppers will find interesting goods there and also at Mukdahan. The handmade lace and tie-dyed mudmee cottons may tempt you, as may such oddities as large washbowls made of aluminum recycled from downed U.S. aircraft. Nong Khai is also a good source for silver. For silk, try Udon Thani and its nearby silk-weaving villages, Khon Kaen, and Si Saket.

Foreigners can cross into Laos at Nong Khai, Nakhon Phanom, and Mukdahan. They require Laotian visas, which can be obtained from the Laotian Embassy in Bangkok, the consulate in Khon Kaen, and (currently) in Nong Khai and at the Friendship Bridge.

Nong Khai

⓭ *615 km (381 mi) northeast of Bangkok, 356 km (221 mi) north of Korat.*

Nong Khai has a delightful frontier-town atmosphere: because Laos has been closed to the world for so long, you feel as if you're at the end of the line. However, times are changing. Laos is opening up, seeking cooperation with Thailand and encouraging tourist travel. Previously the only connection was a scurry of ferries from Tha Sadet, the boat pier, which has a small immigration and customs shed. Now the traffic crosses the Mae Khong on the Friendship Bridge, which opened in 1994, joining Nong Khai and Vientiane, Laos's capital, in a sweeping arc. (If you go across, note that driving in Laos is on the right-hand side.) Non-Thais need Laotian visas. You can get 15-day visas at the Laotian border or, for a slightly higher charge, in Nong Khai (ask at your hotel), but you need to show that you have a return ticket and ample funds to support yourself in Laos. The bridge is about 5 km west of town; a shuttle bus runs to the bridge and Thai passport control from the local bus station. The opening of this bridge has not changed Nong Khai very much, however, as the expected surge in tourism has not occurred.

Fanning out from Tha Sadet, the boat pier, on Rim Khong Road, are market stalls with goods brought in from Laos. On Nong Khai's main street, Meechai Road, old wooden houses—for example, the governor's residence—show French colonial influences from Indochina. **Wat Pho Chai,** the best-known temple, houses a gold image of the Buddha, Luang Pho Phra Sai, that was lost for many centuries in the muddy bottom of the Mae Khong. Its rediscovery, part of the local lore, is told in pictures on the temple's walls. **Village Weaver Handicrafts,** next to the temple, employs 350 families in the production of indigo-dyed mud-mee cotton. You may want to take a B50 tuk-tuk ride 5 km (3 mi) along the Nong Khai–Phon Pisai Road west of town to visit **Wat Khaek** (also called Sala Kaew Koo), something of an oddity created by Luang Pu, a monk who believes that all religions should work together. The temple's gardens are a collection of bizarre statues representing gods, goddesses, demons, and devils from many of the world's faiths, though the emphasis is on Hindu gods.

Lodging

$$ ⊞ **Mekong Royal.** The gleaming white building standing back from the river 2 km (1 mi) out of town was built on the unfulfilled promise that the Friendship Bridge would bring tourists by the busload to Nong Khai. While the furnishings and architecture may not enthrall you, the rooms are spacious, amenities are new, and most of the rooms have great views over the Mae Khong into Laos. Best of all is the large pool, so refreshing in the blistering heat of the I-san. The hotel is part of the Holiday Inn chain. ⊠ *222 Jomanee Beach, 43000,* ☎ *042/420024; 02/272–0087 or 02/272–0089 Bangkok reservations,* ℻ *042/421280; 02/272–0090 in Bangkok. 198 rooms. Restaurant, pool, meeting rooms. AE, DC, MC, V.*

$ ⊞ **Phanthawi.** This is Nong Khai's downtown business hotel. Don't expect more than clean rooms with either air-conditioning or fans. The beds suffice rather than being really comfortable, and the furnishings are sparse. The restaurant, on the open-front ground floor, also serves as a sitting area. The staff speaks limited English, but enough to direct guests to the appropriate bus stations. ⊠ *Haisoke Rd., 43000,* ☎ *042/411568,* ℻ *042/411568. 67 rooms. Restaurant. MC, V.*

En Route   You can take a marvelous scenic trip west along the Mae Khong, on the old dirt road with your own wheels, or on Highway 211 by bus, to **Si Chiang Mai,** 50 km (31 mi) from Nong Khai. This sleepy backwater is famous for producing spring-roll wrappers—you'll see the white translucent rice flour everywhere, spread out on mats to dry. Just out of Si Chiang Mai at road marker 83 you come to **Wat Hin Maak Peng,** a meditation temple run by *mae chee,* Buddhist nuns, and farther on you'll come to **Than Thon waterfall,** a series of rapids in a stream, where Thais picnic and bathe.

Chiang Khan

⑭   *235 km (146 mi) east of Nong Khai, 50 km (31 mi) north of Loei.*

Continuing west from Si Chiang Mai, you'll cross into Loei province and soon come to Chiang Khan, on the banks of the Mae Khong. The village has retained much of its rural charm with old wooden houses along the river. On the eastern edge of town are scores of restaurants with seating areas facing the river and Laos. Downriver, a series of rapids tests the skill of boatmen. From Chiang Khan the road turns south to Loei, the provincial capital, a major stop on bus routes in all directions.

Dining and Lodging

$-$$ ✕🏠 **Chiang Khan Hill Resort.** On two acres atop the bank of the Mae
★ Khong, commanding marvelous views of a series of rapids and the Lao-tian countryside, this resort is worth a trip in its own right. Rooms are in octagonal bungalows, the choicest being the ones with a clear view of the river. The bungalows have a king-size bed, a coffee table and comfortable chairs by the window, and a small but modern bathroom. There's an excellent open-air restaurant where the deep-fried shrimp cakes are crispy and delicious, the *somtan* (a relish) tingles with lime, and the chicken dishes are made from free-range birds. ✉ *Kaeng Khut Khu, 28/2 Mu 4, Chiang Khan,* ☎ *042/821285,* 📠 *042/821414. 40 rooms. Restaurant. MC, V.*

Phu Kra Dueng National Park

⓯ *70 km (42 mi) south of Loei, off the Loei–Khon Kaen highway.*

Loei province's main attraction is Phu Kra Dueng National Park, a lone, steep-sided mountain topped by a 60-square-km (23-square-mi) plateau nearly a mile above sea level. It's wonderfully cool up here, and the profusion of flowers during March and April is brilliant. You reach the plateau by a 9-km (5½-mi) hike through lightly forested fields of daisies, violets, orchids, and rhododendrons, and on top there are well-marked trails to scenic overlooks at the edge of the escarpment. The park is closed during the rainy season (July through October).

Udon Thani

⓰ *564 km (350 mi) northeast of Bangkok, 51 km (32 mi) south of Nong Khai.*

As a major U.S. Air Force base during the Vietnam War, Udon Thani grew in size and importance and, though diminished, the American mil-itary presence remains in a few glitzy bars and in the half Thai–half American young people. A popular hangout for them is the Charoen Hotel on Pho Si Road, where pop singers perform nightly. Tourists come to Udon Thani chiefly as a place to stay while visiting Ban Chiang. The town is known for its *kai yang* (roast chicken), the best of which can be found at the stalls on the corner of Phrajak and Mukkhamontri roads. There is a Western-style shopping center at Jaroensri at the junction of Pho Si and Tahaan roads. At the **Udon Cultural Centre** (✉ Tahaan Road, away from the clock tower) of Udon Teacher's College, an ex-hibit of photographs and artifacts illustrates daily life and regional folk crafts. To buy silk, go to **Ban Na Kha,** a village of silk weavers, about 14 km (8 mi) north on the Nong Khai road.

Ban Chiang

⓱ *60 km (36 mi) east of Udon Thani.*

The chief attraction near Udon Thani is Ban Chiang, where archaeo-logical finds of "fingerwhorl" pottery, skeletons, jewelry, and flint and iron weapons suggest a civilization here more than 7,000 years ago. UNESCO declared it a Heritage Site in 1992. The pottery in particu-lar—red-on-cream with swirling geometric spirals—indicates that this civilization was ahead of its time in cultural development, and even more intriguing is that copper bells and glass beads found here are similar to some found in North and Central America. This poses the question: Did Asians trade with Americans 7,000 years ago, or even migrate halfway around the world? You can reach Ban Chiang from Udon Thani on the local bus, or take a car and driver for about B600. The excavation site is a short walk away at **Wat Pho Si Mai.** The larger of the two **museums** in the center of the village has English explanations. ✉ *Admission.* ⊙ *Wed.–Sun. 9:30–4:30.*

OFF THE BEATEN PATH	One hour by bus northwest of Udon Thani is a 1,200-acre mountain park at **Ban Phue,** where you can rent a motorbike (B40) to get to the top of the mountain, 8 km (5 mi) away. The park is covered with rocks of all sizes, some shaped into Buddhist and Hindu images. **Wat Phra Buddha Baht Bua Bok,** at the top of the hill, is named after the replica of the Buddha's footprint at its base; its 131-ft pagoda is in the style of the revered Wat That Phanom, farther to the east. Take the path to the right of the temple, and within a km (½ mi), you'll reach a **cave** with a series of stick-figure and silhouette paintings thought to be 4,000 years old.

Khon Kaen

⑱ *449 km (278 mi) northeast of Bangkok, 110 km (68 mi) south of Udon Thani.*

South of Udon Thani on the road to Nakhon Ratchasima lies Khon Kaen, whose rapid growth has been assisted by the Thai government in its effort to develop the Northeast. It is now Thailand's third-largest city. Though essentially a businessperson's town, Khon Kaen is also known for its mudmee silk, celebrated each December with a silk fair. At **Chonnabot,** 50 km (30 mi) to the south, you can see the silk being processed, from its cocoon stage through its spinning and dying to its weaving on hand looms. If you don't have time to make the trip, visit **Rin Thai Silk** (✉ 412 Namuang Rd., southeast of the Sofitel, ☎ 043/220705 or 043/221042), an emporium that carries mudmee silks and cottons, both new and old; ready-to-wear items; and local goods, all at reasonable prices.

Lodging

$$–$$$ 🏨 **Sofitel Raja Orchid.** This splendid 25-story hotel dominates the skyline. The soaring lobby is centered by a stylized lotus, the symbol of the I-san, sculpted of glass and copper, silver and gold, and rising like a huge Christmas tree from a marble pool. Carved woods and hand-woven silks add to the luxury, as does the five-bedroom Royal Suite, with its own helipad. You can try Thai, Chinese, Vietnamese, or international cuisine in the sleek restaurants, and in the underground entertainment complex you can drink beer at the Kronen Brauhaus microbrewery, air your lungs at Studio 1 Karaoke, or dance in the dazzling lights at the Wow! Fun House. ✉ *9/9 Prachasumran Rd., 44000,* ☎ *043/322155; 800/221–4542 in U.S.,* FAX *043/322150. 300 rooms. 5 restaurants, 3 bars, pool, health club, dance club, business services, meeting rooms. AE, DC, MC, V.* 🍴

¢–$ 🏨 **Roma Hotel.** An inexpensive place near the bus station, this hotel has a helpful staff, large, sparsely furnished rooms, and bathrooms with hot and cold water. Air-conditioned rooms are better kept up than the fan-cooled ones. ✉ *50/2 Klangmuang Rd., 40000,* ☎ *043/237177,* FAX *043/243458. 46 rooms. Coffee shop. MC, V.*

Nakhon Phanom

⑲ *740 km (459 mi) northeast of Bangkok, 252 km (156 mi) east of Udon Thani.*

Approximately three hours east of Udon Thani by bus is Nakhon Phanom, a sleepy market town on the banks of the Mae Khong and with the best hotel in the area. Foreigners are now allowed to cross the Mae Khong into Laos on one of the regularly scheduled ferries, as long as they have a visa.

Lodging

$$–$$$ 🏨 **Mae Nam Khong Grand View.** The most expensive of Nakhon Phanom's hotels is a modern construction along the river. The concrete structure is not pleasing to the eye, but the carpeted guest rooms are spacious and the tiled bathrooms are modern and clean. The restaurant serves Thai and Western menus, and a live band plays in the nightclub on weekends. ⊠ *527 Sunthon–Wichit Rd.,* ☎ *042/513564,* 𝖥𝖠𝖷 *042/511037. 116 rooms. Restaurant, nightclub. AE, MC, V.*

$–$$ 🏨 **Si Thep Hotel.** This hotel is a good alternative if you don't want to pay luxury prices. The property is about 400 yards from the Mae Khong river, back from a side street off the main road, so all the rooms are quiet. Rooms are standard and the well-used furnishings are slightly depressing, but everything is clean, including the bathrooms. The restaurant has a terrace if you want the evening air instead of air-conditioning. ⊠ *708/11 Si Thep Rd.,* ☎ *042/512395,* 𝖥𝖠𝖷 *042/511346. 87 rooms. Restaurant. MC, V.*

Phra That Phanom

⑳ *50 km (31 mi) south of Nakhon Phanom.*

Take the bus from Nakhon Phanom to Mukdahan to get to Phra That Phanom, northeast Thailand's most revered shrine. No one knows just when Phra That Phanom was built, though archaeologists trace its foundations to the 5th century. The temple has been rebuilt several times—it now stands 171 ft high, with a decorative tip of gold weighing 22 pounds. A small museum to the left of the grounds houses its ancient bells and artifacts. Once a year, droves of devotees arrive to attend the Phra That Phanom Fair during the full moon of the third lunar month, and the village becomes a mini-metropolis, with the stalls of market traders and makeshift shelters for the pilgrims.

Ten kilometers (6 miles) back toward Nakhon Phanom is the small village of **Renu Nakhon,** which has along its main street a row of showrooms and cottage industries similar to those at San Kamphaeng in Chiang Mai. They sell an extensive range of products, including cotton and silk dresses, quilted blankets, and ceramics.

Mukdahan

㉑ *40 km (24 mi) south of Phra That Phanom.*

Mukdahan, Thailand's newest provincial capital, is across the Mae Khong from the Laotian town of Suwannakhet. It buzzes with stalls and shops all along the riverfront, selling goods brought in from Laos—a fascinating array of detailed embroidery; lace; lacquered paintings, trays, and bowls; cheap cotton goods; and a host of souvenir items. When you're not shopping, sample some Thai and Laotian delicacies from one of the numerous riverfront food stalls. Non-Thais with a visa for Laos can cross the Mae Khong.

Lodging

$$ ⊞ **Mukdahan Grand Hotel.** The only Western-style hotel in town is this modern concrete building. Though the staff speaks little English, they are welcoming and helpful. Rooms are plain but adequately furnished with twin- or king-size beds and a table and chairs. The restaurant serves a buffet breakfast, and Thai and Western dishes for lunch and dinner. ⊠ *70 Songnang Sanid Rd., 49000,* ☎ *042/612020,* ⅧX *042/612021. 200 rooms. Restaurant. AE, MC, V.*

Ubon Ratchathani

㉒ *181 km (112 mi) south of Mukdahan, 227 km (141 mi) east of Surin.*

A three-hour bus ride south from Mukdahan takes you to Ubon Ratchathani, southern I-san's largest city. Its best-known tourist attraction is the Candle Procession in late July, when huge beeswax sculptures of Buddhist-inspired mythical figures are paraded through town. At other times, especially after the rainy season, locals make for the food stalls of **Haad Wat Tai Island,** in the middle of the Mun River, connected to the shore by a rope bridge (B1) that sends shivers of apprehension through those who cross. Try the local favorites: *pla chon,* a fish whose name is often translated as "snakehead mullet," or, if your stomach is feeling conservative, the ubiquitous kai yang. Temple enthusiasts should visit both the Indian-style pagoda **Wat Nong Bua,** a copy of one in Bodh Gaya, India, and **Wat Maha Wanaram** (Wat Pa-Yai), which houses a revered Buddha image named Phra Chao Yai Impang, believed to have magical powers. Check out the wax float at the rear of the chedi, used in the Candle Procession.

Lodging

$$ ⊞ **Patumrat Hotel.** Though the nearby Regent Palace is the newest luxury hotel in town, the Patumrat's service and ambience guarantee its position as Ubon's leading hotel. The drawback, as is the Regent's, is its location, a 20-minute walk from the center of town. ⊠ *173 Chayangkun Rd., 34000,* ☎ *045/241501,* ⅧX *045/243792. 137 rooms. Restaurant, coffee shop. AE, DC, MC, V.*

$ ⊞ **Rajthani Hotel.** This modest hotel used by business travelers and tourists is downtown on the main street. The uncarpeted rooms are simply furnished but clean, and bathrooms have hot and cold water. The clerks at the reception desk are friendly but unable to provide much tourist information. ⊠ *297 Khuan Thani Rd., 34000,* ☎ *045/244388,* ⅧX *045/243561. 100 rooms. Restaurant. No credit cards.*

$ ⊞ **Sri Kamol Hotel.** A five-minute walk from the TAT, this clean, modern hotel in the center of town has carpeted rooms with twin- or king-size beds. The furnishings are standard—there's a table with two chairs and a minibar with a small TV on top. The staff is welcoming, and a few of them speak English well. You can often negotiate a discount of 25% on the price of a room. ⊠ *26 Ubonsak Rd., 34000,* ☎ *045/255804,* ⅧX *045/243793. 82 rooms. Restaurant. No credit cards.*

Si Saket

㉓ *40 km (24 mi) west of Ubon Ratchathani, 571 km (357 mi) northeast of Bangkok.*

With the exception of a brand new Buddhist temple, said to be one of the grandest in the Northeast, the town of Si Saket is known more for its pickled garlic, pickled onion, somtam, and, of course, kai yang than its architecture. But in early March, when the colorful lamduan flower blooms, the town comes alive in a riot of yellows and reds, and locals celebrate with the three-day Lamduan Festival. Si Saket can also be used as a base from which to visit Khmer ruins.

$$ ✕🏠 **Manee's Retreat.** In the center of a small village surrounded by
★ paddy fields, Manee has built a stylish wooden house on 9-ft stilts for Westerners who want to see the Thailand that most tourists never get a chance to see. There are only two bedrooms—ideal for two couples traveling together. You can eat Thai or Western food on the balcony, but most visitors eat under the house, often joined by locals who come to check out the foreign guests. Daily activities are arranged by Manee—who speaks fluent English—to fit your interests. Activities include: a trip to the Khmer ruins; a visit to the elephant camp at Surin; and participating in village ceremonies. You can even try your hand at planting rice. Discuss what you want to do before making reservations. Prices vary according to the program but count on about $250 a day for two (that includes everything from food to local transportation). Travel from Bangkok can also be arranged. ⊠ *Ban Nong Wa, Moo 13/29, Kluey Kwang, Huey Tap Tan, Si Saket 33120,* ☎ *01/834–5353. 2 rooms. No credit cards. All-inclusive.*

Prasat Khao Phra Vihan

★ ㉔ *125 km (86 mi) southeast of Si Saket.*

Both Thailand and Cambodia claim that Prasat Khao Phra Vihan is on their soil. The World Court awarded it to Cambodia—but because access from that side requires scaling a cliff, you get to the site from Thailand! The temple is on the outskirts of Guntharalak. Although the 12th-century sandstone laterite ruins are in a state of neglect, enough remains in this commanding location to let your imagination fly back nine centuries to when the Khmer ruled much of southeast Asia. Because brigands and disbanded soldiers caused security problems, the site was closed until 1999. Now you can go by car or by bus from Si Saket down Highway 221 to Guntharalak. You'll need to show your passport to get to the temple. The stiff hike up very steep steps will be rewarded by the summit's sweeping views over Cambodia's jungles. 🏷 *Admission.*

Prasat Hin Wat Sra Kamphang Yai

㉕ *40 km (25 mi) south of Si Saket.*

Prasat Hin Wat Sra Kamphang Yai (Stone Castle), just outside Ban Sa Kamphang, is in better condition than many of the other Khmer sanctuaries in I-san. Thailand's Department of Fine Arts has restored it, re-creating what has been lost or stolen over the last 900 years. Particularly spectacular are the lintels of the middle stupa, which depict the Hindu god Indra riding his elephant Erawan. The main gate, inscribed with Khom letters, is estimated as 10th-century, built during the reign of King Suriyaworamann. The temple behind the prasat is a Thai addition, its walls covered with pictures illustrating Thai proverbs.

Prasat Sikhoraphum

㉖ *85 km (52 mi) west of Si Saket, 40 km (24 mi) east of Surin.*

On the main road west, between Si Saket and Surin, is Prasat Sikhoraphum, a five-prang Khmer pagoda built in the 12th century. The central structure has engraved lintels of Shiva, as well as depictions of Brahma, Vishnu, and Ganesha. Shoppers may want to detour south to **Ban Butom,** 12 km (7½ mi) before Surin, where villagers make straw baskets to be sold in Bangkok. They'll be happy to demonstrate their skill and sell you their wares.

Surin

27 *227 km (141 mi) west of Ubon Ratchathani, 190 km (120 mi) east of Korat.*

Surin is famous for its annual Elephant Roundup in the third week of November. The roundup is essentially an elephant circus, albeit an impressive one, where elephants perform tricks in a large arena and their mahouts reenact scenes of capturing wild elephants. The main show starts at 7:30 AM.

If you want to see elephants at other times, you must travel to **Ban Ta Klang,** a village 60 km (37 mi) north of Surin, off Highway 214. After 36 km (22 mi), at Ban Krapo, take a left and go another 24 km (15 mi) to Ban Ta Klang, home of the Suay people, who migrated from southern Cambodia several centuries ago and whose expertise with elephants is renowned. Until recently, teams of Suay would go into Cambodia to capture wild elephants and bring them back to train them for the logging industry. But civil turmoil in Cambodia and the elephants' vast appetites have led to their replacement by heavy machinery—the animals and their mahouts have become little more than a tourist attraction here and throughout Thailand. Many an elephant and his mahout now travel to Bangkok and even as far as Phuket, where tourists pay B20 to feed the animal a banana or B400 to take an hour's ride.

Recently, TAT and Thai Airways International contributed funds to establish an **Elephant Study Centre** in Ban Ta Klang. A mobile medical unit there provides basic treatment so the animals won't have to go to the elephant hospital in Lampang. There are elephant shows on weekends at the newly built arena. Performances are tentatively scheduled during the winter months for 9:30 AM on Saturday, though times do change, so inquire first (☎ 044/512925 or 044/516053).

On your return south from Ban Ta Klang, 15 km (10 mi) before Surin a small road leads off to the left to **Ban Choke,** a village once famous for its excellent silk. Silver jewelry is now also made there. You can find bargains in bracelets and necklaces with a minimal amount of negotiation.

Lodging

$$ 🏨 **Tharin Hotel.** Surin's newest (and only high-rise) hotel is a 10-minute walk from the center of town. Light flooding in through tall windows reflects off the polished marble in the lobby and reception areas. Rooms are done in light pastels or burnt browns and have wall-to-wall carpeting, TV, telephones, and a table and two chairs. Bathrooms are large. Ask for a corner room and you'll have good city views and lots of light. In the evening, the Darling Cocktail Lounge attracts local swells, and the disco swings on weekends. ⊠ *60 Sirirat Rd., 32000,* ☎ *045/514281,* 🗷 *045/511580. 160 rooms and 35 suites. Restaurant, bar, coffee shop, sauna, nightclub, meeting rooms. AE, MC, V.*

$ 🏨 **Petchkasem Hotel.** Though the Tharin Hotel has smarter creature comforts, the Petchkasem is in the center of town between the bus and railway station. The carpeted guest rooms have air-conditioning, refrigerators, color TV, and not much else. The lobby is a pleasant sitting area, and the staff is helpful. In the evening, hostesses serve drinks in the Bell Cocktail Lounge. ⊠ *104 Jitbamroong Rd., 32000,* ☎ *045/ 511274,* 🗷 *044/511041. 162 rooms. Restaurant, lobby lounge, pool, nightclub, meeting rooms. AE, MC, V.*

¢ 🏨 **Pirom Guest House.** The owners, who speak English well, make this a choice place to stay if you don't mind very basic accommodation. The Piroms will enthusiastically explain the I-san and its traditions to their guests. Mr. Pirom often arranges tours to off-the-beaten-track villages.

There are five small, fan-cooled rooms (no private baths) in the old-fashioned teak house, but you'll spend most of your time in the garden or in the small, homey dining room. The guest house is two blocks west of the market. (The Piroms may move into a newer, larger house, but they will keep the same telephone number.) ✉ *242 Krungsrinai Rd., 32000,* ☎ *044/515140. 6 rooms. Breakfast room. No credit cards.*

Buri Ram

98 km (60 mi) west of Surin, 349 km (220 mi) northeast of Bangkok.

The provincial capital of Buri Ram, less than an hour west of Surin by train or bus, is a rather uninteresting town with little reason for an overnight stay. However, being connected to Bangkok by rail and the Northeast by bus, it is a gateway for those visiting the nearby Khmer prasats.

Prasat Hin Khao Phanom Rung

28 *60 km (34 mi) south of Buri Ram, 65 km (39 mi) southwest of Surin, 90 km (54 mi) east of Korat.*

The restored hilltop sanctuary of Prasat Hin Khao Phanom Rung is 7 km (4½ mi) by bus or taxi from the village of Nang Rung. It is a supreme example of Khmer art, built in the 12th century under King Suriya-woramann II, one of the great Khmer rulers, and restored in the 1980s at a cost of $2 million. It's one of the few Khmer sanctuaries without later Thai Buddhist additions. The approach to the prasat sets your heart thumping—you cross an imposing naga bridge and climb majestic staircases to the top, where you are greeted by the magnificent Reclining Vishnu lintel. This lintel, spirited away in the 1960s, reappeared at the Chicago Art Institute, and after 16 years of protests and negotiations was finally returned to its rightful place in Thailand. Step under the lintel and through the portal into the double-walled sanctuary. Intricate carvings in a style similar to those found in Lopburi cover the interior walls, and in the center of the prasat stands the great throne room dedicated to Lord Shiva.

Prasat Phanom Rung has become very popular with Thais, and in their footsteps have come scores of souvenir and food vendors adjacent to the car park.

Scattered in the area are other Khmer prasats in various stages of ruin, overgrown by vegetation. One of these has been rescued from nature's consumption and prettified by Thailand's Department of Fine Arts. **Prasat Muang Tam** (15 minutes by car south of Phanom Rung; no public bus makes this trip), estimated to be 100 years older than its neighbor, started off as a 10th-century Hindu sanctuary. Its main building symbolically represents the universe, with lesser towers emanating from the center. Today four towers remain, containing Hindu carvings of Shiva and his consort Uma, Varuna on a swan, Krishna with cows, and Indra on the elephant Erawan. The complex is flanked by ceremonial ponds, with five-headed nagas lying alongside.

Prasat Hin Phimae

29 *54 km (34 mi) north of Korat; buses leave for Phimae every 15 mins between 6 AM and 6 PM for the 1¼-hr trip.*

Prasat Hin Phimae, the other great Khmer structure of the Northeast (along with Phanom Rung), was probably built sometime in the late 11th or early 12th century, and though the ruins have been restored, they have not been groomed and manicured. To enter the prasat through the two layers—the external sandstone wall and the gallery—is to step back eight centuries, and by the time you reach the inner sanctuary, you're swept up in the creation and destruction of the Brahman gods engraved on the lintels. Gate towers (*gopuras*) at the four cardinal points guard the entrances, with the main one facing south, toward Angkor. The central white sandstone prang, 60 ft tall, flanked by two smaller buildings, one in laterite, the other in red sandstone, makes an exquisite combination of pink and white against the darker laterite, especially in the light of early morning and late afternoon. The principal prasat is surrounded by four porches, whose external lintels depict Hindu gods and scenes from the *Ramayana*. Inside, the lintels portray the religious art of Mahayana Buddhism.

Though I-san covers a third of Thailand, only recently has it been given any attention for its heritage as part of the Khmer empire. In the 1990s, with the support of Princess Maha Chakri Sirindhorn, the excellent **Phimae National Museum** was founded. Its two floors contain priceless treasures from the early settlers of I-san and from the Dvaravati and Khmer civilizations—notably great works of Khmer sculpture. The museum's masterpiece is a stone statue of King Jayavarman VII of Anghor Thom, found at Phimae. More boundary stones, lintels, and friezes are stacked outside in the garden, and though less interesting to the casual visitor, they are definitely worth a walk past. ⊠ *Tha Songkran Rd.*, ☎ *044/471167*. ⊡ *Admission*. ⊙ *Tues.–Sun. 9–4*.

You may want to drive about 2 km (1⅕ mi) from the ruins to see **Sai Ngam**, the world's largest banyan tree, whose mass of intertwined trunks supports branches that cast a shadow of nearly 15,000 square ft. Some say that it is 3,000 years old. On weekends, the small park nearby has stalls selling *patnee* (noodles) and fried chicken for picnics.

Dining and Lodging

$ ✕ **Tieu Pai.** Phimae ducks are well known for their succulence, and the grilled duck here is worth the trip to Phimae. Other items, such as tom yam kung, supplement the duck dishes. You can sit in the hot shade outside or in the air-conditioning inside. In neither case should you expect ambience. The restaurant is 100 meters beyond the Phimae Museum and across the bridge over the Mun River. ⊠ *Ta Pisu, Ban Lek,* ☎ *044/471983. No credit cards.*

$ ▥ **Phimae Hotel.** Phimae has limited tourist facilities and only very basic hotels, of which the Phimae is about the best, but that isn't saying much. The rooms are clean, but that musty odor of neglected up-country hotels pervades. Only a bottom sheet is provided, along with a blanket, which, with the air-conditioning, you'll need. You may want to request two extra sheets and place the well-used blanket between them. (In these older up-country hotels, management usually supplies extra sheets without cost or question.) ⊠ *305/1–2 Haruthairom Rd., 30100,* ☎ *044/471306,* ℻ *044/471918. 40 rooms. No credit cards.*

Nakhon Ratchasima

③⓪ *54 km (34 mi) southwest of Phimae, 259 km (160 mi) northeast of Bangkok.*

Most tourists use Nakhon Ratchasima (also called Korat) as a base for visiting Phimae and Phanom Rung. With a population of over 300,000, it is I-san's major city and Thailand's second largest, considered the gateway to the Northeast. You will probably not want to spend many daytime hours here, but between 6 and 9 PM head to the **Night Bazaar** in the center of town. A block-long street is taken over by food stands and shopping stalls and is crowded with locals. The huge **local bazaar** for clothes and general merchandise is also fun to walk through. It's on the left-hand side of Chomsuranyart Road; take a right at the end of the Night Bazaar and walk for 200 meters.

A side trip to **Pak Thongchai Silk and Cultural Centre,** 32 km (20 mi) south of Korat, offers a chance to see the complete silk-making process, from the raising of silkworms to the spinning of thread and weaving of fabric. You can also buy silks at some 70 factories in the area. Try the **Srithai Silk** showroom (✉ 333 Subsiri Rd., ☎ 044/441588) in Pak Thongchai. For ceramics, drive out to the village of **Ban Dan Kwian,** 15 km (10 mi) southwest on Route 224. The rust-color clay here has a tough, ductile texture and is used for reproductions of classic Thai designs. **Suwanee Natewong** (✉ 34 Moo 4, Dan Kwian Chok Chai, ☎ 044/375203), on the left as you enter town from Korat, has a wide selection of interesting designs and will ship your purchases if you cannot take them with you.

Korat also serves as a base for trips to **Khao Yai National Park,** southwest of town, which covers 2,168 square km (833 square mi) in four provinces, providing fresh air, hiking, and four golf courses for Thais needing a break from Bangkok.

Lodging

$$–$$$ 🏨 **Royal Princess.** The newest (1994) hotel in town started off well, but cutbacks by the Dusit-Princess hotel group have brought in inferior management; the Sima Thani now has the edge. The expansive lobby gives way to a comfortable lounge. The coffee shop overlooks a small garden and rectangular pool, and the surrounding concrete buildings create a strong glare in the noonday sun. The large rooms are furnished in pastels, and most have two queen-size beds or one king. Bathrooms are functional. The formal restaurant serves the best Cantonese food in town. The hotel's drawback, like that of the Sima Thani, is that it's 3 km (2 mi) from downtown. ✉ 1/37 Surenarai Rd., 30000, ☎ 044/256629, 𝔽𝔸𝕏 044/256601. 186 rooms. Restaurant, coffee shop, pool, 2 tennis courts, health club, business services, meeting rooms. AE, DC, MC, V. ✎

$$–$$$ 🏨 **Sima Thani Hotel.** On the outskirts of Korat (a B40 tuk-tuk ride from the Night Bazaar), this sparkling hotel is well accustomed to tourists and businesspeople. It is designed around a hexagonal atrium lobby. Furnishings in the guest rooms are comfortably unobtrusive. Each room has two queen-size beds, a table and chairs, and a good working desk (but an inadequate reading lamp). Bathrooms come with hair dryers and telephones. The coffee shop–dining room is open 24 hours, the Chinese restaurant is Cantonese, and best of all is the extensive evening buffet outdoors, with musicians and classical I-san dancers every night except Monday. Most of the staff knows some English, and service is extremely professional. ✉ Mittraphap Rd., Tambon Nai Muang, 30000, ☎ 044/243812, 𝔽𝔸𝕏 044/251109. 135 rooms. Restaurant, coffee shop, piano bar, pool, massage, health club, meeting rooms. AE, DC, MC, V.

$$ 🏨 **Rooks Korat.** Even if you're not a golfer, you may well prefer staying at this resort and country club 28 km (17 mi) southwest of Korat. (A songthaew will run you out there for B200.) The cozy, comfortable rooms look out over the par-72 golf course, and the patio with table and chairs is ideal for breakfast or a sundowner. The resort has a good swimming pool, and the terrace alongside it is a pleasant spot for dinner. The restaurant serves adequate food, including excellent crispy fried free-range chicken. Rooks' cost is about half that of the Royal Princess in Korat, and on weekdays, golf greens fees may be included in the room rate. All the prasats around Korat are easily accessible. ✉ Km 22, Korat-Pakthonchai Rd., Ban Laemluak, 30000, ☎ 01/212–0254, 01/212–

2468, or 01/222–1371, ☎ 01/222–1371. 62 rooms. Restaurant, pool, golf course. MC, V.

$ ⊞ **Chansurang.** In the heart of town, minutes away from the Night Bazaar, this was once Korat's main hotel. It then deteriorated, but recent renovations have smartened up the rooms and added modern amenities. The lobby area has been redesigned, and the reception staff gives clients a warm welcome. The restaurant serves Thai dishes, including I-san specialties, and Western food. ✉ 2701/2 Mahadthai Rd., 30000, ☎ 044/257060, ☎ 044/252897. 157 rooms. Restaurant, pool. MC, V.

THE CENTRAL PLAINS AND I-SAN A TO Z

Arriving and Departing

By Airplane

I-SAN

All air traffic to the Northeast radiates from Bangkok, with daily flights on **Thai Airways International** (☎ 02/232–8000 in Bangkok) between the capital and Khon Kaen, Udon Thani, Buri Ram, Nakhon Phanom, Ubon Ratchathani, and Korat.

PHITSANULOK

With three direct flights each day, Thai Airways International connects Phitsanulok with Bangkok (B920) and Chiang Mai (B650). Taxis meet incoming flights.

SUKHOTHAI

The airport, between Sukhothai and Si Satchanalai, is a 35-minute ride from Sukhothai. **Bangkok Airways** (☎ 02/229–3456 in Bangkok) operates a daily direct flight to Sukhothai from Bangkok and Chiang Mai. Alternatively, you can use **Thai Airways International** (☎ 02/232–8000 in Bangkok) into Phitsanulok and take an hour-long bus or taxi ride to Sukhothai.

By Bus

I-SAN

Many of the towns in the Northeast are served by direct air-conditioned and non-air-conditioned buses from Bangkok's **Northern Bus Terminal** (✉ Phaholyothin Rd., ☎ 02/279–4484). Bus fares are slightly lower than train fares. From Phitsanulok, there is daily service to Loei and then on to Khon Kaen and Nong Khai. There are also daily direct buses that connect Chiang Mai and the Northeast's major provincial capitals like Mukdahan and Buri Ram.

From Korat, Thailand is your oyster. There are direct buses to Bangkok (256 km/159 mi), Pattaya (284 km/176 mi), Rayong (345 km/214 mi), Chiang Rai (870 km/539 mi), Chiang Mai (763 km/473 mi), and Phitsanulok (457 km/283 mi).

PHITSANULOK

Buses run frequently to Phitsanulok from Chiang Mai, Bangkok (Northern Terminal), and Sukhothai. Bus service also connects Phitsanulok to eastern Thailand. Long-distance buses arrive and depart from the intercity bus terminal, 2 km (1¼ mi) northeast of town.

SUKHOTHAI

The bus to New Sukhothai from Phitsanulok departs from the intercity bus terminal, makes a stop just before the Naresuan Bridge, and arrives an hour later; you can take a minibus songthaew at the terminal to Old Sukhothai. Buses go directly to New Sukhothai from Chiang Mai's **Arcade Bus Station** (☎ 053/242664); the trip takes five hours and costs B100. The bus trip from Bangkok's **Northern Bus Terminal** (☎ 02/279–4484) takes seven hours and costs B140.

By Train

I-SAN

The Northeastern Line has frequent service from Bangkok to I-san. All trains go via Don Muang airport and Ayutthaya to Kaeng Khoi Junction (the stop after Saraburi), where the line splits. One track goes to Nakhon Ratchasima, continuing east to Buri Ram, Surin, and Si Saket before terminating at Ubon Ratchathani; the other line goes north, stopping at Bua Yai Junction, Khon Kaen, and Udon Thani before arriving at Nong Khai. Both routes have daytime express and local trains and an overnight express train with sleeping cars. The Ubon Ratchathani sleeper leaves Bangkok at 9 PM to arrive at 7:05 AM and departs from Ubon Ratchathani at 7 PM to arrive in Bangkok at 5:20 AM. The Nong Khai sleeper departs from Bangkok at 7 PM to arrive at 7:10 AM and on the return trip leaves Nong Khai at 6:35 PM to be back in Bangkok at 6:10 AM.

PHITSANULOK

Phitsanulok is about halfway between Bangkok and Chiang Mai. On the rapid express it takes approximately six hours from either city. Some trains between Bangkok and Phitsanulok stop at Lopburi and Ayutthaya, enabling you to visit these two historic cities en route. A special express train between Bangkok and Phitsanulok takes just over five hours. Tickets for this service, which cost 50% more than those for regular second-class travel, can be purchased at a separate booth inside the Bangkok or Phitsanulok station; reservations are essential.

Getting Around

I-san

Between cities, there are buses throughout the day, from about 6 AM to 7 PM. Bicycle samlors and songthaews are plentiful in towns. A car with driver can be rented in the major provincial capitals. Reputable self-drive car firms are few and far between—in Nakhon Ratchasima, try **L.A. Trans Services** (☎ 044/267680), which will bring the car to your hotel.

Unless you have your own transportation, the Khmer ruins are best visited by taxi or pick-up, which can be hired for the day (so you can visit more than one site) at railway and bus stations in Buri Ram, Si Saket, and Surin. Always negotiate the price in advance, and bargain hard.

Phitsanulok

Most sights in Phitsanulok are within walking distance, but bicycle samlors are easily available. Bargain hard—most rides are about B20. Taxis are available for longer trips; you'll find a few loitering around the train station.

Sukhothai

Bicycle samlors are ideal for getting around New Sukhothai, but take a taxi (B120) or minibus songthaew (B5) to Old Sukhothai (Muang Kao) and the Historical Park. Minibus songthaews depart from New Sukhothai's bus terminal, 1 km (½ mi) on the other side of Prarong Bridge.

The best means of transportation around the Historical Park is a rented bicycle (B30 for the day). If you don't have much time, you can hire a taxi from New Sukhothai for B300 for a half day. Drivers know all the key sights. Within the park, a tourist tram takes visitors to the major attractions for B20.

Contacts and Resources

Emergencies

NAKHON RATCHASIMA

General Emergencies (☎ 191). **Police** (☎ 044/242010). **Maharat Hospital** (⊠ Chang Phuak Rd., ☎ 044/254990).

NONG KHAI

Police (☎ 042/411020). **Nong Khai Provincial Hospital** (⊠ Meechai Rd., ☎ 042/411504).

PHITSANULOK

Police (☎ 055/240199). **Phitsanuwej Hospital** (⊠ Khun Piren Rd., ☎ 055/252762).

SUKHOTHAI

Police (☎ 055/611199). **Sukhothai Hospital** (☎ 055/611782).

UBON RATCHATHANI

Police (☎ 045/254216). **Rom Gao Hospital** (⊠ Auparat Rd., ☎ 045/254053).

Visitor Information

Contact Tourist Authority of Thailand (TAT) offices for the Tourist Police. **Nakhon Ratchasima TAT** (⊠ 2102–2104 Mittraphap Rd., 30000, ☎ 044/213606). **Phitsanulok TAT** (⊠ 209/7–8 Boromtrailokanat Rd., 65000, ☎ 055/252742), open weekdays 9–4:30. **Ubon Ratchathani TAT** ⊠ 264/1 Khuan Thani Rd., 34000, ☎ 038/377008).

5 THE SOUTHERN BEACH RESORTS

Hidden coves and limpid waters; wide, sweeping bays between headlands; and beaches with untrodden sands or with umbrellas, deck chairs, and Jet Skis. You can choose a luxurious air-conditioned complete resort or sleep under a mosquito net and the stars.

T HE RESORTS OF SOUTHERN THAILAND'S long peninsula between the Andaman Sea and the Gulf of Thailand are pure hedonism. Everything is here for the wanting, from luxury hotels to dirt-cheap bungalows, from water sports to golf, from sleazy bars to elegant dining rooms, from beaches washed by azure waters to verdant hills, from exotic fruit to bountiful seafood and, regrettably, pizza and hamburgers.

Updated by
Nigel Fisher

Pleasures and Pastimes

Beaches

The curving beaches of Phuket, some small and intimate, some large and sweeping, are made for sun-soaked idleness. If Phuket is too commercial, across the water are the bays of Krabi, overhung by limestone cliffs. And others insist that Ko Samui's beaches and its neighboring islands are even better.

Dining

Way down in the south of Thailand, the food can get very spicy; they say the hottest curries come from there. But around the beach resorts seafood is king, lightly sautéed in oil and garlic or spiced up with chilies. Grilled king prawns melt in your mouth. A dish like *her thalee kanom khrok,* which is seafood cooked in coconut milk to which spices, including lemongrass, are added, is delicious. Crabs are a real treat on Phuket. Around Surat Thani the oysters are famous; they are farmed on bamboo poles in river estuaries. Another east coast specialty is salted eggs: coated in a mixture of salt and earth from anthills, they're then rolled in the ashes of rice husks. And in August, try Surat Thani's luscious rambutans. For price categories, *see* Dining *in* Smart Travel Tips A to Z.

Lodging

An attraction of Thailand's beach resorts is the range of accommodations, with hotels and guest houses for every pocket, from the height of luxury to very modest quarters. Phuket is the most developed, Ko Samui comes in second, and Krabi is developing fast. The small island of Ko Phi Phi (*ko* means island), has a score of little bungalow resorts and a couple of midrange resorts. Ko Pha Ngan and Ko Tao, off Ko Samui, have fewer hotels, but plenty of bungalows, and you can be sure there will be more hotels in the near future. Rates fluctuate widely, and in holiday periods they can more than double. For price categories, *see* Lodging *in* Smart Travel Tips A to Z.

Scuba and Snorkeling

The Similan Islands in the Andaman Sea (☞ Makham Bay *and* Guided Tours *in* The Southern Beach Resorts A to Z, *below*) and the Anthong National Park in the Gulf of Thailand, each protected by the government, are superb dive sites where visibility ranges from 60 to 120 ft. Ask at your hotel about taking an overnight dive trip, or investigate a three- to four-day live-aboard cruise. Warning: be sure to wear something to protect your feet when wading among the coral, and be careful when swimming near reefs. Coral gives a nasty abrasion, and an element within it hinders the healing process.

Exploring the Southern Beach Resorts

Along the narrow peninsula that stretches south of Bangkok all the way to the Malaysian border and on to Singapore there are resorts on the west coast facing the Andaman Sea and on the east coast facing the Gulf of Thailand, all reachable from Surat Thani, about 11 hours by train south of Bangkok. Phuket, an island in the Andaman Sea, linked to the mainland by a causeway, was first to be developed, and its expanding popularity has caused tourists to try the beaches of Krabi on the mainland and Ko Phi Phi and other islands in between. Ko Samui, on the Gulf of Thailand, has rapidly grown in recent years to compete with Phuket as an alternative resort area, and it is still less developed.

Great Itineraries

It's unlikely that any traveler, however intrepid, would wander down the peninsula exploring all the towns; southern Thailand is essentially for sun, sea, and sand, and visitors usually settle in at one resort for as many days as they have set aside. For this reason we suggest no itineraries, but simply describe the destinations one by one. Bear in mind that getting to these resorts from Bangkok takes time. By land, count on a good 12 to 14 hours (usually through the night), or by air (including airport transfers), half a day. Should you wish to cover both coasts, there is a six-hour land/boat service between Phuket and Ko Samui, and Bangkok Airways has direct flights.

You can see most of the sights of Phuket in a day, though if you want to swim from every beach you'd need 10 or more. However, you may want to make some day trips. A popular one is to Phang Nga Bay, to see the limestone rocks that tower out of the sea, and the site of the James Bond movie *The Man with the Golden Gun*. Another might be to the Phi Phi Islands for snorkeling. A trip of three days could take you out to the Similan Islands for snorkeling and scuba diving.

A tour of Ko Samui can easily be done in less than a day. For those who are restless lying on beaches, there is a day trip for snorkeling and scuba diving to the Anthong Marine National Park. The adventuresome can take a long-tailed boat to Ko Pha Ngan for a one- or two-night stay and then (again by boat) go on to Ko Tao for another one or two nights. From Ko Tao, take the ferry over to Chumphon on the mainland and pick up the train for Bangkok.

When to Tour the Southern Beach Resorts

The west coast along the Andaman Sea (Phuket and Krabi) has two seasons. During the monsoon season, from May through October, when high seas can make beaches unsafe for swimming, hotel prices are considerably lower. The peak season is the dry period from November through April. Ko Samui and the islands in the Gulf of Thailand have a different weather pattern: the monsoon runs from late October through December (when off-season prices kick in a 40% discount), and peak season runs from January through early July.

PHUKET AND PHUKET BAY RESORTS

Backpackers discovered Phuket in the early 1970s. The word got out about its long, white, sandy beaches and cliff-sheltered coves, its waterfalls, mountains, clear waters, scuba diving, fishing, seafood, and fiery sunsets. Entrepreneurs built massive developments, at first clustering around Patong, then spreading out. Most formerly idyllic deserted bays and secluded havens now have at least one hotel, and hotels are still being built despite a shortage of trained staff and an overburdened infrastructure. Prices have escalated to a point where staying here costs about half as much as in Bangkok. Even the local Director of Tourism admits that Phuket has become overpriced. Charter flights continue to bring tourists from Europe, especially Germany, and during peak season Phuket's 20,000 hotel rooms are jammed to capacity and hotel's add a "peak surcharge" to room rates. Phuket's popularity endures, however, perhaps because it is large enough (so far) to absorb the influx, though more and more visitors are cutting their visits short and moving to less commercial pastures nearby, such as the

Phi Phi Islands or Ao Nang and its 83 offshore islands. Peaceful Phang Nga Bay, north of Phuket, is famous for its karst formations—outcroppings of limestone rising 900 ft straight up from the sea—and offshore caves accessible only by boat.

Phuket is linked to the mainland by a causeway. Its indented coastline and hilly interior make the island seem larger than its 48-km (30-mi) length and 21-km (13-mi) breadth. Before tourism, Phuket was already making fortunes out of tin mining (it is still Thailand's largest tin producer) and rubber plantations. Although the west coast, with its glittering sand beaches, is committed to tourism, other parts of the island still function as normal communities largely untainted by the influx of foreign vacationers. Typically, tourists go directly to their hotels on arrival, spend most of their vacation on the beach, and make only one or two sorties to other parts of Phuket. Renting a car for a couple of days can be a good idea if you want to see the island. Sights and beaches are listed in a counterclockwise itinerary, beginning with Phuket Town, the provincial capital and only real town on the island.

Phuket Town

❶ *862 km (539 mi) south of Bangkok.*

About one-third of the island's population lives in Phuket Town, the provincial capital, but very few tourists stay here. The town is busy, and drab modern concrete buildings have replaced the old Malay colonial-type architecture. Most of the shops and cafés are along Phang-Nga and Rasda roads. By bus, you arrive in Phuket on the eastern end of Phang-Nga Road.

Phuket Town's main street (where many hotel shuttles drop you off) is Rasda Road, and the sidewalk tables in front of the Thavorn Hotel provide a good place to do a little people-watching while sipping a cold beer. Going east from there along Rasda Road, an immediate right puts you on Phuket Road, with the TAT office and Tourist Police on the left. West on Rasda Road after the traffic circle (Bangkok Circle) you come to Ranong Road, with the **local market** on the left, an aromatic riot of vegetables, spices, meats, and sellers and buyers. On the next block of Ranong Road is the **Songthaew Terminal,** where you get the minibus to Patong, Kata, Kamala, Karon, and Surin beaches. Songthaews for Rawai and Nai Harn beaches stop at Bangkok Circle. The **Provincial Town Hall,** diagonally across town from the market, was used as the French Embassy in the movie *The Killing Fields.*

The most relaxing way to see Phuket Town and the island's interior
❷ may be from the top of **Khao Rang** (Rang Hill) northwest of town.

Dining and Lodging

$ ✕ **Natural Restaurant.** It's worth coming into Phuket Town just to dine at this characterful eatery, which has been described as a Swiss Family Robinson tree house, Thai style. Thick vegetation conceals any concrete, signs disappear behind branches, and a waterfall drowns out customer noise. The fare is Thai and good. Though there is an English menu, farangs are rarely seen. A map just southwest of the Central Market will help you find the restaurant. ⊠ *62/5 Soi Phutom, Bangkok Rd.,* ☎ *076/224287. No credit cards. Closed Mon.*

$$$ ⌂ **Metropole.** If you come to Phuket Town on business, you should stay at the best and newest hotel. A sparkling, crisp, marble lobby greets you; there's a spacious lounge bar for cool comfort during the day, and a karaoke bar for fun at night. The very handsome Chinese restaurant, the Fortuna Pavilion, offers a dim-sum lunch. For Western food in a steak-house atmosphere, try the Metropole Café. Guest rooms are

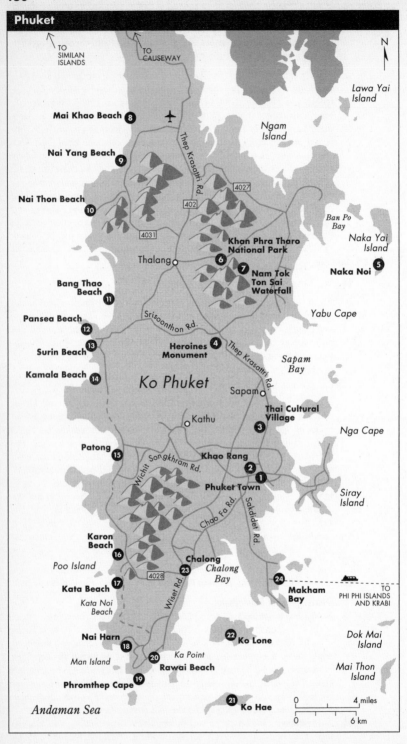

N

TO
SIMILAN
ISLANDS

TO
CAUSEWAY

Lawa Yai Island

Mai Khao Beach 8

Ngam Island

Nai Yang Beach 9

Thep Krasattri Rd.

4027

Nai Thon Beach
10

402

Ban Po Bay

4031

Naka Yai Island

Thalang

Khan Phra Tharo
National Park 6

7 Nam Tok
Ton Sai
Waterfall

Naka Noi 5

Bang Thao
Beach 11

Srisoonthon Rd.

Yabu Cape

Pansea Beach 12

13

Heroines
Monument 4

Thep Krasattri Rd.

Surin Beach

Sapam Bay

Kamala Beach 14

Ko Phuket

Sapam

Nga Cape

Kathu

Thai Cultural
Village 3

Patong 15

Wichit Songkhram Rd.

Khao Rang

2

1

Phuket Town

Chao Fa Rd.

Sakdidet Rd.

Siray Island

Karon
Beach 16

Poo Island

4028

Chalong 23

Chalong Bay

24

TO
PHI PHI ISLANDS
AND KRABI

Kata Beach 17

Wiset Rd.

Kata Noi Beach

Makham
Bay

Dok Mai Island

Nai Harn 18

22 Ko Lone

Man Island

20

Ka Point

Mai Thon Island

Rawai Beach

Phromthep Cape 19

Andaman Sea

21 Ko Hae

0   4 miles

0   6 km

bright, with picture windows and pastel furnishings. ⊠ *1 Soi Surin, Montri Rd., Phuket Town 83000,* ☏ *076/214022,* ꬰ *076/215990. 248 rooms. 2 restaurants, lobby lounge, pool, health club, business services, meeting rooms. AE, DC, MC, V.*

Thai Cultural Village

❸ *5 km (3 mi) north of Phuket Town.*

The Thai Cultural Village has a 500-seat amphitheater, where it presents various aspects of southern Thai culture: classical Thai dance, shadow puppet shows, Thai boxing exhibitions, sword fighting, an "elephants-at-work" show, and more. ⊠ *Thepkasati Rd.,* ☏ *076/214860.* ꬰ *Admission.* ⊘ *Show times: 10:15, 11, 4:45, 5:30.*

Heroines Monument

❹ *12 km (7 mi) north of Phuket Town.*

On the airport highway at a crossroads, you'll notice a statue of two women. In 1785 these sisters rallied the Thais to ward off a siege by the Burmese, who had sacked Ayutthaya four years earlier.

The **National Museum** nearby has exhibits displaying the way of life and history of Phuket, including dioramas of the heroines. ☏ *076/311426.* ꬰ *Admission.* ⊘ *Wed.–Sun. 10–4.*

Naka Noi

❺ *26 km (16 mi) northeast of Phuket Town.*

By taking the road east at the crossroads you'll arrive at Ban Po Bay, where you can take a 20-minute boat ride to Naka Noi, the Pearl Island. After you tour the island and perhaps look in at the Pearl Extracting Show at 11 AM, visit the small **restaurant** (☏ *076/213723*) for refreshments. Lodging is also available.

Khan Phra Tharo National Park

❻ *19 km (12 mi) north of Phuket Town.*

Turning inland from Ban Po on the small, partially unpaved road heading for Thalang, you'll traverse Khan Phra Tharo National Park, the last remaining virgin forest on Phuket.

❼ You may want to stop at **Nam Tok Ton Sai Waterfall,** a few minutes off the road. It's a popular picnic spot all year, but the falls are best during the rainy season.

Mai Khao Beach

❽ *37 km (23 mi) northwest of Phuket Town.*

From Thalang, a few miles northwest of the Heroines Monument intersection, the main road continues north to the airport and the causeway. If you take the airport road west for 5 km (3 mi) to the shore, you'll get to Mai Khao Beach. This is Phuket's northernmost beach and the island's largest, often ignored by Western tourists because at low tide it turns slightly muddy, and its steep drop-off makes it unpopular with swimmers. The absence of farangs attracts Thais, who appreciate its peacefulness. Giant sea turtles like it, too: they come between November and February to lay their eggs.

Nai Yang Beach

❾ *34 km (20 mi) northwest of Phuket Town.*

Nai Yang Beach is really a continuation south of Mai Khao—making a 10-km (6-mi) stretch of sand. It curves like a half-moon, with casuarina trees lining the shore. It is popular with Thais, and it now has a resort, Pearl Village. Another, larger resort is under construction, perhaps spelling an end to the beach's quiet.

Nai Thon Beach

❿ *30 km (18 mi) northwest of Phuket Town.*

Tucked in the center of a headland that separates Nai Yang and Bang Tao Bay is Nai Thon Beach. Its rough waters keep swimmers away, and the village remains a peaceful fishing port.

Bang Thao Beach

⓫ *22 km (14 mi) northwest of Phuket Town.*

South of the headland sheltering Nai Thon, the shore curves in to form Bang Thao Beach, formerly the site of a tin mine. Chemical seepage had left the place an ecological disaster, and it remained an eyesore until about 10 years ago, when a Thai developer bought the land and started a cleanup. He built one hotel, then another, and another, until the whole bay became a resort area with five major hotels and their 2,000 rooms and 27 restaurants. All the hotels—the Banyan Tree, Dusit Laguna, Laguna Beach Club, Sheraton Grande Laguna, and Allamanda—cater to the affluent tourist. A free shuttle service travels between them, guests can use the pool facilities of any hotel in the group, and a cross-dining plan permits guests of one hotel to dine at any other. The Dusit and the Sheraton have the best beaches.

Dining and Lodging

$$$$ ✕▥ **Banyan Tree Phuket.** Of the five resort hotels on Laguna Beach, this is the most exclusive—and expensive. It's built along classical European lines, but with teak floors and Thai fabrics. Many guests come for rejuvenation treatments that include herbal massages, special diets, and exercise. When not being pampered at the spa, you can stay in your private villa—a secluded enclave whose bathroom, with an extra outdoor shower, is as big as the huge bedroom. The king-size bed is enthroned on a raised platform and, lying on it, wrapped in your toga, you look out onto your private garden. At the end of the garden there's a open-sided gazebo where, if the mood takes you, a masseuse will come and perform miracles on your body. Thirty-four of these villas have their own 9-by-3-meter pools (B5,000 extra). Should you tire of the hotel's two restaurants, you can join the hoi polloi at any of the restaurants at the other Laguna Beach hotels and bill your meals to your room. Your only worry will be the mosquitoes, who'll visit your ankles when the sun goes down. ✉ *33 Moo 4 Srisoonthorn Rd., Cherngtalay, Thalang, Phuket 83110,* ☎ *076/324374,* ℻ *076/324356. 98 villas. 2 restaurants, pool, massage, spa, 5 tennis courts, health club, squash. AE, MC, V.* ✎

$$$ ✕▥ **Dusit Laguna.** Facing a mile-long beach and flanked by two lagoons, this hotel is popular with upscale Thais seeking refuge from the more commercial Patong and with foreigners who want to stay in a sedate, quiet resort yet like to be near a more lively hotel (the Sheraton) when the mood strikes. The hotel rooms, with picture windows opening onto private balconies, have pastel decor and spacious bathrooms. There's barbecue dining on the terrace and, after dinner, dancing to the latest beats. European fare is served at the Junkceylon; Thai cuisine, to the tune of traditional Thai music, is served in the Ruen Thai restaurant. Evening entertainment changes nightly and may consist of a song-and-dance troupe of transvestites or classical Thai dance. The cross-dining plan with the other four resorts in the Laguna complex extends your choices of where to eat and be entertained. ⊠ *390 Srisoonthorn Rd., Cherngtalay, Thalang, Phuket 83110,* ☎ *076/324320; 02/236–0450 Bangkok reservations,* FAX *076/324174. 233 rooms and 7 suites. 4 restaurants, pool, putting green, 2 tennis courts, windsurfing, boating, meeting rooms, travel services. AE, DC, MC, V.* 🍃

$$$ ✕🛏 **Sheraton Grande Laguna.** Another Laguna Beach hotel, this one is built around a lagoon. The beach is just across a grassy lawn, and a 323-meter narrow pool meanders through the hotel complex before opening up into two larger, swimmable pools. The large rooms are furnished minimally and decorated with indigenous art. All have small private balconies. Bathrooms have a sunken tub that looks appealing but takes forever to fill, so you tend only to use it for a shower. The service is swift and polite. For more privacy and personal attention, rent one of the 85 one- or two-bedroom "villa suites" in a separate enclave with its own pool, and receive a complimentary breakfast as well as evening cocktails. Guests can dine at a range of restaurants, the best of which is the Marketplace, a group of food stands that present a sampling of Asian foods, from grilled Thai lobster to Mongolian hot pot. There are several other casual restaurants; the more formal Tea House for Chinese seafood; and, for Thai food, the Chao Lay, built on stilts over the lagoon. ⊠ *Bang Thao Bay, 10 Moo 4 Srisoonthorn Rd., Cherngtalay, Thalang, Phuket 83110,* ☎ *076/324101,* FAX *076/324108. 258 rooms and 85 suites. 5 restaurants, 2 pools, 18-hole golf course, 4 tennis courts, windsurfing, boating, nightclub. AE, DC, MC, V.* 🍃

Pansea Beach

★ ⑫ *21 km (12 mi) northwest of Phuket Town.*

South of Bang Thao, in a small bay sheltered by a headland, stretches Pansea Beach, virtually a private enclave for two splendid hotels.

Dining and Lodging

$$$$ ✕🛏 **Amanpuri.** For taste and elegance, there is no finer place in Thailand—nor any quite as expensive. The most basic accommodation costs $370, but a room with a better view costs $850. The completely open main building, with polished floors, modern bamboo furniture, and thatch roof, looks over a serene, black-lined swimming pool surrounded by tall palms. A sweeping staircase leads down to the secluded beach. Guests stay in individual pavilions, staggered up the hillside and reached by an elevated boardwalk whose style is distinctly Thai, with broad eaves and swooping roofs. Each suite has a private sundeck with a gazebo; the furnishings are handcrafted of local woods. A split-level bar perched on the hill has a romantic view of the sunset across the Andaman Sea, and in the beautiful dining room the culinary delights prepared by an enthusiastic French chef (with an Italian touch) will tempt you to return. Try the fresh fish on a bed of vegetables, topped with a sauce sparked by fresh ginger and lemongrass. Thirteen privately owned villas, each with several bedrooms and a pool, are also rented out. ⊠ *Pansea Beach, Cherngtalay, Phuket 83110,* ☎ *076/324333; 02/ 287–0226 Bangkok reservations; 800/447–7462 U.S reservations,* FAX *076/324100. 40 pavilions and 30 villas. 2 restaurants, bar, pool, 2 tennis courts, windsurfing, boating, shops, travel services. AE, V.* 🍃

$$$$ 🛏 **Chedi.** There's a special ambience and superior service here, a resort
★ that is exclusive without being overly formal and stiff. As you enter the lobby, you are greeted by a sweeping view of the Andaman Sea and a hexag-

onal pool, with gardens below that abut the sands of the virtually private beach. Although all the chalets along the hillside face the sea, it is hidden from most of them by swaying palms. One that does have a sea view is No. 106. Each chalet has its own sundeck; the interior is but pleasantly uncluttered and accentuated by shining wood floors and woven palm walls. The bathrooms, a bit skimpy, have only showers and no baths. The Chedi used to be a bargain but the rates have steadily climbed to around $220— still, that is $150 cheaper than the Amanpuri next door. ⊠ *118 Moo 3, Pansea Beach, Cherngtalay, Phuket 83110,* ☎ *076/324017,* ℻ *076/ 324252. 110 rooms. Restaurant, outdoor café, pool, 2 tennis courts, windsurfing, boating, business services, meeting rooms. AE, DC, MC, V.* ✎

Surin Beach

⑬ *20 km (12 mi) northwest of Phuket Town.*

Surin Beach, adjoining Pansea Beach to the south, has a long stretch of golden sand, but it's not good for swimming because of strong currents. On the headland south of Surin you'll find several small, romantic coves. Each requires a climb down a cliff, where, with luck, the tiny beach surrounded by palms and rocks is your personal haven. One particularly peaceful cove is **Laem Sing.**

Kamala Beach

⑭ *18 km (11 mi) west of Phuket Town.*

South of a headland below Surin Beach is Kamala Beach, a small curving strip of sand with coconut palms and a few bungalows, a resort hotel, and a delightful, tiny, open-air restaurant called the White Orchid. Beyond this restaurant a small dirt road leads over a rugged cliff to Patong—passable, but very tricky and not advised even if you are an experienced dirt-track motorcyclist. It's best to drive back to the main road that sweeps its way down the west coast.

Dining

$ ✕ **White Orchid.** At the far end of the Kamala Bay Terrace Resort, be-
★ yond the Kamala Hotel, where the road peters out to a rutted track, is Eed's little restaurant, with six or seven tables under a thatched cover and two more sitting under palm trees at the water's edge. The menu is limited to what Eed buys that day in the market. If she has the tiger prawns, be sure to have those, and start with her spring rolls. Although most of what she and her sister cook is Thai, she does a couple of Western dishes as well. All is clean, and Eed will prepare the food according to your taste. Not only is Eed warm and welcoming, but she speaks English and French, too. ⊠ *Kamala Bay,* ☎ *01/892–9757. No credit cards.*

$ ⌸ **Seaside Inn.** A line of bungalows facing a courtyard constitutes this motel-like inn in the center of Kamala village, just across the road from the beach. The owner is helpful, and the air-conditioned rooms are modern and clean, with tiled floors. The queen-size beds have firm mattresses, the minibar supports the cable TV, and there is a small kitchenette for preparing simple meals. The large bathrooms have hot and cold water, and the accommodation here is a bargain at B1,000—far below the prices generally charged on Phuket. ⊠ *88/6 Moo 3, Rimhad Rd., Kamala Beach, Phuket 83000,* ☎ ℻ *076/270894. 14 rooms. MC, V.*

Nightlife

The newest extravaganza on the island is **Phuket Fantasea** (⊠ 99 Moo 3, Kamala Bay, ☎ 078/271222), a Las Vegas-type show with Thai chorus girls doing modern and classical dance, 30 elephants doing animal tricks, and humans doing magic tricks, all for B1,000. ▱ *Admission.* ☺ *Open daily 5:30–10:30 PM. Showtime 9 PM.*

Patong

⑮ *13 km (8 mi) west of Phuket Town.*

Patong is Phuket's mini Pattaya, complete with German restaurants, massage parlors, hustlers selling trinkets, and places like Tatum's, a combined coffeehouse, disco, and go-go bar. Within a half-mile radius around Soi Bangla there are 150 bars and a number of gay clubs. The 90 lodgings, ranging from deluxe hotels to small cottages—more than 6,000 double rooms in all—attest to Patong's popularity among charter groups. From about 7 PM on, the main street is lined for about 3 km (2 mi) with stalls selling, among other things, junk jewelery, wood carvings, and watches. Restaurants down side streets offer seafood and Western food, and beyond these, one bar crowds out another. Special buses bring hotel guests to Patong for the evening, allowing time for dinner, shopping, and a turn around the café-bars.

Dining and Lodging

$$ ✕ **Baan Rim Pa.** For classical Thai cooking, come to this restaurant on a cliff at the north end of Patong Beach. The large, open terrace is one of the most attractive settings on Phuket, and the food is prettily presented in traditional style. In fact, the head chef started the Thai Cooking School and has constructed set menus to make ordering simpler for non-Thais. Therein lies the warning: if you like hot and spicy fare, you may be disappointed. ⊠ *100/7 Kalim Beach Rd., Patong,* ☎ *076/340789. AE, MC, V.*

$$ ✕ **Chao Lay at Coral Beach Hotel.** Perched on a bluff overlooking the Andaman Sea and the beach, the Chao Lay open-front restaurant is an ideal spot to enjoy fantastic views and Thai cooking. Dishes include tom kha gai, mee krob, spring rolls, and grilled seafood. ⊠ *104 Moo 4, Patong Beach,* ☎ *076/321106. Reservations essential. AE, DC, MC, V.*

$$ ✕ **Mallee's Seafood Village.** This restaurant in the center of Patong offers a wide-ranging international menu. Two Thai dishes worth trying are the charcoal-grilled fish in banana leaves and the steamed fish in a tamarind sauce. If you want Chinese food, try the shark steak in a green-pepper sauce; for European fare, consider the veal sausage with potato salad. On the other hand, you may simply want to sit at one of the sidewalk tables and indulge in pancakes with honey. ⊠ *94/4 Taweewong Rd., Patong,* ☎ *076/321205. AE, DC, MC, V.*

$$ ✕ **Suang Sawan.** Since they cater to vacationing foreigners, restaurants in Phuket are usually not as good (or as cheap) as those in Bangkok or other parts of Thailand. What distinguishes restaurants here is location—as is the case with Suang Sawan. Sitting above the sea, north of Patong, the panorama of coastline below makes this a splendid place to dine on seafood. Try the *pla gaprong nam manao* (sea bass steamed in a spicy lime broth). ⊠ *255 Phrabarama Rd., Patong,* ☎ *076/344175. MC, V.*

$$$ ✕🏨 **Diamond Cliff Hotel.** North of town and away from the crowds, this is one of the smartest and most architecturally pleasing resorts in Patong. The beach across the road has mammoth rocks that create the feeling of several private beaches. The swimming pool is built on a ledge above the main part of the hotel, providing an unobstructed view of the coast. Rooms are spacious, full of light, and decorated in pale colors that accentuate the open feel of the hotel. Dining is taken seriously, with fresh seafood cooked in European or Thai style. Guests can eat indoors or on the restaurant's terrace looking out to sea. ⊠ *61/9 Kalim Beach, Patong, Kathu District, Phuket 83121,* ☎ *076/340501; 02/246–4515 Bangkok reservations,* FAX *076/340507. 140 rooms. Restaurant, bar, lobby lounge, pool, boating, travel services. AE, MC, V.* 🐾

$$ 🏨 **Paradise Resort.** There are many similar moderately priced hotels in Patong. This one on the strip facing the beach has more appeal than

those in the thick of restaurants, shops, and bars. The Paradise has reasonably large rooms and clean bathrooms, a pool, and a coffee shop–dining room for light Thai and Western fare. ✉ *93 Taweewong Rd. (next to the Holiday Inn), Patong, Phuket 83121,* ☎ *076/340172,* FAX *076/295467. 16 rooms. Restaurant, pool, travel services. MC, V.*

$$ ☷ **Phuket Cabana.** This hotel's attraction is its location: in the middle of Patong, facing the beach. Both guests and staff are laid-back, but the basic resort amenities are here, with a good tour desk and a reputable dive shop to arrange outings. Modest rooms are in chalet-type bungalows furnished with rattan tables and chairs. The Charthouse restaurant serves grilled Western food and a decent selection of Thai dishes. ✉ *80 Taweewong Rd., Patong Beach, Phuket 83121,* ☎ *076/340138,* FAX *076/340178. 80 rooms. Restaurant, pool, dive shop, travel services, airport shuttle. AE, MC, V.*

$ ☷ **Bangla Bang.** If you want to be encircled by the bars and restaurants of Patong and want your lodgings cheap, try this hotel, down a small soi and therefore relatively quiet. The air-conditioned rooms are clean, with enough space for a queen-size bed or two twins. Bathrooms have hot water. The owner is chatty and knows the local scene. ✉ *29/2 Bangla Rd., Patong, Phuket 83150,* ☎ *076/344528,* FAX *076/344529. 17 rooms. MC, V.*

Karon Beach

⑯ *20 km (12 mi) southwest of Phuket Town.*

Over the headland south of Patong is beautiful Relax Bay, surrounded by verdant hills and virtually taken over by the huge Le Meridien Hotel. Occasionally, cruise ships anchor offshore, doubling the already large crowd of vacationers. A little way farther south is Karon Beach, divided into two sections: Karon Noi, a small area under development with a rather scruffy beach, and Karon Yai. Because of its good swimming and surfing, the latter part is becoming increasingly popular, and several hotels and a minitown have sprung up, making it just another strip of beach with hotels and some shops one block in from the seafront.

Dining and Lodging

$$ ✕ **On the Rock.** This 100-seat restaurant on three levels, perched on the rocks overlooking Karon Beach, is wonderfully romantic. Three baby reef sharks glide lazily in an aquarium tank, glancing at the diners. Seafood is the specialty: try the *her thalee kanom khrok* (mackerel with fresh tomato and onion) and the *pla goh tod na phrik* (snapper in a pepper and chili sauce) with rice. Those not partial to Thai fare can choose Italian pasta dishes. ✉ *Marina Cottages, south end of Karon Beach,* ☎ *076/381625. AE, MC, V.*

$$$$ ☷ **Le Meridien.** This self-contained resort occupying a small bay is designed to keep you so fully occupied that you never need to bother with the rest of Phuket. The U-shape bay is very pretty, though undercurrents can curtail swimming and the water is often rather murky. Most of the hotel guest rooms, which are furnished in rattan and teak, have lovely sea views. Guests (mostly on packaged holidays from Europe) seem to focus, however, on the two large swimming pools, complete with an island planted with palm trees. The complex, on 48 acres with long passageways and multiple shops, restaurants (buffet meals are the norm), and bars, has the feel of an international vacation camp, but if you're looking for one place to meet all your holiday needs, Le Meridien could be your answer. ✉ *Karon Beach, Box 277, Phuket 83000,* ☎ *076/ 340480,* FAX *076/340479. 470 rooms. 7 restaurants, 3 bars, 2 pools, 4 tennis courts, health club, squash, meeting rooms. AE, DC, MC, V.* ☙

$–$$ ☷ **Marina Cottages.** The 50 small cottages here, straddling the divide
★ between Karon and Kata beaches, all have verandas with views of ei-

ther the ocean or palm trees. Those closer to the beach are more spacious than those up the hill, but all have air-conditioning, tiled floors, balconies, and private bathrooms. The pool, nestled among rock outcroppings, is surrounded by tropical foliage. Though prices have increased, this hotel remains one of the better values on the island. ⊠ *Box 143, Phuket 83000,* ☎ *076/330625,* FAX *076/330516. 104 rooms. 2 restaurants, pool. AE, MC, V.* 🍷

$ 🏨 **Ruan Thep Inn.** Just a stone's throw from the beach is a small collection of air-conditioned bungalows with decent-sized rooms and clean bathrooms. A small restaurant satisfies the appetite, though there are plenty more eateries a short walk north, in the heart of Karon Beach. ⊠ *120/4 Moo 4, Patak Rd., Karon Beach, Phuket 83000,* ☎ *076/330281. 14 rooms. MC, V.*

Kata Beach

⑰ *22 km (13 mi) southwest of Phuket Town.*

Kata Beach is the next beach south of Karon Beach. The sunsets are as marvelous as ever, but the peace and quiet are fading fast. Club Mediterránée has been followed by other large hotels, but there are still stretches of sand with privacy, and the center of town has only a modest number of bars. Nearby, on lovely Kata Noi Beach (*noi* means "little") in the shelter of a forest-clad hill, is the Kata Thani Hotel, popular with tour groups.

Dining and Lodging

$$$ ✕🏨 **Boathouse Inn & Restaurant.** With all 33 rooms looking onto Kata
★ Beach, an excellent Thai restaurant facing the Andaman Sea, and a relaxing beach bar, this small hotel is a very comfortable retreat. The Thai-style architecture adds a traditional touch to the otherwise modern amenities, such as bedside control panels and a Jacuzzi pool. Guest rooms are furnished in reds and browns and have air-conditioning, private safes, and bathrooms with baths and massage showers. Though the restaurant is air-conditioned, it's best to sit on the veranda listening to gentle music from a small band. Try the *kung thot keeow*: fried shrimp paste with green curry, full of herbs and spices, garnished with basil leaves and strips of red chili, and served on thin, crisp pastry shells. The hotel also offers Thai cooking courses. ⊠ *2/2 Patak Rd., Kata Beach, Phuket 83100,* ☎ *076/ 330015; 02/253–8735 Bangkok reservations.,* FAX *076/330561. 36 rooms. Restaurant, bar, beauty salon, travel services. AE, DC, MC, V.* 🍷

$ ✕🏨 **Friendship Bungalows.** A four-minute walk from the beach, two rows of single-story buildings contain modest, sparsely furnished, but spotlessly clean rooms, each with its own bathroom (there is usually hot water). The owners are extremely hospitable and encourage guests to feel at home. The small restaurant-bar on a terrace offers good Thai food; Western food is also available. Your leftovers will probably be enjoyed by the two monkeys on the restaurant's wall, who play there all day. ⊠ *6/5 Patak Rd., Kata Beach, Phuket 83130,* ☎ *076/330499. 23 rooms. Restaurant. No credit cards.*

$$–$$$ 🏨 **Kata Beach Resort.** The fact that this hotel is owned by a Thai family (rather than a conglomerate) is reflected in staff loyalty and their enthusiasm for the hotel, which in turn makes the guest feel truly welcome. All rooms have balconies, but try to get a room that looks out to sea and faces Crab Island. Even if your wedding was a long time ago, the honeymoon rooms are a good choice for view and space. Your one complaint here will be the tantalizing smell of the breakfast buffet wafting through the lobby in the morning. The Nero restaurant is worth a dinner when you need a break from buffet dining. The beach is long and wide, and most water sports are provided free of charge by the hotel. ⊠ *5/2 Moo,*

Patak Rd., Kata Beach, Phuket 83100, ☎ *076/330530,* FAX *076/330128.*
267 rooms. 3 restaurants, pool, health club, water sports. AE, MC, V.☙

$$–$$$ 🏨 **Kata Thani.** Practically all of Kata Noi is taken up by this resort.
All the large guest rooms have balconies facing the beach, though this
means walking down long corridors to reach your room from the
lobby. Between the hotel rooms and the sandy, golden beach are grass
lawns and two large pools, one with a pool bar. There are street restaurants when you tire of the three hotel dining rooms. (The hotel has another self-contained building, the Bhuri, which is back from the beach
and not particularly recommended.) ⊠ *3/24 Patak Rd., Kata Noi, Phuket*
83100, ☎ *076/330124,* FAX *076/330426. 433 rooms. 3 restaurants, 2*
pools, 4 tennis courts, health club, water sports. AE, MC, V.☙

Nai Harn

★ ⑱   *18 km (11 mi) southwest of Phuket Town.*

The road south of Kata cuts inland across the hilly headland to drop
into yet another gloriously beautiful bay, Nai Harn. Protected by Man
Island, this deep bay has been a popular anchorage for international
yachtsmen. On the north side, a huge, white-stucco, stepped building,
the Phuket Yacht Club, rises from the beach in stark contrast to the
verdant hillside. From the Yacht Club's terrace, the view of the sun dropping into the Andaman Sea is superb. The public beach, with a few
stalls for snacks, is good for sunning and swimming.

Dining and Lodging

$$$$ ✕🏨 **Royal Meridien Phuket Yacht Club.** Set in a picturesque, westward-
facing bay, this stepped, modern, luxury hotel (now managed by Meridien) looks like an ambitious condominium complex. Architecture aside,
its comfort, service, amenities, and secluded location make it extremely
pleasant. A 1998 refurbishment has brought this hotel back up to speed
even though it has lost its role as headquarters for the King's Regatta in
December. The guest rooms are large and have separate sitting areas and
private balconies overlooking the beach and the islands (balconies on
upper floors are completely secluded). Make a point of dining in the Chart
Room, an open-sided restaurant that overlooks the bay. Try the baked
fresh fish stuffed with prawns in a tasty mixture of Thai spices. ⊠ *Nai*
Harn Beach, Phuket 83130, ☎ *076/381156; 02/251–4707 Bangkok reser-*
vations; 071/537–2988 in U.K.; 800/526–6566 in U.S., FAX *076/381164.*
100 rooms and 8 suites. 2 restaurants, bar, pool, 2 tennis courts, spa,
health club, windsurfing, boating, travel services. AE, DC, MC, V.☙

Phromthep Cape

⑲   *18 km (11 mi) southwest of Phuket Town.*

From the cliff top at Phromthep Cape, the southern point of Phuket Island, the panorama includes Nai Harn Bay and the island's coastline.
At sunset, the view is supreme. This evening pilgrimage has become so
popular that policemen organize parking, and a row of souvenir stands
lines the parking lot. But once you get away from the congestion you
can enjoy the colors of the setting sun in contemplative solitude.

Rawai Beach

⑳   *16 km (10 mi) southwest of Phuket Town.*

Around the corner from Phromthep, facing south, is Rawai Beach, whose
shallow, muddy beach is not very attractive, but whose shoreline, with
a fishing village set in a coconut grove, has the charm you may have
wanted to find in Phuket.

At the southern end of Rawai Beach lies the small village of **Chao Le,** whose inhabitants are descendants of the original tribes of Phuket. Called Chao Nam (Water People) by the Thais, they tend to shy away from the modern world, preferring to stay among their own. They are superb swimmers, able to fish at 90 ft in free dives. One of the three tribes of the Chao Nam is believed to be descended from the sea gypsies who pirated 17th-century trading ships entering the Burmese-Singapore waters. Of the three Chao Nam villages on Phuket, the one at Rawai Beach is the easiest to visit.

East of Rawai is **Ka Point.** Most of the promontory is owned by the huge Mercure Hotel Phuket Island Resort, a virtual town with several restaurants, two swimming pools, and a minibus to take guests from one facility to another.

Ko Hae

㉑ *8 km (5 mi) offshore from Chao Le.*

Cruise boats leave Rawai and Chalong, farther up the coast, for popular Ko Hae (Coral Island), 30 minutes from shore, which has clear water for snorkeling and superb beaches for sunbathing. There is a café on the island and a resort with 40 bungalows.

Ko Lone

㉒ *6 km (4 mi) north of Ko Hae.*

North of Ko Hae is Ko Lone, another island reached by boat from Rawai or Chalong, with a 30-room resort on its northern shore. Hiring a boat for half a day costs B800.

Chalong

㉓ *11 km (7 mi) south of Phuket Town.*

Chalong Bay is a huge, horseshoe-shape bay, whose entrance is guarded by Ko Lone and whose waters are the temporary resting place for yachts making passage from Europe to Asia. Commercial fishing boats also anchor here, and you can catch a boat to Ko Hae and Ko Lone from the jetty. The town of Chalong has several good, inexpensive, outdoor seafood restaurants—try Kan Eang for delicious crabs and prawns. Boats also make the short run over to Ko Raya, a small, tranquil island where Jet Skis are banned. The island has a couple of spotless beaches, Ao Tok (best for sunsets) and Ao Siam. Should you wish to spend the night, five small resorts can accommodate you at prices ranging from B500 to B1,000. Book through **Pal Travel Services** (☎ 076/340551, ext. 1150).

A bit inland from Chalong Bay you'll find **Wat Chalong,** the largest and most famous of Phuket's 20 Buddhist temples—all built since the 19th century. It enshrines the gilt statues, wrapped in saffron robes, of two revered monks who helped quell an 1876 rebellion.

Dining

$$ ✕ **Jimmy's Lighthouse Bar and Grill.** This pub-restaurant, formerly called Latitude 8, is still a hangout for sailors, though many of the sailing crowd now go next door to the marina, and the crowd that gathers here is partly tourists. The food, both Thai and Western, has improved, and it's good both for lunch and dinner. ⊠ *45/33 Chao Fa Rd., Chalong,* ☎ *076/381709. No credit cards.*

$$ ✕ **Kan Eang.** There are now two Kan Eang restaurants in Chalong.
★ Thais make a point of going to Kan Eang 1; the food is more authentic and spicier than at nearby Number 2, which is next door and in

from the bay. At Number 1, get a table next to the seawall under the coconut palms and order some delicious seafood. Choose spicy dishes carefully, and be sure that your waiter understands whether you want Thai *pet* (spicy hot) or to farang taste. Include the succulent and sweet crabs in your order. ✉ *Chalong,* ☎ *076/381323. AE, MC, V.*

Makham Bay

㉔ *11 km (6 mi) east of Chalong Bay, 9 km (5 mi) south of Phuket Town.*

East of Chalong Bay lies a peninsula with the town of Makham Bay, where you can catch the ferryboat to the Phi Phi Islands and then on to Krabi.

OFF THE BEATEN PATH | **THE SIMILAN ISLANDS** – With some of the world's most interesting marine life, these islands off the west coast of Phuket in the Andaman Sea are renowned for snorkeling and diving. No hotels are permitted, though there are camping facilities. The underwater sights rival those of the Seychelles and the Maldives, and visibility ranges from 60 to 120 ft. You'll dive in water 10 ft deep down to about 120 ft. The most comfortable way to visit the islands is to take a cruise boat with a sleeping cabin from Phuket. You can also travel 80 miles north of Phuket airport to the mainland and up the coast to Tha Talamu in Phang Nga province, from where boats make the 70-minute run out to the islands on day trips. Over the last few years, the mainland coast has blossomed with hotels and dive operators, and it has its own lovely beaches for swimming and sunning. The **Khaolack Laguna Resort** (✉ 27/3 Moo 1, Bang Naisie, Takua Pah, Phang Nga 82100, ☎ 076/420200, FAX 076/420206) has 58 cottages and 32 hotel rooms amid tropical foliage and set back from the sandy cove, as well as a pool and restaurant.

Ko Phi Phi

In Phuket Bay, 90 mins southeast of Phuket Town; 2 hrs southwest of Krabi.

The Phi Phi Islands used to be idyllic retreats, with secret silver-sand coves, unspoiled beaches, and limestone cliffs dropping precipitously into the sea. But their proximity to busy Phuket and the easy 90-minute journey by ferry from Makham Bay have meant that tourists coming to escape Phuket's commercialism simply bring it with them. Ko Phi Phi became in some ways the poor man's Phuket, with very modest bungalow accommodations for the budget traveler, but in the late 1990s the cheap bungalows on the better beaches gave way to more expensive accommodations and backpacker lodgings were pushed to the outskirts of the main shopping street and the bays beyond. The main street, crowded with gift shops, travel agencies, and inferior restaurants, is extremely tacky, but even so it draws tourists in droves, and in high season, Ko Phi Phi is a zoo.

Of the two main islands, only **Phi Phi Don** is inhabited. It's shaped like a butterfly, with two hilly land portions linked by a wide sandbar 2 km (1¼ mi) long. Most accommodations and the main mall with its shops and restaurants are on this sandbar, where boats come into a village called **Ton Sai**. No vehicles are allowed on the island; you can disembark at hotels on the north cape if you wish. In the evening, visitors stroll up and down the walkway along the sandbar, where small restaurants display the catch of the day on ice outside. Later in the evening, bars and discos keep the young from their beds. Away from Ton Sai, where travel is either by serious hiking or by boat, Ko Phi Phi quiets down with some very high-priced resorts, such as the P. P. Palm, in an oasis of greenery fronting a beach.

The most popular way to explore is by either a cruise boat or a long-tail boat that seats up to six people. One of the most exciting trips is to the other main island, **Phi Phi Lae.** The first stop is **Viking Cave,** a vast cavern of limestone pillars covered with what look like prehistoric drawings but are actually only a few centuries old, depicting Portuguese or Dutch cutters. The boat continues on, gliding by cliffs rising vertically out of the sea, for an afternoon in **Maya Bay.** Here the calm, clear waters, sparkling with color from the live coral, are ideal for swimming and snorkeling. You can take a 45-minute trip by long-tail boat to circular **Bamboo Island,** with a superb beach around it. The underwater colors of the fish and the coral are brilliant. The island is uninhabited, but you can spend a night under the stars.

Dining and Lodging

Restaurants on Phi Phi consist of a row of closely packed one-room cafés down the narrow mall. The menus offer mostly fish dishes—you choose your fish from the ice bin outside, and the chef cooks it according to your instructions. Prices are well under B200 for two people, including a couple of Singha beers. The open-air restaurants to the left of the pier cost more, but the food is essentially the same. The two luxury accommodations are off by themselves, 15 minutes by boat or a stiff 45-minute hike from the isthmus.

$$$–$$$$ ✕⌸ **P. P. Palm Beach Travelodge Resort.** This isolated retreat built on a terrace at the north end of the island has standard double rooms, as well as larger deluxe rooms in bungalows with sea views at twice the price. All rooms are air-conditioned and have small refrigerators and color TV. A new management is refurbishing all rooms with the intention of making this the most exclusive resort on Ko Phi Phi. The terraced restaurant, serving Thai and European cuisines, has splendid views of the sea, and the fish is absolutely fresh. ✉ *Cape Laemthong, Phi Phi, 81000,* ☎ *01/229–1052; 076/214654 Phuket reservations,* 𝖥𝖠𝖷 *01/229–1922. 100 rooms. Restaurant, snorkeling, windsurfing, boating, travel services. AE, V.*

$$–$$$ ⌸ **PP Princess.** In the center of the isthmus, this complex of bungalows in a coconut grove looks a little like a modern housing development, but its air-conditioned units with shiny wood floors are spacious and comfortable. The main building houses a restaurant and a huge lobby where guests, sometimes arriving in large groups, are processed before being shunted off to their bungalows. The complex faces Lohdalum Bay, though only a few bungalows have views. ✉ *Lohdalum Bay, Phi Phi, 81000,* ☎ *075/622079,* 𝖥𝖠𝖷 *075/612188. 79 rooms. Restaurant, bar, dive shop. AE, DC, MC, V.*

$$ ⌸ **Cabana Hotel.** Facing the sea amid coconut palms, this property offers smart accommodations in the center of Phi Phi at Ton Sai village, just five minutes from the ferry docks. Rooms are either in the hotel around the swimming pool or in small wood bungalows with a more rustic flavor—the ambience is set by the cane furniture. All rooms have air-conditioning. The outdoor restaurant, like most other restaurants on the island, specializes in fish. ✉ *Ton Sai Beach, Phi Phi, 81000,* ☎ *075/620634,* 𝖥𝖠𝖷 *075/612132. 100 rooms. Restaurant, pool. AE, DC, MC, V.*

$$ ⌸ **Pee Pee Island Village.** This hotel on the north cape offers modest accommodations in small thatched bungalows. It provides the same water sports and tours as its neighbor, P. P. Palm Beach, but the atmosphere here is more laid-back—and the hotel less expensive. The views are less impressive, however, although guests do have panoramas of the sea and palm-clad hills. ✉ *Cape Laemthong, Phi Phi, 81000,* ☎

01/476–7517; 076/215014 in Phuket, ℻ 01/229–2250. 65 rooms. Restaurant, snorkeling, boating, travel services. AE, V.

$ ▦ **Andaman Beach Resort.** About a 15-minute walk east from the pier is Laem Hin and a small beach that escapes most of the human traffic of Ton Sai. The Andaman has a range of comfortable bungalows, each with its own bathroom, on a lawn that reaches down to the sand. ⊠ *Laem Hin Beach, Phi Phi, 81000,* ☎ *01/228-4368,* ℻ *01/228–4368. 33 bungalows. No credit cards.*

Phang Nga Bay

★   *100 km (62 mi) north of Phuket, 93 km (56 mi) northwest of Krabi.*

Phang Nga Bay, made famous by the James Bond movie *The Man with the Golden Gun,* lies at the top of Phuket Bay. There are little islands to explore, as well as offshore caves and startling karst formations rising out of the sea. You really need a full day to see everything and to appreciate the sunsets, which are particularly beautiful on **Ko Mak.**

The best—really the only—way to visit this bay is by boat. A number of agencies on Phuket run half-day trips, or you can hire a boat locally. There are two inlets, just before you reach Phang Nga town, from which long-tail and larger boats depart. Most tour buses go to the western inlet, where costs run B1,300 for two hours (you're unlikely to see the Kao Kien cliff paintings), negotiable to B900. The second inlet, signposted "Ferry," has fewer foreign tourists and better prices—about B800 for three hours. **Mr. Kean** (☎ 076/43061) is a reliable organizer who rides around in his songthaew. Most tourists don't arrive from Phuket until 11 AM, so if you get into the bay before then, it will be more or less yours to explore, with a boatman as your guide. To get an early start, you may want to stay overnight in the area.

There are several key sights. **Ko Panyi** has a Muslim fishing village built on stilts, restaurants charging 300% above a reasonable price, and lots of souvenir shops selling high-priced junk. The beautiful **Ko Phing Kan,** now known as James Bond Island, is well worth a visit. **Ko Tapu** looks like a nail driven into the sea. **Tham Kaeo grotto** is an Asian version of Capri's Blue Grotto. **Kao Kien** has overhanging cliffs with primitive paintings, thought to be 3,500 years old, of elephants, fish, and crabs. **Tham Lot** is a large cave with stalactites that have been carved into an archway large enough for cruise boats to pass through.

Dining and Lodging

$$ ✕▦ **Phang Nga Bay Resort.** This modern hotel's raison d'être is as a base for exploring the bay, and you can hire a boat here to do so. It's on an estuary 1½ km (1 mi) from the coast, and it doesn't have panoramic views, but the rooms are comfortable and modern, the bathrooms are clean and large, and the dining room serves reasonable Chinese, Thai, and European food. ⊠ *20 Thaddan Panyee, Phang Nga 82000,* ☎ *076/440723 or 01/917–4147,* ℻ *076/440726. 88 rooms. Restaurant, coffee shop, pool, 2 tennis courts. AE, MC, V.*

¢   ▦ **Phang Nga Bay National Park.** Before the dock area and the Phang Nga Bay Resort is the Phang Nga National Park, with chalet-style accommodation. There are two units to each chalet, and each unit has two bedrooms. The rooms are spartan and the mattresses very hard. Bathrooms have squat toilets (don't use toilet paper—it clogs the drains), and showers are bowls of cold water poured over your body—all typical aspects of traditional Thai living that are not for everyone. The restaurant alongside a tidal creek has superb, spicy Thai food. ⊠ *80 Mu 1, Phang Nga Bay 82000,* ☎ *076/411136. 6 rooms. Restaurant. No credit cards.*

KRABI

867 km (538 mi) south of Bangkok, 180 km (117 mi) southeast of Phuket, 43 km (27 mi) by boat east of Ko Phi Phi.

Krabi, the provincial capital of the region, lies across Phuket Bay on the mainland. Once a favorite harbor for smugglers bringing alcohol and tobacco from Malaysia, it has become a fishing port and gateway to the province's islands, particularly Ko Lanta and Ko Phi Phi, and the famous beaches at and around Ao Nang. Krabi is a pleasant, low-key town, but most visitors stop here only to do some shopping, cash traveler's checks, arrange onward travel, and catch up on the news at one of the restaurants on Uttarakit Road. With the opening in 1999 of an airport 12 km (7½ mi) from town, however, one can expect Krabi to mushroom in size and increase its tourist infrastructure.

Between Krabi and Ao Nang Beach lies **Susan Hoi** (Shell Cemetery Beach), aptly named for the 75-million-year-old shells that have petrified into bizarrely shaped rock slabs.

Dining and Lodging

$$ ✕ **Isouw.** This floating restaurant just across from the Night Market can be a cool place in which to sit, enjoy lunch, and watch the river traffic. It specializes in grilled fish with sweet-and-sour sauce, and the mee krob here has an abundance of fresh, sweet shrimp. ✉ *Krabi,* ☎ *075/611956. Reservations not accepted. No credit cards.*

$–$$ ⊞ **Thai Hotel.** Though it is primarily for business travelers, this new hotel ranks as Krabi's best. If you've missed your onward connections, the location is convenient—just a block from the pier. Rooms are uniform and have a two-tone blue color scheme. Many have a queen-size as well as a single bed, just in case you bring your mother-in-law. Bathrooms are modern and functional. ✉ *7 Isara Rd., 81000,* ☎ *075/611474,* FAX *075/620564. 151 rooms. Restaurant. MC, V.*

$ ⊞ **Grand Tower Hotel.** Extremely popular with backpackers of all ages, this modern, five-story guest house has large, fan-cooled rooms and clean, modern bathrooms. The café serves basic Western fare, and the tour desk operators are knowledgeable. Many of the long-distance private bus companies stop here. ✉ *73/1 Uttarakit Rd.,* ☎ *075/621456,* FAX *075/611741. 40 rooms with bath. Restaurant, travel services. MC, V.*

Ao Nang

★ *20 km (12 mi) from Krabi Town.*

Ao Nang, less than 20 minutes (a B20 songthaew ride) by road from Krabi, was discovered by backpackers in the early 1990s. Now it's being discovered by land speculators. Already, smart modern hotels have replaced most of the thatched bungalows, and the rutted roads are paved. Further growth can be expected with the opening of the Krabi airport. But even with the development, the beaches here are some of Thailand's most attractive, and the fascinating 83 offshore islands and limestone karsts will always remain. Days are spent on the beach or exploring the islands by boat. The snorkeling and scuba diving are good, particularly around Turtle Island and Chicken Island. Long-tail boats for hire line the beaches for trips to other islands or to other beaches along the coast.

Around a headland farther on from Ao Nang Bay is **Haad Noppharat Thara,** a beach (and part of a National Park) less populated than Ao Nang that's famous for its rows of casuarina trees. You can walk out to the little rocky island at low tide, but don't linger there too long. When the tide comes in, so does a current. For total seclusion, hire a long-tail boat to take you (15 minutes) to the offshore islands. You can also take a boat back toward Krabi to the beaches of **Nam Mao and Railay** (the shuttle boat between Ao Nang and Railay costs B30). You can stay at Railay, in the luxury Rayavadee Resort or in a backpacker-type bungalow, and have a meal at one of the restaurants.

Dining and Lodging

$$$$ ✕🏨 **Rayavadee Premier Resort.** A true retreat laid out on 26 landscaped
★   acres, this resort is on the mainland but is accessible only by boat (20 minutes from Krabi town or 10 minutes from Ao Nang Bay). Its gardens and coconut groves lead down to white-sand beaches on three sides. Such privacy comes dearly: prices start at $330. Circular Thai-style pavilions have spacious living rooms downstairs and curving staircases to the magnificent bedrooms and sumptuous bathrooms with huge, round tubs. The use of highly polished wood and tile floors adds to the cool luxury. Because nearly all the pavilions are between the two beaches that flank the headland, you are never more than a five-minute walk from a beach. Krua Pranang, the Thai restaurant in a breezy pavilion, serves food as exciting as it is delicious. For an appetizer, try the *mieng kana* (Chinese broccoli leaves filled with lime, chili, shallots, and ginger) or the fried sweetened beef and papaya salad served with steamed rice. For entrées, the steamed fish with pickled plum and the tom kha gai are two tasty choices. If you plan to arrive at the hotel directly from Bangkok, you will need to fly into Phuket by 3:30 PM, have a hotel car take you the two hours to a ferry landing, and then take a 10-minute boat ride to the resort. ✉ *67 Mu 5, Susan Hoy Rd., Tambol Sai Thai, Krabi 81000,* ☎ *075/620740,* ☎ *075/620630. 98 pavilions. 2 restaurants, bar, snack bar, in-room safes, in-room VCRs, pool. AE, DC, MC, V.* ☙

$$–$$$ ✕🏨 **Krabi Resort.** What was once a small collection of thatched cottages on Ao Nang has mushroomed into a large resort. Rows of attractive wood bungalows are staggered back from the beach. (The first two rows closest to the beach cost 15% more, at B3,000.) Furnishings are wood and wicker. A concrete two-story building at the back of the property offers 40 standard hotel rooms for the same price as the bungalows in the last two rows. There is also a pool in the garden. The restaurant, popular with guests from other hotels, is alongside the beach adjoining several other dining establishments, all of which specialize in local seafood. ✉ *55–57 Pattana Rd., Amphoe Muang, Krabi 81000,* ☎ *075/ 637030; 02/208–9165 Bangkok reservations,* ☎ *075/637051. 103 rooms. Restaurant, pool, boating, nightclub. DC, MC, V.*

$ ✕🏨 **Emerald Bungalows.** On the quiet, sandy beach of Haad Noppharat, just north of Ao Nang, this hotel offers an array of bungalows with private baths. Those facing the beach are the best and most expensive (B1,200). The restaurant serves seafood and Thai dishes and is the place for socializing and reading. ✉ *Haad Noppharat Beach, Moo 4, Tambol Ao Nang (2/1 Kongca Rd., Krabi 81000),* ☎ *075/611106. 36 rooms. Restaurant. No credit cards.*

$$–$$$ 🏨 **Ao Nang Villa.** At the other end of the beach from the Krabi Resort, where bungalows used to be, stands a three-story hotel facing the beach, which curves around a good-sized swimming pool and gardens. All rooms have balconies facing the pool. The restaurant pavilion, in gardens of its own next door, serves dinner both under its roof and on the surrounding lawn. A few good twin-bed bungalows still remain, kept only for those in the know. These are fan-cooled and smallish, but with private bathrooms (cold water only) and full access to all the hotel's amenities; they can, with some negotiation, be a great bargain. ✉ *113 Ao Nang Beach, Krabi 81000,* ☎ *075/637270,* ☎ *075/637274. 62 rooms. Restaurant, pool, tennis court. MC, V.*

$$ 🏨 **Ban Ao Nang Resort.** The rooms at this three-story hotel are quite large and have decent bathrooms. All but a few are air-conditioned; the others come with a fan and are about B500 cheaper. The nicest rooms overlook the swimming pool. Those at the back have views of tropical undergrowth and are only to be taken as a last resort. The staff is friendly and helpful. The beach and the main street of Ao Nang are 100 meters down a slight hill. Meals are served buffet-style. ✉ *31/3 Moo 2, Ao Nang, Krabi 81000,* ☏ *075/637072,* 🖷 *075/637070. 108 rooms. Restaurant, pool. MC, V.*

$$ ⊞ **Phra Nang Inn.** Krabi's prices have doubled in the last two years, and this hotel is no exception, but it does have rustic charm and a good location across the road from the beach. Rooms are furnished in soft colors, some with four-poster and some with two queen-size beds. The staff is extremely accommodating; hopefully their attitude won't change with the new management. The dining room serves Thai and international fare. ✉ *119 Mu 2, Ao Nang, Krabi 91000,* ☏ *075/637130,* 🖷 *075/637134. 83 rooms. Restaurant. AE, DC, MC, V.* ✍

¢–$ ⊞ **Railay Bay Bungalows.** This is one of a couple of modest resorts facing the same pretty beach as the Dusit Rayavadee. (Cocos, the cheapest, with tiny units and shared baths, gets an active, friendly, backpacking clientele.) The Railay Bay's bungalows start at B400 for a small fan-cooled unit that's back from the beach and go up to B700 for a larger unit closer to the water. There is even one air-conditioned bungalow at B1,600. The two tightly packed rows of bungalows are perpendicular to the beach, extending inland from the beachfront restaurant, which serves inexpensive seafood, Thai dishes, and European breakfasts. ✉ *Railay Beach, Ao Nang, Krabi 81000,* ☏ *01/228–4112,* 🖷 *01/228–4516. 30 rooms. Restaurant. No credit cards.*

¢ ⊞ **Inter House.** On the small street that runs parallel to the beach road are a number of guest houses. Inter House is noteworthy for its friendly owner, Mrs. Chotika Boonrungsri, and the clean, fan-cooled rooms that are large enough for two queen-size beds (B500). It has no restaurant, but there is a local Thai eatery next door. ✉ *245/11 Moo 2, Ao Nang Arcade, Ao Nang, Krabi 81000,* ☏ *075/637508 or 01/968–9846. 5 rooms. No credit cards.*

¢ ⊞ **Jinda Guest House.** Cheap bungalows are hard to find in Ao Nang, but there are four guest houses in a row up the main street, 200 yards from the beach. There isn't much difference between them; they all charge B200 for a fan-cooled room and shared bathroom. You may want to try the Jinda first, since breakfasts are quite reasonable and the owner speaks a little English. ✉ *Moo 2, Ao Nang, Krabi 81000,* ☏ *01/607–8556. 9 rooms with shared bath. No credit cards.*

KO SAMUI AND NEARBY ISLANDS

In the southern Gulf of Thailand lies Ko Samui, the world's coconut capital, discovered by backpackers several years ago and now regarded as an alternative to Phuket. Already too commercial for some people, it still has far fewer hotels, restaurants, and bars than Phuket, and it is a haven of tranquillity compared with seedy Pattaya. The island's best food, both Thai and Western, is found at the major hotels; the greatest number of local restaurants are in Chaweng, but little distinguishes one from another. Just look to make sure that the seafood is fresh. Lamai Beach has a noisy and more developed nightlife. The quieter beaches, such as Bophut, are on the island's north shore. The TAT has a list of guest houses on the islands, and most travel agencies can make reservations at some of them and at the hotels.

Ko Samui is half the size of Phuket, and could be easily toured in a day. But tourists come for the sun and beach, not for sightseeing, and they usually stay put. We cover the island clockwise. The best beaches, with glistening white sand and clear waters, are on the east coast; the others have either muddy sand or rocky coves. The waters around Ko Samui are already less clear than they were years ago, but the sea surrounding the smaller islands nearby is still crystal clear. Ko Pha Ngan, north of Ko Samui, though in the process of being discovered by tourists and land developers, is still one of the world's most idyllic places. Ko Tao, north of Ko Pha Ngan, is now a haven for backpackers and has fantastic snorkeling. The tiny islets of the Angthong Marine National Park, east of Ko Samui, are also superb for snorkeling and scuba diving.

New Port

❶ *500 km (310 mi) south of Bangkok, 20 km (12 mi) by boat east of Don Sak, which is 27 km (18 mi) from Surat Thani.*

The car ferry from Don Sak on the mainland arrives at New Port, south of the main town, Na Thon. Unless a hotel van is waiting for you, take a songthaew first to Na Thon, and then another to reach your final destination.

Na Thon

❷ *30 km (18½ mi) by boat east of Surat Thani, 6½ km (4 mi) north of New Port.*

Compared with the other sleepy island villages, Na Thon is a bustling town. The passenger ferry from Surat Thani docks here; shops, travel agencies, and restaurants line the waterfront, and local businesses and banks are on the parallel street one block back. Though Na Thon has a hotel, tourists seldom stay in town.

Maenam

❸ *10 km (6 mi) northeast of Na Thon.*

On the north coast east of Na Thon, the first major tourist area is Maenam. Its long, curving, sandy beach is shaded by trees and lapped by gentle waters that are great for swimming. Inexpensive guest houses and the luxury Santiburi resort share the 5-km (3-mi) stretch of sand.

Lodging

$$$$ 🏠 **Santiburi.** Set in 23 acres of gardens paralleling the beach is an ex-
★ clusive hideaway. The standard suites are private bungalows with highly polished wood floors, even in the huge bathrooms, which have two black washbasins, black oval bathtubs, and separate black-tile shower stalls— a typical case of modern Thai opulence. The contemporary Thai furnishings give an open feel that's enhanced by a glass panel between the living room and bedroom. Sliding doors to the patio add to the openness at the expense of privacy. Each bungalow has its own TV, VCR, and CD player, with free CDs and videotapes. The main building, a modern Thai pavilion overlooking the oval swimming pool, has European and Thai restaurants—the Sala Thai has superb dishes. Guests also amble up to the beach bar for informal meals. From this secluded resort oasis you can walk to the main road and take a songthaew to any part of the island. ✉ 12/12 Moo 1, Tambol Maenam, Ko Samui 84330, ☎ 077/425031; 02/238–4790 Bangkok reservations; 800/223–5652 in U.S., FAX 077/425040. 75 suites. 2 restaurants, snack bar, pool, 2 tennis courts, health club, squash, boating. AE, DC, MC, V. 🐾

Bophut

❹ *11 km (7 mi) east of Na Thon.*

A small headland separates Maenam from the next bay, Bophut. The beach is quite narrow but wide enough for sunbathing and jogging. During rainy season the runoff waters make the sea slightly muddy,

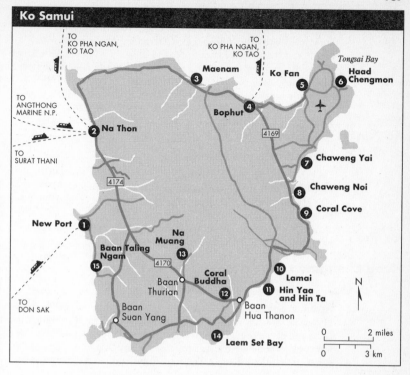

Ko Samui

TO
KO PHA NGAN,
KO TAO

TO
KO PHA NGAN,
KO TAO

Tongsai Bay

Maenam

3

Ko Fan

5

6 **Haad Chengmon**

TO
ANGTHONG
MARINE N.P.

Bophut

4

2 **Na Thon**

4169

TO
SURAT THANI

7 **Chaweng Yai**

4174

8 **Chaweng Noi**

9 **Coral Cove**

New Port

1

Na Muang

Baan Taling Ngam

13

4170

15

Coral Buddha

10 **Lamai**

Baan Thurian

12

11 **Hin Yaa and Hin Ta**

Baan Hua Thanon

Baan Suan Yang

N

TO
DON SAK

14 **Laem Set Bay**

0   2 miles

0   3 km

but otherwise this village community is a low-key resort in contrast to
the burlesque of Chaweng beach. Prices here are also less than in
Chaweng or Lamai. Hotels and guest houses range from backpacker
hangouts to fancier places, and a line of pleasant restaurants faces the
seafront. Bophut also serves as the point from which high-speed boats
go to Ko Tao every morning at about 8:30.

Dining and Lodging

$–$$ ✕ **La Sirene.** For a touch of French cooking—the owner is from Nice—
try this small bistro on the waterfront. A four-course menu beginning
with some homemade pâté followed by medallions of beef or pork in
a mustard sauce, salad, and then dessert runs about B220. À la carte
dishes, including Thai ones, are also offered. A few tables are inside,
but the delight is to sit on the deck overlooking the boats moored a few
yards offshore. ⊠ *65/1 Bophut Beach,* ☎ *077/425301. No credit cards.*

$ ✕ **Happy Elephant.** Owner Khun Sasothon displays the day's seafood
specialty on ice in front of his Thai restaurant. Choose the fish and
specify how you'd like it done, have a drink at the bar, and then, when
dinner is ready, sit outside on the deck above the beach and dine under
the stars, watching the twinkling lights of Ko Pha Ngan across the sea.
Other dishes are also served—the *tom yam pla nam sai* (clear spicy soup
with fish) is strongly recommended. ⊠ *79/1 Moo 1, Bophut Beach,*
☎ *077/245347. No credit cards.*

$ 🏨 **The Lodge.** Looking a bit like an English roadside inn, this small,
two-story, vine-clad hotel has clean, modern rooms, all facing the sea.
The spacious air-conditioned rooms (B1,000) have minimal but adequate furnishings and wood floors, with ceiling fans and lockboxes.
Bathrooms have both showers and tubs, with hot and cold water. The
TV has CNN, and best of all, each room has a balcony. ⊠ *91/1 Moo
1, Bophut Beach, Ko Samui 84140,* ☎ *077/425337,* FAX *077/425336.
10 rooms. Restaurant, bar. No credit cards.*

$ 🏨 **Peace Bungalows.** Just to the west of the main street of Bophut, the Pupaiboon family has a collection of bungalows. The smaller ones are fan-cooled; the larger ones are air-conditioned and popular with Thai families. All are well-maintained and clean. The large grass lawn shaded by coconut palms leads down to the beach. It has one of the better hotel restaurants on the island, serving zesty Thai food as well as international dishes. ⊠ *Bophut Beach, Ko Samui 84320,* ☎ *077/ 425357,* 🖷 *077/425343. 36 rooms. Restaurant. MC, V.*

Ko Fan

❺   *18 km (11 mi) east of Na Thon.*

On the north shore of Ko Samui near the northeast tip is Ko Fan, a little island with a huge sitting **Buddha image** covered in moss. Try to visit at sunset, when the light off the water shows the statue at its best. Back across the causeway, on the beach facing the seated Buddha, there are a number of guest houses and bungalows frequented by backpackers who find Bophut too noisy and expensive.

Haad Chengmon

❻   *20 km (12½ mi) east of Na Thon.*

Continue east along the north coast to Haad Chengmon (*haad* means "beach"), which is dominated by the headland Laem Rumrong. This is the end of the road for the few songthaews that take this route, and few tourists come here. The several guest houses and one upscale resort scattered along the shoreline don't disturb the peace and tranquillity.

Dining and Lodging

$$$$ ✕🏨 **Tongsai Bay Hotel.** The Tongsai Bay is an elegant resort retreat whose service is not as good as it should be for the price. Set on 25 acres stepped up from the bay, it has whitewashed, red-tile hillside cottages with balconies looking out to sea (when the view is not blocked by foliage), and 24 rooms in the three-story main building. The cottage rooms are stylishly furnished, and some of the split-level rooms incorporate the natural rock wall, although they are too closely clustered together. The dining room has beautiful views; reserve a table on the terrace. Ko Samui is known for huge succulent oysters and king prawns, and Tongsai gets the best. The duck in tamarind sauce is also excellent. A shuttle will take you to Na Thon and Chaweng. ⊠ *Tongsai Bay, Ko Samui 84140,* ☎ *077/421451; 02/254–0023 Bangkok reservations,* 🖷 *077/421462; 02/253–3190 Bangkok reservations. 80 rooms. Restaurant, bar, pool, 2 tennis courts, windsurfing, boating. AE, DC, MC, V.*

$$$ 🏨 **Boat House Hotel.** This imaginative property across the bay from Tongsai comprises 34 rice barges converted into duplex suites. The whalelike boats in tightly packed rows 100 yards in from the shore look like a Jonah's nightmare, but onboard, they're superb. Each has an enclosed upper deck with a lounge and wet bar and, below, a sitting area, bedroom, and large bathroom with a grand oval tub. The hulls are original; the uncluttered interiors and upper decks are new, with highly polished teak and mahogany beams and paneling. The double beds are just a foot off the floor, while high above are suspended fishing nets. Another 176 rooms were built in two wings between the barges and the road. They're less expensive (B3,200 versus B5,400 for a barge suite) but have no sea view. Coral reefs are exposed at low tide, but the swimming is safe and in sheltered waters. The hotel is a little off the beaten track. ⊠ *Chengmon Beach, Ko Samui, Surat Thani 84140,* ☎ *077/421451; 02/254–0023 Bangkok reservations,* 🖷 *077/421462. 34 boat suites, 176 rooms. 2 restaurants, pool, 4 tennis courts, windsurfing, boating, travel services. AE, DC, MC, V.*

Chaweng

20 km (12½ mi) east of Na Thon.

If you have your own transportation—and don't mind bumping over rutted, unpaved surfaces—the road continues around the peninsula for 6 km (3¾ mi) to Chaweng Beach (also served by songthaew from Bophut). Of the 11 beach areas of Ko Samui, Chaweng has the finest glistening white sand. It is also the most congested, crammed with guest houses, hotels, shops, restaurants, and tourists. All this commercial activity enlivens both sides of the one unpaved road, a block in from the beach. It could be seen as a miniature version of Patong Beach on Phuket, but in contrast to the tacky, neon-lit commercialism there, the chaotic mishmash of buildings and shacks on Chaweng's strip is more fun and more Thai.

❼ **Chaweng Yai** (*yai* means "large"), the northernmost section, is separated from Chaweng Noi (*noi* means "little") by a small point, Laem Koh Faan. Chaweng Yai is divided by a reef into two sections, of which the northern one is a quiet area popular with backpackers. The southern part is crowded with hotels and scantily clad tourists, young and old (Thais find it offensive that Western women sunbathe topless, and although they usually say nothing, they smile scornfully). Here you will find anything you want, from scooter rentals to money changers and nightclubs, like the currently popular **Reggae Pub** (☎ 077/422331), with its many bars and dance floors.

❽ South of this busy beach is **Chaweng Noi,** which is not as fully developed and whose beach has livelier waves. The salt air has yet to be tainted by the odor of suntan oil, but there are already many hotels and more on the way.

Dining and Lodging

$ ✕ **Nakorntorung.** There are prettier places to dine than this open-sided restaurant with concrete floor, Formica-topped tables, and toilet rolls for napkins, but it is hard to find better seafood, Thai curries, and soups. That's why locals come here, as does a smattering of Westerners who recognize good food and are not put off by the service—the staff is friendly and helpful, just slow. The restaurant is on the main street in the southern part of town, diagonally across from the Beachcomber Resort. ✉ *2 Chaweng Beach Rd., Chaweng,* ☎ *077/422500. No credit cards.*

$$$ 🏨 **The Imperial Samui.** This resort is attractively laid out at the top of a landscaped garden terrace with steps leading down to the beach. Guest rooms, which fan out from the main building, are standard, with modern furnishings and little appeal except for the view of the beach. One disadvantage is that wherever you go on the property you must go up or down steps. Attention is focused on the swimming pool, which contains a small island, complete with three coconut trees. The hotel is at the south end of Chaweng Noi, where the beach isn't crowded and the sea is clean. The restaurant tends to serve too many boring, although bountiful, buffets. ✉ *Chaweng, Ko Samui 84140,* ☎ *077/421390,* 🗚 *02/253–3190 Bangkok reservations. 77 rooms. Restaurant, bar, pool, windsurfing, boating. AE, DC, MC, V.* 🐾

$$$ 🏨 **Poppies.** At the far southern end of Chaweng is without doubt the most attractive of all its hotels. Though away from the noisy hoi polloi, it's within walking distance of shops and nightlife. Each cottage has either a queen or two twin beds and a living room with a sofa bed. Cottages have air-conditioning and a ceiling fan. Roof panels, doors, and floors are all teak, and Thai cotton and silk are used. Bathrooms have a sunken tub and shower set in marble. With a ratio of 3.5 staff members to every cottage, you can be assured that service is swift and attentive. Poppies restaurant, between the pool and the beach, offers seafood, Thai, and international fare served either under the sky or in the sala-style dining room. ✉ *South Chaweng Beach, Box 1, Chaweng, Ko Samui 84320,* ☎ *077/422419,* ℻ *077/422420. 26 cottages. Restaurant, pool. AE, MC, V.* 😊

$$ ⌂ **Amari Palm Reef Hotel.** The part of Chaweng beach on which this hotel is set is too shallow for swimming; you must walk 500 yards south for that. Half the rooms, in two wings that overlook the pool and garden, are simply functional, with small bathrooms and showers only. The more attractive accommodations are across the road from the beach in small compounds of teak, Thai-style bungalows. Mattresses are on low platforms above the polished mahogany floor. The large cottages have sleeping lofts, air-conditioning, and small terraces. The hotel has a swimming pool with a swim-up bar. The dining room (mostly Western fare) is one floor up, with a view; the Thai restaurant is in a wood-paneled room to the rear. The staff is enthusiastic and friendly. ✉ *14/3 Moo 2, Tambon Bophut, Chaweng, Ko Samui 84140,* ☎ *077/422015; 02/255–4588 Bangkok reservations,* ℻ *077/422394. 104 rooms. 2 restaurants, bar, 2 pools, 2 tennis courts, squash. MC, V.* 😊

$$ ⌂ **Central Samui Hotel.** Set back from the beach, this hotel may not be quite as smart as its neighbor, the Imperial Samui, but it costs less. Guest rooms come with fans or, for a few more dollars, air-conditioning. Equipment for water sports is available, and the restaurant offers views over the gulf. ✉ *Chaweng Noi Beach, Ko Samui 84140,* ☎ *077/421384,* ℻ *077/421385. 50 rooms. Restaurant, bar, coffee shop, windsurfing. AE, MC, V.*

$–$$ ⌂ **Fair House.** This hotel on the beach at Chaweng Noi used to have small, simple bungalows with air-conditioning. Only a couple of these are left, and a modern resort has been constructed, separated from the beach by a swimming pool. Furnishings are simple but adequate—queen-size or twin beds, two cane chairs, a small coffee table, and a TV on the minibar. Showers have hot and cold water. The open-front dining room has broad sea views, and the Thai cuisine—with a few Western dishes—is remarkably good. ✉ *Chaweng, Ko Samui 84140,* ☎ *077/422327,* ℻ *077/422255. 36 rooms. Restaurant, bar, pool. MC, V.*

$ ⌂ **Montien.** Decent-sized bungalows, each with a patio given privacy by tropical foliage, line up perpendicular to the beach. Well-placed bedside lights make for easy reading indoors. A separate washbasin just outside the bathroom is convenient, and there's a hot-water shower. The ambience is spare, but at B1,200 the Montien is good value, especially if you want to be in the heart of Chaweng's action. ✉ *5 Moo 2, Chaweng, Ko Samui 84140,* ☎ *077/422169,* ℻ *077/422145. 25 rooms. Restaurant, bar. MC, V (adds 5% to bill).*

$ ⌂ **O. P. Bungalow.** Among the inexpensive bungalow hotels that line the middle part of Chaweng Beach protected by a reef, this quiet property is efficiently run, and it has clean, simple rooms with hot-water showers. The narrow property has four rows of cottages stretching back from the beach to the road (rates are higher closer to the beach). The rooms have tile floors and most have twin beds. Room 502, with a double bed and close to the beach, is a good one to request. An open-sided coffee shop down at the beach has reasonably priced Thai and Chinese food. ✉ *111 Chaweng Beach Rd., Chaweng, Ko Samui, Surat Thani 84320,* ☎ *077/422424,* ℻ *077/422425. 38 rooms. Restaurant. No credit cards.*

Coral Cove

❾ *21 km (13 mi) southeast of Na Thon.*

Beyond the Imperial Samui Hotel is Coral Cove, popular with scuba divers. But you don't have to be a diver to enjoy the underwater scenery: just walk waist-high into the water and look through a mask to see the amazing colors of the coral. For a Thai seafood lunch, walk up the rocks to Coral Cove Bungalows, where you also can rent snorkeling equipment.

Lamai

⓾ *18 km (11 mi) southeast of Na Thon.*

A rocky headland separates Chaweng from Ko Samui's second most popular beach, Lamai. It lacks the glistening white sand of Chaweng, but its clear water and rocky pools made it the first area to be developed on Ko Samui (investors later shifted their get-rich plans to Chaweng). Lamai has more of a steeply shelving shoreline than Chaweng, so few families come here, but it does make the swimming better. It's not as honky-tonk or congested as Chaweng, though there are plenty of restaurants and bars and enough shops to stir your acquisitive instincts.

Every visitor to Ko Samui makes a pilgrimage to Lamai for yet another reason: at the point marking the end of Lamai beach stand two rocks, **⓫** named **Hin Yaa** (Grandmother Rock) and **Hin Ta** (Grandfather Rock). Erosion has shaped the rocks to resemble weathered and wrinkled intimate private parts. It's nature at its most whimsical.

Lodging

$–$$ 🏨 **Golden Sand Beach Resort.** The open lobby and reception area of this hotel are off Lamai's main street. Guest rooms, in two-story buildings, angle out from the reception room and overlook a palm-fringed garden. Although the rooms are small, most have air-conditioning (a few less expensive ones are fan-cooled) and each has its own balcony and private bathroom with a shower. The most expensive rooms have a sea view. The coffee shop offers Thai, Chinese, and Western fare, and a beach bar stays open late. ⊠ *124/2 Lamai Beach, Ko Samui, Surat Thani 84310,* ☎ *077/424031,* 🅵🅰🆇 *077/424430. 82 rooms. Coffee shop, bar. MC, V.*

$–$$ 🏨 **Pavilion.** Not too far from the action but far enough to offer a little respite from the tawdriness of downtown, the Pavilion has standard rooms in its hotel and some more expensive but much nicer octagonal thatched bungalows on its grounds. The hotel restaurant has good seafood and the beachside pool is a nice alternative to the sands. ⊠ *120 Lamai Beach, Ko Samui 84310,* ☎ *077/424427,* 🅵🅰🆇 *077/424211. 45 rooms. Restaurant, pool. MC, V.*

En Route About 4 km (2½ mi) from Lamai beach, at the small Chinese fishing village of Baan Hua Thanon, the road that forks inland (the direct route **⓬** to Na Thon) leads to the **Coral Buddha,** a natural formation carved by years of erosion. Beyond the Coral Buddha, toward Na Thon, lies the village of Baan Thurian, famous for its durian trees, where a track to the right climbs up into jungle-clad hills to the island's best waterfall, **⓭** **Na Muang.** The 105-ft falls are spectacular—especially just after the rainy season—as they tumble from a limestone cliff to a small pool. You can bathe in the pool, getting cooled by the spray and warmed by the sun. For a thrill, swim through the curtain of falling water; you can sit on a ledge at the back to catch your breath.

Laem Set Bay

⓮ *17½ km (11 mi) south of Na Thon.*

This small rocky cape on the southeastern tip of the island is away from the crowds. It's a good 3 km (2 mi) off the main circle road, and without your own transport it's hard to reach, but it's worth the effort to get there to have a meal at the Laem Set Inn. You may also want to visit the nearby **Samui Butterfly Garden,** two acres of meandering walks enclosed by nets that take you through kaleidoscopic clouds of butterflies. ☒ *Admission.* ☉ *Daily 10–4.*

Dining and Lodging

$–$$$$ ✕☒ **Laem Set Inn.** The Perrys (he's British, she's Thai) have created a unique retreat here, with widely varying rates. The buildings are reconstructions of traditional Thai houses or genuine old houses they saved from destruction. The top-priced Kho-Tan suite (two bedrooms, B9,250), an old rosewood house found on nearby Kho-Tan and reassembled here overlooking the sea, has its own pool. Another suite was made from the old Ko Samui post office. The small, thatched cottages (B1,250) with woven bamboo walls are more modest, with small bathrooms and showers only, but they have lofts for a child or for storage. Dining is given serious attention, and the kitchen has won accolades from the international press. The beach is a mix of sand and coral, with a picturesque sprinkling of rocks. The inn provides kayaks, snorkeling equipment, and mountain bikes at no charge. ☒ *110 Moo 2, Hua Thanon, Ko Samui, Surat Thani 84310,* ☏ *077/424393 or 077/ 233300,* 𝖥𝖠𝖷 *077/424394. 4 rooms, 3 suites, 9 cottages. Restaurant, pool, snorkeling, boating, bicycles. MC, V.*

Baan Taling Ngam

⑮ *3 km (2 mi) south of New Port.*

The south and west coasts are less developed; their beaches are not so golden, the water not so clear, and the breezes not so fresh. But there is one very good reason for coming to the west coast, and that is a luxury hotel directly west of the village of Baan Taling Ngam, on a pretty stretch of shore with magnificent views.

Dining and Lodging

$$$$ ✕☒ **Le Royal Meridien Baan Taling Ngam.** The name of this expensive luxury hotel, now under Meridien management, means "home on a beautiful cliff," which eminently suits the small and appealing hotel set dramatically on a 200-ft cliff facing west across the sea. Sunsets are phenomenal—be sure you come at least once for a sundowner. The equally stunning swimming pool is set so that its water, flowing over one side, seems to disappear over the cliff. Most of the 42 guest rooms are built into the cliffside, and each has a private terrace. The contemporary furnishings are given warmth by a generous use of wood paneling. Seven suites and a pool down by the beach are reached by golf carts, and above the main building there are 33 private, two-bedroom villas that the hotel leases. You'll dine elegantly on Thai and European fare at the Lom Talay; seafood is served at the more casual Promenade. Baan Taling Ngam is secluded, and some may find it inconveniently far from most of the island's attractions—you'll need transportation whenever you leave the property. ☒ *295 Moo 3, Baan Taling Ngam, Ko Samui 84140,* ☏ *077/ 423019; 0800/40–40–40 in U.K.; 800/225–5843 in U.S.,* 𝖥𝖠𝖷 *077/ 423220. 42 rooms, 7 suites, 33 villas. 2 restaurants, pool, 2 tennis courts, health club, travel services. AE, DC, MC, V.* ✆

OFF THE BEATEN PATH   **ANGTHONG MARINE NATIONAL PARK** – You should take one full day for a trip out to the 40 islets that make up the Angthong Marine National Park, which covers some 250 square km (90 sq mi). The water, the multicolor coral, and the underwater life are amazing, and the rocky islets form weird and wonderful shapes. Boats leave Na Thon daily at 8:30 AM for snorkeling and scuba diving; the cost is B250 and the trip takes about one hour.

Ko Pha Ngan

12 km (7½ mi) by boat north of Ko Samui.

Since Ko Samui is no longer off the beaten track, travelers looking for the simple beach life now head for Ko Pha Ngan, which is at the turning point of its development. A decade ago, the few international wanderers stayed in fishermen's houses or slung hammocks on the beach. Now cheap, simple guest bungalows have sprung up on most of the best beaches, and investors are buying up beach property. Land worth a million baht three years ago can bring as much as 45 million baht today. For now, though, the lack of transportation to and on the island limits Ko Pha Ngan's transformation, and one of the world's most idyllic places has yet to be spoiled.

Since the island's unpaved roads twist and turn, it's easier to beach-hop by boat. In fact, if you want to find the beach that most appeals to you, take a ferry trip around the island—it takes about nine hours with stops along the way. The southeast tip of the island is divided by a long promontory into **Haad Rin West** and **Haad Rin East,** the island's most popular and crowded areas, sometimes referred to as the back-packers' ghetto. Boats from **Thong Sala,** the major town, take 40 minutes to reach Haad Rin East; their departure is timed to meet arriving passengers from the interisland boat.

If Haad Rin is too crowded, catch the onward boat up the east coast to **Haad Tong Nai Pan,** a perfect horseshoe bay divided by a small promontory. On the beach of the southern and larger half are several guest houses and a couple of small restaurants. The northern bay, ★ **Tong Nai Pan Noi,** is the smaller and quieter of the two. Telephone cables have yet to link it with the world, and though there is a road, no self-respecting kidney will take the incessant bouncing of the four-wheel-drive vehicle negotiating its curves and ruts. Glistening white sand curves around the turquoise waters of this half-moon bay, and coconut trees behind the beach hide the houses of the villagers. At the ends of the bay are two small resorts.

Dining and Lodging

$ ✕ **Pannoi's.** The owner of this local restaurant goes fishing in the evening for the next day's menu. The guests, barefoot and shirtless, sit at rough-hewn wood tables set in the sand. A meal may consist of tender and succulent *ma pla* (horsefish, much like snapper) and a plateful of barbecued prawns with garlic and pepper. ⊠ *Haad Tong Nai Pan Noi,* ☎ *no phone. No credit cards.*

$–$$ ✕⌸ **Panviman Resort.** This resort has thatched cottages and stone-and-
★ stucco bungalows (B3,500), some cooled by fan and others by air-conditioning. Each bungalow has a balcony, a large bedroom, and a spacious bathroom with a cold-water shower. During the day, electricity is turned off and the rooms become stifling, but who wants to be inside? There are also twin-bed, fan-cooled hotel rooms (half with ocean views) that cost B1,200. The circular wood restaurant, cooled by the breezes blowing over the promontory, serves Western food, but the Thai dishes are better and more extensive. Ask for a light hand in the chili department. Guests gather here to watch a nightly video. ⊠ *Haad Tong Nai Pan, Ko Pha Ngan,* ☎ ⅎ *077/377048,* ☎ *02/587–8491 Bangkok reservations,* ⅎ *02/587–8493 in Bangkok. 15 rooms, 10 bungalows, 15 cottages. Restaurant. MC, V.*

$ ⌸ **Tong Tapan Resort.** These small thatched cottages on stilts perched on the side of the hill are home to international backpackers. ⊠ *North end of Haad Tong Nai Pan Noi,* ☎ *no phone. 22 rooms. No credit cards.*

Ko Tao

47 km (29 mi) by boat north of Ko Pha Ngan.

Small Ko Tao is an island 4 km (2½ mi) wide and 8 km (5 mi) long, with unpaved roads. Only five years ago the island was likened to a second home for Robinson Crusoe. Today it is inundated with backpackers, hanging out and dreading the day when they might actually have to go to work. It's on the scheduled route of ferries out of Ko Pha Ngan and Ko Samui, and two boats a day make the three-hour (express boat) or six-hour (regular ferry) run between Ko Tao and Chumphon on the mainland. The island used to make its living from coconuts, but tourism is taking over despite the rugged interior and few beaches, and more than two dozen small bungalow developments offer basic accommodation. Since the peace and quiet has gone, the main reason to come here is the snorkeling. In fact, speedboats now leave from Ko Samui's Bophut pier at 8:30 AM, taking snorkelers on day trips to Ko Tao and neighboring Ko Nang Yuan (about B1,300).

Most of the bungalows on Ko Tao are on **Haad Sai Ri**, a sweeping crescent beach north of **Ban Mae Hut**, the village where the ferries dock. One of the better places is **Sea Shell Bungalows** (☎ 01/229–4621). Rooms here (B800) are fan-cooled and have private bathrooms. On the south shore of the island at **Haad Chalok Kao**, the **Ko Tao Cottage International Dive Resort** (☎ 01/229–3662, FAX 01/229–3751) has fan-cooled bungalows for less than B1,000 a night. If both of these are full, go to the Ko Tao Tourism Centre, a commercial travel office, and ask the owner, Khun Aka, to find you a bungalow. This office is to the right as you exit the ferry terminal building and about 165 yards up the dirt road.

Ko Nang Yuan is a teeny island, or rather three islands linked by a sandbar, where the snorkeling is excellent. It's 15 minutes off the north coast of Ko Tao and tends to be flooded with visitors arriving on the 10 AM ferry who depart at 4 PM. The only residents on the island are guests at the **Ko Nang Yuan Dive Resort** (☎ 01/229–5085, FAX 01/229–5212), which has simple rooms at B800 and more spacious ones with air-conditioning at B2,500. It's the only lodging on the island, so make sure you can stay there *before* the last ferry leaves.

Chumphon

400 km (240 mi) south of Bangkok, 50 km (21 mi) by boat east of Ko Tao.

Chumphon is often seen as the gateway to the south, since trains and buses connect it to Hua Hin and Bangkok in the north, to Surat Thani and Phuket farther south, and to Ranong to the southwest. Ferries to Ko Tao dock at Pak Nam at the mouth of the Chumphon River, 11 km (7 mi) southeast of town. Most boat services run a free shuttle between the docks and the city. **Songserm Travel Centre** (✉ 66/1 Thatapao Hotel, Chumphon, ☎ 077/502764) coordinates its ferry with its bus service to and from Bangkok.

You'll find little of specific interest in Chumphon, but people here are very friendly. If you are overnighting here or have a couple of hours before catching onward transportation, visit the Night Market. If you have more time, just north of Chumphon there's an excellent beach, **Ao Thong Wua Laen,** with a superb hotel. You can catch a songthaew (B25) on the street across from the bus station or take the hotel's minivan (B120). The curving beach is 3 km (2 mi) of white-yellow sand with a horizon dotted by small islands famous as the nesting place of swifts. Swifts make nests that the Chinese like to serve as bird's nest soup. Never venture onto these islands—they are patrolled by armed guards who will shoot you on sight to protect the fortune of the concessionaire. Just offshore is, however, safe. Dive boats go out to nearby reefs where there is some spectacular coral.

There are several restaurants and guest houses along Thong Wua Laen beach as well as picnic and camping spots. But even on national holidays the beach is far from crowded.

Lodging

$–$$ ⌸ **Chumphon Cabana Resort.** This excellent resort at the south end of Thong Wua Laen beach consists of 40 bungalows hidden in lush foliage and another 100 hotel rooms in three low-rise buildings. Each of the hotel rooms has a private balcony. Furnishings are simple but pleasant, and the bamboo-walled bungalows are especially romantic. The public areas are open-sided and spacious, but most guests, when not out diving or getting some sun, sit around the airy, open restaurant beside the beach. The staff is super friendly and, even if you are not staying at the hotel, will help you make travel arrangements. The hotel also should be commended for spending a few extra million and building an ecologically friendly resort with an infrastructure designed to protect the environment. A PADI-registered dive shop is attached to the hotel. ⊠ *69 Moo 8, Saplee, Pathui, Chumphon 86230,* ☎ *077/ 560245 up to 9,* FAX *077/560247,* ☎ FAX *02/427–0122 Bangkok reservations. 140 rooms. Restaurant, dive shop, meeting rooms. MC, V.*

¢ ⌸ **Marokot.** This is not the most luxurious or the most prestigious hotel in Chumphon, but the rooms are clean, the air-conditioning is efficient, the queen-size beds are firm and comfortable, and the bathrooms have hot and cold water. The staff is very helpful and the hotel's location is a short walk from Songserm's bus and ferry pickup point, the city bus terminal, and the Night Market. Best of all, the price for a room is only B300. ⊠ *102–112 Thannon Songkla, 86000,* ☎ *077/503628,* FAX *077/ 570196. 46 rooms, most with air-conditioning. No credit cards.*

SOUTHERN BEACH RESORTS A TO Z

Arriving and Departing

By Airplane

KO SAMUI

The island's small airport, on the northeast tip, is served by **Bangkok Airways** (☎ 077/425012 at Ko Samui airport; 02/229–3456 in Bangkok), which runs five very expensive flights daily between Bangkok and Ko Samui (B3,950 one way), between Phuket and Ko Samui (B2,550 one way), and between Singapore and Ko Samui (about B14,000). Reservations are crucial during peak periods. **Thai Airways International** (☎ 077/273355) flies to Surat Thani on the mainland, from which you must transfer to Ko Samui.

Taxis meet arrivals; the price is fixed (usually B200) for trips to various parts of the island. Some hotels have a limo or van service at the airport, but these cost the same as a taxi. Songthaews sporadically go between the airport and Na Thon for B30.

KRABI

Krabi has a new airport into which **Thai Airways International** (☎ 076/ 620070) runs two flights a day to and from Bangkok.

PHUKET

Bangkok Airways (⊠ Yaowarat Rd., Phuket Town, ☎ 076/212311 or 076/212341) now offers two flights daily between Chiang Mai and

Phuket, Ko Samui and Phuket, and U-Tapao (Pattaya) and Phuket. **Thai Airways International** (✉ 78 Ranong Rd., Phuket Town, ☎ 076/211195 domestic, 076/212499 international) has daily 70-minute flights from Bangkok and 30-minute flights from Hat Yai. The airline also has direct flights from Chiang Mai, Penang (Malaysia), and Singapore.

Phuket's airport is at the northern end of the island. Most of the hotels are on the west coast, and many send minivans to meet arriving planes. These are not free—just convenient. For Phuket Town (32 km/20 mi southeast of the airport) or Patong Beach, take a Thai Airways minibus—buy the ticket (B80 and B120, respectively) at the transportation counter in the terminal. Songthaews run sporadically between the airport and Phuket Town for B30.

By Boat

Songserm Travel Centre (☞ Travel Agencies, *below*) operates many of the boats to and from Ko Pha Ngan, Ko Tao, Ko Phi Phi, and Ko Samui.

KO PHA NGAN AND KO TAO

From Surat Thani, Songserm express boats depart for Thong Sala on Ko Pha Ngan at 7 AM, 9 AM, and 2 PM (sometimes more often), stopping en route at Na Thon on Ko Samui. From Chumphon on the mainland, two ferries (one Songserm express taking just over two hours and one slow boat taking just over six hours) travel daily to Ko Tao and on to Ko Pha Ngan and Ko Samui. (These ferries are frequently cancelled during the monsoon season.) From Ko Samui, you can also take a small ferryboat from Bophut to Haad Rin at about 10 AM, and in good weather (but not when the seas are high), a long-tail boat leaves Maenam for Haad Tong Nai Pan at about 9 AM. A speedboat seating a score of passengers departs for Ko Tao every morning from Bophut at 8:30.

The State Railway offers a combined ticket that takes you by train to Chumphon and by ferry to Ko Tao and Ko Pha Ngan.

KO PHI PHI

Boats leave Makham Bay on Phuket twice a day (9:30 and 1) for the two-hour journey; those run by Songserm Travel Centre are the best. Two to four ferries a day make the two-hour trip between Krabi and Phi Phi Don.

KO SAMUI

From Surat Thani, two ferries cross to Ko Samui. The Songserm passenger boat leaves several times a day for Na Thon from its terminal 8 km (5 mi) out of town (a Songserm bus collects passengers from the row of travel agencies on the Surat Thani waterfront). The ride takes about two hours, after which the ferry goes on to Ko Pha Ngan. The other ferry, which takes cars and cargo, leaves from Donsak, 45 minutes by bus from Surat Thani, and lands at New Port. This ferry takes about 90 minutes. Combined bus-ferry tickets are available from one of the many tour or bus companies in Surat Thani. The last ferry to Ko Samui leaves around 4 PM, and the last ferry from Ko Samui departs at 3 PM. Times vary, so be sure to check the schedule.

KRABI AND AO NANG

Two to four ferries a day make the two-hour run between Krabi and Ko Phi Phi. Bookings can be made on the dock at Phi Phi Don or any travel agency; the fare is B160. Ferries also go once a day between Ko Phi Phi and Ao Nang.

By Bus

KRABI AND AO NANG

Air-conditioned buses depart from Bangkok's Southern Bus Terminal at 7 PM and 8 PM for the 819-km (509-mi) journey (B850) to Krabi, which takes about 12 hours. From Phuket, buses usually leave in the morning for the 180-km (112-mi) trip (B150). Songthaews go from Krabi to Ao Nang for about B20.

PHANG NGA BAY

First get yourself to the one-horse town of Phang Nga, served by frequent buses from Krabi and Phuket, then take a songthaew 10 km (6¼ mi) to the bay. At the bay, hire a long-tail boat to tour the islands.

PHUKET

Non-air-conditioned buses leave throughout the day from Bangkok's Southern Bus Terminal. One air-conditioned bus leaves in the evening. Tour companies also run coaches that are slightly more comfortable, and often the price of a one-way fare includes a meal. The bus trip from Bangkok to Phuket takes 12–13 hours. A bus plies between Phuket and Surat Thani with timed connections for the Ko Samui ferry. There's also service between Phuket and Trang, Hat Yai, and Satun.

SURAT THANI

This town, at the crossroads of railway and bus lines, is the jumping-off point for many southern beach resorts. Buses from Bangkok's Southern Bus Terminal cost less than the train (about B255 for air-conditioned buses), but they are also less comfortable. Private tour companies use more comfortable, faster buses. Express buses also go to Surat Thani from Phuket (5 hrs), Krabi (4 hrs), and Hat Yai (7 hrs).

By Train

KO SAMUI

The State Railway of Thailand sells a combined ticket that includes rail fare (a berth in air-conditioned second class), bus connection, and ferry ride, for B610. Passengers leave Bangkok at 7:15 PM and arrive in Ko Samui at about 10 AM the following day.

PHUKET

The closest train station is at Surat Thani, where trains connect to Bangkok and Singapore. A bus service links Phuket with Surat Thani (5 hr) and the overnight train, which takes 11 hours to Bangkok. The State Railway of Thailand, in conjunction with Songserm Travel Centre, issues a combined train (second-class air-conditioned sleeper) and bus ticket (B670).

SURAT THANI

Many express trains from Bangkok's Hualamphong railway station stop at Surat Thani on their way south. The journey takes just under 12 hours, and the best trains are the overnighters that leave Bangkok at 6:30 PM and 7:20 PM, arriving in Surat Thani soon after 6 AM. First-class sleeping cabins are available only on the 7:20 train. Two express trains make the daily run up from Trang and Hat Yai in southern Thailand.

Getting Around

Ko Pha Ngan

The twisting, rutted, unpaved roads can be painful for the bony. You may want to consider using the long-tail boats out of Thong Sala that travel to all the bays on the island.

Ko Phi Phi

On these islands the way to get around is on foot or by cruise boat or long-tail boat.

Ko Samui

Na Thon is the terminus for songthaews, which take either the north route around the island via Chengmon to Chaweng on the east coast, or the southern route along the coast to reach Lamai. Between Chaweng and Lamai you change songthaews at a transfer point for either the northern or southern route. The fare from Na Thon to Chaweng, the most distant point, is B30. Songthaews for the northern trip start from the waterfront north of the pier; those on the southern route start from south of the pier.

After about 6 PM songthaews become private taxis, and fares need to be established before setting out. During the day, songthaews may be rented as private taxis. The trip from Na Thon to Chaweng, for example, costs B250.

If you really want to explore Ko Samui, it's best to rent your own transportation. Jeeps are expensive (around B1,200 plus B175 for the Collision Damage Waiver [CDW]), but they're the safest, although most people choose motor scooters (about B175 per day), which can be rented at most of the resorts. Gravel, potholes, and erratic driving make riding dangerous, and each year some travelers return home with broken limbs, and though crash helmets are now mandatory, some never return at all.

Avis has counters at the Santiburi Hotel (☏ 077/425031), the Imperial Tongsai Bay Hotel (☏ 077/421451), and at the airport. **Hertz** is represented at the airport and at most of the luxury resorts.

Phuket

Ten-seat songthaews have no regular schedule, but all use Phuket Town as their terminal. Songthaews leave from Ranong Road near the day market and Fountain Circle, plying back and forth between most beaches; a few also make the trip to the airport. If you want to get from one beach to another, you will probably have to go back into Phuket Town and change songthaews. Fares range from B20 to B40.

Taxi fares are usually fixed between different destinations. If you plan to use taxis frequently, get a list of fares from the TAT office, because drivers are not above charging more. A trip from Phuket Town to Patong Beach is B140 and to Bang Tao is B200.

Your own transport is, of course, the most convenient for exploring. If on motor scooter, watch out for potholes and loose gravel that can cause a spill; crash helmets are required by law. Some minor roads are not paved. Many hotels have rental desks, but their prices are 25%–40% higher than those outside hotels or in Phuket Town, where a scooter costs B150 a day and a jeep is B750.

At **Pure Car Rent** (✉ 75 Rasda Rd., Phuket Town, ☏ 076/211002), prices for a jeep start at B770 per day, plus a CDW of B120 per day. Motor scooters begin at B150 a day. The larger, 150-cc scooters are safer. **Avis** (☏ 076/327358), **Budget** (☏ 076/205396), and **Hertz** (☏ 076/321190) have offices at the airport, as well as at some hotels.

Contacts and Resources

Emergencies
General Emergencies: ☏ 1699.

KO SAMUI
Tourist Police (☏ 077/421281 in Na Thon). **Hospital** (☏ 077/421230); also **Surat Thani Hospital** (☞ *below*).

PHUKET
Police (☏ 076/212046). **Tourist Police** (☏ 1699). **Ambulance** ☏ (076/212297). **Bangkok Phuket Hospital**(☏ 076/254421).

Tourist Police (☎ 077/281300 or 1699). **Surat Thani Hospital** (⊠ Surat-Phun Phin Rd., ☎ 077/272231).

Guided Tours

A half-day Phuket sightseeing tour includes Wat Chalong, Rawai Beach, Phromthep Cape, and Khao Rang. Other half-day tours take in the Thai Cultural Village and the cultured-pearl farms on Naka Noi Island. Make arrangements at your hotel.

A full-day boat tour goes from Phuket to Phang Nga Bay and other islands. **World Travel Service** (☞ Travel Agencies, *below)* runs a comprehensive tour to Phang Nga Bay. Another full-day tour visits the Phi Phi Islands for swimming and caving. The daylong Ko Hav (Coral Island) tour takes you snorkeling and swimming.

Full-day cruises to the Similan Islands, costing B1,500, are run by **Songserm Travel Centre** (☞ *below*). The boat trip takes about 10 hours from Phuket, and about four hours from Thap Lamu Port, two hours north on the west coast. **Marina Divers** (⊠ Karon Villa Hotel, Karon Beach, Phuket, ☎ 076/381625) runs diving trips to the Similan Islands. The **Siam Cruise Co.** (⊠ 33/10–11 Chaiyod Arcade, Sukhumvit Soi 11, Bangkok 10110, ☎ 02/255–8950) operates two- and three-night cruises to the Similans on the luxury cruise ship *Andaman Princess*. **PIDC Divers** (⊠ 1/10 Viset Rd., Chalong Bay, Phuket, ☎ 076/381219), operates the 66-ft MV *Andaman Seafarer* for four- and six-day live-aboard dive excursions that cost approximately $520 and $720, respectively.

Travel Agencies

Chan Phen Tour (⊠ 145 Uttarakit Rd., Krabi, ☎ 075/612404, ℻ 075/612629) is one of a number of travel agencies on Uttarakit Rd. **Chok Anan** (⊠ Ratchadamnoen Klang Ave., Bangkok, ☎ 02/281–2277) runs buses from Bangkok to Surat Thani. **Dive Deep** (⊠ Chaweng Beach Resort, Ko Samui, ☎ 077/230155) runs trips from Ko Samui to Angthong National Marine Park, Ko Tao, and Sail Rock. **Lao Ruam Kij** (⊠ 11 Khongka Rd., ☎ 075/611930) is a travel agency in Krabi.

Songserm Travel Centre (⊠ 121/7 Soi Chapermla, Phyathai Rd., Bangkok 10400, ☎ 02/252–9654 and 02/251–8994) has branches in Ko Pha Ngan (⊠ Ferry terminal, Thong Sala, ☎ 077/281639); Ko Samui (64/1–2 Na Thon, ☎ 077/421316); Phuket (⊠ 51 Satoon Rd., Phuket Town, ☎ 076/222570, ℻ 076/214391); and Surat Thani (⊠ In the ferry terminal, ☎ 077/272928).

Travel Accommodation Centre (⊠ Seafood Village, Ao Nang, ☎ 075/637311, ℻ 075/637311) is extremely knowledgeable and helpful in finding lodging on east coast resorts, including Phuket. **World Travel Service** (⊠ Hotel Phuket Merlin, Phuket Town, ☎ 076/212866, ext. WTS; Phuket Yacht Club, ☎ 076/214020, ext. WTS) is reliable.

Visitor Information

Ko Samui TAT (⊠ Na Thon, ☎ 077/421281). **Krabi TAT** (⊠ Uttarakit Rd., ☎ 075/612740). **Phuket TAT** (⊠ 73–75 Phuket Rd., near bus terminal, Phuket Town, ☎ 076/212213). The TAT desk at Phuket airport offers limited help. The **Surat Thani TAT** office (⊠ 5 Talat Mai Rd., ☎ 077/281828) also handles Ko Phi Phi, Ko Pha Ngan, and Ko Tao.

6 BACKGROUND AND ESSENTIALS

The Kaleidoscope

Sacred Structures and Sculptures:
From the Wat to Images of the Buddha

Map of Thailand

Smart Travel Tips A to Z

THE KALEIDOSCOPE

THE KINGDOM OF THAILAND is unique among Southeast Asian nations in having developed its culture independently of Western colonialism. As far back as 6800 BC, pottery was being made in Thailand, and excavations at Ban Chiang indicate that bronze was being cast in 2000 BC—about the same time as Mesopotamia is thought to have entered the Bronze Age. The Austroasiatic-speaking Mon inhabited the region; the ancestors of the Thais were still living in southwestern China (they would move during the 6th and 13th centuries into the Chao Phraya River basin). The Mon established the area's first recognizable civilization in Dvaravati, a collection of city-states, and their influence stretched over most of present-day Thailand.

The Khmer Empire emerged in the 6th century, expanding its kingdom across modern-day Cambodia and, by the 10th century, into Thailand. By the early 13th century, the Khmers had outspent themselves on temples and battles with Vietnam. In 1238, two Thai princes overthrew the Khmer outpost at what is now Sukhothai, establishing the first Thai state and beginning the Sukhothai period. Nineteen-year-old Rama (later known as Ramkhamhaeng, or Rama the Bold) took the throne in 1278 and expanded his kingdom to include parts of Laos, southern Burma (Myanmar), and the southern peninsula around Nakhon Si Thammarat. To protect his northern flank in Chiang Mai, Rama made treaties with the Lanna and Phayao kingdoms.

Not only was Rama an outstanding warrior, but he also made two significant contributions to Thai culture. He revised and adapted the Khmer alphabet to the requirements of the Thai language, and he invited Sri Lankan monks to purify the Khmer-corrupted Theravada (sometimes called Hinayana) Buddhism and establish the religion in a form that is, for the most part, practiced today.

By 1350, Sukhothai's strength had waned sufficiently for the dynamic young state of Ayutthaya to usurp the reins of power. By 1432 Ayutthaya had sacked Angkor, forcing the Khmers to set up a new capital at Phnom Penh. Sukhothai fell to Ayutthaya in 1438, and for four centuries and 33 kings, Ayutthaya was Thailand's heart and mind. A brief interlude occurred when the Burmese attacked Ayutthaya in 1568 and defeated the Thais. For 10 years Ayutthaya paid tribute to Burma until King Naresuan amassed an army and defeated the Burmese at Nong Sarai in 1593. For the next 150 years, Ayutthaya prospered. In the 1650s, its population exceeded that of London and—according to many foreign travelers—its golden spires, waterways, and roads made it a glorious capital.

In 1766 the Burmese attacked the city again. After a 15-month siege, they finally captured Ayutthaya. Golden Buddhas were melted down, treasuries ransacked, and buildings burned. Thais who hadn't escaped were killed or enslaved; by the time the Burmese left, Ayutthaya's population had dropped from 1 million to 10,000.

Under General Taksin, the Thais regrouped, established a capital on the Chao Phraya River at Thonburi (opposite present-day Bangkok), and began expelling the Burmese from Thailand. Although he was a commoner, Taksin was a brave and clever enough warrior to rise through the ranks and eventually be crowned king. Unfortunately, he went insane, and in 1782 the warrior Chao P'ya Chakri, one of Taskin's supports, was invited to accept the throne. Taksin was executed (no one was allowed to touch a king, so he was put in a sack and beaten to death), and Chao P'ya Chakri became the first king of the current Chakri dynasty. (The present monarch, King Bhumibol Adulyadej, is the ninth in the line.) One of the first acts of Chao P'ya Chakri, or Rama I (all kings of the dynasty are given the title Rama), was to make Bangkok the capital.

Western powers were first welcomed when they arrived in 1512, but the French (from whom the Thai word *farang*, meaning foreigner, is derived) tried to replace the government with a puppet regime. As a result, the Thais not only threw out the French but also closed their doors to all outsiders until the middle of the 19th century. When the West again threatened Thailand's sovereignty, King Mongkut (Rama IV, 1851–68) kept the colonial forces at bay through a series of adroit treaties. His efforts were continued by King Chulalongkorn (Rama V, 1868–1910), who secured colonial recognition of Thai sovereignty by ceding to the British a little of what is now Malaysia and to the French a little of Cambodia.

Under King Chulalongkorn, slavery was abolished, hospitals and schools were established, and some upper-class Thais received a European education so they could replace Western advisers. Under King Prajadhipok (Rama VII, 1925–35), the world's economic depression brought its share of discontent to Thailand. The pressure for sweeping reform ended in 1932 when a group of mid-ranking military officers demanded the establishment of a constitutional monarchy similar to that of Great Britain.

Since then, quasi-military governments and a strong bureaucracy have administered the country. Changes in government have been by coup as often as by election. Despite such upheavals, the nation's policies have been remarkably consistent in fostering its industrial economy. Since World War II, Thailand has been demonstratively pro-American, receiving in return billions of dollars that increase and decrease proportionately to America's fear of communism. Thailand's own communist rebellion, centered in the poor north, was crushed in the 1980s with harsh military might. Calls for democracy were also met with a heavy hand. Student demonstrators battled with police in 1973 and again in 1976, when hundreds were savagely beaten, many were lynched, and a few were burned alive.

Protests in 1992 against the military-controlled government also met with a bloody crackdown in which as many as 200 demonstrators were killed. This protest, however, had positive results. An elected government (albeit a corrupt one) was returned to power, and a new constitution was drawn up—one designed to permit fair elections, reduce corruption, and ensure that the government responds to the people. Only time will tell whether or not it has the desired result.

Throughout all this, the monarchy has had a stabilizing influence. The much-loved king is seen as the father of the nation, and the queen has won the heart of every Thai. The trust and respect for the royal family had a calming effect during the 1992 democracy demonstrations and the economic crisis of 1997–98. The monarchy binds Thai society, allowing the nation a chance to progress peacefully into the 21st century.

— Nigel Fisher

SACRED STRUCTURES AND SCULPTURES: FROM THE WAT TO IMAGES OF THE BUDDHA

Nearly every element of Thai religious structures, which constitute 95% of classical Thai architecture, symbolizes some aspect of Thai Theravada Buddhism. Many such buildings have a cylindrical or pyramidal shape that symbolizes a hierarchy of perfection. Some early cities had a massive central tower that represented Mount Meru, the city of Brahma and the home of the gods. The tower's upper portion was divided into seven levels and subdivided into 33 lesser tiers to symbolize the 33 heavens. At the summit in the 33rd heaven sat Indra, who presided over the universe. By its very height, the central tower pierced the sky, becoming one with the heavens themselves.

The principal building materials have varied with the ages. Khmer and Lop Buri architects built in stone and laterite; Sukhothai and Lanna builders worked with laterite and brick. Ayutthaya and Bangkok architects opted for brick cemented by mortar and covered with one or more coats of stucco. In early construction, walls were often several feet thick; when binding materials and construction techniques improved they became thinner.

Multi-tier buildings often have a horizontal, squat look. The Thais, however, abhor straight lines and true perpendiculars, so the outlines of their religious buildings are often graceful arcs—providing both stability and a sense of height—rather than steep, unvarying lines. The overall effect is one of soft sinuosity that belies the basic block-like shapes and the thick, heavy walls and columns.

Thai religious sculpture went far beyond mere symbolism. To the Buddhist artist and his patron, the sacred images that fill Thailand's temples are never just works of art but rather are sacred objects. The donor gains merit for his act but remains anonymous, as does the artist. The image must be blessed by Buddhist priests when it's made and again when moved. Heavy punishment was exacted for damaging an image.

Wats

Wat translates loosely to mean a religious complex. It can actually be one Buddhist temple or monastery or several buildings in or around a single compound. The monks who live in or near a wat are regarded as upholders and interpreters of Buddhism, as teachers, as arbiters, as counselors, and as practitioners of herbal medicine. Thus, the wat is the focal point of community life.

Wats are erected as acts of merit, allowing the donor to be reborn as a higher being, or in memory of great events. You can tell much about a wat's origins by its name. A wat *luang* (royal wat) for example, was constructed or restored by royals and may have the words *rat, raja,* or *racha* in its name (e.g., Ratburana or Rajapradit). The word *phra* may indicate that a wat contains an image of the Buddha. In many cases, a wat may be named for the *chedi* (a building with relics of the Buddha or his scriptures or the ashes of a donor) that was the first of its structures to be built. Wats that contain an important relic of the Buddha have the words *maha* (great) and *that* (relic) in their names. Thailand's nine major wat mahathats are in Chiang Rai, Chai Nat, Sukhothai, Phitsanulok, Ayutthaya, Bangkok, Yasothon, Phetchaburi, and Nakhon Si Thammarat.

Thai wats, especially in the later periods, were seldom planned as entire units, so they often appear disjointed and crowded. To appreciate a wat's beauty you often have to look at its individual buildings.

The *bot,* the wat's main structure, holds a Buddha image and serves as a congregation and ordination hall for the monks. The *viharn* holds the principal Buddha image and serves as the general sermon hall for monks and worshipers alike. It's not essential for a wat to have a viharn, and the rules attending its design and orientation aren't as strict as those for a bot.

The bot and viharn should face water because Buddha is said to have sat under a Bodhi tree facing a river when he attained Enlightenment. If the site lacks a natural body of water, the monks may dig a pond. If no water whatever is available, the bot, the viharn, and the images they contain face the rising sun. The importance of water was carried still further during the Ayutthaya period by Mahayana Buddhist belief, which likened a religious building to a boat carrying pilgrims to salvation. In the late Ayutthaya and early Bangkok periods this was represented by a curved line along the building's base corresponding to the deck line of a boat. Such structures are called *thawing samphao* (ship's hull) bots or viharns.

Bots can have a rectangular or cruciform shape. Their interiors often contain many rows of columns—surmounted by capitals in the shapes of lotus buds or water lilies—and ceilings ornamented with lotus or star-cluster motifs. The Buddha image is kept far from the entrance. If there's more than one image, the one in front, called the "presiding image," is generally more important. Around the image there may be disciples in attitudes of worship.

A series of meditation galleries known as the *phra rabieng* (cloister) may surround a bot. Such galleries are colonnaded with one side open to the bot. Some hold rows of Buddha images; others are painted with scenes from the Thai literary classic, the *Ramakien.* Bots are also surrounded by consecrated ground. Holes are dug at the four corners and the axes of the four cardinal points. Eight *luk nimit* (stone spheres)—and, often, gold and jewelry—are placed in holes and covered with earth. Atop each luk nimit is a *bai sema* (boundary stone), which may be shaped like a leaf and carved in intricate relief or may consist of two thin slabs placed close together. A ninth luk nimit is buried at the site of the main Buddha image. The bai sema denote where all earthly power ends; not even a king may issue orders within their bounds.

The outer walls of bots and viharns are either whitewashed or highly decorated. The predilection for elaborate decoration stems not only from a Thai love for bright color but from a Hindu and Khmer credo that a temple is more than a repository for a Buddha image, it is the transposition to earth of a heavenly world. Porcelain mosaic pieces, patterned ceramic tiles, gold leaf, paint, faience, and marble are among the things that lend a glittering fairytale-like aspect to architectural surfaces.

The chedi is another important wat structure. It came to Thailand from India via Sri Lanka, and it was originally used to hold relics of the Buddha. Later it held his scriptures or marked a site where a king or abbot was cremated. Today, anyone with sufficient money can build one to hold his or her ashes. (Stouter versions of the chedi were originally called *stupas;* today the terms are used interchangeably.) A chedi's base has three platforms representing the three worlds: hell, earth, and heaven. The top spire has up to 33 rings representing the 33 Buddhist heavens. While Sukhothai architects adopted the Sri Lankan bell-shape chedi, Ayutthayan architects gave it a square form.

Wats may also have a *sala kanprien,* where monks say prayers between noon and 1 PM; a cruciform-shape *prasad* that's reserved for royal use; a square *mondop,* which can serve as a library or a reliquary container; a *prang* (spire), towering above the compound; and a *ho trai,* which is set on stilts and very elaborately decorated as befits a structure holding holy scriptures. Wat courtyards often contain an open-walled sala—where monks take their midday meal and travelers find overnight shelter—as well as towers whose bells toll the hours or alert the community to an emergency.

During the early Ayutthaya period, wat interiors were illuminated by the light passing through vertical slits in the walls (wider, more elaborate windows would have compromised the strength of the walls and, hence, the integrity of the structure). In the Bangkok period, the slits were replaced by proper windows set below wide lintels that supported the upper portions of the brick walls. There are usually five, seven, or nine windows on a side in accordance with a Thai preference for odd numbers. The entrance doors are in the end wall facing the Buddha image; narrower doors may flank the entrance door.

Window shutters and door leaves may be carved in relief and covered with gold leaf, inset with mirrored tiles, covered in mythical scenes rendered in mother-of-pearl, or done in lacquer and gold. During the late Sukhothai and early Ayutthayan periods, the principal subjects of the door leaves were a pair of *deva* (angels with swords), who served as wat guardians. In the middle and late Ayutthayan period, door leaves either had intricate floral patterns or featured the earth, devas, and vines—among whose tendrils animals and birds frolicked. Peacocks and such mythical creatures as *nagas* (snakes believed to control the irrigation waters of rice fields) are also depicted.

Roofs, which are covered in glazed clay tiles or wooden shakes, generally consist of three overlapping sections, with the lower roof set at gentle slopes, increasing to a topmost roof with a pitch of 60°. Eave brackets in the form of a naga with its head at the bottom often support the lower edges of the roofs. In the north, the eave bracket is a triangular piece with the naga's head at the top and its tail curving back along its body to end at the wall; the lower portion of the bracket is a filigree of foliage. Along the eaves of many roofs are wat-style wind chimes: a row of small brass bells with clappers attached to thin brass pieces shaped like Bodhi tree leaves.

At both extremities of the roof peaks on bots, viharns, and sala kanprien is a curious figure—sometimes presented as the head of a naga—known as a *chofa,* which literally translates to "bunch of sky." None of these buildings is regarded as consecrated until the chofa has been fixed in place.

Sculpture

How did sculptors know how to portray the Buddha? They often relied on ancient texts that outlined the *lakshanas* (guidelines by which sages could recognize future Buddhas). Characteristics cited in Sanskrit poetry include legs like a deer, thighs like the trunk of a banana tree, arms smooth and rounded like the trunk of an elephant, hands like lotus flowers just beginning to bloom with the fingertips turned back like petals, a head shaped like an egg, a chin like a mango stone, a nose like a parrot's beak, eyebrows like drawn bows, and hair like the stings of scorpions.

The more commonly used source, however, was a series of 32 lakshanas from Pali religious texts. They included feet with 108 auspicious signs (Buddhist lore suggests that the Buddha flew to Thailand and implanted his foot on a mountaintop, leaving behind the 108 auspicious signs in the whorls and lines of its imprint), wedge-shape heels, long fingers and toes of equal length, legs like an antelope, arms long enough that he could touch either knee without bending, skin so smooth that dust wouldn't adhere to it, a body as thick as a banyan tree, long eyelashes like those of a cow, 40 teeth, a hairy white mole between his *urna* (eyebrows), deep blue eyes, and an *ushnisha* (protuberance) atop his head—either a turban, a topknot, or a bump on his skull. To these, sculptors added ear lobes elongated by heavy earrings worn in the Buddha's youth—a reference to his royal upbringing—and a flame atop the ushnisha to signify his great intellect.

Tradition decrees four positions for the Buddha image: seated (the Maravijaya or Victory over Mara, being the most common), standing, walking (rare, generally confined to the

Sukhothai period), and reclining (as the Buddha was at his death). Seated images are depicted with their feet in the Vajrasena or "adamantine" position with both soles pointing upward, the Virasana or "hero" pose with one leg atop the sole of the other foot, or seated in the so-called European fashion on a throne with his feet placed firmly on the ground.

Buddhist iconography calls for the Buddha's hands to be placed in *mudras* (gestures) representing various events in his lifetime. The mudras are of Indian origin, but sometime during the reign of King Rama III (1824–1851) a list of 40 of the most common was prepared. The six most often seen are the Vitarka Mudra (Argumentation or Preaching), Varada Mudra (Bestowing Charity), Bhumisparsa Mudra (Calling the Earth to Witness), Dhammachakra Mudra (Setting in Motion the Wheel of the Law or the Buddhist Doctrine), Dhyani or Samadhi Mudra (Meditation), and the Abhaya Mudra (Calming or Dispelling Fear).

Some images were painted, though those that have survived from earlier ages bear only a few smudges of color. Images were often decorated with jewelry or crowns (which seems contrary to the Buddha having foresworn all accoutrements and material possessions.) The emerald Buddha, the realm's most sacred image, wears a different set of clothes for each season. In a holy ceremony at Wat Phra Kaew presided over by the king, the image's clothes are changed at the beginning of the hot, the rainy, and the cold seasons.

The adorned Buddhas shouldn't be confused with another category of images: Boddhisatvas and Boddhisattas. In Mahayana Buddhism, a Boddhisatva is an emanation of the five Dhyani Buddhas identified in the Mahayanan sutras. Of these emanations, the Avalokitesvara, related to the Amithaba Buddha of the west, was the most popular among sculptors of the Srivijaya and late Lop Buri periods. The Boddhisatva Avalokitesvara may be portrayed with four arms (the usual number) or as

many as 11 heads and 22 arms. He has a heavily ornamented body, and may have an antelope skin flung over his left shoulder or a tiger skin tied at his waist. The key identifying mark is his hair, which is tied in a chignon and decorated with an image of Amithaba meaning "infinite light," a reference to his transcendental nature. Alternatively, he may be portrayed as an ascetic.

Theravada Buddhism, the school that Thailand ultimately adopted, recognizes the Boddhisattas, the Buddhas-to-be identified in the Chadok Tales. Images of these are more difficult to distinguish because they lack precise identifying marks; but, then, Thai sculptors produced very few of them. The most noted was a series of 500 that were sculpted in the 15th century.

Two other popular subjects were the Dhammachakra or Wheel of the Law and the Buddhapada or Buddha's footprint. The Wheel of the Law represents the Buddha's Doctrine and is the object referred to in the mudra for "Setting the Wheel of Law in Motion." It was first devised in India during the reign of the 3rd-century BC Buddhist ruler Asoka. As a subject for sculpture, it was popular in Thailand only among Mon artists. Buddha footprints, with their 108 auspicious signs that would guide sages in recognizing Buddhas-to-be, were especially popular among the sculptors of Ayutthaya period.

To a limited extent, Thai sculptors produced images of the trinity of Hindu deities. Though images of Brahma the Creator are rare, there are dozens of statues of Vishnu the Preserver and Siva the Destroyer. Vishnu was popular because his avatar, Rama, was the hero of the *Ramakien*. Several rulers of Sukhothai (Ramkamhaeng) and Ayutthaya (Ramathibodi and Ramesuan) incorporated his name into their own as have the kings of the present dynasty (Rama I, II, III . . .) Another avatar of Vishnu, Narayana (Phra Narai in Thai) has also enjoyed great popularity. In the Bangkok period he's portrayed riding Vishnu's vehicle in the pediments of the major wats. In statues carved in-the-round,

Vishnu himself is depicted with a smooth, unadorned body and standing with his four arms outstretched. Prior to the 8th century AD Vishnus wore cylindrical miters or hats; those after that date wore crowns. Statues of Siva are somewhat rarer. The Hindu deity was portrayed in the standing position with a smooth, unadorned body bearing several pairs of arms but wearing a tall chignon with an ornament instead of a miter like Vishnu.

Thai sculptors worked with many different materials, but bronze was the most popular. Many early bronze Buddhas were covered in gold leaf. In the Lop Buri period the image's eyes were fashioned of metal, while in the Lanna and Bangkok periods they were made of colored gemstones or enamel. Good stone is scarce in Thailand, but there are several pieces, notably Hindu figures, that testify to the skill of Thai sculptors. Artists also carved in wood, though few statues have survived.

Stucco—made of lime, sand, and, often, rice husks—was employed for both wat decoration and sculpture. The wet substance was either shaped by hand or pressed into molds. Sukhothai sculptors applied it in layers to create large pieces. The material was usually shaped over a framework of bamboo, wood, or thin tin rods. Large free-standing images were generally made of brick or laterite and covered with stucco. The finished images were nearly always painted. The skin areas of many stucco Buddha images were covered in gold leaf, and Mon sculptors introduced the practice of inlaying the stucco with colored stones, bits of ceramic, or mother-of-pearl.

Although terra-cotta is difficult to work with, the Thai's have used it for figures, votive tablets, and architectural details since Neolithic times. Like stucco, it was shaped by hand or in elaborate molds. Ceramics have also occupied a major place in Thai sculpture, especially during the Sukhothai period. Images at Wat Mangkon provide good examples of the art; some were several feet tall, fired in one piece, and coated in gray or off-white glazes. Throughout history, Thai architects borrowed ideas from Indian, Sri Lankan, and Kampuchean (Cambodian) structures, and Thai artists often used symbolic elements that began as Hindu concepts. Just as the Christians found it expedient to adopt pagan celebrations and symbols as their own, Buddhists modified Hindu elements to fit their needs. Despite the antecedents, what emerged were architectural and artistic styles that are uniquely sacred and uniquely Thai.

ESSENTIAL INFORMATION

BOOKING

When you book, **look for nonstop flights** and **remember that "direct" flights stop at least once.** Try to avoid connecting flights, which require a change of plane.

On popular tourist routes during peak holiday times, domestic flights are often fully booked. Make sure you have reservations, and make them well in advance of your travel date. Flights should be reconfirmed when you arrive in Thailand.

CARRIERS

When flying internationally, you must usually choose between a domestic-carrier, the national flag carrier of the country you are visiting, and a foreign carrier from a third country. National flag carriers have the greatest number of nonstops. Domestic carriers may have better connections to your home town and serve a greater number of gateway cities. Third-party carriers may have a price advantage.

About 70 airlines serve Bangkok, and more are seeking landing rights. Northwest Airlines is the major U.S. carrier, flying daily from six U.S. cities, with the best connection times in Tokyo. East-coast travelers departing from New York or Washington, D.C., should consider using British Airways or Virgin Atlantic/Thai Airways via London for 19-hour flights to Bangkok. Singapore Airlines flies from Newark via Amsterdam to Bangkok.

➤ Major Airlines: **Asiana Airlines** (☎ 800/227–4262). **British Airways** (☎ 800/247–9297). **Cathay Pacific** (☎ 800/233–2742). **China Airlines** (☎ 800/227–5118). **EVA Air** (☎ 800/695–1188). **Gulf Air** (☎ 800/553–2824). **Japan Airlines** (☎ 800/525–3663). **Korean Air** (☎ 800/438–

5000). **Northwest Airlines** (☎ 800/447–4747). **Singapore Airlines** (☎ 800/742–3333). **Thai Airways** (☎ 800/426–5204). **United Airlines** (☎ 800/241–6522).

➤ From the U.K.: **British Airways** (☎ 020/8897–4000 or 0345/222111 outside London). **Qantas** (☎ 0345/747767 or 0800/747767). **Thai Airways** (☎ 020/7499–9113).

CHECK-IN & BOARDING

Assuming that not everyone with a ticket will show up, airlines routinely overbook planes. When everyone does, airlines ask for volunteers to give up their seats. In return, these volunteers usually get a certificate for a free flight and are rebooked on the next flight out. If there are not enough volunteers, the airline must choose who will be denied boarding. The first to get bumped are passengers who checked in late and those flying on discounted tickets, so **get to the gate and check in as early as possible,** especially during peak periods.

Always **bring a government-issued photo I.D. to the airport.** You may be asked to show it before you are allowed to check in.

CUTTING COSTS

The least expensive airfares to Thailand must usually be purchased in advance and are nonrefundable. It's smart to **call a number of airlines, and when you are quoted a good price, book it on the spot**—the same fare may not be available the next day. Always **check different routings** and look into using different airports. Travel agents, especially low-fare specialists (☞ Discounts & Deals, *below*), are helpful.

A number of Web sites offer lower fares when you **book tickets on the Internet;** try cheaptickets.com, expedia.com, priceline.com, or ticket-planet.com. These sites will find schedules, discounts, fares, and packages for you; you can even order and pay for tickets and reserve seats and meals on-line.

Consolidators are another good source. They buy tickets for scheduled international flights at reduced rates from the airlines, then sell them at prices that beat the best fare available directly from the airlines, usually without restrictions. Sometimes you can even get your money back if you need to return the ticket. Carefully read the fine print detailing penalties for changes and cancellations, and **confirm your consolidator reservation with the airline.**

For independent travelers, most airlines offer special "Circle Pacific" fares. The pricing and routing of these tickets depend on the arrangements that the airline has with the local carriers of the region. The tickets must be purchased 14–30 days in advance, and they carry cancellation penalties. You usually can add on extra stopovers, including Australian and South Pacific destinations, for a nominal charge (about $50). Several airlines work together to offer "Around the World" fares, but you must follow a specific routing itinerary and cannot backtrack. "Around the World" itineraries usually include a couple of Asian destinations before continuing through Africa and Europe.

➤ CONSOLIDATORS: **Cheap Tickets** (☎ 800/377–1000). **Discount Airline Ticket Service** (☎ 800/576–1600). **Unitravel** (☎ 800/325–2222). **Up & Away Travel** (☎ 212/889–2345). **World Travel Network** (☎ 800/409–6753).

ENJOYING THE FLIGHT

Some carriers have prohibited smoking throughout their systems; others allow smoking only on certain routes or even certain departures on that route. For flights within Asia, many airlines still have smoking sections, so **contact your carrier regarding its smoking policy.**

FLYING TIMES

Bangkok is 17 hours from San Francisco, 18 hours from Seattle and Vancouver, 20 hours from Chicago, 22 hours from New York and Toronto, 11 hours from London, and 10 hours from Sydney. Add more time for stopovers and connections, especially if you are using more than one carrier.

TRAVEL WITHIN THAILAND

Thai Airways connects Bangkok with all major cities and tourist areas in Thailand, except Ko Samui. Bangkok Airways has numerous daily flights between Bangkok and Ko Samui, using 40-seat planes. It also flies daily between Ko Samui and Phuket, daily from Bangkok to Angkor Wat in Cambodia, twice a week to Krabi, and three times a week to Chiang Mai via Sukhothai. Its fares are competitive with those of Thai Airways. The new and fast-growing Angel Airlines flies between Bangkok and Chiang Mai, Phuket, Udon Thani, and Singapore; between Chiang Mai and Phuket, Udon Thani, and Singapore; and between Phuket and Singapore.

Thai Airways offers a "Discover Thailand Pass." For $179 you can take four flights to any of the airline's Thailand destinations. You must purchase the pass outside Thailand. Be aware that this pass has its limitations: For example, if you fly from Chiang Mai to Surat Thani, you must change planes in Bangkok, meaning that you will use two of your four flights.

➤ AIRLINES: **Angel Airlines** (☎ 02/535–6287 at Don Muang airport office). **Bangkok Airways** (✉ 60 Queen Sirikit National Convention Centre, New Ratchadaphisek Rd., Klongotey, Bangkok, ☎ 02/229–3456 or 02/229–3434). **Thai Airways International** (✉ 485 Silom Rd., Bangkok, ☎ 02/232–8000).

AIRPORTS

The major gateway to Thailand is Bangkok's Don Muang International Airport, which is about 15 mi (25 km) north of Bangkok. Bangkok is going ahead with plans for a second airport at Nang-Ngu Kao, 32 km (20 mi) east of town, to relieve congestion at Don Muang, but its projected opening date of late 2004 may be delayed by a year or two.

Bangkok Airways built an airport outside Sukhothai, which was once slightly off the beaten track. Now a daily flight arrives from Chiang Mai and Bangkok. The airline has also initiated direct flights between Bangkok and Siem Reap and between Singapore and Ko Samui. (Because Bangkok Airways is the only carrier with rights on Samui, flights there are already very expensive and are likely to become truly exorbitant.) There's also a new airport at Krabi with flights to and from Bangkok.

➤ AIRPORT INFORMATION: **Don Muang International Airport** (☎ 02/535–2081).

TRANSFERS

Bangkok has nonstop airport shuttles that serve the train stations as well as hotels (☞ see Arriving and Departing in Bangkok A to Z). Shared hotel vans and taxis are also a popular mode of transport. It helps to **have a hotel brochure or an address in the local language for the driver.**

From the center of Bangkok to Don Muang, allow about 40 minutes in light traffic, 90 minutes at rush hour.

BUS TRAVEL

Long-distance buses are cheaper and faster than trains and reach every corner of the country. The level of comfort depends on the bus company, however, luxury "super buses" with extra-wide reclining seats, air-conditioning, video, scheduled box or buffet meals, and rest rooms are available. Be aware that air-conditioned buses are always so cold that you'll want to bring an extra sweater.

CUTTING COSTS

A typical fare for the nine-hour trip between Chiang Mai and Bangkok is anywhere from B300 to B570 depending on the travel agent with whom you book. Travel agents on Khao San Road in Bangkok offer some of the cheapest deals for private buses.

FARES & SCHEDULES

Travel agents have bus schedules and can make reservations and issue tickets.

BUSINESS HOURS

BANKS & OFFICES

Thai and foreign banks are open weekdays 8:30–3:30, except for public holidays. Most commercial concerns in Bangkok operate on a five-day week and are open 8–5. Government offices are generally open 8:30–4:30 with a noon–1 lunch break.

GAS STATIONS

Gas stations in Thailand are usually open at least 8–8 daily; many, particularly those on the highways, are open 24 hours a day.

MUSEUMS & SIGHTS

Each museum keeps its own hours and it may select a different day of the week to close; it's best to call before visiting. Wats are generally open to visitors from 7 or 8 in the morning to 5 or 6 PM.

SHOPS

Many stores are open daily 8–8.

CAMERAS & PHOTOGRAPHY

Remember to ask permission or smile and make eye contact with people and children before photographing them.

➤ PHOTO HELP: **Kodak Information Center** (☎ 800/242–2424). *Kodak Guide to Shooting Great Travel Pictures,* available in bookstores or from Fodor's Travel Publications (☎ 800/533–6478; $16.50 plus $5.50 shipping).

FILM & DEVELOPING

Expect to pay around U.S. $3.75 for a roll of Kodak 200 ASA 120 with 36 exposures. For Fuji 200 ASA 115 with 36 exposures you will be charged around U.S. $3.50.

The cost of developing film is usually 30 baht, plus 4 baht to 6 baht per exposure. That works out to about $5.70 for a 36-exposure roll of film. The quality is usually commensurate with that of a one-hour developing shop back home; you will find Kodak and other film stores throughout the more touristed sections of Thailand.

CAR RENTAL

Cars are available for rent in Bangkok and in major tourist destinations, however the additional cost of hiring a driver is small and the peace of mind great. If a foreigner is involved in an automobile accident, he or she—not the Thai—is likely to be judged at fault.

Rates in Thailand begin at $39 a day and $336 a week for an economy car with unlimited mileage. This includes neither tax, which is 7% on car rentals, nor the collision damage waiver, which is about $10 a day. It is better to make your car-rental reservations in Thailand as you can usually secure a discount.

In Chiang Mai, Ko Samui, Pattaya, and Phuket, **consider renting a jeep or motorcycle,** popular and convenient ways to get around. **Be aware that motorcycles skid easily on gravel roads** or on gravel patches on the pavement. On Ko Samui, a sign posts the year's count of foreigners who never made it home from their vacation!

➤ MAJOR AGENCIES: **Alamo** (☎ 800/ 522–9696; 0208/759–6200 in the U.K.). **Avis** (☎ 800/331–1084; 800/ 879–2847 in Canada; 02/9353–9000 in Australia; 09/525–1982 in New Zealand). **Budget** (☎ 800/527–0700; 0144/227–6266 in the U.K.). **Dollar** (☎ 800/800–6000; 0208/897–0811 in the U.K., where it is known as Eurodollar; 02/9223–1444 in Australia). **Hertz** (☎ 800/654–3001; 800/ 263–0600 in Canada; 0208/897– 2072 in the U.K.; 02/9669–2444 in Australia; 03/358–6777 in New Zealand). **National InterRent** (☎ 800/227–3876; 0345/222525 in the U.K., where it is known as Europcar InterRent).

INSURANCE

When driving a rented car you are generally responsible for any damage to or loss of the vehicle as well as for any property damage or personal injury that you may cause. Before you rent see what coverage your personal auto-insurance policy and credit cards already provide.

REQUIREMENTS & RESTRICTIONS

In Thailand, your own driver's license is acceptable unless your current driver's license is not written in English, in which case you must obtain an international driving license. It's a good idea for anyone to have an international driver's permit; it's available from the American or Canadian Automobile Associations, and, in the United Kingdom, from the Automobile Association or Royal Automobile Club. Having one in your wallet may save you a problem with the local authorities.

SURCHARGES

Before you pick up a car in one city and leave it in another, **ask about drop-off charges or one-way service fees,** which can be substantial. Note, too, that some rental agencies charge extra if you return the car before the time specified in your contract. To avoid a hefty refueling fee, **fill the tank just before you turn in the car,** but be aware that gas stations near the rental outlet may overcharge.

CAR TRAVEL

GASOLINE

A liter of gasoline costs approximately B14–B16. Many gas stations stay open 24 hours and have clean toilet facilities and minimarkets.

PARKING

In cities, the larger hotels, restaurants, and department stores have garages or parking lots. Rates vary, but count on B10 an hour. If you purchase anything, parking is free, but you must have your ticket validated.

ROAD CONDITIONS

The major roads in Thailand tend to be very congested, and street signs are often in Thai only. But the limited number of roads and, with the exception of Bangkok, the straightforward layout of cities combine to make navigation relatively easy. **Avoid driving at night in rural areas,** especially north and west of Chiang Mai and in the south beyond Surat Thani, as highway robberies have been reported.

RULES OF THE ROAD

Drive on the left; speed limits are 60 kph (37 mph) in cities, 90 kph (56 mph) outside, and 130 kph (81 mph) on expressways.

The main rule to remember is that traffic laws are routinely disregarded. Bigger vehicles have the unspoken right of way, motorcyclists seem to think they are invincible, and bicyclists often don't look around them. Drive carefully.

If you are renting a motorcycle, **wear a helmet**; they are now required by law, and this law is periodically enforced, particularly in Phuket.

CHILDREN IN THAILAND

Youngsters are welcome in Thailand. You will be amazed at how many people will want to hold and play with your kids, and at how their presence will actually open conversations and cut through cultural boundaries. If you are renting a car, don't forget to **arrange for a car seat** when you reserve.

FLYING

If your children are two or older, **ask about children's airfares.** Usually, infants under two not occupying a seat fly at greatly reduced fares or even for free. When booking, **confirm carry-on allowances** if you're traveling with infants. In general, for babies charged 10% of the adult fare you are allowed one carry-on bag and a collapsible stroller; if the flight is full, the stroller may have to be checked or you may be limited to less.

Experts agree that it's a good idea to use safety seats aloft for children weighing less than 40 pounds. Airlines set their own policies: U.S. carriers usually require that the child be ticketed, even if he or she is young enough to ride free, since the seats must be strapped into regular seats. Do **check your airline's policy about using safety seats during takeoff and landing.** And since safety seats are not allowed just everywhere in the plane, get your seat assignments early.

When reserving, **request children's meals or a freestanding bassinet** if you need them. But note that bulk-head seats, where you must sit to use the bassinet, may lack an overhead bin or storage space on the floor.

LODGING

Most hotels in Thailand allow children under a certain age to stay in their parents' room at no extra charge, but others charge for them as extra adults; be sure to **find out the cutoff age for children's discounts.**

SIGHTS & ATTRACTIONS

Places that are especially appealing to children are indicated by a rubber duckie icon in the margin.

SUPPLIES & EQUIPMENT

Supplies are easy to find in the major supermarkets in Thailand; you can get both Huggies and Pampers brand diapers in small to extra-large sizes. Expect to pay $5.07 for a 16-diaper package of small Pampers baby-dry or $8.89 for a 24-diaper package of large. Baby bottles, food, and toys are also easily found.

COMPUTERS ON THE ROAD

The business centers of many hotels provide Internet access. In modern upscale hotels, you'll often find in-room phone jacks for your laptop. They use the same connecting module as in the United States (different from that used in Great Britain). Most Internet servers have arrangements with roaming services that have partners in different cities throughout Asia, however be aware that AOL does not have an access number in Thailand. You can establish an e-mail address free of charge with an ad-driven provider such as www.hot-mail.com, whose international service can be accessed by any server.

In Thailand's major cities, as throughout Southeast Asia, cyber cafés are springing up all over; Bangkok, for example, has half a dozen or more in any given tourist or business section of the city, such as Silom Road or Khao San Road. The Internet café prices are considerably cheaper (about 1 baht per minute) on Khao San Road than in other tourist spots of the city, where the prices can be as high as 10 baht per minute.

CRUISE TRAVEL

Some cruise lines, including Cunard and Royal Viking, call at major Southeast Asian ports as part of their around-the-world itineraries. Cunard's Sea Goddess provides a luxury trip in the Gulf of Thailand and through the Straits of Malacca into the Andaman Sea. Seabourn Cruises spends 14 days cruising the waters of Southeast Asia, including the Gulf of Thailand. If a slow boat sounds tempting, contact Freighter World Cruises for a listing of current cargo ships en route to the region.

Plan to spend at least four weeks cruising from the West Coast of the United States to Southeast Asia, as these ships usually visit ports in the Pacific and Australia along the way.

➤ CRUISE LINES: **Cunard's Sea Goddess** (⊠ 555 5th Ave., New York, NY 10017, ☎ 212/880–7500 or 800/ 221–4770). **Freighter World Cruises** (⊠ 180 South Lake, Suite 335, Pasadena, CA 91101, ☎ 818/449– 3106 or 800/531–7774). **Royal Viking** (☎ 800/426–0821). **Seabourn Cruises** (San Francisco St., San Francisco, CA 94133, ☎ 415/391–7444 or 800/929–9595).

CUSTOMS & DUTIES

When shopping, **keep receipts** for all purchases. Upon reentering the country, **be ready to show customs officials what you've bought.** If you feel a duty is incorrect or object to the way your clearance was handled, note the inspector's badge number and ask to see a supervisor. If the problem isn't resolved, write to the appropriate authorities, beginning with the port director at your point of entry.

IN THAILAND

One liter of wine or liquor, 200 cigarettes or 250 grams of smoking tobacco, and all personal effects may be brought into Thailand duty-free. Visitors may bring in any amount of foreign currency; amounts taken out may not exceed those declared upon entry. Narcotic drugs, pornographic materials, and firearms are strictly prohibited.

If you are bringing any foreign-made equipment from home, such as cam-

eras, it is wise to carry the original receipt with you or register it with U.S. Customs before you leave (Form 4457). Otherwise, you may end up paying duty on your return.

IN AUSTRALIA

Australian residents who are 18 or older may bring home $A400 worth of souvenirs and gifts (including jewelry), 250 cigarettes or 250 grams of tobacco, and 1,125 ml of alcohol (including wine, beer, and spirits). Residents under 18 may bring back $A200 worth of goods. Prohibited items include meat products. Seeds, plants, and fruits need to be declared upon arrival.

➤ INFORMATION: **Australian Customs Service** (Regional Director, ⊠ Box 8, Sydney, NSW 2001, ☎ 02/9213– 2000, FAX 02/9213–4000).

IN CANADA

Canadian residents who have been out of Canada for at least 7 days may bring home C$500 worth of goods duty-free. If you've been away less than 7 days but more than 48 hours, the duty-free allowance drops to C$200; if your trip lasts 24–48 hours, the allowance is C$50. You may not pool allowances with family members. Goods claimed under the C$500 exemption may follow you by mail; those claimed under the lesser exemptions must accompany you. Alcohol and tobacco products may be included in the 7-day and 48-hour exemptions but not in the 24-hour exemption. If you meet the age requirements of the province or territory through which you reenter Canada, you may bring in, duty-free, 1.14 liters (40 imperial ounces) of wine or liquor *or* 24 12-ounce cans or bottles of beer or ale. If you are 16 or older you may bring in, duty-free, 200 cigarettes and 50 cigars. Check ahead of time with Revenue Canada or the Department of Agriculture for policies regarding meat products, seeds, plants, and fruits.

You may send an unlimited number of gifts worth up to C$60 each duty-free to Canada. Label the package UNSOLICITED GIFT—VALUE UNDER $60. Alcohol and tobacco are excluded.

➤ INFORMATION: **Revenue Canada** (⊠ 2265 St. Laurent Blvd. S, Ottawa, Ontario K1G 4K3, ☎ 613/993–0534; 800/461–9999 in Canada, FAX 613/957–8911, www.ccra-adrc.gc.ca).

IN NEW ZEALAND

Homeward-bound residents 17 or older may bring back $700 worth of souvenirs and gifts. Your duty-free allowance also includes 4.5 liters of wine or beer; one 1,125-ml bottle of spirits; and either 200 cigarettes, 250 grams of tobacco, 50 cigars, or a combination of the three up to 250 grams. Prohibited items include meat products, seeds, plants, and fruits.

➤ INFORMATION: **New Zealand Customs** (Custom House, ⊠ 50 Anzac Ave., Box 29, Auckland, New Zealand, ☎ 09/359–6655, FAX 09/359–6732).

IN THE U.K.

From countries outside the EU, including Thailand, you may bring home, duty-free, 200 cigarettes or 50 cigars; 1 liter of spirits or 2 liters of fortified or sparkling wine or liqueurs; 2 liters of still table wine; 60 ml of perfume; 250 ml of toilet water; plus £136 worth of other goods, including gifts and souvenirs. If returning from outside the EU, prohibited items include meat products, seeds, plants, and fruits.

➤ INFORMATION: **HM Customs and Excise** (⊠ Dorset House, Stamford St., Bromley, Kent BR1 1XX, ☎ 0207/202–4227).

IN THE U.S.

U.S. residents who have been out of the country for at least 48 hours (and who have not used the $400 allowance or any part of it in the past 30 days) may bring home $400 worth of foreign goods duty-free.

U.S. residents 21 and older may bring back 1 liter of alcohol duty-free. In addition, regardless of your age, you are allowed 200 cigarettes and 100 non-Cuban cigars. Antiques, which the U.S. Customs Service defines as objects more than 100 years old, enter duty-free, as do original works of art done entirely by hand, including paintings, drawings, and sculptures.

You may also send packages home duty-free: up to $200 worth of goods for personal use, with a limit of one parcel per addressee per day (except alcohol or tobacco products or perfume worth more than $5); label the package PERSONAL USE and attach a list of its contents and their retail value. Do not label the package UNSOLICITED GIFT or your duty-free exemption will drop to $100. Mailed items do not affect your duty-free allowance on your return.

➤ INFORMATION: **U.S. Customs Service** (⊠ 1300 Pennsylvania Ave. NW, Washington, DC 20229, www.customs.gov; inquiries ☎ 202/354–1000; complaints c/o ⊠ Office of Regulations and Rulings; registration of equipment c/o ⊠ Resource Management, ☎ 202/927–0540).

DINING

Food is a consuming passion for Thais; they constantly eat and snack. Throughout the day, roadside food carts replace one another, each vendor stirring up a different tasty morsel, depending on the time of day. Thai food is eaten with a fork and tablespoon, with the spoon held in the right hand and the fork used like a plow to push food into the spoon. Chopsticks are used only for Chinese dishes, such as noodle recipes. After you have finished eating, place your fork and spoon on the plate at the 5:25 position; otherwise the server will assume you would like another helping.

The restaurants we list are the cream of the crop in each price category. Price categories throughout the chapter are based on the following ranges:

CATEGORY	COST*
$$$$	over $20
$$$	$10–$20
$$	$4–$10
$	under $4

per person, including service charge; a 7.5% government tax (VAT) is added to restaurant bills

MEALS & SPECIALTIES

The range of Thai cuisine is vast; no restaurant worth its salt has fewer than 100 dishes on its menu. There are seasonal delights, and of course, regional differences and specialties. You'll find a delicious spicy pork sausage in the north, and northern cuisine is usually eaten with sticky rice kneaded into balls and dipped in various sauces. Thais know that eating out can be cheaper than eating in, and that inexpensive restaurants often serve food that's as good as, and sometimes better than, the fare at fancy places.

Thai cuisine's distinctive flavor comes particularly from the use of fresh Thai basil, lemongrass, tamarind, lime, and citrus leaves. And though some Thai food is as hot as the fires of hell, an equal number of dishes are mild—and the hot ones can be tempered. Instead of salt, Thais use *nam pla*, a fish sauce served with meals.

Thai foods vary from super-hot dishes with loads of garlic and chilies to blander, simpler noodles and rice-based meals where the hot spices are served on the side, so you can adjust the incendiary level to your own taste.

If you're not sure what to order, start with some staples such as pad Thai, which is fried noodles with tofu, vegetables, eggs, and peanuts. Another frequently ordered dish is tom yam kung, which is prawn and lemongrass soup with mushrooms.

MEALTIMES

Restaurants tend to open in late morning and serve food until 9 or 10 at night. Outdoor vendors can be found 24-hours a day.

Unless otherwise noted, the restaurants listed in this guide are open daily for lunch and dinner.

RESERVATIONS & DRESS

Reservations are always a good idea: we mention them only when they're essential or not accepted. Book as far ahead as you can, and reconfirm as soon as you arrive.

Because Thailand has a hot climate, jackets and ties are rarely worn at dinner except in expensive restaurants, usually in the big hotels. We mention dress only when men are required to wear a jacket or a jacket and tie.

WINE, BEER & SPIRITS

Thai beers include Singha, Amarit, and Kloster; Singha is the most common of the three. You will also readily find Carlsberg, which is jointly owned by Danish and Thai business interests and heavily promoted in the country. San Miguel and Tuborg are other contenders in the market.

Rice whiskey, which tastes sweet and has a whopping 35 percent alcohol content, is another favorite throughout Thailand. Mekong is by far the most popular rice whiskey, but you will also see labels such as Sang Thip, Kwangthong, Hong Thong, Hong Ngoen, Hong Yok, and Hong Tho. Wine is increasingly available. However, the locally produced wines are likely to leave you with a nasty headache the next day, and the imported ones may do damage to your wallet. Imported wines are also likely to be in poor condition due to the tropical heat.

DISABILITIES & ACCESSIBILITY

Thailand has yet to develop facilities for people with disabilities, and pavements are totally unsuitable for wheelchairs. But traveling with a car and driver is relatively affordable here, and the Thais are so helpful that a person with disabilities can expect to have a great deal of friendly assistance.

RESERVATIONS

When discussing accessibility with an operator or reservations agent, **ask hard questions.** Are there any stairs, inside *or* out? Are there grab bars next to the toilet *and* in the shower/tub? How wide is the doorway to the room? To the bathroom? For the most extensive facilities meeting the latest legal specifications, **opt for newer accommodations.**

DISCOUNTS & DEALS

DISCOUNT RESERVATIONS

To save money, **look into discount reservations services** with toll-free numbers, which use their buying power to get a better price on hotels, airline tickets, even car rentals. When booking a room, always **call the hotel's local toll-free number** (if one is available) rather than the central reservations number—you'll often get a better price. Always ask about special packages or corporate rates.

When shopping for the best deal on hotels and car rentals, **look for guaranteed exchange rates,** which protect you against a falling dollar. With your rate locked in, you won't pay more, even if the price goes up in the local currency.

➤ AIRLINE TICKETS: ☎ 800/FLY–4–LESS.

➤ HOTEL ROOMS: **Steigenberger Reservation Service** (☎ 800/223–5652, www.srs-worldhotels.com). **Travel Interlink** (☎ 800/888–5898, www.travelinterlink.com). **Vacation-Land** (☎ 800/245–0050, www.vacation-land.com).

PACKAGE DEALS

Don't confuse packages and guided tours. When you buy a package, you travel on your own, just as though you had planned the trip yourself. Fly/drive packages, which combine airfare and car rental, are often a good deal.

ECOTOURISM

Thailand tour agencies increasingly try to be eco-friendly, particularly on jungle treks in northern Thailand. In Chiang Mai, many people are now talking about the need to preserve the forests and the hill-tribe groups who live off this land. It is a delicate balance—some argue that if the hill-tribe people are moved out, the land will be taken over by big corporations who will deforest the region (or set up hotels). Others say that the hill tribe people slash and burn the forests and are causing erosion problems in the region. There is also an issue of whether these hill-tribe people are getting a fair share of money they generate—tourists come to see them, yet they remain poor. It's up to you how you want to play a part in this issue—there are travel agents who assert that the hill tribes will benefit from your visit. Ask tough questions.

Avoid dining in restaurants that serve exotic animals as main courses.

Pay the extra few baht to buy water in glass bottles that can be recycled. Sometimes water comes in reusable plastic containers, which are clearly marked as such. However, as it stands now, too many plastic bottles are often simply strewn about, leaving an eyesore on street corners, and worse, on beaches and in riverbeds.

ANIMAL RIGHTS

The elephant has a long history in Thailand (elephants were used to haul timber and move huge objects, including the teak pillars used in royal palaces and temples) and is revered for its strength, courage, and intelligence. In recent years, however, mechanization and restrictions on teak logging have made the domesticated elephant obsolete, and elephants and their mahouts have come to rely on the tourist industry as their only source of income. To make sure they are not mistreated, animal rights groups, including Friends of the Asian Elephant, now monitor the treatment of elephants used in shows and treks. If you are going on an elephant-back trek and have concerns, check out how various companies treat their animals. Find out, for example, how many hours the elephants are worked each day and whether you will be riding in the afternoon heat.

Elephants shouldn't work more than five hours per day, and they should rest during the afternoon as they can become ill and thus temperamental if forced to work in the midday heat. A stick with a sharp hooked spike at the end is used by the mahout to control his elephant. If you see extensive overuse of these sticks, notify Friends of the Asian Elephant, who will investigate the situation. Be as specific as you can in your complaint: note the trek company or elephant show, the address, the mahout's name, the elephant's name, and how frequently the mistreatment occurred.

➤ CONTACTS: **Friends of the Asian Elephant** (✉ 350 Moo 8, Ram-Indra Rd., Soi 61, Tharaeng, Bangkhen, Bangkok 10230, ☎ 𝔽𝔸𝕏 02/945-7124, www.elephant.tnet.co.th).

ELECTRICITY

To use your U.S.-purchased electric-powered equipment, **bring a converter and adapter.** The electrical current in Thailand is 220 volts, 50 cycles alternating current (AC); wall outlets take either two flat prongs, like outlets in the United States, or Continental-type plugs, with two round prongs.

If your appliances are dual-voltage, you'll need only an adapter. Don't use 110-volt outlets marked FOR SHAVERS ONLY for high-wattage appliances such as blow-dryers. Most laptops operate equally well on 110 and 220 volts and so require only an adapter.

EMBASSIES AND CONSULATES

Most nations maintain diplomatic relations with Thailand and have embassies in Bangkok; a few have consulates also in Chiang Mai. Should you need to apply for a visa to another country, the consulate hours are usually 8–noon.

➤ IN BANGKOK: **Australian Embassy** (37 Sathorn Tai Rd., ☎ 02/287–2680). **Canadian Embassy** (15th Floor, Abdulrahim Bldg., 990 Rama IV, ☎ 02/636–0540). **New Zealand Embassy** (93 Wireless Rd., ☎ 02/254–2530). **British Embassy** (1031 Wireless Rd., ☎ 02/253–0191). **U.S. Embassy** (120-122 Wireless Rd., ☎ 02/205–4000).

➤ IN CHIANG MAI: **Australian Consulate** (✉ 165 Sirman Khalajan, ☎ 053/221083). **British Consulate** (✉ 201 Airport Business Park, 90 Mahidon, ☎ 053/203–405). **U.S. Consulate** (✉ 387 Wichayanom Rd., ☎ 053/252629).

EMERGENCIES

Thais are generally quite helpful, so you should get assistance from locals if you need it. The Tourist Police will help you in case of a robbery or rip-off.

Many hotels can refer you to an English-speaking doctor. For serious health situation, it's best to be treated in your own country; otherwise consider flying to Singapore, which has the region's best medical facilities.

➤ CONTACTS: **Police** (☎ 191). **Tourist Police** (☎ 1699).

ENGLISH-LANGUAGE MEDIA

Thailand has by and large a free press, with only a modicum of self-censorship (particularly when referring to the monarchy) in evidence.

BOOKS

Major hotels have bookstores and tourist areas have second-hand shops where you should be able to trade or buy inexpensive books written in a variety of languages.

NEWSPAPERS & MAGAZINES

There are two English-language newspapers published daily in Thailand: *The Bangkok Post* (morning edition) and *The Nation* (afternoon edition). The former has more of an international news staff, which is evident in the more Western-style reporting.

The Bangkok Metro magazine tells readers what's hip and happening in Bangkok. It also gives some listings for Pattaya, Phuket, and Chiang Mai.

Popular newspapers and magazines—from the *International Herald Tribune* to *Time* magazine—are widely available throughout Thailand.

RADIO & TELEVISION

Bangkok has five VHF-TV networks, with English shows aired periodically during the day, although mostly in the mornings. Satellite and cable TV are widely available, where you can expect to see HBO, MTV Asia, CNN International, and BBC World Service Television.

There are literally hundreds of radio stations available in Thailand. Check out 107 FM for CNN hourly updates. Radio Bangkok, at 95.5 FM, also has English-speaking DJs.

ETIQUETTE & BEHAVIOR

Displays of anger, raised voices, and confrontations are considered very bad form. Thais disapprove of public nudity and of public shows of affection. **Do not step over a seated person** or someone's legs. Don't point your feet at anyone; keep them on the floor, and take care not to show the soles of your feet. **Never touch a person's head,** even a child's (the head is considered sacred), and avoid touching a monk if you are a woman.

When visiting temples, **don't wear shorts or tank tops.** Remove your shoes before entering the temple and don't **point your toes at any image of the buddha.**

GAY & LESBIAN TRAVEL

Thailand has always shown tolerance toward homosexuality, though public affection between couples (homo- or heterosexual) is frowned on. In Bangkok, Patpong III has many gay bars, and you'll also find them in Chiang Mai, Pattaya, and Phuket.

➤ GAY- & LESBIAN-FRIENDLY TRAVEL AGENCIES: **Different Roads Travel** (✉ 8383 Wilshire Blvd., Suite 902, Beverly Hills, CA 90211, ☎ 323/651–5557 or 800/429–8747, FAX 323/651–3678, leigh@west.tzell. com). **Kennedy Travel** (✉ 314 Jericho Turnpike, Floral Park, NY 11001, ☎ 516/352–4888 or 800/237–7433, FAX 516/354–8849, main@kennedytravel.com, www. kennedytravel.com). **Now Voyager** (✉ 4406 18th St., San Francisco, CA 94114, ☎ 415/626–1169 or 800/255–6951, FAX 415/626–8626, www.nowvoyager.com). **Skylink Travel and Tour** (✉ 1006 Mendocino Ave., Santa Rosa, CA 95401, ☎ 707/546–9888 or 800/225–5759, FAX 707/546–9891, skylinktvl@aol.com, www. skylinktravel.com), serving lesbian travelers.

HEALTH

Although Thailand does not require or suggest vaccinations before traveling, the United States Centers for Disease Control offer the following recommendations:

Tetanus and polio vaccinations should be up-to-date, and you should be immunized against (or immune to) measles, mumps, and rubella. If you plan to visit rural areas, where there's questionable sanitation, you'll need a vaccination as protection against hepatitis A.

Be aware that a high percentage of sex workers in Thailand are HIV positive, and unprotected sex is extremely risky.

FOOD & DRINK

In Thailand the major health risk is traveler's diarrhea, caused by eating contaminated fruit or vegetables or drinking contaminated water. So **watch what you eat.** Avoid ice, uncooked food, and unpasteurized milk and milk products, and **drink only bottled water** or water that has been boiled for at least 20 minutes, even when brushing your teeth. Mild cases may respond to Imodium (known generically as loperamide) or Pepto-Bismol (not as strong), both of which can be purchased over the counter; paregoric, another antidiarrheal agent, does not require a doctor's prescription in Thailand. Drink plenty of purified water or tea—chamomile is a good folk remedy. In severe cases, rehydrate yourself with a salt-sugar solution (½ teaspoon salt and 4 tablespoons sugar per quart of water).

MEDICAL PLANS

No one plans to get sick while traveling, but it happens, so **consider signing up with a medical-assistance company.** Members get doctor referrals, emergency evacuation or repatriation, hot lines for medical consultation, cash for emergencies, and other assistance.

➤ MEDICAL-ASSISTANCE COMPANIES: **International SOS Assistance** (✉ 8 Neshaminy Interplex, Suite 207, Trevose, PA 19053, ☎ 215/245–4707 or 800/523–6586, FAX 215/244–9617, www.internationalsos.com; ✉ 12 Chemin Riantbosson, 1217 Meyrin 1, Geneva, Switzerland, ☎ 4122/785–6464, FAX 4122/785–6424, www. internationalsos.com; ✉ 331 N. Bridge Rd., 17-00, Odeon Towers, Singapore 188720, ☎ 65/338–7800, FAX 65/338–7611, www.international-sos.com).

SHOTS & MEDICATIONS

According to the U.S. government's National Centers for Disease Control(CDC) there is a limited risk of malaria, hepatitis B, dengue, rabies, and Japanese encephalitis in certain rural areas of Thailand. In most urban or easily accessible areas you need not worry. However, if you plan to visit remote regions or stay for more than six weeks, **check with the CDC's International Travelers Hotline.** In areas where malaria and dengue, both of which are carried by mosquitoes, are prevalent, use mosquito nets, wear clothing that covers the body, apply repellent containing DEET, and use spray for flying insects in living and sleeping areas. Also **talk to your doctor about taking antimalarial pills.** There is no vaccine to combat dengue, so if it's in the area, travelers should use aerosol insecticides indoors as well as mosquito repellents outdoors. Both Ko Samet and northern Thailand are known to have malarial mosquitoes, so take extra precautions if you visit these areas.

➤ HEALTH WARNINGS: **National Centers for Disease Control** (CDC; National Center for Infectious Diseases, Division of Quarantine, Traveler's Health Section, ✉ 1600 Clifton Rd. NE, M/S E-03, Atlanta, GA 30333, ☎ 888/232–3228, FAX 888/232–3299, www.cdc.gov).

HOLIDAYS

New Year's Day (January 1); Chinese New Year (February 12, 2002 and February 1, 2003); Magha Puja (on the full moon of the third lunar month); Chakri Day (April 6); Songkran (April 13–15); Coronation Day (May 5); Visakha Puja, May (on the full moon of the sixth lunar month); Queen's Birthday (August 12); King's Birthday (December 5). Government offices, banks, commercial concerns, and department stores are usually closed on these days, but smaller shops stay open.

INSURANCE

The most useful travel insurance plan is a comprehensive policy that includes coverage for trip cancellation and interruption, default, trip delay, and medical expenses (with a waiver for preexisting conditions).

If you're traveling internationally, a key component of travel insurance is coverage for medical bills incurred if you get sick on the road. Such expenses are not generally covered by Medicare or private policies. U.K. residents can buy a travel insurance policy valid for most vacations taken during the year in which it's purchased (but check pre-existing-condition coverage). British and Australian citizens need extra medical coverage when traveling overseas.

Always **buy travel policies directly from the insurance company**; if you buy them from a cruise line, airline, or tour operator that goes out of business you probably will not be covered for the agency or operator's default, a major risk. Before making any purchase, **review your existing health and home-owner's policies** to find what they cover away from home.

LANGUAGE

Thai is the country's national language. As it uses the Khmer script and is spoken tonally, it is confusing to most foreigners. In polite conversation, a male speaker will use the word "krap" to end a sentence or to acknowledge what someone has said. Female speakers use "ka." It is easy to speak a few words, such as "sawahdee krap" or "sawahdee ka" (good day) and "khop khun krap" or "khop khun ka" (thank you). With the exception of taxi drivers, Thais working with travelers in the resort and tourist areas of Thailand generally speak sufficient English to permit basic communication.

LODGING

Every town of reasonable size offers accommodations. In the smaller towns the hotels may be fairly simple, but they will usually be clean and certainly inexpensive. In major cities or resort areas there are hotels to fit all price categories. At the high end, the luxury hotels can compete with the best in the world. Service is generally superb—polite and efficient—and most of the staff usually speak English. At the other end of the scale, the lodging is simple and basic—a room with little more than a bed. The least expensive places may have Asian toilets (squat type with no seat) and a fan rather than air-conditioning.

All except the budget hotels have restaurants and offer room service throughout most of the day and night. Most will also be happy to make local travel arrangements for you—for which they receive commissions. All hotels advise that you use their safe-deposit boxes.

During the peak tourist season, October–March, hotels are often fully booked and charge peak rates. At special times, such as December 30–January 2 and Chinese New Year, rates climb even higher, and hotel reservations are difficult to obtain. Weekday rates at some resorts are often lower, and virtually all hotels will discount their rooms if they are not fully booked. Don't be reticent about asking for a special rate. Breakfast is rarely included in the room tariff. Hotel rates tend to be lower if you reserve through a travel agent (in Thailand). The agent receives a reduced room rate from the hotel and passes some of this discount on to you.

The lodgings we list are the cream of the crop in each price category. We always list the facilities that are available—but we don't specify whether they cost extra: when pricing accommodations, always ask what's included and what costs extra.

Price categories throughout the book are based on the following ranges:

CATEGORY	COST*
$$$$	over $160
$$$	$100–$160
$$	$60–$100
$	$20–$60
¢	under $20

*per double room, including service and tax

Assume that hotels operate on the **European Plan** (EP, with no meals) unless we specify that they use either the **Continental Plan** (CP, with a Continental breakfast) or the **Modified American Plan** (MAP, with breakfast and dinner) or are **all-inclusive** (including all meals and most activities).

HOSTELS

No matter what your age, you can **save on lodging costs by staying at hostels.** In some 5,000 locations in more than 70 countries around the world, Hostelling International (HI), the umbrella group for a number of national youth-hostel associations, offers single-sex, dorm-style beds and, at many hostels, rooms for couples and family accommodations.

HOTELS

All hotels listed have private bath unless otherwise noted.

MAIL & SHIPPING

Thailand's mail service is reliable and efficient. Major hotels provide basic postal services. Bangkok's central general post office on Charoen Krung (New Road) is open weekdays 8–6, weekends and public holidays 9–1. Up-country post offices close at 4:30 PM.

OVERNIGHT SERVICES

You can ship packages via DHL Worldwide, Federal Express, or UPS.

➤ CONTACTS: **DHL Worldwide** (✉ 22nd Floor, Grand Amarin Tower, Phetburi Tat Mai, Bangkok, ☎ 02/207–0600). **Federal Express** (8th Floor, Green Tower, Rama IV, Bangkok, ☎ 02/367–3222). **UPS** (16/1 Soi 44/1, Sukhumvit, Bangkok, ☎ 02/712–3300).

POSTAL RATES

Airmail postcard rates to countries outside the Pacific Rim are B12; the minimum rate for airmail letters is B17. Allow about 10 days for your mail to arrive at its overseas destination. For speedier delivery, major post offices offer overseas express mail service (EMS), whose minimum rate (for 200 gr) is B350.

RECEIVING MAIL

You may have mail sent to you "poste restante" at the following address: Poste Restante, General Post Office, Bangkok, Thailand. There is a B1 charge for each piece collected. Thais write their last name first, so be sure to have your last name written in capital letters and underlined.

SHIPPING PARCELS

Parcels are easy to send from Thailand. Parcel rates vary by weight, country of destination and shipping style (air or surface). Expect to pay between B700 and B1,100 for a kilo package and then an additional B300 to B350 per added kilo.

MONEY MATTERS

It is possible to live and travel quite inexpensively if you do as Thais do— eat in local restaurants, use buses, and stay at non-air-conditioned hotels. Once you start enjoying a little luxury, prices jump drastically. For example, crossing Bangkok by bus is less than 15¢, but by taxi the fare may run to $10. Prices are typically higher in resort areas catering to foreign tourists, and Bangkok is more expensive than other Thai cities. Imported items are heavily taxed.

Sample prices: buffet breakfast at a hotel, $8; large bottle of beer at a hotel, $6, but in a local restaurant it will be under $3; dinner at a good restaurant, $15; 1-mile taxi ride, $1.50; museum entrance, 50¢–$2.

Prices throughout this guide are given for adults. Substantially reduced fees are almost always available for children, students, and senior citizens. For information on taxes, *see* Taxes, *below*.

ATMS

24-hour automatic teller machines are widely available throughout Thailand. Some Thai ATMs take Cirrus, some take Plus, some take both.

CREDIT CARDS

Credit cards are accepted in restaurants, hotels, and shops. You may be levied a 3 to 5 percent charge despite the fact that this is technically against Thai law, but you will likely receive a favorable exchange rate from your home bank that could make up the difference.

Throughout this guide, the following abbreviations are used: **AE**, American Express; **DC**, Diner's Club; **MC**, Master Card; and **V**, Visa.

➤ REPORTING LOST CARDS: **American Express** (☎ 800/327–2177); **Discover Card** (☎ 800/347–2683); **Diners Club** (☎ 800/234–6377); **Master Card** (☎ 800/307–7309); and **Visa** (☎ 800/847–2911).

CURRENCY

The basic unit of currency is the baht. There are 100 satang to one baht. There are five different bills, each a different color: B10, brown; B20, green; B50, blue; B100, red; B500, purple; and B1,000, beige. Coins in use are 25 satang, 50 satang, B1, B5, and B10. The B10 coin has a gold-color center surrounded by silver.

The baht, formerly pegged to the U.S. dollar, is at press time undergoing considerable fluctuation. All hotels will convert traveler's checks and major currencies into baht, though exchange rates are better at banks and authorized money changers. The rate tends to be better in Bangkok than up-country and is better in Thailand than in the United States. Major international credit cards are accepted at most tourist shops and hotels.

At press time, B44 = US$1, B63 = £1, B28 = C$1, B23 = $A1, B18 = NZ$1.

CURRENCY EXCHANGE

Changing "old" U.S. $100 (the ones with the small heads) is increasingly difficult as these notes have been successfully counterfeited in the region. Bring the new "big head" U.S. $100. Clean, crisp notes are also preferred.

For the most favorable rates, **change money through banks.** Although ATM transaction fees may be higher abroad than at home, ATM rates are excellent because they are based on wholesale rates offered only by major banks. You won't do as well at exchange booths in airports or rail and bus stations, in hotels, in restaurants, or in stores. To avoid lines at airport exchange booths, **get a bit of local currency before you leave home.**

➤ EXCHANGE SERVICES: **International Currency Express** (☎ 888/278–6628 for orders, www.foreignmoney.com). **Thomas Cook Currency Services** (☎ 800/287–7362 for telephone orders and retail locations, www.us.thomas-cook.com).

TRAVELER'S CHECKS

Do you need traveler's checks? It depends on where you're headed. If you're going to rural areas and small towns, go with cash; traveler's checks are best used in cities. Lost or stolen checks can usually be replaced within 24 hours. To ensure a speedy refund, buy your own traveler's checks—don't let someone else pay for them: irregularities like this can cause delays. The person who bought the checks should make the call to request a refund.

PACKING

Pack light, because porters can be hard to find and baggage restrictions are tight on international flights—be sure to check on your airline's policies before you pack. And either leave room in your suitcase or bring expandable totes for all your bargains.

Light cotton or other natural-fiber clothing is appropriate for Thailand; drip-dry is an especially good idea, because the tropical sun and high humidity encourage frequent changes of clothing. Avoid exotic and delicate fabrics because you may have difficulty getting them laundered.

Thailand is generally informal: a sweater, shawl, or lightweight linen jacket will be sufficient for dining and evening wear, except for top international restaurants, where men will still be most comfortable in a jacket and tie. A sweater is also a good idea for cool evenings or overly air-conditioned restaurants, buses, and trains.

The paths leading to temples can be rough; **bring a sturdy pair of comfortable walking shoes.** Slip-ons are preferable to lace-up shoes, as they must be removed before you enter shrines and temples.

Bring a hat and sunscreen for the tropical sun. Mosquito repellent is a good idea, and toilet paper is not always supplied in public places.

PASSPORTS & VISAS

When traveling internationally, **carry your passport even if you don't need one** (it's always the best form of I.D.) and **make two photocopies of the data page** (one for someone at home and another for you, carried separately from your passport). If you lose your passport, promptly call the nearest embassy or consulate and the local police.

ENTERING THAILAND

Australian, Canadian, U.S., and U.K. citizens—even infants—need only a valid passport and an onward ticket to enter Thailand for stays of up to 30 days. New Zealanders are permitted to stay up to 90 days with a valid passport and onward ticket.

The Immigration Division in Bangkok issues Thai visa extensions, but if you overstay by a few days, don't worry; you'll simply pay a B200 per diem fine as you go through immigration on departure.

➤ VISA EXTENSIONS: **Immigration Division** (Soi Suan Phlu, Sathorn Rd., Bangkok, ☎ 02/287–3101).

REST ROOMS

Western toilets are usually available, although you still may find squatters in older buildings. Toilet paper is rarely provided, so it's a good idea to carry tissues. Often a bucket is placed under a tap next to the loo; you are expected to fill the bucket with water and flush out the toilet manually.

SAFETY

Thailand is a safe country, but normal precautions should be followed: be careful late at night, watch your valuables in crowded areas, and lock your hotel rooms securely. Credit-card scams—from stealing your card to swiping it several times when you use it at stores—are a frequent problem. Don't leave your wallet behind when you go trekking and make sure you keep an eye on the card when you give it to a salesperson.

While it's never wise to become involved in a brawl, it is particularly foolish to do this in Thailand: (a) many of the locals are accomplished martial artists and/or carrying weapons; and (b) as a foreigner you will likely be deemed at fault, even if you weren't.

LOCAL SCAMS

Beware of touts, particularly taxi drivers, offering to take you to "their" guesthouse or "their brother's" shop; it's a sham. The driver will be given a commission on your spendings.

WOMEN IN THAILAND

Women should take normal precautions; take care when walking alone on beaches or desolate areas, particularly late at night. Dress conservatively, and don't respond to verbal comments and/or harassment. If you're lost or need assistance, try to consult local women when possible.

SENIOR-CITIZEN TRAVEL

To qualify for age-related discounts, **mention your senior-citizen status up front** when booking hotel reservations (not when checking out) and before you're seated in restaurants (not when paying the bill). When renting a car, ask about promotional car-rental discounts, which can be cheaper than senior-citizen rates.

TAXES

A 10% value added tax is built into the price of all goods and services, including restaurant meals, and is essentially nonrefundable.

TELEPHONES

AREA & COUNTRY CODES

The country code for Thailand is 66. When dialing a Thailand number from abroad, drop the initial 0 from the local area code. The country code is 1 for the United States and Canada, 61 for Australia, 64 for New Zealand, and 44 for the U.K.

DIRECTORY & OPERATOR ASSISTANCE

If you wish to receive assistance for an overseas call, dial100/233–2771. For local telephone inquiries, dial 100/183, but you will need to speak Thai. In Bangkok, you can dial 13 for an English-speaking operator.

INTERNATIONAL CALLS

To make overseas calls, you should use either your hotel switchboard—Chiang Mai and Bangkok have direct dialing—or the overseas telephone facilities at the central post office and telecommunications building. You'll find one in all towns. In Bangkok, the overseas telephone center, next to the general post office, is open 24 hours; up-country, the facilities' hours may vary, but they usually open at 8 AM and some stay open until 10 PM. Some locations in Bangkok have AT&T USADirect phones, which connect you with an AT&T operator.

LONG-DISTANCE CALLS

Long-distance calls can only be made on phones that accept both B1 and B5 coins. For a long-distance call in Thailand, dial the area code and then the number.

LONG-DISTANCE SERVICES

AT&T, MCI, and Sprint access codes make calling long distance relatively convenient, but you may find the local access number blocked in many hotel rooms. First ask the hotel operator to connect you. If the hotel operator balks, ask for an international operator, or dial the international operator yourself. One way to improve your odds of getting connected to your long-distance carrier is to travel with more than one company's calling card (a hotel may block Sprint, for example, but not MCI). If all else fails, call from a pay phone.

➤ ACCESS CODES: **AT&T USADirect** (☎ 0019–991–1111; ☎ 800/222–0300 for other areas). **MCI World-Phone**(☎ 001–999–1–2001 not from pay phones; ☎ 800/444–3333 for other areas). **Sprint International Access** (☎ 001–999–13–877; ☎ 800/877–4646 for other areas).

PUBLIC PHONES

Public telephones are available in most towns and villages and take B1 coins or both B1 and B5 pieces. Long-distance calls can be made only on phones that accept both B1 and B5 coins. For a long-distance call in Thailand, dial the area code and then the number.

TIME

Thailand is seven hours ahead of Greenwich Mean Time. It is 12 hours ahead of New York, 15 hours ahead of Los Angeles, 7 hours ahead of London, and 3 hours behind Sydney.

TIPPING

In Thailand, tips are generally given for good service, except when a price has been negotiated in advance. A taxi driver is not tipped unless hired as a private driver for an excursion. With metered taxis in Bangkok, however, the custom is to round the fare up to the nearest 5 baht. Hotel porters expect at least a B20 tip, and hotel staff who have given good personal service are usually tipped. A 10% tip is appreciated at a restaurant when no service charge has been added to the bill.

TOURS & PACKAGES

Because everything is prearranged on a prepackaged tour or independent vacation, you'll spend less time planning—and often get it all at a good price.

BOOKING WITH AN AGENT

Travel agents are excellent resources. But it's a good idea to collect brochures from several agencies as some agents' suggestions may be influenced by relationships with tour and package firms that reward them for volume sales. If you have a special interest, **find an agent with expertise in that area**; ASTA (☞ Travel Agencies, *below*) has a database of specialists worldwide.

Make sure your travel agent knows the accommodations and other services of the place they're recommending. Ask about the hotel's location, room size, beds, and whether it has a pool, room service, or programs for children, if you care about these. Has your agent been there in person or sent others whom you can contact?

Do some homework on your own, too: local tourism boards can provide information about lesser-known and small-niche operators, some of which may sell only direct.

BUYER BEWARE

Each year consumers are stranded or lose their money when tour operators—even large ones with excellent reputations—go out of business. So **check out the operator.** Ask several travel agents about its reputation, and try to **book with a company that has a consumer-protection program.** (Look for information in the company's brochure.) In the United States, members of the National Tour Association and the United States Tour Operators Association are required to set aside funds to cover your payments and travel arrangements in the event that the company defaults. It's also a good idea to choose a company that participates in the American Society of Travel Agents' Tour Operator Program (TOP); ASTA will act as mediator in any disputes between you and your tour operator.

Remember that the more your package or tour includes the better you can predict the ultimate cost of your vacation. Make sure you know exactly what is covered, and **beware of hidden costs.** Are taxes, tips, and transfers included? Entertainment and excursions? These can add up.

➤ TOUR-OPERATOR RECOMMENDATIONS: **American Society of Travel Agents** (☞ Travel Agencies, *below*). **National Tour Association** (NTA; ✉ 546 E. Main St., Lexington, KY 40508, ☎ 606/226–4444 or 800/682–8886, www.ntaonline.com). **United States Tour Operators Association** (USTOA; ✉ 342 Madison Ave., Suite 1522, New York, NY 10173, ☎ 212/599–6599 or 800/468–7862, FAX 212/599–6744, ustoa@aol.com, www.ustoa.com).

TRAIN TRAVEL

The State Railway of Thailand has three lines, all of which have terminals in Bangkok. The Northern Line connects Bangkok with Chiang Mai, passing through Ayutthaya and Phitsanulok; the Northeastern Line travels up to Nong Khai, near the Laotian border, with a branch that goes east to Ubon Ratchathani; and the Southern Line goes all the way south through Surat Thani—the stop for Ko Samui—to the Malaysian border and on to Kuala Lumpur and Singapore, a journey that takes 37 hours. (There is no train to Phuket, though you can go as far as Surat Thani and change to a scheduled bus service.)

To save money, look into rail passes. But be aware that if you don't plan to cover many miles, you may come out ahead by buying individual tickets.

Many travelers assume that rail passes guarantee them seats on the trains they wish to ride. Not so. You need to book seats ahead even if you are using a rail pass; seat reservations are required on some trains, and are a good idea on trains that may be crowded— particularly in summer on popular routes. You will also need a reservation if you purchase overnight sleeping accommodations.

For information on schedules and passes, call the Bangkok Railway Station.

➤ TRAIN STATIONS: **Bangkok Railway Station** (☎ 02/223–3762 or 02/223–0341).

CLASSES

Most trains offer second- or third-class tickets, but the overnight trains to the north (Chiang Mai) and to the south offer first-class sleeping cabins. Couchettes, with sheets and curtains for privacy, are available in second class. Second-class tickets are about half the price of first-class, and since the couchettes are surprisingly comfortable, most Western travelers choose these. Do not leave valuables unguarded on these overnight trains.

DISCOUNT PASSES

The State Railway of Thailand offers two types of rail passes. Both are valid for 20 days of unlimited travel on all trains in either second or third class. The **Blue Pass** costs B1,100 (children B750) and does not include supplementary charges such as air-conditioning and berths; for B3,000 (children B1,500), the **Red Pass** does. Currently, a special discounted rate, available for nonresidents of Thailand, gives a reduction of B1,000 for the Red Pass and B400 for the Blue Pass.

FARES & SCHEDULES

Train schedules in English are available from travel agents and from major railway stations.

An air-conditioned, second-class couchette, for example, for the 14-hour journey from Bangkok to Chiang Mai is B625; first class is B1,190.

PAYING

Tickets may be bought at railway stations. Travel agencies can also sell tickets for overnight trains.

RESERVATIONS

Reservations are strongly advised for all long-distance trains.

TRANSPORTATION AROUND THAILAND

BICYCLE RICKSHAWS

For short trips, bicycle rickshaws are a popular, inexpensive form of transport, but they become expensive for long trips. (Note that they aren't allowed in central Bangkok.) Fares are negotiable: **Be very clear about what price is agreed upon.** Drivers have a tendency to create misunderstandings leading to a nasty scene at the end of the trip.

SAMLORS

Usually called tuk-tuks for their spluttering sound, these three-wheel cabs are slightly less expensive than taxis and, because of their maneuverability, the most rapid form of travel through congested traffic. All tuk-tuk operators drive as if your ride will be their last, but, in fact, they are remarkably safe. Tuk-tuks are not very comfortable, though, and they subject you to the polluted air, so they're best used for short journeys.

TAXIS

Most Bangkok taxis now have meters installed, and these are the ones tourists should take. In other cities, fares are still negotiated. Taxis waiting at hotels are more expensive than those flagged down on the street. **Never enter an unmetered taxi until the price has been established.** Most taxi drivers do not speak English, but all understand the finger count. One finger means B10, two is for B20 and so on. Ask at your hotel what the appropriate fare should be. **Never pay more than what the hotel quotes,** as they will have given you the high price. If in doubt, accept 65%–75% of the cabbie's quote.

With any form of private travel, **never change your initial agreement on destination and price unless you clearly establish a new "contract."** Moreover, if you agree to the driver's offer to wait for you at your destination and be available for your onward or return journey, you will be charged for waiting time, and, unless you have fixed the price, the return fare can be double the outbound fare.

TRAVEL AGENCIES

A good travel agent puts your needs first. Look for an agency that has been in business at least five years, emphasizes customer service, and has someone on staff who specializes in your destination. In addition, **make sure the agency belongs to a professional trade organization.** The American Society of Travel Agents (ASTA), with 27,000 agents in some 170 countries, is the largest and most influential in the field. Operating under the motto "Integrity in Travel," it maintains and enforces a strict code of ethics and will step in to help mediate any agent-client disputes if necessary. ASTA also maintains a Web site that includes a directory of agents. (If a travel agency is also acting as your tour operator, *see* Buyer Beware *in* Tours & Packages, *above*.)

➤ LOCAL AGENT REFERRALS: American Society of Travel Agents (ASTA; ☎ 800/965–2782 24-hr hot line, FAX 703/684–8319, www.astanet. com). Association of British Travel Agents (✉ 68–71 Newman St., London W1P 4AH, ☎ 0207/637–2444, FAX 0207/637–0713, abta.co.uk, www. abtanet.com). Association of Canadian Travel Agents (✉ 1729 Bank St., Suite 201, Ottawa, Ontario K1V 7Z5, ☎ 613/521–0474, FAX 613/521–0805, acta.ntl@sympatico.ca). Australian Federation of Travel Agents (✉ Level 3, 309 Pitt St., Sydney 2000, ☎ 02/9264–3299, FAX 02/9264–1085, www.afta.com.au). Travel Agents' Association of New Zealand (✉ Box 1888, Wellington 10033, ☎ 04/499–0104, FAX 04/499–0827, taanz@ tiasnet.co.nz).

VISITOR INFORMATION

➤ TOURIST INFORMATION: Tourism Authority of Thailand (✉ 5 World Trade Center, Suite 3443, New York, NY 10048 U.S., ☎ 212/432–0433, FAX 212/912–0920; ✉ 611 North Larchmont Blvd., 1st floor,, Los Angeles, CA 90004 U.S., ☎ 213/461–9814, FAX 213/461–9834). Inquiries from Canada should be directed to the Los Angeles office.

➤ IN THE U.K.: Thailand Tourist Board (✉ 49 Albemarle St., London W1X 3FE, ☎ 0207/499–7679).

➤ IN AUSTRALIA AND NEW ZEALAND: Tourism Authority of Thailand (✉ 75 Pitt St., Sydney 20000, NSW, ☎ 2/9247–75719).

➤ U.S. GOVERNMENT ADVISORIES: U.S. Department of State (✉ Overseas Citizens Services Office, Room 4811 N.S., 2201 C St. NW, Washington, DC 20520, ☎ 202/647–5225 for interactive hot line, 301/946–4400 for computer bulletin board, FAX 202/647–3000 for interactive hot line).

WEB SITES

Do check out the World Wide Web when you're planning. You'll find everything from up-to-date weather forecasts to virtual tours of famous cities. Fodor's Web site, www.fodors. com, is a great place to start your online travels. Other sites worth checking out are: www.tat.or.th, www.amazingsiam.com, www. thailand-travelsearch.com, and www. nectec.or.th for more information on Thailand.

WHEN TO GO

Thailand has two climatic regions: tropical savannah in the northern regions and tropical rain forest in the south. Three seasons run from hot (March through May) to rainy (June through September) and cool (October through February). Humidity is high all year, especially during the hot season. The cool season is pleasantly warm in the south, but in the north, especially in the hills around Chiang Mai, it can become quite chilly. The cool season is the peak season. Prices are often twice as high then as in the low seasons, yet hotels are often fully booked.

CLIMATE

➤ FORECASTS: Weather Channel Connection (☎ 900/932–8437), 95¢ per minute from a Touch-Tone phone.

The following are average daily maximum and minimum temperatures forBangkok. The north will generally be a degree or two cooler.

Jan.	89F	32C	May	93F	34C	Sept.	89F	32C
	68	20		77	25		75	24
Feb.	91F	33C	June	91F	33C	Oct.	88F	31C
	72	22		75	24		75	24
Mar.	93F	34C	July	89F	32C	Nov.	88F	31C
	75	24		75	24		72	22
Apr.	95F	35C	Aug.	89F	32C	Dec.	88F	31C
	77	25		75	24		68	20

FESTIVALS AND SEASONAL EVENTS

The festivals listed below are national and occur throughout the country unless otherwise noted. Many events follow the lunar calendar, so dates vary from year to year.

➤ JAN.: **New Year celebrations** are usually at their best around temples. In Bangkok, special ceremonies at Pramanae Ground include Thai dancing.

➤ FEB.: **Magha Puja**, held on the full moon of the third lunar month, commemorates the day when 1,250 disciples spontaneously heard Lord Buddha preach the cardinal Doctrine. The **Flower Festival**, held in Chiang Mai during the early part of the month when the province's flowers are in full bloom, features a parade with floral floats, flower displays, and beauty contests.

➤ APR.: **Songkran** marks the Thai New Year and is an occasion for setting caged birds and fish free, visiting family, dancing, and splashing everyone with water in good-natured merriment. The festival is at its best in Chiang Mai.

➤ MAY: On the full moon of the sixth lunar month, the nation celebrates the holiest of Buddhist days, **Visakha Puja**, commemorating Lord Buddha's birth, enlightenment, and death. Monks lead the laity in candlelight processions around their temples.

➤ AUG.: On the 12th, **Queen Sirikit's birthday** is celebrated with religious ceremonies at Chitlada Palace, and the city is adorned with lights.

➤ NOV.: Held on the full moon of the 12th lunar month, **Loi Krathong** is the loveliest of Thai festivals. After sunset, people make their way to a body of water and launch small lotus-shape banana-leaf floats bearing lighted candles to honor the water spirits and wash away the sins of the past year. Of all Bangkok's fairs and festivals, the **Golden Mount Festival** is the most spectacular, with sideshows, food stalls, bazaars, and large crowds of celebrants.

➤ DEC.: On the 5th, the **King's birthday**, a trooping of the colors is performed in Bangkok by Thailand's elite Royal Guards.

Thailand

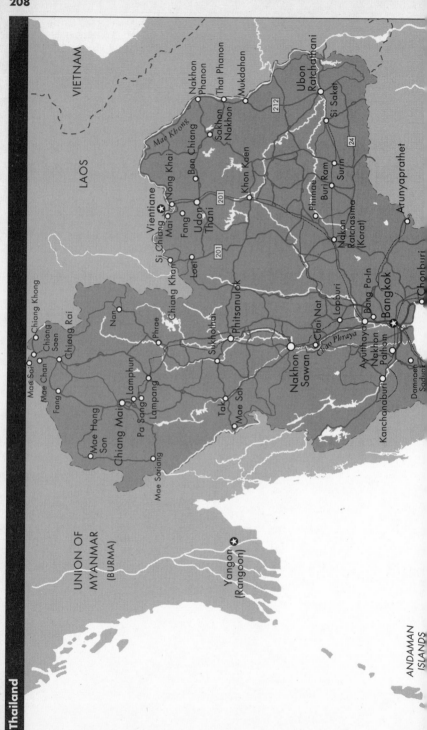

VIETNAM

LAOS

Mae Khong

Nakhon Phanon

That Phanon

Mukdahan

Ubon Ratchathani

Si Saket

212

Ban Chiang

Sakhan Nakhon

24

Vientiane

Nong Khai

Khon Kaen

201

Phimae

Buri Ram

Surin

Arunyaprathet

Si Chiang Mai

Fang

Udon Thani

Nakon Ratchasima (Korat)

Loei

201

Chonburi

Chiang Khong

Chiang Khan

Chiang Saen

Chiang Rai

Nan

Phrae

Phitsanulok

Chai Nat

Lopburi

Bang Pa-In

Bangkok

Mae Sai

Mae Chan

Chiang Mai

Lamphun

Sukhothai

Chao Phraya

Ayuthaya

Nakhon Pathom

Mae Hong Son

Fang

Pa Sang

Lampang

Nakhon Sawan

Damnoen Saduat

Kanchanaburi

Mae Sariang

Tak

Mae Sot

UNION OF MYANMAR (BURMA)

Yangon (Rangoon)

ANDAMAN ISLANDS

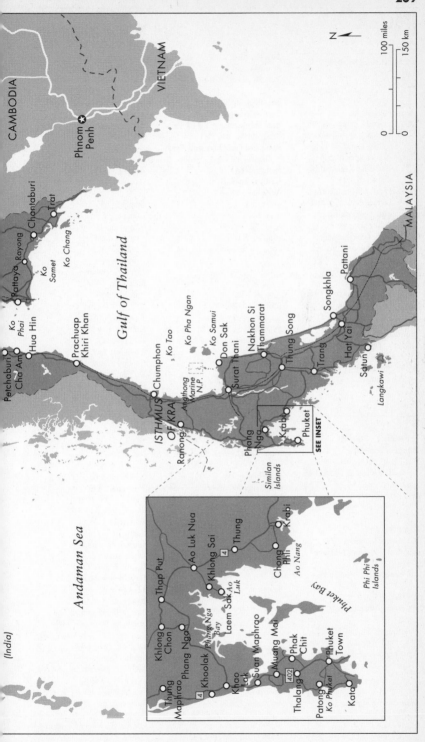

CAMBODIA

VIETNAM

Phnom Penh

100 miles

150 km

N

Gulf of Thailand

Chontaburi

Trat

Pattaya   Rayong

Ko Chang

Ko Samet

Ko Phai

Hua Hin

Prachuap Khiri Khan

Petchaburi

Cha Am

Ko Tao

Ko Pha Ngan

Chumphon

Ko Samui

Don Sak

Nakhon Si Thammarat

Surat Thani

Thung Song

Songkhla

Pattani

Trang

Hat Yai

Satun

Langkawi

ISTHMUS OF KRA

Angthong Marine N.P.

Ranong

Phang Nga

Krabi

Phuket

SEE INSET

Similan Islands

MALAYSIA

Andaman Sea

(India)

Thung Maphrao

Phang Nga

Khlong Chon

Thap Put

Ao Luk Nua

Khlong Sai

Thung

Krabi

Chong Phil

Ao Nang

Khoolak

Phang Nga Bay

Laem Sak

Ao Luk

Khao Lak

Suan Maphrao

Muang Mai

Phak Chit

Thalang

Patong

Ko Phuket

Kata

Phuket Town

Phuket Bay

Phi Phi Islands

INDEX

Icons and Symbols

★ Our special recommendations

✕ Restaurant

🏠 Lodging establishment

✕🏠 Lodging establishment whose restaurant warrants a special trip

🖐 Good for kids (rubber duck)

☞ Sends you to another section of the guide for more information

✉ Address

☎ Telephone number

🕐 Opening and closing times

💷 Admission prices

💷 Sends you to www.fodors.com/urls for up-to-date links to the property's Web site

Numbers in white and black circles ③ ❸ that appear on the maps, in the margins, and within the tours correspond to one another.

A

Air travel, *190–191*
Bangkok, 59–60
Bangkok excursions, 86
Central Plains and I-san, 143
with children, 194
northern Thailand, 117–118
southern beach resorts, 175–176
Airports, *191–192*
Aisawan Thippaya, *74*
Angthong Marine National Park, *172*
Ao Nang, *163–165, 176–177*
Ao Noi, *77*
Ao Thong Wua Laen, *174–175*
Ayutthaya, *21, 66, 71–73, 86, 87, 88, 89*
Ayutthaya Historical Study Centre, *73*

B

Baan Taling Ngam, *172*
Bamboo Island, *161*
Ban Butom, *138*
Ban Chiang, *125, 134–135*
Ban Choke, *139*
Ban Dan Kwian, *142*
Ban Houie Sai, *112*
Ban Mae Hut, *174*

Ban Na Kha, *134*
Ban Phe, *84*
Ban Phue *(mountain park), 135*
Ban Prathap Chai, *117*
Ban Ta Klang, *139*
Ban Sop Ruak, *93, 113*
Bang Pa-In, *66, 74*
Bang Sai Folk Arts and Craft Centre, *74*
Bang Saray, *84*
Bang Thao Beach, *152–153*
Bangkok, *18–63*
architecture, 18
arts, 18, 55
bars, 53–54
cabaret, 54
children, attractions for, 28, 29
classical Thai dance, 55
cultural shows, 54
dance clubs, 54
dining, 18, 26, 30–31, 34–41
dinner cruises, 54–55
emergencies, 62
English-language bookstores, 62
ferries, 19
guided tours, 63
helicopters, 60
itineraries, 20–21
jazz bars, 55
lodging, 18–19, 41–53
mototaxi, 61
nightlife, 19, 53–55
outdoor activities, 55–56
pubs, 53–54
river boats, 19
shopping, 19, 56–59
skytrain, 61–62
spectator sports, 56
taxis, 60, 62
telephones, 63
transportation, 59–62
travel agencies, 63
visitor information, 63
when to go, 20
Bangkok excursions, *65–89*
architecture, 65
beaches, 65, 76–77
children, attractions for, 68, 80–81
dining, 65, 69–70, 73, 75–76, 77–78, 81–82
Eastern Seaboard, 79–86
emergencies, 89
itineraries, 66
lodging, 65, 69–70, 73, 75–76, 77–79, 82–83, 84, 85, 86
nightlife and the arts, 65, 83
north from Bangkok, 71–73
outdoor activities, 65, 70, 83–84
shopping, 70
taxis, 87–88

tour operators, 89
transportation, 86–89
visitor information, 89
west of Bangkok, 66–71
western Gulf Coast, 76–79
when to go, 66
Banglampoo *(Bangkok), 28*
Beaches
Ao Nang, 163–165
Baan Taling Ngam, 172
Bang Thao, 152–153
Bangkok excursions, 65, 76–77
Bophut, 166–167
Chalong, 159–160
Chaweng, 169–170
Chengmon, 168
Chumphon, 174–175
Coral Cove, 170–171
Haad Nopphharat Thara, 163
Hua Hin, 76–77
Kamala, 154
Karon, 156–157
Kata, 157–158
Ko Fan, 168
Ko Hae, 159
Ko Lone, 159
Ko Pha Ngan, 173
Ko Phi Phi, 160–162
Ko Tao, 174
Laem Set Bay, 171–172
Lamai, 171
Mai Khao, 151
Makham Bay, 160
Maenam, 166
Nai Harn, 158
Nai Thon, 152
Nai Yang, 152
Nam Mao, 164
Pansea, 153–154
Phang Nga Bay, 162
Railay, 164
Rawai, 158–159
Similan Islands, 160
Surin Beach, 154
Susan Hoi, 163
Bicycle rickshaws, *207*
Boat travel
Bangkok, 61
Bangkok excursions, 86
northern Thailand, 118
southern beach resorts, 176
Bophut, *166–167*
Bottle Museum, *81*
Buddhist monument, *67–68*
Buri Ram, *140*
Bus travel, *192*
Bangkok, 60, 61
Bangkok excursions, 87
Central Plains and I-san, 143–144
northern Thailand, 118
southern beach resorts, 176–177
Business hours, *192*

NOTES

NOTES

NOTES

NOTES

NOTES

NOTES

NOTES

NOTES

FODOR'S THAILAND

EDITORS: Carissa Bluestone, Mayanthi Fernando

Editorial Contributors: Mick Elmore, Nigel Fisher, Lara Wozniak

Editorial Production: Tom Holton

Maps: David Lindroth, *cartographer;* Rebecca Baer; and Bob Blake, *map editors*

Design: Fabrizio La Rocca, *creative director;* Guido Caroti, *art director;* Jolie Novak, *senior picture editor,* Melanie Marin, *photo editor*

Cover Design: Pentagram

Production/Manufacturing: Colleen Ziemba

COPYRIGHT

Seventh Edition

ISBN 0–679–00792–X

ISSN 1064–0993

IMPORTANT TIP

Although all prices, opening times, and other details in this book are based on information supplied to us at press time, changes occur all the time in the travel world, and Fodor's cannot accept responsibility for facts that become outdated or for inadvertent errors or omissions. So always confirm information when it matters, especially if you're making a detour to visit a specific place.

SPECIAL SALES

Fodor's Travel Publications are available at special discounts for bulk purchases for sales promotions or premiums. Special editions, including personalized covers, excerpts of existing guides, and corporate imprints, can be created in large quantities for special needs. For more information, contact your local bookseller or write to Special Markets, Fodor's Travel Publications, 280 Park Avenue, New York, NY 10017. Inquiries from Canada should be directed to your local Canadian bookseller or sent to Random House of Canada, Ltd., Marketing Department, 2775 Matheson Boulevard East, Mississauga, Ontario L4W 4P7. Inquiries from the United Kingdom should be sent to Fodor's Travel Publications, 20 Vauxhall Bridge Road, London SW1V 2SA, England.

PRINTED IN THE UNITED STATES OF AMERICA

10 9 8 7 6 5 4 3 2 1

PHOTOGRAPHY

Photographers/Aspen: *Paul Chesley, cover. (Wat Po Temple, Bangkok)*

The Atlanta, *14C.*

Black Star: *John Everingham, 12B. David McIntyre, 6 bottom left.*

Tibor Bognar, *6A, 6B, 8A, 8B, 14A.*

Corbis: *7C. Michael Freeman, 13E. Wolfgang Kaehler, 11A. Kevin R. Morris, 11B. Roman Soumar, 10C. Jay Syverson, 14B. Luca I. Tettoni, 7D. Michael S. Yamashita, 12A.*

Jack Hollingsworth, *4–5, 9C.*

Houserstock: *Steve Bly, 12C. Jan Butchofsky-Houser, 10A.*

Hua Hin Golf Tours, *2 bottom left.*

The Image Bank: *Eric Meola, 7E.*

Liaison Agency: *Richard Vogel, 9E.*

The Oriental Bangkok, *14E.*

Panviman Resort, *14D.*

PhotoDisc, *2 bottom center, 14G.*

PictureQuest: *Flat Earth, 2 top left, 2 top right, 2 bottom right, 3 top left, 3 top right, 3 bottom left, 3 bottom right, 14F.*

Stone: *David Hanson, 11C.*

Luca Tettoni, *14H.*

Travel Stock: *Buddy Mays, 10B.*

Nik Wheeler, *1, 9D, 13D, 16.*

ABOUT OUR WRITERS

Every trip is a significant trip. Acutely aware of that fact, we've pulled out all stops in preparing *Fodor's Thailand*. To help you zero in on what to see in Thailand, we've gathered some great color photos of the key sights. To show you how to put it all together, we've created multiday itineraries and neighborhood walks. And to direct you to the places that are truly worth your time and money this year, we've rallied the team of endearingly picky know-it-alls we're pleased to call our writers. Having seen all corners of Thailand, they're real experts. If you knew them, you'd poll them for tips yourself.

Mick Elmore arrived in Bangkok on Thanksgiving Day 1991 ending a four-month drive from Melbourne, Australia, with Peter Goldie in a beat-up old Chrysler. He's been stuck in traffic ever since. A journalist since 1984—first in Texas, then in Australia—he is now based in Bangkok, where he writes for wire services and magazines. Mick updated the Bangkok and Side Trips out of Bangkok chapters.

Nigel Fisher, who updated Bangkok Dining and Lodging, Northern Thailand, the Central Plains and I-san, and the Southern Beach Resorts, is editor of the monthly travel publication *Voyager International*. He has traveled extensively throughout Asia and the world, and uses Bangkok as his Eastern base.

Lara Wozniak, who updated the Smart Travel Tips A to Z, is a U.S. lawyer and senior features writer for *Hong Kong iMail,* a daily English-language newspaper in Hong Kong. She regularly contributes to American and British newspapers and magazines. She also wrote the Nepal chapter for *Fodor's Nepal, Tibet, and Bhutan 1st Edition.*

Don't Forget to Write

Keeping a travel guide fresh and up-to-date is a big job. So we love your feedback—positive and negative—and follow up on all suggestions. Contact the Thailand editor at editors@fodors.com or c/o Fodor's, 280 Park Avenue, New York, NY 10017. And have a wonderful trip!

Karen Cure
Editorial Director